Testing Older Adults

Contributors

David Arenberg, Ph.D.

Kenneth D. Cole, Ph.D.

Michael Duffy, Ph.D.

Carol J. Dye, Ph.D.

Marla Hassinger, Ph.D.

Christopher Hertzog, Ph.D.

Thelma Hunt, Ph.D., M.D.

Iseli K. Krauss, Ed.D.

Asenath La Rue, Ph.D.

Clyde J. Lindley, M.A.

Bernice A. Marcopulos, Ph.D.

Samuel J. Popkin, Ph.D.

John D. Ranseen, Ph.D.

E.A. Robertson-Tchabo, Ph.D.

James M. Schear, Ph.D.

David Schlenoff, Ed.D.

Frederick A. Schmitt, Ph.D.

Steve Shindell, Ph.D.

Glenn Smith, Ph.D.

McCay Vernon, Ph.D.

Testing
Older Adults

A REFERENCE GUIDE FOR
GEROPSYCHOLOGICAL ASSESSMENTS

Thelma Hunt, Ph.D., M.D.

Clyde J. Lindley, M.A.

General Editors

Foreword by James E. Birren, Ph.D.

8700 Shoal Creek Boulevard
Austin, Texas 78758
(512) 451-3246

Printed in the United States of America

Library of Congress Cataloging-in-Publication Data

Testing older adults : a reference guide for geropsychological
  assessments / Thelma Hunt, Clyde J. Lindley, general editors ;
  foreword by James E. Birren.
     p.   cm.
  Includes bibliographies and indexes.
  ISBN 0-89079-218-6
  1. Aged—Psychological testing. I. Hunt, Thelma. II. Lindley,
  Clyde J.
  RC953.T47   1989
  155.67—dc20   89-10327
                                                        CIP

8700 Shoal Creek Boulevard
Austin, Texas 78758

10 9 8 7 6 5 4 3 2 1   89 90 91 92 93

Contents

IV. LIFE-SPAN DEVELOPMENT PERSPECTIVES

Foreword

JAMES E. BIRREN, PH.D.

Although the impetus for the development of mental tests began early in this century with their use with children, the end of the century is marked by rapid expansion in the use of psychological measurements with older persons. Also, the creation of the National Institute on Aging has been accompanied by rising public interest in the biological, social, and psychological functioning of mature and older adults. Not only are older individuals more interested in their well-being with advancing age, there are more of them. There are many concerns of an aging society for which the services of psychologists will be increasingly sought.

Many decisions involving older persons are facilitated by the availability of psychological measurements. The health community increasingly seeks the assistance of psychologists in determining the level of functioning of an older person. Furthermore, the health professions are increasingly relying upon diagnostic information provided by psychological and neuropsychological measurements. Thus, the separation of what may be a relatively normal process from underlying pathology places demands upon psychologists and the repertory of available psychological tests.

There is also the matter of assessing the process of measuring change in the patient's status in response to a wide array of therapies that may include drugs, activity and exercise, or individual or group psychotherapy. Indeed, the approval of drugs for public use in turn often depends upon the adequacy of psychological measurements that will tell us the efficacy of new pharmacological agents.

Many tests have not been standardized or much used in the age range where frequent differential diagnosis is called for. However, data from longitudinal studies suggest that it is in the mid-80s when functional capacities are most likely to change. Therefore, increasingly we will have to have instruments that are standardized and validated for use with the very old.

To the above should be added the use of psychological measurements in determining competencies of individuals in matters of guardianship or employability in the marketplace. Increasingly, litigation is brought about over age issues, frequently to be resolved by a psychologist whose charge it is to asses the competency of the individual to perform work tasks.

Such tasks, however, are not easy ones. Often there are increasing intra- and interindividual differences with age, which confound problems of establishing norms and test validity. It is also becoming apparent that the assessment of the individual in the high technology laboratory or professional center does not necessarily yield information about the capacity of a handicapped older person to live at home. Thus, the question of ecological validity of a test can be raised in estimating predictability from measurements carried out in a controlled environment to the natural environment in which individuals live. The competency of older individuals in activities of daily living in specific environments is only partially assessed by instruments used in an unfamiliar context.

In addition to the broad issue of the ecological validity of measurements for older adults, there are issues to be studied about the factor structure of tests over the life span. Fundamental issues arise as to whether a test measures the same thing throughout the 60 or more years of adult life. There are questions to be resolved about the relative weighting of cognitive tests that show increments with age and those that show declines.

Mental tests have come of age; that is, they are being applied to many problems of assessment in an adult population. Usefulness of such measurements rests upon a base of scientific research that is being built up in the area of application to older adults. In some respects, psychologists are better prepared to face the contemporary picture of assessment in an aging society by having a long history of the development of the mental tests with children. We cannot rely, however, on the instruments of the past used with children for application with adults. The demands of assessment in an aging population are much too rigorous for such an easy adaptation. The chapters of this book provide perspectives on the many facets of test assessment of older individuals in a modern society. The issues are not simple; they represent a vast frontier for the useful roles of psychology and psychologists.

This book is timely in that it offers a systematic measurement approach for the psychologist to the wide range of demands that are increasingly being made to provide professional assessment.

Institute for Advanced Study in Gerontology and Geriatrics
Ethel Percy Andrus Gerontology Center
University of Southern California, Los Angeles

Preface

This book adds a fourth to the series of companion volumes that cover a life-span approach to the presentation of psychological tests and test problems. The titles previously published in this series are *Testing Children,* edited by S. Joseph Weaver, Ph.D. (1984); *Testing Adults,* edited by Dennis P. Swiercinsky, Ph.D. (1985); and *Testing Adolescents,* edited by Robert G. Harrington, Ph.D. (1987).

Testing Older Adults may be said to have a dual purpose. As necessary preludes to its main purpose of discussing psychological testing of older persons, the text makes reference to facts, theories, and opinions regarding the elderly. An understanding of the older person and the aging process is a sine qua non background for selecting, administering, and interpreting psychological tests with this population in relation to the problems at hand. Normal aging and pathological aging require differentiation when interpreting tests.

In the practice of psychology, the subdivisions of the life span have not been clearly defined by age designations nor have tests been specifically classified in this manner. Both life-span subdivisions and test classifications overlap. However, as professionals, we still talk about tests for children, tests for adolescents, tests for adults, and now tests for the elderly (older adults). Under the circumstances and limitations of scientific knowledge, the tests included as appropriate for consideration in this volume must be regarded as a matter of somewhat arbitrary decision-making on the part of the editors. Inclusions or exclusions were also influenced by the contents of contributions from the various chapter contributors.

In guiding the content of this book and then in reviewing the contributions to its content, the editors have been very cognizant of the changes in social and legal concepts and definitions with respect to the older person. An effort has been made in discussions of tests to emphasize the importance of understanding these changes. Test users must become more clearly aware of what it means to be an "older person." They must have a knowledge about the aging process and realize that attitudes, expectancies, and cooperativeness become increasing factors in testing as age increases. They must keep in mind that the results of tests today may have more far-reaching cultural-social values than in the past. Professionals must be able to interpret adult test norms and their applicability in terms of the era in which they were developed (probably when adult test participation may have been far removed from what it would be today). A mass of misinformation about adults stemming from interpretation of early testing data has to be corrected. One must be wary of age curves on abilities, and especially of the establishment of the age variant in the statistics.

Testing Older Adults was undertaken with a broad coverage outline in mind; this encompassed constructing a picture of the older person as one who calls for special consideration in testing, reviewing the related "state of the science," and venturing projections with respect to the needs facing us as professionals. The authors of the chapters in *Testing Older Adults* were invited to contribute because of their already established contribution to testing the older person or their promise in terms of ongoing research. They were given general guidelines of expected coverage, and all chapters were reviewed and coordinated with other chapters by the editors.

It was decided early in planning the book that recognizable consideration should be given to some general emerging problems that are closely related to the older person. One of these is the evaluation of competency (actually, varied competencies, in the national scene, in the community, on the job, in the home, and in managing one's self). This issue is not limited, of course, to testing the older person. To be practically understandable and maximally useful, test results must not only convey comparison with norms of one's age (say, age 60—including do-nothings, near do-nothings, doing-littles, average doing persons, above average performers, and persons of high competency). Many commonly used tests supply norms that permit adult comparisons only with 16 years of age or over groups, or only up to a 16-year-old group. These norms problems have been specifically addressed in *Testing Older Adults*.

Another emerging problem relates to the older person as the older worker. Tests must assess for work potentials and work performance, not just for relative placement on older age norms or for comparisons with younger person norms. The jobs or responsibilities that may be given older workers may demand abilities and aptitudes not significantly related to pure age norms (older or younger). Norms must be developed according to these needs. They often have to be "local" norms, specific to a situation at hand.

In developing the outline for this book and inviting participants, cognizance has also been given to the particular problems of the older person that create calls for the help of psychological tests. These include common adjustment problems, depression, impairment in physiological functioning, memory dysfunction, stress (physiological and psychological), and psychological concerns (as sexual dysfunction, loss of ego, social inadequacy, suicide threats, etc.). Particular attention has also been given to the contributions which psychological testing can made to professions concerned with medical care, nursing home care, counseling, and forensic problems of the older person.

ACKNOWLEDGMENTS

Our first thanks must go to our chapter contributors, who so generously shared their valuable insights and professional expertise. We are greatly indebted to them for the wealth of experience and creativity contained within this volume.

We appreciate both the confidence in our abilities to edit and develop this book and the suggestions with respect to its content that were conveyed by Daniel J. Keyser and Richard C. Sweetland of Test Corporation of America (TCA). They, along with Clark Smith of TCA, provided motivation and support to our endeavors.

The editing of this book and our contributions to its writing would have been impossible without the encouragement and concrete help of Jane Guthrie, our guiding editor at the Test Corporation of America. She was in constant communication with us, providing assistance and guidance in dealing with problems that arose. She also contributed at various stages of progress valuable ideas and motivational influences affecting the book's content and the authorship of its chapters. Credit is also due to the other members of the TCA staff who through their assistance made these efforts possible and fruitful.

In selecting possible contributors for the chapters, we sought persons competent not only in the field of testing but also in the field of gerontology. We are indebted to many colleagues who made valuable suggestions. We are particularly grateful to James L. Fozard, Associate Scientific Director, Baltimore Longitudinal Studies of Aging, National Institutes of Aging. He recommended outstanding persons for consideration for each of the chapters. Similarly, we received author recommendations from Cecil Peck, formerly Director, Clinical Psychology and Deputy Director, Mental Health and Behavioral Sciences, Veterans Administration Central Office; from David Arenberg, National Institutes of Aging, who also accepted co-authorship of a chapter; from Ilene Siegler, Duke University Medical Center; and from Paul Costa and Robert McCrae of the National Institutes of Aging.

Great thanks for professional review of many of the individual chapters is due C. James Klett, formerly Chief of the Veterans Administration Cooperative Studies Coordinating Center. His critical comments were most constructive and helpful. Similarly, our gratitude is extended to Mary Anne Nester, psychologist with the U.S. Office of Personnel Management, for her critical reviews of three chapters dealing with visual disabilities, hearing disabilities, and motor impairment. Her comments were valuable and appreciated.

We recognize the valuable contributions in library assistance made by Joanna Chen Lin, Librarian, Gerontological Research Center, National Institutes of Aging, Baltimore, and Wendy Carter, Reader Service Specialist, Veterans Administration Central Office Library, Washington, D.C.

And we acknowledge that we could not have carried through without the knowledgeable secretarial assistance of Natalie Neviaser.

Thelma Hunt & Clyde J. Lindley
Washington, D.C.

1

Introduction: Historical Perspective and Current Considerations

THELMA HUNT, PH.D., M.D.

Defining the role of psychological testing, developing specifically appropriate tests, and relating these issues to the practical demands placed upon the older person are recently emerging considerations. This slowly appearing attention to tests for the older adult involves complex related factors and conditions. These are the concerns of the chapters of this book.

A brief critical look at some of the important factors and events in the general history of psychological testing provides an appropriate background for testing older adults.

The era surrounding World War I was quite important in the history of test development and applications. Standardized testing in the schools had come into prominence prior to the war. At first the tests were of the recall type; later experimentation involved short-answer alternate-choice and multiple-choice forms. Group intelligence tests were developed to furnish an alternative to compiling time-consuming individual mental test scores (e.g., from the Binet Intelligence Scale). The development of group tests outside the school situation was hastened by the need for an ability test that could help classify the hundreds of thousands of recruits for both military and related services during World War I.

The group test needs were approached by a government-appointed committee of psychologists headed by Robert M. Yerkes, at that time president of the American Psychological Association. During an impressively short period of time (reportedly 3 months), the committee reviewed already available pertinent information, developed a great deal of preliminary test materials, and carried out unofficial trials of the materials. The immediate result was the development of the Army Alpha and Army Beta tests. Some prominent authorities in testing have viewed these two tests as very important to the stimulation and development of the testing field (Hunt, 1936).

Early contributors to testing were more experimentally oriented and interested than they were practically concerned. Even Edward K. Strong, whose interest test has withstood the longest and most varied history imaginable, developed his test from a theoretical motivational urge. As a rule, the theory that provided a foundation for test development did not focus on or even attend to the needs of older adults. The Binet Intelligence Scale (Binet-Simon Scale), which appeared in 1905 and introduced IQ ratings, was based upon an age-growth concept. The 1911 revision (the year of Binet's

1

death) extended the original coverage from a narrower range to what was designated as a range extending to adult age (15- to 16-year level in terms of mental age ratings). While used in much adult testing in clinical settings during the early years of testing, in 1939 the Wechsler-Bellevue Scale began replacing it in the testing of older persons.

In testing younger persons the primary emphasis has been prediction—of scholastic success, of job success, or of response to therapy. There are exceptions, of course, as when the function of testing is mainly a diagnostic one. By contrast, the emphasis in testing the older person has focused not on predictions, but on status quo evaluations.

Some interesting psychometric observations may be noted. For example, most tests currently available for adults were not developed for assessment in situations and challenges that characterize the older person's life. Most were originally developed or have been adapted from other tests that assess functioning in academic contexts (i.e., the classroom) or in academically oriented counseling centers (Cornelius & Caspi, 1987). Further, most of the early measures of abilities and general aptitudes were sensorimotor tests, with erroneous concepts of the relationship between sensorimotor functions and mental abilities and no knowledge or recognition of age changes in these functions. Such errors continue to haunt us, especially when testing older persons.

Views of the older person must be fitted into a correct developmental concept of abilities as related to age. Many of us have grown up with the concept of a developmental graph of the relationship between ability and age in which the line of relationship gradually ascends to around age 15 to 16, then flattens out to an unchanging relationship or actually shows a decline in the final decades of life. This graph needs scrutiny and greater scientific support. Some older persons may still be in a developmental stage for certain functions measured by psychological tests to which they may be subjected. There is no set *age of maturity,* universally applicable to all tests.

The progress of psychological testing has been very much intertwined with practical concerns that often involve evaluation of the older person. The question of maturity age for a given ability or characteristic, for example, is answerable only by study of persons of increasing age. Predictions about vocational success made from high school testing requires criterion studies of older persons. Longitudinal studies extending to older adult ages are obviously required in the development of new tests or the application of older ones to the problems of the older adult.

Growing applications of testing older persons have had effects upon the site of testing and the emphases of testing. The setting has tended with testing the older person to move from academia (schools, colleges, etc.) to expanded testing in employment services, job placement centers, retirement centers, hospitals, nursing homes, and other places of older person activities. In these changes the test professional has had to be especially concerned that staff are well trained in the test functions that they perform. Outside the academic setting they are farther from their academic experiences and basic test training.

Older persons must be involved in confirming theoretical concepts about the nature of abilities. For example, Cattell's theories postulate a *fluid* intelligence and a *crystallized* intelligence. The former is the underlying basic potentiality in the organism (human), capable of functioning even in old age; the latter is more or less fixed by the influences of experience. The search for tests to confirm Cattell's theory has involved testing older persons.

Pursuing theoretical ideas a bit farther, Matarazzo (1972) views tests as having produced a *psychometric* intelligence versus a *functional* intelligence. In the extremity of example, psychometric intelligence is completely and adequately expressed in terms of the test (evaluating instrument) result (an age quotient measure, a percentile, or a standard score). In his development of intelligence test measures, Wechsler emphasized a global concept in which the functioning of the intelligence was a part of the measurement. The Comprehension section of the Wechsler Verbal scale particularly illustrates his emphasis upon the functioning of intelligence. Not only must the test subject comprehend the question and give the correct response, but he or she must answer questions about the "why." Wechsler's global concept is quite pertinent to testing older persons.

Tests of older persons should make further contribution to the issue of "primary mental abilities." The concept originated with the work leading to Thurstone's factor analytic study of the mid-1930s. At the time of the study, Thurstone drew on all types of tests that had been utilized in "mental ability" tests to date and six factors emerged. Are any left out because of the limitations of those with which he started? Some professionals think so. Accepting their opinions, a new tryout test for factor analytic study should be constructed with components added to cover all types of tests now in use in presumably mental test measurements. Furthermore, in future studies of "primary mental abilities," the age range in studies should be expanded.

As noted, tests historically have been developed mainly in a context of theory and research. Subsequent needs, only partially met and still with us, have to do with practical applications, including applications to older adults. Perhaps to blast off their easy chairs those who are derelict in these duties, the author of a recent article in the *American Psychologist* said:

> Despite the proliferation of tests, the numerous exchanges about the appropriate and inappropriate interpretations and uses of tests, and the substantial advances in the science of psychology, the statistical sophistication of psychometrics and the technology supporting testing, the fundamental nature of widely used standardized tests has changed relatively little during the last half century. (Linn, 1986, p. 1153)

This may be an extreme statement, but in looking at the publication dates on many of the tests in frequent use, one can see much truth in it. For the typical user, earlier tests as compared with newer ones are more familiar, they have been easier to give, they have been easier to score, the types of ratings suggested have been easier to understand, and they have been more readily available to minimally trained users. Unfortunately these older tests have limitations when used with older adults. Most have not been developed or standardized for an older adult population. When using these tests the psychologist must of necessity rely on clinical judgment in evaluating and interpreting test results, and this implies confirming impressions through interviews and behavioral observations.

The meaning that underlies testing has received too little attention. The purpose of psychological testing is not accomplished by obtaining and reporting an IQ or percentile rating. The psychologist and/or test user must know what abilities are tapped, for example, by the Wechsler Similarities test or Digit-Symbol test and take into account the established relationship between test scores and the purposes for which the test is used (validity determination). The surface has hardly been scratched with respect to understanding the meaning of typical standardized tests administered to the older person.

Test norms are a recurring problem. By definition, norms for a test permit comparisons of an individual's score to scores made by persons in a group to which the individual belongs or might become a part. The group must be *meaningful* in relation to the purpose of the testing. Adequate data for meeting these problems have been rare in testing older persons.

More concern needs to be given to validity studies. In the typical psychometric frame of reference, validity studies concern themselves with the relationship of predictors and the thing to be predicted. In situations in which psychological tests are used, the tests are the predictors. Too often in the testing of older persons the tests have not been based sufficiently upon study of potential factors upon which predictions might be made, nor are they inclusive enough of the various factors making up the totality of predictive factors. On the other side of the equation the situation is no better. What is to be predicted, if in reality the tests are actually used for predicting in older adult testing, is rarely adequately defined. Even in the case of the older person entering or returning to the workplace, the criterion measures of work to be performed are likely to be difficult to quantify, variable from person to person in a study, and not distributed in a manner favorable to statistical studies.

Tests of older persons necessitate some modifications in the stringency of ordinarily used directions for administration and scoring. What modifications are needed? Which of the needed ones are permissible? How must tests be interpreted in relation to the modifications?

Recent observations (Hayes, Nelson, & Jarrett, 1987) have been made of the possible practical utility, under special circumstances, of unreliable, invalid assessment procedures. A functional approach to test utilization sometimes means strong acceptance and use of something in particular from a test that in totality shows a low validity coefficient. The "something" may be an item or small part from a test or it may be a behavior associated with the test administration. For example, Verbal IQ on a WAIS may be of little value in dealing with the problems of a non-community acceptance and withdrawing behavior of an aged woman, but individual information and comprehension responses, or lacks of response, may give important leads to dealing with the behavioral problems.

The long recognized problem of test anxiety is of particular concern in the testing of older persons. Test anxiety is an emotional state associated with the test situation, whatever the test may be (a pencil-and-paper ability test, a manual dexterity test, a physical fitness test, etc.). Unless the aim is to evaluate anxiety, the anxiety becomes an extraneous factor interfering with the assessment of what is needed, presumably under circumstances with the absence of anxiety. Older persons are more likely than younger ones to suffer the anxiety problems that affect test results. They are far removed from the school-associated experiences that involve tests, and they may experience anxiety relating to lack of information about tests. Older examinees are concerned both about whether they will do well on the tests and how the test will relate to their problems/needs. Few studies have examined a realistic relationship between anxiety and the test performance of older persons.

Computerized testing has expanded the scope of tests available to clinical workers. With proper training and instructions, it has augmented the information obtained on persons with whom psychologists deal in teaching or diagnostic pursuits. But caution must be exercised; one does not substitute a computerized description of a personality represented by a given MMPI test profile for a clinician's analysis of the profile. But computerized testing is with us, and many view that its advantages outweigh its disadvantages.

Widespread utilization of computerized testing has recently been proposed by the United States Employment Service (USES) and U.S. Armed Forces. The USES functions for persons who want a job. The proposed system of computerized testing will greatly facilitate "matching" of persons with jobs. Similarly proposed universal Army use of computerized testing of applicants wishing to enter the Army will greatly facilitate classification, assignment for training, and placement for work duty. These are examples of uses with persons generally below the age of the older person, but, as the older person comes more and more into view as a personnel concern, the principles apply to more situations.

Comments about computerized testing of older persons must not be left without mention of its limitations. Older persons are not as available for such testing as are younger persons. They are not likely to be found in organized groupings, as in a classroom. They are not likely to be as easily put in contact with a computer outlet. They may not be accustomed to computers and may resist participation in programs in which computers play a part. Computerized testing with older persons may be very time-consuming and expensive.

Testing of older persons must satisfy the basic needs of psychological testing in the current era. Tests must be characterized by a fairness to all. Fairness in testing burgeoned as a result of the concerns of the Equal Employment Opportunity Commission (EEOC) beginning in the 1960s. The early concerns dealt primarily with unfairness as it related to racial characteristics and secondarily to educational and cultural factors associated with race. Now unfairness has entered as a consideration of suitability of tests in other contexts, including use with older persons. Testing of older persons must continue to contribute to solving the general psychological test problems that remain unsolved or only partially solved. These include many age-old issues: Is Binet's concept of intelligence still acceptable today? What is the age of maturity of functions being tested? For purpose of establishing and stating test norms for persons over 16 years of age, what age groupings are justifiable?

The differential diagnosis between organic and functional disorders relating to brain functioning has been of key importance to medical specialists and neuropsychologists dealing with neurological functioning and neurological impairment. What did the patient have to begin with? What aspects of the patient's original inheritance have been lost? What are the prospects? Early in the history of psychological testing, psychologists sensed their role in these problems and developed tests and instructions for their use and interpretation that might help the medical clinician, as well as contribute to their own professional advancement and needs. Wechsler's earliest test (the Wechsler-Bellevue Intelligence Scale) developed during his service as a psychologist in the psychopathic division of the Bellevue Hospital set forth the basics of subtest differentiation in the diagnosis of organic versus functional disorders. This marked the beginning of clinical neuropsychology (the study of the effects of brain disorders on behavior). The approaches have developed into a complex and significant specialty, carried on more recently through pioneering work by Halstead, Luria (1966), and others. With an increasing population of older persons, trained specialists are needed in this area of performance; few clinical psychologists currently are adequately trained.

Psychologists and other professionals involved in testing and test interpretation for older adults must be attitudinally and work-wise oriented toward cooperation in multidisciplinary professional relationships. Referrals for testing the older person may come from a variety of professional sources. Educational administrators may need assistance in selection and promotional procedures for teaching related personnel. Vocational counselors need psychometric experts to ensure maximum utilization of available test data. Community agencies furnish the setting for accomplishing many of the needed interdisciplinary relationships of psychometrists dealing with the older person. Interdisciplinary relations with the medical profession have historically (and presently) furnished the most outstanding and publicized examples of concerns stemming from the relationships. In a physical sense, Nature itself forges the relationships: Medicine is concerned with the body; the nervous system (including the brain) is crucial to the functioning of the body; the brain, the spinal cord, the neurons, and the sensory and response organs that the nervous system coordinates are the basic introductory topics of the study of psychology.

Medicine and psychology share responsibilities in relation to behavior. Mr. "X" cannot walk because a bone in his leg is fractured. Mr. "Y" cannot walk because his nervous system cannot properly coordinate the elements involved in kinesthesis. Mr. "Z," suffering from no physical or neurological ailments, cannot walk because he is suffering from a psychologically regressive disorder taking him back to early childhood. Rehabilitation for the first two of these is the responsibility of the physician; for the third the responsibility lies with the psychologist (or other psychotherapist). But cooperative medical-psychological considerations are needed in diagnosis and treatment planning. Neuropsychologists (those especially trained in medical-psychological relationships) should have much to contribute in such cases.

Levinson (1986) has strongly recommended multidisciplinary approaches in studying adult development. He emphasizes adult development as a link between psychology and other disciplines, including sociology, biology, and history. Levinson sees the fragmentation of approaches produced by competing disciplines as an adverse deterring factor in study of the life course, but he sees improvement on the way:

> The recognition is slowly dawning that the many specialties and theoretical approaches are not isolated entities but aspects of a single field: the study of the individual life course. During the next decade, this study will emerge as a new

multidisciplinary field in the human sciences, linking the various disciplines. (1986, p. 4)

Levinson also sees the social sciences as suffering from lack of interdisciplinary cooperation in studying the sociocultural factors in life development and from lack of coordination with the sciences in studying the individual. To quote further:

> It is necessary, instead, to create a new perspective that combines development and socialization and that draws equally on biology, psychology, and social science, as well as on the humanities. Movement in this direction is not easy, violating as it does the current vested interests of each discipline involved. (1986, p. 13)

Most of the problems of older persons are complex and call for contributions from a number of professions. Cooperative multidisciplinary relationships is the message. Within their own categories of competing disciplines, psychologists and psychometrists should stay mindful of a few additional points:

1) Look with favor on marrying a statistical test score with a personal rating;

2) Keep a balance between personal views on behavior as an organicist or as a psychogeneticist; and

3) Give equal respect to the experimental psychologist in the laboratory and the practical psychologist in the workplace.

We learn from the past what to do in the present and what to project into the future. Psychology's past reveals multidisciplinary origins and relationships. Assessment of the older person emphasizes the multidisciplinary approach in practice.

REFERENCES

Cornelius, S.W., & Caspi, A. (1987). Everyday problem solving in adulthood and old age. *Psychology and Aging, 2,* 144-153.
Hayes, S.C., Nelson, R.O., & Jarrett, R.B. (1987). The treatment utility of assessment. *American Psychologist, 42,* 963-974.
Hunt, T. (1936). *Measurement in psychology.* New York: Prentice-Hall.
Levinson, D.J. (1986). A conception of adult development. *American Psychologist, 41,* 3-13.
Linn, R.L. (1986). Educational testing and assessment. *American Psychologist, 41,* 1153-1160.
Luria, A.R. (1966). *Higher cortical functions in man.* New York: Basic Books.
Matarazzo, J.D. (1972). *Wechsler's measurement and appraisal of adult intelligence.* Baltimore: Williams & Wilkins.

2

Who Is the Older Person?

CLYDE J. LINDLEY, M.A.

As borne out by the U.S. Senate Special Committee on Aging's (1987-1988) report, one of the most significant factors affecting America's present and future course is the aging of its population. During the past several years our concepts and attitudes about older persons have undergone great changes, and these changes are dynamic and ongoing. Contributing to the change is the increasing realization that the average age of the nation's population is rising and that the shift in population composition will have important effects upon the country's economics, politics, and social problems.

Some professionals view older adults as a differentiated category of human beings and believe that there are specific tests, theories, methodologies, or bases of test interpretations for such a category. In contrast, a more accurate and holistic view defines the older person from a functional rather than chronological age standpoint.

The importance of a broad knowledge of the older adult and the personal, family, social, economic, medical, and political circumstances surrounding his or her life cannot be overemphasized. The psychologist or psychometrist responsible for testing the older person must be aware of these facts and circumstances. In addition to the requisite knowledge and understanding of the aging process, it is critical for clinicians to realize the significance to the older person of what his or her old age means.

Interest is awakening in securing more and better information about older persons. In recognition of this, the American Psychological Association began to publish a new journal, *Psychology and Aging,* in March 1986. A burgeoning professional and scientific literature from various disciplines emphasizes the aging process and its complexity. Tremendous research activity is underway at the National Institute on Aging, in various aging centers, at universities and university medical schools, within the Veterans Administration Geriatric Research and Education Centers (GREC), and elsewhere. Despite these activities, Birren (1987), an outstanding scientist in research on aging, points to the inadequacy of scientific knowledge about aging. He indicates the need for studies ranging from the most basic to the evaluation of applications. Birren advocates, among other things, strengthening our understanding of *normal aging* by emphasizing "the interactive influences of behavioral and social factors as they parallel physiology" (p. 2). Maddox (1987) stresses a somewhat related theme by stating that the most important problems in aging are interdisciplinary and not the exclusive domain of any single discipline. Multidisciplinary research efforts require a high degree of cooperation among scientists (Lindley, 1959).

THE CONCEPT OF YOUNG-OLD VERSUS OLD-OLD

An older person is often viewed as old by the criterion of chronological age. The U.S. Census Bureau defines the elderly as those aged 65 and over, and the Social Security Administration uses 65 for the age for beginning to pay full benefits. Retirement from the world of work may begin well before age 65. Complicating this age criterion is the fact that some people are old (biologically) well before age 65, while others seem younger at 70 to 75 and older. The concept of *young-old* (65-74 years of age) and *old-old* (75 years of age and older) has been proposed to differentiate between the physical, psychological, and situational characteristics of the two age groups (Neugarten, 1974, 1977; Poon, 1980). Neugarten (1977) indicated that the young-old group is characterized by a period of early adjustment to old age status and retirement, by continued physical vigor, and by developing potentially new opportunities for community involvement. The old-old group is more often characterized by a greater loss of peers, increasing sensory deficits, and consequent restrictions in social functioning. Feifel and Strack (1987) suggest that the reviews of studies of the old-old and the young-old indicate there are generally diminished biopsychosocial characteristics that differentiate the two groups (e.g., reduced physical and mental activities, shrinking social support).

Another report describes young-olds (aged 55 to 74) as persons in their later middle-age who are healthy and fully functioning (Neugarten, 1975). The old-olds are those aged 75 and over who often have multiple chronic diseases and/or disabilities, and who are dependent on others for support. Manton, Siegler, and Woodbury (1986) warn that this characterization has stereotyped the old-old and ignores the importance of functioning in later life. They indicate there are subgroups within the elderly that do not conform to the young-old/old-old pattern.

Feifel and Strack (1987) interviewed and tested 109 fairly healthy males, 53 in the young-old group and 56 in the old-old group, on a variety of features that helped define adaptation to old age (Poon, 1980). The major finding of the study was the broad similarity between the groups. No important differences occurred in such areas as fear of death, religious belief, life values, general mood, self-concept, and perceived social support. "Overall, in examining Neugarten's premise, old-old seems to be young-old more often than not" (p. 411). Differences between the two age groups did not occur in personality, attitudinal, or other psychological domains.

In summary, it appears that old-age classifications such as the young-old and old-old may be convenient in demographic analyses, but too frequently mask the distinctive individual patterns of adaptation to changes that occur with increasing age. In the words of Feifel and Strack (1987), "Older people are different not only from the young, but also from each other, even within the same age category. . . . Basic material for scrutiny should be not the young-old or old-old individual but the whole person"[1] (p. 412).

Instead of using chronological age as a criterion, functional age has been suggested (Salthouse, 1986). This generally refers to the person's ability to be self-maintaining, to engage in intellectual activity, and to pursue directed activities such as

---

1. Many research studies will of necessity use groupings of age ranges for convenience, not based on differential characteristics of the different age groups.

working. But there is little agreement on how to assess functional age (Zopf, 1986). The Duke OARS (Older Americans Resources and Services) longitudinal studies on assessment of functional status of older persons (Maddox, 1972; Maddox et al., 1979) focused on measures of impairment physically, emotionally, or in capacity for self-care. Most older adults (almost 7,000 males and females) were not significantly impaired on the initial and subsequent evaluation. However, the risk of impairment did rise with age. Zopf (1986) discusses the fact that in large population studies there is close proximity of chronological age to physiological age, functional age, and the aging process. He cautions that the wide individual variations within the large populations do not warrant any interpretation that the elderly are all alike in their characteristics. Groups of older persons are as heterogeneous as other groups, with the exception that all of the members are at least age 65. A basic fact is that people age differently (Maddox, 1987), that the elderly are very heterogeneous in their characteristics, and the outstanding characteristic is their diversity.

COMMON MYTHS AND MISCONCEPTIONS

There is another complicating factor in understanding the older person. Despite all the factual information now available in the United States, there is a mass of misinformation about older persons and many unfounded inferences about the aging process. These misconceptions about aging have led to an abundance of myths (Palmore, 1974, 1977, 1982, 1984; Butler, 1980; Peterson, Hall, & Peterson, 1988). Butler (1978), for example, has noted the misconception that older persons are prone to hypochondriasis. The early stereotypes characterized older people as unhappy, lonely, in poor health with chronic conditions, as complainers and cranks, lacking in personal initiative, dependent on others, miserable, and waiting to die. Old age implies a condition in which life is no longer enjoyable. Another common belief is that older persons have lost interest in and capacity for sexual relations. Foner and Schwab (1981) discuss several stereotypes, such as that most people 65 and over suffer a mild to severe form of senility, that intelligence declines with age, that most people lose muscular strength as they age, and that people 65 and over are slower at accomplishing tasks than younger people (because of age).

The attitudes of younger adults toward older adults is often disdainful. Older men are frequently referred to as "old-timers," "Pops," and "dirty old men" (Rubinstein, 1986). Young adults regard old adults as being of lower status and prestige (Birren & Cunningham, 1985); as a consequence, young adults may have a negative attitude toward growing old. Many people in the United States do view aging as a negative aspect of life:

> Old people often are invisible in the media unless they are surprisingly *youthful*, contradict the stereotypes for a *person of their age*, or simply live an unusually long time. On the street, they are often ignored as if they were invisible, unless they become a *problem*. (Kimmel, 1988, p. 175)

In the work environment a common belief is that older workers are not productive. Stagner (1985) has found that employers believe that older persons in the workplace are less capable, less efficient, and less productive. Craft, Doctors, Shkop, and Benecki (1979) report that in a simulated hiring study, managers evaluating résumés believed that older candidates were more likely opinionated, less serious, and less ambitious. (Additional attitudes about older workers and facts refuting these beliefs are discussed in the chapter "Assessment of Older Persons in the Workplace.")

Older persons are believed to be more conservative and less flexible. This conservatism has been interpreted sometimes to result from increasing age. However, the social and cultural forces influencing attitude change appear to affect both older and younger persons alike. Older persons don't necessarily become more conservative—such results are probably a result of cohort effects associated with earlier socializations.

Even the term *elderly* itself has some unfavorable connotations. Maddox (1987) called attention to the "inappropriateness of broad references to 'the elderly' as though some dominant internal mechanism associated with age homogenized them into an undifferentiated lump of humanity" (p. 558).

Many of these stereotypes and prejudices about older persons persist among the professional groups responsible for the care of the elderly. In an editorial in the *Journal of the American Medical Association,* Welte (1987) states that elderly patients are often assumed to have a poor prognosis, cognitive impairment, decreased quality of life, limited life expectancy, and reduced social worth simply because of their age. Butler (1969) has used the term "ageism" to connote discrimination against the elderly. Interviewers often view older job applicants as "more difficult to train and place into jobs, more resistant to change and less suitable for promotion and expect them to have lower job performances" (Avolio & Barrett, 1987, p. 56). Welte points out that this "ageism" should be avoided when selecting treatments and predicting outcomes for elderly patients. Palmore (1974) pointed out that lack of knowledge about aging is common in the general public and also among medical and helping professions working directly with the aged. Lay persons, as a result of observing complaining older persons, may develop a negative stereotype of older persons, while medical personnel stigmatize them by calling them old "crocks" (Costa & McCrae, 1985).

Some of the biases and myths related to the older person are, in fact, not entirely unrealistic. As pointed out by Gatz and Pearson (1988), psychologists' concept of ageism needs revision as their basis for providing psychological services. One of the dangers is that generalized ideas about ageism may adversely affect specific cases. For example, a treatable case of depression may be ignored if overlooked as a part of a global concept of age. In addition, psychologists may develop an "antidiscrimination response" whereby they emphasize the competencies of older persons and excuse their shortcomings, which results in failure to recognize legitimate psychological problems with potential for remediation. Gatz and Pearson indicate that another possibility is that professionals overestimate the occurrence of a particular problem, for example, progressive dementia, when many patients may in fact have a reversible condition. This can be very serious because it neglects other symptoms that need evaluation and intervention. Gatz and Pearson (1988) conclude by stating some of the problems of research related to ageism:

Age is a weak stereotype; people may hold negative stereotypes, and yet they may feel called upon to express more acceptable sentiments; people may discount elderly people who serve as positive exemplars because they are not "typical" old persons; and individuals may simultaneously hold multiple stereotypes of the aged. (p. 187)

RESEARCH FINDINGS ON OLDER ADULTS AND AGING

Research studies of the aging process in older persons contradict the many myths and negative views. Butt and Beiser (1987), in analyzing the results of a multination[2] international survey on human values and well-being over the life span, found in several different countries that the vast majority of the population over 65 years of age is reported to be well and independent. Clearly the stereotype that older persons are unhappy with the processes of aging is untrue. According to the results of the 1985 Health Interview Survey conducted by the National Center for Health Statistics (1987), 70% of elderly people in the United States living in the community describe their health as excellent, very good, or good compared with others their age; only 30% report that their health is fair or poor. Old people are not unhappy with the process of aging and do not necessarily feel lonely or isolated. Studies of happiness with the Affect Balance Scale (ABS) failed to indicate age differences on the scale, with the conclusion that happiness is not age linked (George, 1987). Contrary to expectations many older persons over age 65 have the ability to engage in sexual relations (Bray, 1984). This has been confirmed for most men and the majority of women by the Duke OARS longitudinal studies (Palmore, 1974). Masters and Johnson (1966) report that healthy older persons can engage in sexual relations through their 70s and 80s.

Studies of older people in retirement communities generally emphasize how involved and active these retirees are. They report they are not lonely, that they feel they have a family (a peer group they live with), that they didn't come to the retirement community to die, and that they don't even think of getting old in the community (Barron, 1988). Subjects report a very active life, and idleness is almost unspeakable. Similar conditions exist at the more than 600 other retirement communities in the U.S. Of course, there is obviously another side to this "happy" picture of retirement communities. The viability of retirement communities is a problem, and they have their lives and life stages as do the individuals living in them (La Greca, Strieb, & Folts, 1985). The older persons living there get older and develop health problems that may require movement to full-care facilities, and some persons die there.

The U.S. Senate Special Committee on Aging (1987-1988) reports that most older persons have a very favorable positive attitude toward their health. Longitudinal studies on personality in aging (Costa, McCrae, & Arenberg, 1983) indicate that personality is not likely to change simply as a result of growing older; that is, a very flexible person does not become rigid or stubborn. Costa and McCrae's (1980) research contradicts the notion that aging persons are hypochondriacs; they are no more so than younger persons. These researchers found that poor psychological

---

2. Australia, Brazil, Canada, France, India, Italy, Japan, Korea, the Philippines, Singapore, the United Kingdom, the United States and West Germany.

adjustment produces excessive health complaints unrelated to age. They also report that personality structure remains highly stable over the adult life span. In a later study Costa and McCrae (1985) state that as individuals age, there is consistent evidence of age-related increases for complaints in the sensory, cardiovascular, and genitourinary systems, as well as in total number of complaints. However, changes are not consistently seen in other systems. They interpret this as an increase in complaints that are actually related to health changes. Costa and McCrae state categorically that the increased somatic complaints are not due to hypochondriacal behavior. They admit that there are some hypochondriacs among older persons, but argue that hypochondriasis is no more prevalent in older age groups than in any other age groups. Increasing age by itself does not appear to modify personality functioning.

THE DEMOGRAPHICS OF AGING

Considerable demographic information is now available about the trends and projections of our older population (Schick, 1986; U.S. Senate Special Committee on Aging, 1985-1986; U.S. Senate Special Committee on Aging, 1987-1988; *Statistical Abstracts of the United States, 1985,* 1984). There is a growing awareness of the aging of our population and its future implications. These data provide an essential background for understanding the older person. Table 1 illustrates the present large numbers of older persons in the population and the rapid growth in the next 50 years. In 1980, 25.5 million persons (11%) in the United States were age 65 and over. Fifty years later this number grows to 64.5 million (21%)! The 85-plus population is growing especially rapidly. By 2030 this group is expected to be almost four times as large. The 67-74 group is projected to be over two times its size by 2030. Similarly, the 75-84 group is almost three times as large.

Other selected demographic facts about the growth of the older population are quoted from the report of the U.S. Senate Committee on Aging (1987-1988):

The older population grew more than twice as fast as the rest of the population during the last two decades.

The elderly population is growing older. In 1986, 41 percent of the elderly population was age 75 and older. By the year 2000, half of the elderly population is projected to be 75-plus.

Elderly women now outnumber elderly men three to two.

The ratio of elderly persons to persons of working age has grown from seven elderly per 100 persons age 18 to 64 in 1900 to 19 per 100 today. By 2010, there are expected to be 22 elderly persons per 100 of working age and by 2050, 38 per 100.

The number and proportion of older veterans is increasing. By the year 2000, close to two-thirds, 63 percent, of all 65-plus males will be veterans, compared to a little over one-fourth, or 27 percent in 1980.

More than half of the elderly live in just eight states: California, New York, Florida, Pennsylvania, Texas, Illinois, Ohio, and Michigan.

TABLE 1

ACTUAL AND PROJECTED GROWTH OF THE OLDER POPULATION, 1980–2030
(NUMBERS IN THOUSANDS)

Age	1980	1990	2000	2010	2020	2030
All ages total population	226,505	249,657	267,955	283,238	296,597	304,807
55-64	21,700	21,051	23,767	34,848	40,298	34,025
65-74	15,578	18,035	17,677	20,318	29,855	34,535
75-84	7,727	10,349	12,318	12,326	14,486	21,434
85 and over	2,240	3,313	4,926	6,551	7,081	8,612
65 and over	25,544	31,697	34,921	39,195	51,422	64,581

Sources: 1900–80: U.S. Bureau of the Census, *Decennial Censuses of Population.*
1900–2050: U.S. Bureau of the Census, *Projections of the Population of the United States by Age, Sex, and Race: 1983-2080.* (Current Population Reports, Series P-25, No. 952, May 1984). Projections are middle series.

(*Note:* Table adapted from Table 1-2, 1987-1988, *Aging America,* U.S. Senate Special Committee on Aging.)

In 1980, for the first time, more elderly lived in the suburbs than in the central cities.

On average, older persons change residences one-fourth as often as younger persons, but those who move out-of-state tend to move to the Sunbelt.

A new trend, called "countermigration," has emerged in which some 60-plus persons who migrated to the Sunbelt in their early retirement years return to their home states or the homes of family and friends.

Life expectancy at age 85 has increased 24 percent since 1960 and is expected to increase another forty percent by 2040 (Soldo and Manton, 1985).

More people are also surviving into their 10th and 11th decades. The upward trend in life expectancy is continuing; Americans who reached their 65th birthdays in 1985 could expect, on average, to live another 16.8 years.

The ratio of females to men varies dramatically with age. In the under-20 age group, for instance, there were 34.5 million females versus 36.1 million males in 1986. The 30-to-34 year age group was evenly balanced at about 10.4 million each. But for the 65- plus age group, there were 17.4 million women and 11.8 million men. Elderly women now outnumber elderly men three to two, a considerable change from 1960 when the ratio of elderly females to elderly males was six to five.

This disparity becomes more marked in the upper age ranges. In 1986, there were 83 men between 65 and 69 years for every 100 women in that same group. Among those 70-74, there were 74 men for every 100 women; for those 75-79, 64 men; for those 80-84, 53 men and for 85+, only 40 men. (pp. 1, 14, 15, 20, 23, 25)

The second division of the U.S. Senate Special Committee on Aging Report is concerned with incomes of differing age- and sex-determined population groups (1987-1988):

Older persons have substantially less cash income than those under 65.

Elderly persons are more likely than other adults to be poor.

The old-old (85 years of age or older) have significantly lower money incomes than the young-old (65 to 74 years of age).

In 1986, the median income of elderly women was slightly more than half (56 percent) the median income of elderly men, $6,425 versus $11,544. Nearly three-quarters (71.8 percent) of the elderly poor population are women.

Nonwhite elderly individuals have substantially lower money incomes than their white counterparts. (p. 2)

The Senate Committee Report on Aging includes facts on retirement—a topic of almost universal concern to the older worker:

> In this century, retirement has become an expected part of an individual's life course. In 1900, the average male spent three percent of his lifetime in retirement. In 1980, he was spending nearly one-fifth, or 13.8 years of his life in retirement.

> Age 65 is commonly thought of as the "normal" retirement age. However, almost two-thirds of older workers retire before age 65.

> The labor force participation of men and women drops rapidly with increasing age. For instance, according to labor force statistics for 1986, 55 percent of 60- to 64-year-old men were in the labor force compared to 25 percent of 65- to 69-year-old men, and ten percent of those age 70-plus.

> In 1986, almost three-quarters (72 percent) of 65-plus workers were in managerial and professional; technical, sales, and administrative support; and service occupations.

> Three-quarters of the labor force would prefer to continue some kind of part-time work after retirement. In 1986, of the elderly who were at work in non-agricultural industries, 48 percent of the men and 61 percent of the women were on part-time schedules.

> For those elderly who desire to work, unemployment creates serious problems. Older workers who lose their jobs stay unemployed longer than younger workers, suffer a greater loss, and are more likely to give up looking for another job. (pp. 2, 3)

Another section of the Senate Committee Report on Aging deals with the health of the older person:

> Contrary to stereotype, most older persons view their health positively. Although most older people have at least one chronic condition, seven out of ten noninstitutionalized elderly describe their health as good or excellent compared to others their age.

> One out of four elderly have at least a mild degree of functional disability, but the chance of becoming disabled increases with age. Half of the oldest-old have some functional disability.

> Cross-sectional data have shown that the likelihood of having a chronic illness increases with age. More than four out of five persons 65 and over have at least one chronic condition and multiple conditions are commonplace among the elderly.

> Many psychiatric problems are not as common for older persons as for younger persons. However, an important health problem of older age is cognitive impairment (which can be related to a number of sources, including Alzheimer's dis-

ease). A recent study has shown that 63 percent of the elderly in nursing homes have at least a mild form of cognitive impairment.

Three out of four elderly die from heart disease, cancer, or stroke. Though heart disease has been declining, it remains the major cause of death today.

The elderly are the heaviest users of health services. They account for 30 percent of all hospital discharges, 20 percent of all doctor visits, and one-third of the country's personal health care expenditures even though they constitute only 12 percent of the population. Health care use is greatest in the last year of life and among the old-old.

Only about five percent of the elderly live in nursing homes at any given time. In 1985, an estimated 1.3 million elderly persons lived in nursing homes.

"Informal supports"—the help of friends, spouses, and other relatives—provide valuable assistance to the elderly. (p. 3)

Selected social aspects of the life of older persons are discussed in another section of the Report:

Most elderly men are married and live in a family setting, while most older women are widows. In 1986, 67 percent of women age 75-plus were widowed while 68 percent of the men in this age group were married. In 1986, 51 percent of the women age 75-plus lived alone, while only 19 percent of men in this age category lived alone.

The gap in educational attainment between the elderly and nonelderly is closing. In 1986, elderly people had completed an average of 11.8 years of school compared to 12.6 years for all adults.

In 1985, 75 percent of the households maintained by an older person were owner-occupied and about 83 percent of these were owned free and clear.

Significant numbers of elderly persons live in inadequate housing and do not have telephones. (p. 4)

GENERAL ASSESSMENT CONSIDERATIONS

The demographic material quoted from the U.S. Senate Special Committee on Aging reports facts and trends that must be of concern to test developers and test users for the older population. The first and most noticeable message conveyed by the Senate report is the complexity of the problems. It underscores the difficulty of the tasks that the psychologist faces in conducting psychological assessment in a climate in which the changes in population ages, economic, social, and health factors are so interrelated. This complexity is acknowledged by researchers studying aging. Confounding the problem is the fact that there is no strong consensus regarding the basic nature of aging and the aging process.

Older persons needing psychological evaluation present collectively a widely varying possible list of complaints or problems. Many referrals to the psychologist have a high incidence of problems with medical, psychological, and social components. The components may not be clearly discernible and they may interact with each other. They are very likely to reach the psychologist doing the testing from a referral based upon a complaint, with little or no background related to the complaint. In order to interpret psychological testing the complaint must be placed in its proper context.

The complaint often can be viewed as "the tip of the iceberg." As an example, an older worker may complain about stress and increased anxiety from overwork in a new job assignment that he or she states is beyond his or her capabilities. Although some situational work factors contribute to the problem, the main source of the anxiety may be primarily home related rather than work related. Though not evident in the case history, through pre-testing interviews and verbal interaction prior to actual testing the psychologist may sense the realistic difficulties. They can then be pursued as background for selecting and interpreting the tests and as facts important to diagnosis/treatment. The interrelatedness of physical, mental, and social functioning in making accurate assessments is stressed by Kane and Kane (1981).

Psychologists testing older persons must recognize and understand the increasing health problems, health concerns, and health-related complaints of older persons (Woodward & Wallston, 1987) and the relationships between health and behavior (Siegler & Costa, 1985). Rowe (1985) reports that elderly persons living in the community have 3.5 "disabilities" per person; those institutionalized have 6 per person—probably relating to differences in general state of health, as well as stage of development of the disability. In the area of mental health, the needs of older persons are not being met (Roybal, 1988).

The increasing health concerns relate to a large extent to population demographics. An increasing proportion of the population is coming into the older person classification, and the older persons themselves are getting older. Sensorimotor disturbances and complaints are common; not major catastrophic losses, but more or less minor interferences with life's activities. In the sensory category, self-centered concerns are most often encountered with respect to vision and hearing because of their importance and exteroceptive nature.

Older persons are likely to encounter visual decline sufficient to influence daily task performances to some degree; for a significant minority these changes are severe (Kline & Schieber, 1985). Some visual loss occurs in practically all older adults through the normal process of aging (Kosnik, Winslow, Kline, Rasinski, & Sekuler, 1988). Decline in near vision increases most rapidly with age. Older persons generally have slower response time in performing visual tasks and experience difficulties both in adapting to glare or dim light and in adapting when going from light places/ rooms to dark places/rooms (or vice versa). In the testing situation particular concerns relate to adequate lighting (without glare), the size of the print on pencil-and-paper tests (the Wide Range Achievement Test-Revised, as an example, has a large-print edition), the vision requirements for reacting to exposure of Bender Visual Motor Gestalt cards, and color vision and appreciation of texture and shading necessary for normal use of the various cards of the Rorschach. Poor vision may affect locomotion and be a constant worry to the older person.

Age changes in hearing are often characterized as progressive, irreversible, and detrimental to successful adaptation in the later years of life (Olsho, Harkins, &

Lenhardt, 1985). Older persons referred for evaluation for other problems may have moderate hearing impairment, which has implications for testing. If the testing room (situation) has much background noise, this may be very disruptive and affect the person's interaction with examiner during the interview and scores on oral tests such as parts of the Wechsler Adult Intelligence Scale (WAIS) and its revision, the WAIS-R. Following oral directions may be difficult because of misunderstanding what is said by the examiner.

On the motor (response) side of the sensorimotor process, older persons may show symptoms of slowness, incoordinations, contractures, and tremors among an extensive list of differentiated motor disturbances. Paralyses on the one end of the scale and convulsions on the other represent extremes of motor disturbance. Some degree of motor loss is to be expected with old age and is usually adjusted to adequately. Older people frequently complain of foot problems:

> The ability to ambulate freely and move about, to render care for oneself, and to remain an active and productive member of society is often lost when foot problems become painful and in fact incapacitate the person from the normal activities of daily living. Ambulation is many times the key or the catalyst between an individual retaining dignity and remaining in a normal living environment or being institutionalized. (Helfand, 1984, p. 291)

Slowing of response time (reaction time) with increasing age is well documented (Salthouse, 1985). The slowing, however, may be related to health factors or to lack of use of a specific activity. Healthier adults will generally have faster reaction times than those less healthy of comparable age. Timed tests may put older persons at a disadvantage when their slowness is due to the fact that they have not used the test skills/abilities for a long time. Some health problems (i.e., arthritis) that involve hand-wrist-finger functions will have a direct relation to slowed reaction time, and as a consequence, invalidate timed performance tests.

Many minor, perhaps normal, physical-psychological deficits in the older person are not a part of the test-awareness of the psychologist administering psychological tests. Rating on "ability to follow instructions" can erroneously relate mainly to motor ability if measured by a finger-tapping test in a person with motor impairments involving the fingers. Failure to recognize minor motor difficulties may significantly affect IQ ratings on the WAIS.

It is obvious that minor problems in vision, hearing, and motor areas are often interrelated and may have a very real impact on psychological test results. Before administering psychological tests the psychologist should be alert to the existence of any of these problems and to their interrelationships. Where feasible, the problems should be counteracted by modifications in the test environment or test materials. If the problems cannot be counteracted, then test interpretations and test reports must be made in the light of the problems.

In addition to the effects of minor sensorimotor disturbances of which psychologists must be cognizant when selecting and administering psychological tests, another physiological concern needs to be mentioned: the effect of drug-induced states produced by medication that the older person may be taking. Drowsiness, headaches, irritability, anxiety, incoordination, and a host of other drug effects upon behavior, sensitivities, and emotions may interfere with psychological testing. An older person who is incapable of learning a task or who receives an IQ of 65 on a test because of drowsiness and inability to maintain sustained attention from phenobarbital medication should not be judged inherently incapable and of low intellect.

Psychologists testing older persons frequently meet problems of memory and memory evaluations (Gilewski & Zelinski, 1986). Older persons coming to a psychologist or professional counselor more often than not express a concern about whether their memory is slipping. They seem, as commonly pointed out in discussions of memory, to be able remember very well, with many details, events of long ago, but have trouble with current daily things. Actually, reasonably healthy older adults usually test within normal limits on memory tests. Their deficits or claimed deficits in everyday memory are likely to be attention or motivationally related. Also, the number of things impinging upon the adult for possible memory is likely to increase with age, at least during the functional years of life. Anxieties about the result may cause the older person to assume erroneously decreasing memory powers. However, claimed deficits of anxieties about memory should be investigated for possible serious disorders.

Broader cognitive deficits often appear in older adults who perform less well than younger age groups on tasks of reasoning, problem solving, and concept formation. New evidence has recently been reported that disease or declining health rather than age per se is in large part responsible for lowered cognitive and intellectual functioning (Manton et al., 1986). However, abilities involving practical intelligence or social competence have received much less attention. Cornelius and Caspi (1987) constructed an Everyday Problem-Solving Inventory to assess this latter area. Everyday problem-solving performance displayed a linear increase with age, with older adults performing better than younger adults. Older adults did not show a decline in performance.

In the behavioral area, there may be lack of orientation, confusion about time, inadequate knowledge of environmental aspects of living, disturbances in self-concept, and other varying degrees of incompetence in coping with and adjusting to life. Because of loss of friends, loved ones, or spouse, many older persons experience loneliness and depression. All of these complaints and symptoms must be carefully explored to determine how they affect the functional capacity of the older person.

In evaluating an older person, the psychologist must carry out the procedures involved in the context of valid information about older persons in general. Such information forms the basic background for selecting, conducting, and interpreting the test(s). The concept of "valid information about older persons in general" is hard to establish and is not incorporated in the *musts* of many professionals administering tests. It is not significant of "mental lapse" that a particular older person cannot recite one of the multiplication tables if over 50% of older persons of the same chronological age fail such a task. In order to make use of the particular older person's performance, the broader picture of older persons in general must be incorporated into the interpretation. Also, there must be incorporated knowledge about the particular person, experiences of the person, and circumstances of the test administration.

The situational factors of the older person's living are important in interpreting test results. Situational factors like health, income, and housing can be used in grouping and classifying people, but it is not the situation per se that is likely to be significant. Rather, the significance lies in the way persons (older persons) experience and feel about these factors (Ogilvie, 1987). Here again is evidence of the heterogeneity of older persons as a group. They are not alike. They feel differently and react differently to the situational factors.

Because much of psychological testing is concerned with the process of aging, attention needs to be given to such considerations and studies of human aging as those of Rowe and Kahn (1987). These scientists distinguish between *usual aging* and *successful aging*. The former refers to the commonly accepted idea of aging, in and of itself, as the determining factor in producing age-associated cognitive and physiological deficits, with the consequent neglect of the substantial heterogeneity within age groups. Successful aging, by contrast, involves recognition of the importance of extrinsic factors, and the interaction between psychosocial and physiological variables, that have the potential for health promotion and disease prevention in the elderly. This tends to counteract the emphasis on "normal" aging, which tends to create a gerontology of the usual.

It has been the aim of this chapter to discuss the rather multitudinous array of things that must form the background for professionals working with the older person. In order to plan and administer programs of testing with the proper concerns, the professional worker must know who the older person is, appreciate his or her characteristics, and be familiar with the typical physical, psychological, social, and economic problems faced by older adults.

REFERENCES

Avolio, B.J., & Barrett, G.V. (1987). Effects of age stereotyping in a simulated interview. *Psychology and Aging, 2,* 56-63.
Barron, S. (1988). Oh, to be a kid again. *The Washingtonian, 23*(6), 149-159.
Birren, J.E. (1987). A view from the social and behavioral sciences. *Comprehensive Gerontology Bulletin, 1,* 2-3.
Birren, J.E., & Cunningham, W.R. (1985). Research on the psychology of aging: Principles, concepts and theory. In J.E. Birren & K.W. Schaie (Eds.), *Handbook of the psychology of aging* (2nd ed., pp. 3-34). New York: Van Nostrand Reinhold.
Bray, G.P. (1984). Sexuality in the aging. In T.F. Williams (Ed.), *Rehabilitation in aging* (pp. 81-95). New York: Raven.
Butler, R.N. (1969). Ageism: Another form of bigotry. *The Gerontologist, 9,* 243-246.
Butler, R.N. (1978). The doctor and the aged patient. In W. Reichel (Ed.), *The geriatric patient* (pp. 199-206). New York: H. P. Publishing.
Butler, R.N. (1980). Ageism: A foreword. *Journal of Social Issues, 36*(2), 8-11.
Butt, S.D., & Beiser, M. (1987). Successful aging: A theme for international psychology. *Psychology and Aging, 2,* 87-94.
Cornelius, S.W., & Caspi, A. (1987). Everyday problem solving in adulthood and old age. *Psychology and Aging, 2,* 144-153.
Costa, P.T., Jr., & McCrae, R.R. (1980). Still stable after all these years: Personality as a key to some issues in aging. In P.B.B. Baltes & O.G. Brim, Jr. (Eds.), *Life-span, development and behavior* (Vol. 3, pp. 66-103). New York: Academic Press.

Costa, P.T., Jr., & McCrae, R.R. (1985). Hypochondriasis, neuroticism, and aging: When are somatic complaints unfounded? *American Psychologist, 40,* 19-28.

Costa, P.T., McCrae, R.R., & Arenberg, D. (1983). Recent longitudinal research on personality in aging. In K.W. Schaie (Ed.), *Longitudinal studies of adult psychological development* (pp. 222-265). New York: Guilford.

Craft, J.A., Doctors, S.I., Shkop, Y.M., & Benecki, T.J. (1979). Simulated management perceptions, hiring decisions and age. *Aging and Work, 2,* 95-100.

Feifel, H., & Strack, S. (1987). Old is old is old? *Psychology and Aging, 2,* 409-412.

Foner, A., & Schwab, K. (1981). *Aging and retirement.* Monterey, CA: Brooks/Cole.

Gatz, M., & Pearson, C.G. (1988). Ageism revised and the provision of psychological services. *American Psychologist, 43,* 184-188.

George, L.K. (1987). Affect Balance Scale. In G.L. Maddox (Ed.), *The encyclopedia of aging* (p. 13). New York: Springer.

Gilewski, M.J., & Zelinski, E.M. (1986). Questionnaire assessment of memory complaints. In L.W. Poon (Ed.), *Handbook for clinical memory assessment* (pp. 93-107). Washington, DC: American Psychological Association.

Helfand, A.E. (1984). Common foot problems in the aged and rehabilitative management. In T.F. Williams (Ed.), *Rehabilitation in the aging* (pp. 291-303). New York: Raven.

Kane, R.A., & Kane, R.L. (1981). *Assessing the elderly: A practical guide to measurement.* Lexington, MA: Lexington Books.

Kimmel, D.C. (1988). Ageism, psychology, and public policy. *American Psychologist, 43,* 175-178.

Kline, D.W., & Schieber, F.B. (1985). Vision and aging. In J.E. Birren & K.W. Schaie (Eds.), *Handbook of the psychology of aging* (2nd ed., pp. 296-331). New York: Van Nostrand Reinhold.

Kosnik, W., Winslow, L., Kline, D., Rasinski, K., & Sekuler, R. (1988). Visual changes in daily life throughout adulthood. *Journal of Gerontology: Psychological Sciences, 43,* 63-70.

La Greca, A.J., Strieb, G.F., & Folts, W.E. (1985). Retirement communities and their life stages. *Journal of Gerontology, 40*(2), 211-218.

Lindley, C.J. (1959). Cooperative research—a realistic appraisal. In C.J. Lindley (Ed.), *Transactions of the third VA research conference, chemotherapy in psychiatry* (pp. 21-24). Washington, DC: U.S. Veterans Administration.

Maddox, G.L., Fillenbaum, G., & George, L. (1979). Extending the uses of the LRHS data set. *Public Data Use, 7,* 57-62.

Maddox, G.L. (1972). Interventions and outcomes: Notes on designing and implementing an experiment in health care. *International Journal of Epidemiology, 1,* 339-345.

Maddox, G.L. (1987). Aging differently. *The Gerontologist, 27,* 557- 564.

Manton, K.G., Siegler, I.C., & Woodbury, M.A. (1986). Patterns of intellectual development in later life. *Journal of Gerontology, 41,* 486-499.

Masters, W., & Johnson, V. (1966). *Human sexual response.* Boston: Little, Brown.

National Center for Health Statistics. (1987, October). Current estimates from the National Health Interview Survey, United States, 1986. *Vital and Health Statistics* (Series 10, No. 164).

Neugarten, B. (1974). Age groups in the young-old. *Annals of the American Academy of Political and Social Science, 415,* 187-198.

Neugarten, B. (1975). The future and the young old. *The Gerontologist, 15,* 4-9.

Neugarten, B. (1977). Personality and aging. In J.E. Birren & K.W. Schaie (Eds.), *Handbook of the psychology of aging* (pp. 626-649). New York: Van Nostrand Reinhold.

Ogilvie, D.M. (1987). Life satisfaction and identity structure in late middle-aged men and women. *Psychology and Aging, 2,* 217-224.

Olsho, L.W., Harkins, S.W., & Lenhardt, M.L. (1985). Aging and the auditory system. In J.E. Birren & K.W. Schaie (Eds.), *Handbook of the psychology of aging* (2nd ed., pp. 332-377). New York: Van Nostrand Reinhold.

Palmore, E.B. (1974). *Normal aging, Vol. 2.* Durham, NC: Duke University Press.

Palmore, E.B. (1977). Facts on aging: A short quiz. *The Gerontologist, 17,* 315-320.

Palmore, E.B. (1982). Attitudes toward aging. *Research on Aging, 4,* 333-348.

Palmore, E.B. (Ed.). (1984). *Handbook on the aged in the United States.* Westport, CT: Greenwood.

Peterson, C.C., Hall, L.C., & Peterson, J.L. (1988). Age, sex, and contact with elderly adults as predictors of knowledge about psychological aging. *International Journal of Aging and Human Development, 26,* 129-137.

Poon, L.W. (Ed.). (1980). *Aging in the 1980's.* Washington, DC: American Psychological Association.

Rowe, J.W. (1985). Health care of the elderly. *New England Journal of Medicine, 312,* 827-835.

Rowe, J.W., & Kahn, R.L. (1987). Human aging: Usual and successful. *Science, 237,* 143-150.

Roybal, E.R. (1988). Mental health and aging. *American Psychologist, 43,* 189-194.

Rubinstein, R.L. (1986). *Singular paths: Old men living alone.* New York: Columbia University Press.

Salthouse, T.A. (1985). Speed of behavior and its implications for cognition. In J.E. Birren & K.W. Schaie (Eds.), *Handbook of the psychology of aging* (2nd ed., pp. 400-422). New York: Van Nostrand Reinhold.

Salthouse, T.A. (1986). Functional age: Examination of a concept. In J.E. Birren, P.K. Robinson, & J.E. Livingston (Eds.), *Age, health and employment* (pp. 78-92). Englewood Cliffs, NJ: Prentice-Hall.

Schick, F.L. (1986). (Ed.). *Statistical handbook on aging Americans.* Phoenix, AZ: Oryx.

Siegler, I.C., & Costa, P.T., Jr. (1985). Health behavior relationships. In J.E. Birren & K.W. Schaie (Eds.), *Handbook of the psychology of aging* (2nd ed., pp. 144-166). New York: Van Nostrand Reinhold.

Stagner, R. (1985). Aging in industry. In J.E. Birren & K.W. Schaie (Eds.), *Handbook of the psychology of aging* (2nd ed., pp. 789-817). New York: Van Nostrand Reinhold.

U.S. Bureau of the Census. (1984). *Statistical abstracts of the United States* (105th ed.). Washington, DC: U.S. Department of Commerce.

U.S. Senate Special Committee on Aging. (1985-1986). *Aging America: Trends and projections.* Washington, DC: U.S. Senate.

U.S. Senate Special Committee on Aging. (1987-1988). *Aging America: Trends and projections.* Washington, DC: U.S. Department of Health and Human Services.

Welte, T. (1987, July). Age as a risk factor for inadequate treatment. *Journal of the American Medical Association,* pp. 258-516.

Woodward, N.J., & Wallston, B.S. (1987). Age and health care beliefs: Self-efficacy as a mediator of low desire for control. *Psychology and Aging, 2,* 3-8.

Zopf, P.E., Jr. (1986). *America's older population.* Houston: Cap and Gown Press.

3

Psychometric Considerations in Testing the Older Person

CHRISTOPHER HERTZOG, PH.D., JAMES M. SCHEAR, PH.D.

The purpose of this chapter is to provide a basic introduction and review of principles of psychometric theory as they apply to testing the older person. The proper application of testing and test scores in clinical assessment requires taking into account the characteristics of the assessment instruments themselves. In order for professionals to be intelligent users of testing information, they must be knowledgeable of the specific technical criteria that enable and also limit legitimate interpretation of test results. Technical standards for tests include areas of validity, reliability, background information on test development and revision, information on scales and norms, and the recommended content of technical manuals and user's guides. There are well-established standards for tests that make it possible to determine if a particular test has appropriate measurement properties. These technical standards are specified in several resources, including the 1985 *Standards for Educational and Psychological Testing* jointly authored by the American Educational Research Association (AERA), the American Psychological Association (APA), and the National Council on Measurement in Education (NCME).

There is an extensive literature on the subject of clinical assessment of the older person that focuses on both cognitive and personality assessment (e.g., Gallagher, Thompson, & Levy, 1980; Kaszniak, in press; Poon, 1986; Raskin & Jarvik, 1979; Schaie & Schaie, 1977; Schear, 1984; Storandt, Siegler, & Elias, 1978; Zarit, Eiler, & Hassinger, 1985). Given the quality of this literature and the space limitations here, our discussion is limited to a consideration of psychometric issues such as validity and reliability and their relevance for testing and assessment of older persons. Although it will be necessary to describe some of the content to be found in the literature cited above, it will not be reviewed in detail.

The authors wish to express appreciation to Dr. Susan Sato for her helpful comments on earlier drafts of the chapter. This work was supported, in part, by a Research Career Development Award from the National Institute on Aging (K04-AG00335) to the first author and by the Veterans Administration Medical Research Service funds awarded to the second author.

TECHNICAL GUIDELINES FOR PSYCHOMETRIC TESTS AND THEIR USE

Measurement Principles: Reliability and Validity

Because this book addresses a multidisciplinary audience, it may be helpful to define some basic psychometric terms and principles that are relevant to the ensuing discussion. A *measure* is a quantitative representation of an empirically observable attribute. The term *instrument* is often used interchangeably with *measure*. A common distinction is drawn between two types of measures: tests and scales. The distinction is somewhat arbitrary, for both types of measures are designed to characterize the individual's level on an underlying attribute. In practice, the term *test* refers to measures based upon responses to items in which responses may be objectively classified as correct or incorrect according to an external standard. *Scale*, on the other hand, is a term commonly reserved for measures of attributes that cannot be objectively determined, instead requiring the rating of the attribute by some observer (e.g., the person him- or herself, a clinician, or an informant). Although there are multiple scaling techniques provided by psychometrics, the most common is the use of summative scales with multiple Likert rating scale items. An example is the Profile of Mood States (McNair, Lorr, & Droppleman, 1971), which asks individuals to rate the degree to which a set of adjectives accurately describes their current mood (e.g., depressed, elated). Multiple items are included for each construct to be rated. Often such scales include multiple subscales measuring multiple, related constructs (e.g., depression, anxiety, hostility). After individuals rate themselves on all items, the rating responses are summed over items measuring the same attributes.

It is critical that tests employed for assessment of older individuals have known and acceptable levels of reliability and validity. Test *reliability* is concerned with the consistency of measurement—the extent to which the test would, in principle, return the same score for the same individual if administered in the same setting. *Validity* is a more diverse and complicated concept; as treated in modern measurement theory, it derives from the critical/realist perspective that assumes there exists, in the world, attributes that determine directly the behavior of individuals in situations. These attributes (of persons and situations) are assumed to be latent constructs that can be identified theoretically and then, with appropriate methods, measured empirically (Cook & Campbell, 1979; Cronbach, 1970; Cronbach & Meehl, 1955; Messick, 1981). Validity, then, is defined as the extent to which a test actually measures the construct it was designed to measure. Traditionally, this concept of validity has been termed *construct validity* in order to separate it from related concepts such as *content validity*, *predictive validity*, and *concurrent validity* (e.g., Cronbach, 1970). The new *Standards for Educational and Psychological Testing* (AERA, APA, & NCME, 1985) acknowledges that all forms of validity are based, explicitly or implicitly, on issues involving the construct validity of the test. Issues of criterion-related validity (including both concurrent and predictive validity), for instance, involve the extent to which the test can be used to predict a criterion measure at the same or a later point in time. For example, one could ask whether an admissions examination like the Graduate Record Examination has predictive validity for academic success in graduate school. Although one need not, strictly speaking, know why the exam predicts the desired criterion in order to use it for predictive purposes, a purely empirical approach to prediction has problems of introducing artifact or bias for unknown reasons. Moreover, the current perspective acknowledges that predictive validity occurs because of relations between underlying constructs. A test, due to the construct it measures, can predict other constructs (or, more precisely, other measures of different constructs) because these attributes are related.

There are multiple research methods for determining reliability and validity of measures that will not be considered in detail here (see Allen & Yen, 1979, and Nunnally, 1978, for sound introductions). However, normal professional standards demand that, before a clinician or researcher selects a test or scale, he or she must evaluate the candidate instrument. The first question to ask is, has reliability and validity been estimated using appropriate techniques?

The most common methods of estimating reliability include correlations among alternate forms, test-retest designs, and internal consistency methods (e.g., split-half techniques). Each reliability design and estimation technique has its own problems. Test-retest designs use the correlation of a test at two separate administrations as a basis for estimating reliability. This design assumes that individual differences in the underlying construct are perfectly stable between first test and retest. Under this assumption, less than perfect correlations reflect the influence of random measurement error. However, any influences that cause shifts in individual differences in the underlying attributes between test and retest sessions (e.g., practice effects, reductions in test anxiety due to exposure to the testing environment) are confounded with measurement error and will cause an underestimate of the test's reliability. This example illustrates that selection of a reliability estimate depends upon what is known about behavior of the construct, so that reliability depends upon the accuracy of our theories about the constructs that are being measured. Thus, before one accepts at face value the reliability estimate reported in a test or scale manual, one should ponder whether the technique of reliability estimation is appropriate for a given construct.

Internal consistency methods of estimating reliability are the most commonly employed technique, especially when using self-report scales. Internal consistency captures the idea that a test or a psychological scale has multiple constituent items, and that the consistency of individual differences in responses on items measuring the same construct provides a basis for estimating reliability of the overall test or scale. Tests of intelligence, memory, and other forms of cognition typically use multiple items to increase the reliability and validity of the overall test score. The use of multiple items is also a common feature of most psychological scales.

Reliability for summative scales is most commonly estimated from internal consistency methods such as Cronbach's *coefficient alpha*. It is important for the test consumer to realize that any internal consistency reliability statistic is just an *estimate* of reliability. Just like the reliability estimate based upon the test-retest correlation, the accuracy of an internal consistency reliability estimate depends upon the truth of a set of assumptions. For this reason, internal consistency methods are only appropriate for certain types of scales and tests. Internal consistency estimates vary in their assumptions, but all methods assume that all the items in a subscale measure one and only one underlying construct. This assumption is sometimes termed *homogeneity* (e.g., McDonald, 1978). A good operational definition of homogeneity is that, when factor analysis is used on the test items, a single factor accounts for all the item correlations. Internal consistency estimates of reliability can grossly underestimate the reliability of a measure when items in a test or scale are not factorially homogeneous. An example would be a general test of intelligence like the Wechsler Adult Intelligence Scale-Revised (WAIS-R) Full Scale IQ score (Wechsler, 1981). The WAIS-R Full Scale score may have good predictive validity for a criterion like educational attainment because it combines heterogeneous ability constructs that have independent value in educational settings (Matarazzo, 1972). However, the reliability of the Full Scale IQ score would be seriously underestimated by internal consistency methods. Similarly, Anastasi (1982) reviews evidence that the split-half reliability estimate is inappropriate for speeded tests of intelligence. When the test score depends primarily upon the number of items answered in a fixed time limit, then item responses ought to be highly correlated because of the low difficulty of each item response. Under these circumstances, a split-half correlation would overestimate the true reliability. Alternate forms or test-retest reliability estimates would be more appropriate bases for estimating reliability.

The important message from the preceding discussion is that a reliability estimate must be considered carefully, not just accepted at face value. The same issues apply for assessing construct validity, although the fundamental problems in validity make it easier to appreciate the limits of evidence for construct validity. Because it is easier to estimate reliability than to demonstrate validity, the consumer of a test should expect (but critically evaluate) reliability estimates. However, reliability is necessary but not sufficient for justifying use of a scale. Accepted standards also demand evidence for the construct validity of a test, and test users should be wary of any test that provides evidence for reliability but not validity.

Demonstration of construct validity is admittedly difficult. A minimal criterion is that, if a test or scale is being employed for a given purpose, it has demonstrated criterion-related validity relevant to that purpose. For example, it is appropriate to require that a neuropsychological test for frontal lobe damage (like the Wisconsin Card Sorting Test) has been shown to have predictive validity for actual frontal lobe dysfunction. Given the latent (unobservable) nature of constructs, construct validity cannot be directly assessed. Instead, it requires use of theoretical inference, using a set of propositions about empirically observable phenomena (associated with the test) that would be true *if* the test truly measures the construct of interest. The concept of a body of evidence consistent with theory about the underlying construct was termed *nomological net* by Cronbach and Meehl (1955; see also Cook & Campbell, 1979). The extent of evidence required for an inference of construct validity in part depends on the degree of confidence one can have in selected observations. In the case of frontal lobe damage, it is reasonable to expect that the test correlates more highly with evoked potentials and neuroradiologic procedures of the frontal regions than with distal brain areas (e.g, occipital or parietal lobes). Given our assumption that such physiological criteria are reasonable reflections of the activities of the underlying CNS, such evidence for validity may suffice. However, evidence for the validity of a self-report measure of some attribute like neuroticism may be more complicated due to the alternative interpretations that might apply to empirical phenomena (e.g., avoidance behaviors) that are theoretically relevant to the construct.

This sort of issue leads to complex research designs for assessing construct validity (e.g., Blalock, 1982, 1985; Campbell & Fiske, 1959; Cook & Campbell, 1979). For example, Hertzog, Hultsch, and Dixon (1987) conducted an elaborate study of the construct validity of two metamemory questionnaires. Metamemory is defined as a set of beliefs and knowledge of one's own memory functioning. The design employed by Hertzog et al. (1987) included (a) multiple measures of meta-memory construct, (b) multiple measures of related constructs (e.g., locus of control, personality), and (c) multiple memory tasks so that the predictive validity of meta-memory for actual memory performance could be assessed. A high degree of correla-tion between alternative measures of metamemory (*convergent validity*), coupled with low relationships to related (but theoretically distinct) constructs (termed *dis-criminant validity*) suggested that the questionnaires were measuring something unique (see Cook & Campbell, 1979). However, predictive validity to memory per-formance was relatively low, with correlations between multiple measures of self-rated memory capacity and actual memory performance ranging between .2 and .3. This finding was *not* taken as evidence of a lack of construct validity, however, because it is likely that individuals' beliefs about their own memory ability are inac-curate. That is, the questionnaires could validly measure beliefs about memory, but these beliefs could in turn be inaccurate. In other words, there may truly be a low degree of relationship between the memory beliefs construct and the memory ability construct; under this argument, predictive validity of metamemory for actual mem-ory becomes an empirical question about construct relationships and not a basis for evaluating the construct validity of the metamemory questionnaire.

A major problem for these types of construct validity studies is that correlations are used as a basis of inference, but correlations among scales may underestimate the degree of relationship among constructs because of attenuation due to random mea-surement error (unreliability). Assessment of construct validity often requires use of statistical techniques that can correct for unreliability, such as structural equation models (see Bentler, 1978; Dwyer, 1983; Schaie & Hertzog, 1985).

It is obvious, then, that a major problem for evaluating a candidate measure is that the rules for inferring construct validity are complex and even controversial. Consumers should not necessarily rely on assertions in the test manual regarding demonstrations of validity. Fortunately, it is possible for the clinician or researcher to access reviews of candidate tests (e.g., Keyser & Sweetland, 1985-1988). However, the consumer may need some background in psychometrics to appreciate fully the validity and reliability data and the conclusions of the reviewers. If the user lacks the expertise in psychometric concepts to make responsible decisions regarding test use, the possibility of retaining outside consultants with such expertise should be strongly considered.

Demonstrating Validity and Reliability in Specific Populations

The consumer of a test must appreciate that an empirical demonstration of relia-bility and validity is specific to the population that is under study, an issue with obvious relevance to the problem of testing older persons:

Where there are generally accepted theoretical or empirical reasons for expecting that reliabilities or standard errors of measurement differ substantially for different populations, estimates should be presented for each major population for which the test is recommended. (AERA, APA, & NCME, 1985, p. 22)

Further,

When selecting the type and content of items for tests and inventories, test developers should consider the content and type in relation to cultural backgrounds and prior experiences of the variety of ethnic, cultural, age, and gender groups represented in the intended population of test takers. (AERA, APA, & NCME, 1985, p. 26)

It is important, then, for a test user to be sure that a test has demonstrated validity and reliability *in the specific population* in which the test is to be used. Validity and reliability of a test in one population does not necessarily imply that the degree of validity and reliability generalizes to other populations. Moreover, as most professionals who interact with older persons know, the population of older individuals is heterogeneous, containing persons of varied backgrounds, health status, sensory and perceptual deficits, and other characteristics that may influence responses on tests and questionnaires. Thus, consumers of tests for older persons should pay careful attention to the validation sample used for the test. Did it contain older persons of any kind? Did it contain representative samples of subgroups of older persons for whom the professional wishes to use the test? Whether the validity of a test generalizes to a population for whom the test was not validated is an empirical question and cannot be assumed to be true.

Quantitative Aspects and Norms

Before discussing quantitative aspects and norms, it is important to introduce and briefly define some terms that are central to test construction and measurement.

Raw scores are those expressed in the original unit of measurement used by the measure. Raw test scores are expressed in units of measurement that are arbitrary and determined by the test's construction (number of items, scaling technique, etc.). *Transformed* or *scaled scores* are mathematical transformations of raw scores so that the scaled scores have useful properties. Transformations ought to consider the nature of the scales of measurement, because certain transformations will alter properties of the scores in (possibly) undesirable ways. Usually, the types of scales measured in psychometrics are either *ordinal* (numbers indicate rank ordering of values, but the quantitative difference between points on an ordinal scale do not reflect degree of difference) or *interval* (numbers reflect both rank ordering and relative difference in amount of the measured attribute). Most of the discussion that follows applies only to interval scales.

A common set of scale transformations assumes a normal distribution, or the familiar bell-shaped curve. Figure 1 displays a normal distribution. An important feature of the normal distribution is that the shape of the distribution may be summarized in terms of two parameters: the *mean* and the *variance*. The square root of the variance, the *standard deviation,* is most often used to describe distance from the mean in a normal distribution.

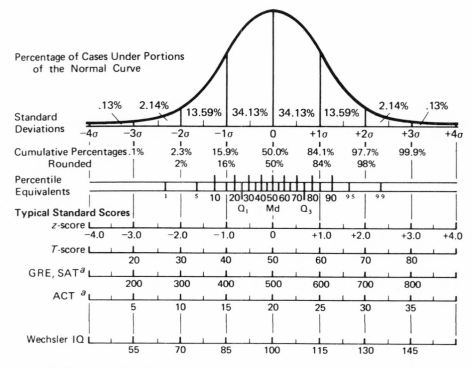

FIGURE 1. The normal distribution and standard score scales based on standard deviation units from the normal distribution. (Adapted from *Test Service Bulletin No. 48* by permission of The Psychological Corporation.)

Discussion in the previous section noted that it is crucial to attend to the population in which a test has been validated. An additional reason to ensure that the population must be assessed is so that norms for tests can legitimately be applied. Norms define the distribution of test scores so that the numbers can be related to location in the distribution of scores on some theoretical population (e.g., male Caucasians):

> Norms that are presented should refer to clearly described groups. These groups should be the ones with whom users of the test will ordinarily wish to compare the people who are tested. (AERA, APA, & NCME, 1985, p. 33)

Many different kinds of *norms* may be appropriate for a given test use: local norms, based on sampling from the population or specified groups in a particular locality; state or regional norms; norms based on national probability sampling; and norms based on a wide variety of occupational and educational classifications. All these definitions imply identification of a target population. However, whenever the target is a special subpopulation, such as the elderly, then one must have published norms for that subpopulation.

There are a number of issues associated with the use of norms for the elderly. The most common norm is to use normal distribution theory to convert raw scores into scaled scores based upon the normal distribution. Then the scaled scores can be used as the basis for evaluating the deviation of the person from the population mean by using normal deviates. Figure 1 shows that a person's deviation from the mean can be captured by a z-score, or *standard score*, defined as

$$z = (X_i - MN(X))/SD(X)$$

where X is some quantitative variable (test scores), X_i is the score of a given individual on X, MN(X) is the population mean of X, and SD(X) is the population standard deviation of X. The standard score is simply a linear transformation of the raw score. The mean of the distribution is now 0 and the standard deviation is 1.0. This linear transformation converts the raw score into *standard deviation units*. A z of +1.0 is one standard deviation above the population mean. A z of -2.0 is two standard deviations below the mean. The z-score standardization will not affect the correlation of the test score with other measures, but it does make it easier to understand the score of an individual in terms of his or her relative standing in the normal distribution.

Figure 1 further illustrates a basic principle in psychological statistics and applied psychometrics. Calculation of a z-score is assumed to enable conversion to percentile rank in the overall distribution. A z-score of +1.00 means that a person is scoring at the 84% point of the cumulative normal frequency distribution. In plain English, this person scores as high or higher than 84% of the total distribution of persons in the population.

There are a number of other scalings that convert raw scores into transformed scores based upon the mean and standard deviation of a parent population. Generally, IQ scores, standard scores, T-scores, and so on are variants on the theme—scores are converted to standard deviation units and then re-expressed in some metric. Traditionally, the IQ transformation of intelligence test scores is set up so that the rescaled population mean is 100 and the rescaled standard deviation is 15. Thus an IQ of 130 is 2 standard deviations above the mean, translating to a percentile rank of approximately the top 2.5% of the distribution.

The WAIS-R is a common test in use for clinical and neuropsychological assessment of older persons. One of the major advantages and benefits of the WAIS-R, in addition to the content validity of its selection of tests for measuring intelligence, is that its norms are based on large and well-defined standardization samples that include large groups of older persons. The WAIS-R manual (Wechsler, 1981) provides clear instructions on how to score and calculate scaled scores. An important issue is whether the norm is expressed in terms of the overall population or expressed relative to a subpopulation (e.g., the elderly). After raw scores are calculated for all WAIS-R subtests, the WAIS-R involves two additional transformations: scaled scores and IQ scores. *Scaled scores* are linear transformations of the raw scores, using the mean and standard deviation of a reference group of 20- to 34-year-old individuals in the standardization sample. The WAIS-R scaled scores have been rescaled so that the reference group has a mean of 10 and a standard deviation 3 for all subtests. Two benefits of scaled scores are 1) the ability to sum scores of different subtests to arrive at Verbal, Performance, and Full Scale scores, correcting for differences in units of measurement in each scale, and 2) the ability to compare each examinee's score to the reference group distribution.

However, a more common set of norms in the WAIS-R is the IQ norms. These norms have been adjusted to be specific to each age decade (25-34, 34-45, etc.). The IQ scores are scaled so that mean age differences are removed, and the IQ score is relative to a person's parent group. Given that there are substantial mean age differences on many WAIS-R subtests (Wechsler, 1981), the same raw score will convert to a different IQ score depending upon the age of the examinee. This property is useful if one is seeking to understand the person's score relative to his or her own age group. For example, the WAIS-R Performance Scale sums several tests that shows robust age differences. The mean Performance Scale score for persons aged 25-34 is 49.89 (S.D. = 11.63), whereas the mean Performance Scale score for the 70-74 group is 30.62 (S.D. = 8.40) (see Wechsler, 1981, Table 7). The IQ transformation takes this difference into account. A person between the ages of 25 and 34 whose Performance Scale score is 60 is assigned an IQ score of 114. A person aged 70-74 who achieves a Performance Scale score of 60 receives an IQ score of 145! This difference reflects the fact that a young adult scoring 60 on the test is about 1 standard deviation above his group mean, but a 70- to 74-year-old person scoring 60 is about 3 standard deviations above the mean of the 70-74 age group. Thus, while the scaled scores reflect standing relative to the reference group and can be compared directly across different age groups, the IQ scores are normed to the specific age group.

Recognition of this issue leads scientists interested in charting age changes to use raw scores or scaled scores rather than WAIS-R IQ scores. It would be inappropriate to use WAIS-R IQ scores for studies of age differences in WAIS-R performance, as it statistically removes mean age differences. For the clinician, a choice of the scaled score norms or the IQ norms for describing performance depends upon whether one wants to know the individual's relative standing to same-aged peers or to the young reference group.

The selection of norms may have profound implications for clinical assessment of older persons. For example, a group of scientists interested in aging and memory deficits have proposed a new nosological category termed *age associated memory impairment* (Crook et al., 1986). Crook et al. (1986) propose three general criteria for a diagnosis of age-associated memory impairment, two of which exclude 1) other pathological conditions known to affect memory and 2) examinee or informant complaint of impaired memory. Their third proposed criterion is memory task performance 1 standard deviation below the performance of a young adult reference group on memory tasks (e.g., the Wechsler Memory Scale). Although use of the young reference group can be justified on the basis of a conception of age-related decline from young adult levels of memory, the use of a 1 S.D. criterion suggests that substantially more older persons will be classified as memory impaired by this criterion than by a criterion of 1 S.D. below older persons' memory performance. Certainly, research on the false positive rate of such a classification criterion is warranted.

Psychometric Theory: Multiple Components of Test Scores

Problems of construct validity and interpretation of tests can be represented by reference to a multiple component theory of test scores (e.g., Embretson, 1983,

1985). The basic idea is that test score performance is determined by multiple cognitive processes. A componential perspective conceptualizes the intelligence test as an information-processing task (e.g., Carroll, 1980; Sternberg, 1977, 1985). The componential perspective argues that solving test items requires multiple steps in transforming information presented in a test item into a cognitive representation appropriate for identifying the correct answer. An implication of the componential perspective is that individual differences in item response times and accuracy of item responses are determined by multiple components that may or may not represent processes involved in the latent cognitive ability construct the test was designed to measure. One implication of the componential perspective is that age-related declines in test performance may reflect age declines in cognitive processes that are required for test performance but are not directly involved in the cognitive ability under study.

The same concept applies to other types of scales, such as self-rated attributes like depressive affect. Generically, the issue is the influences of variables other than the desired attribute (construct). In personality research, many influences on personality scales have been studied, including response sets. Sociological methodologists have termed these sources of invalidity *systematic errors of measurement* in order to differentiate them from random measurement error (e.g., Blalock, 1982).

The concept of multiple determinants translates into the statistical model of multiple components and multiple components of variance in test scores. The classic psychometric model represents the test as a linear sum of weighted components, where the weights are determined by the causal influence of components on overall test performance; for example,

$$X_i = w_1 {}^*C_{1i} + w_2 {}^*C_{2i} + w_3 {}^*C_{3i} + e_i$$

where X_i is the test score of the ith individual, the w's are invariant weights for all individuals, and each C_i is a component score for the ith individual. The fundamental problem for research at the interface of cognitive psychology and psychometrics is identifying and measuring the sources of these components of variance. The problem for test interpretation is taking into account the relative importance of different influences on components of variance when evaluating the meaning of the overall test score. More complicated versions of this model are required for componential modeling of test items (e.g., Embretson, 1983, 1985), but the concept helps us understand why there may be concern about differential validity of tests for older persons. Basically, concerns about equivalent measurement properties (age-related measurement equivalence; see below) involve concern that different age groups have a different constituent components and/or different component weights. The discussion will return to this issue in the context of reviewing some recent research on the measurement properties of tests and scales in older populations.

ISSUES FOR TEST USAGE WITH OLDER PERSONS

There are a number of specific issues associated with using tests for older persons, many of which have been considered at length in the methodological literature (especially in the domain of life-span developmental psychology; see Baltes, Reese,

& Nesselroade, 1977; Nesselroade & Labouvie, 1985; Nesselroade & Reese, 1973; Schaie, 1973, 1977; Schaie & Hertzog, 1982, 1985). However, the implications of these more theoretical treatments for testing are often obscure to the practitioner in the area. Likewise, clinicians have presented a variety of ideas on the topic of assessment in clinical practice (see Kaplan, 1979; Kramer & Jarvik, 1979; Poon, 1980, 1986; Schear, 1984). The discussion that follows will examine some of these theoretical issues and their implications for test users.

Measurement Equivalence

Given the elimination of test variation due to environment, variation in examiner behavior, and so on, one must still be concerned that the test has equivalent measurement properties in populations of different ages. In essence, if any kind of quantitative comparisons are to be made across different ages, one needs to know not only that a test is reliable and valid for older persons but also that it has equivalent reliability and validity in different age groups. Can we argue that a test measures the same latent construct in the same way for persons of different ages or for different groups of persons? Can we argue that any difference in a test score represents quantitative differences in the same underlying processes, or is it possible that the test has different measurement properties? Baltes and Nesselroade (1970, 1973) have argued that quantitative comparisons of test scores are not justified unless the property of measurement equivalence holds across the persons studied.

Although measurement equivalence is primarily a problem for the scientist using test scores to draw inferences about changes in attributes, the issue is relevant to the clinician as well. On what basis can one use published norms if it is suspected that the individual being evaluated may differ from the reference population on attributes salient for test score performance? In the clinical situation, some clinicians have suggested that it may be necessary to dispense with standardized procedures to gain more useful insights about a subject's ability level (Schear, 1984). In so doing, however, the data are no longer used according to standardized procedures and the relationship between the score and norms is no longer appropriate. However, the clinical information may be helpful in adjusting the inferences made by the clinician in the final analysis. For example, when a subject is working on an item beyond the time limit of the test, it may be very informative as well as helpful to the subject's motivation to let him or her continue and successfully complete the item. On a qualitative basis, the failure on the standardized procedures may not provide information about the ability to actually complete the task (see Albert, 1981, and Albert & Kaplan, 1980, for descriptions of such a qualitative approach in neuropsychology).

A great deal of methodological progress has been made in techniques for using multivariate statistics (e.g., factor analysis, structural equation models, item response theory) to assess measurement equivalence across developmental levels (Baltes et al., 1977; Hertzog, 1987, 1989; Schaie & Hertzog, 1985). In particular, several authors have shown how confirmatory factor analysis can be used for assessing equivalence of a test's item factor structure across age groups (e.g., Hertzog, 1989; Liang, 1985; Rock, Werts, & Flaugher, 1978). These techniques have yet to be applied to many tests and self-report scales used by gerontologists.

What have we learned from the studies that have been done? Many scales and tests designed for use with the elderly have been shown to have acceptable levels of reliability and factorial validity in older populations. For tests of psychometric intelligence, widely used in the scientific and clinical assessment of older persons, there is evidence that such tests have equivalent factor structure across different groups of normal adults, even though there are reliable age changes in mean levels of intelligence test performance (Hertzog, 1987; Hertzog & Schaie, 1986, 1988). It is important to note that much of this evidence has been gained from confirmatory factor analytic studies that avoid some of the interpretational problems associated with exploratory factor analysis. The early literature, based upon exploratory factor analysis, was contradictory and complex (see Reinert, 1970). The more recent confirmatory analyses, reviewed by Hertzog (1987), suggest that there is a basic level of factorial invariance (equal unstandardized factor pattern weights) but that psychometric abilities have higher correlations in older populations (Cunningham, 1981). Additional work on this problem is needed, especially given the results of Hertzog (in press) discussed below, but there is some reason for optimism about the measurement equivalence of many psychometric tests in older populations.

Consequently, psychometric equivalence of intelligence tests in older populations might seem a relatively safe bet. After all, psychometricians devoted much of the early twentieth century to an intensive effort to develop and refine measures of multiple abilities. However, assumptions of measurement equivalence for the proliferating number of self-report scales and experimentally based tasks and tests in the literature may be another matter. Liang (1984, 1985) and others have conducted an extensive series of studies examining the properties of measures of subjective well-being, depression, and the like. The results of such studies are generally encouraging, in that measurement properties of subsets of Likert scale items often seem to be equivalent across multiple age groups. But it is also clear that scales may not always factor as their manuals would predict (see Hertzog, 1989).

Confirmatory factor analytic techniques can also be applied at the level of the summative scales formed from multiple items. For example, Hertzog and Nesselroade (1987) examined the measurement properties of summative scales measuring state anxiety. They found that alternate forms of a precursor of the Curran and Cattell (1976) state anxiety scale were in fact parallel, having equal true score variances, measurement error variances (and hence, equal reliabilities). Analysis of one study showed an estimated reliability of .89 for the state anxiety scales in an older population.

The unavoidable message is that a test that has not been explicitly shown to have equivalent measurement properties for older persons may produce invalid results when administered to them. Given the current state of knowledge about aging, plus the tendency for test authors not to extensively validate tests and questionnaires in older populations, it is likely that testers of older persons will employ tests and questionnaires anyway, even if their measurement properties are not well known. However, if measurement equivalence has not been demonstrated, and if test validity for older persons has not been established, then consumers of test results may be open to criticisms of age bias/discrimination in the use of tests in assessing elderly individuals (Schaie, 1988).

Nondevelopmental Influences

Even if a test is assumed to have equivalent measurement properties for older persons, it is still necessary to consider whether there are influences other than age that affect interpretation of test scores relative to test norms. The classic case is the influence of generational (cohort) differences on age differences in test scores. The age norms for the WAIS and WAIS-R discussed previously are based upon cross-sectional standardization samples. Although a matter of controversy, some gerontologists have argued that cross-sectional data do not constitute an appropriate basis for age norms due to confounded generational differences. This issue is considered at length by Schaie (1973) and Schaie and Schaie (1977). Cross-sectional data for a representative sample may be appropriate for assessing where a current set of older persons stands relative to the overall population, and for assessing the relative standing of an individual vis-à-vis his or her peers. The chief problem is that, given substantial cohort differences, new norms may be needed for each cohort. That is, cross-sectional age norms may not generalize to other cohorts at the same ages, so that such norms become rapidly obsolete. Moreover, it may be inappropriate to conclude that, if an older person performs poorly with respect to a young adult reference group, that it is the aging process that has caused this relatively poor standing.

Inferences Regarding Intraindividual Development

Aging, like any form of development, is generally conceptualized as changes occurring within a given individual as he or she grows older. Implicitly then, we can only measure development directly by measuring the same person over time. Baltes et al. (1977) termed within-person change "intraindividual change," and contrasted this with interindividual differences (differences between different persons). Gerontologists are wont to forget that comparisons between different persons in gerontological research and practice are essentially done for reasons of efficiency and convenience. One needs to make rapid inferences about the changes in an older individual and cannot wait to study the person as he or she changes over time. A clinician testing an older person for age-associated memory impairment wants to know if the older person has declined in his or her memory capacity. Often, this is assessed by comparing a person's test scores to an appropriate age norm. If a person has declined, their performance is likely to be impaired relative to their same-aged peers. However, this is not, strictly speaking, correct. Decline in the best and brightest may reduce them to average levels of performance, relative to their peers. Conversely, an educationally disadvantaged individual may perform relatively poorly but may have maintained performance levels with advancing age. Such a person may have started (and stayed) at a low level of performance. Inferences about actual intraindividual change from between-person differences (e.g., age norms) can be improved by using stratified norms that take into account background variables such as education, although such information may not always be available.

If one adopts an intraindividual change perspective, then an interesting new avenue for testing and test evaluation may involve repeated testing of the same individuals. There are problems with repeated measures tests, including practice effects, reactive effects of testing, and so on (e.g., Cook & Campbell, 1979). Nevertheless, the opportunity to collect baseline data on an individual—in essence, using the person's past performance as the basis for inferring change—presents some exciting possibilities that could be realized if background test data on standard tasks were routinely collected (as, for example, blood pressure is routinely collected as part of a doctor's visit). In such cases one would want to know whether observed change was reliably different from baseline, using a standard error of measurement based upon intraindividual variability in scores rather than the between-persons standard deviation.

Normative and Nonnormative Aging

Knowledge about the ways in which age-related variables influence test performance is an important part of assessing test scores of elderly persons. A gross way of classifying aging effects is in terms of normative or primary aging (e.g., Baltes & Willis, 1977; Birren, 1964). These are aging-effects changes due to biological aging processes that are expected to affect all individuals, although possibly at different rates, as compared to changes associated with nonnormative (often pathological) conditions. An example of the latter would be Alzheimer's disease. The probability of experiencing a nonnormative pathological condition may be related to age, as is the case for Alzheimer's disease, but it is still considered a secondary disease process, distinct from biological aging per se.

Both normative aging effects and nonnormative influences are candidates for influencing various kinds of test scores. The issue, for the test user, is whether these influences affect the measures instead of the latent constructs under study. To the extent that a test of verbal intelligence is adversely impacted by age- or disease-related changes in variables influencing test performance, then poor test performance can possibly lead to misdiagnosis. The normative aging effects and nonnormative influences can be illustrated in a number of ways.

Speed of Processing and Test Performance

Speed of information processing is arguably one of the best demonstrated normative age changes in the psychological studies of aging (e.g., Birren, 1965; Salthouse, 1985). It is well known that as persons age, their speed of information processing slows. Further, pathological conditions such as cardiovascular disease result in even greater impairment of information processing speed than is caused by primary aging alone (i.e., Spieth, 1965).

Hertzog (in press) recently reported a study that suggests that speed of information processing can have both construct-relevant and performance-specific influences on intelligence test performance by older persons. Hertzog defined construct-relevant influences of speed as those that are related to the ability under study. Age changes in information processing efficiency ought to affect intellectual abilities, especially if efficiency of information processing is a defining characteristic of intelligence. However, as pointed out by Lorge (1936) and many others, age changes in speeded tests may affect test performance without affecting the ability construct the test was designed to measure.

Hertzog (in press) measured multiple intellectual abilities in a cross-sectional sample of adults and also administered a measure of how fast persons could mark the type of computerized answer sheets often used for intelligence tests when the test booklets already provided the correct answers. All the examinees had to do was to find the appropriate spot on the answer sheet and mark it. Speed on this task ought to be related to basic information processing speed—how fast one can shift attention, locate a desired point in a display, and make the mark. However, this process may or may not be related to the abilities the tests were designed to measure. Hertzog (1989) also found that the relationship of the speed of answer-sheet marking to one measure of verbal intelligence—Thurstone's Primary Mental Abilities Verbal Meaning subtest (Thurstone & Thurstone, 1949)—increased with increasing age. Table 1 reports the relevant correlations. This pattern was not observed for other vocabulary tests given in the battery. Furthermore, the Verbal Meaning showed significant age differences, favoring younger adults, whereas the other vocabulary tests used by Hertzog (in press) did not. The explanation seems to be that the Verbal Meaning test is more influenced by speed, and that age-related slowing causes declines in test score performance independent of any change in verbal comprehension.

On the other hand, Hertzog (in press) found that other measures of speed had strong correlations with many different intellectual abilities (such as inductive reasoning and spatial visualization). Hertzog (in press) found, as had others (e.g., Horn, Donaldson, & Engstrom, 1981), that partialling for perceptual speed measures

TABLE 1

CORRELATIONS OF PMA SUBTESTS AND ANSWER SHEET VARIABLES
IN FOUR SEPARATE AGE GROUPS

| | Age Groups | | | |
	Students	Middle-Aged	Young-Old	Old-Old
N	202	166	219	178
Age range	18-26	43-54	55-66	67-78
V - VA	23	38	45	59
R - RA	18	15	40	32
S - SA	35	40	38	39
N - NA	19	39	32	41

Note: Decimal points for correlations have been omitted.

V: PMA Verbal Meaning	VA: Verbal Meaning Answer Sheet
S: PMA Space	SA: Space Answer Sheet
R: PMA Reasoning	RA: Reasoning Answer Sheet
N: PMA Number	NA: Number Answer Sheet

attenuated age differences in these more complex intellectual abilities. Although it seems likely that speed cannot account for all age changes in abilities (Botwinick, 1977), to what extent might a person be classified as impaired due to the negative impact of cognitive slowing? Salthouse (1985) provides a clear and compelling review of research in the area that suggests that much of the age-related decline in intelligence test performance may be related to normative slowing (see also Birren, Woods, & Williams, 1980).

One implication of this literature—and the Hertzog (in press) study in particular—for test selection with older persons seems clear. Unless the purpose of the testing is to assess speed of information processing, testers should consider avoiding tests that are highly speeded, as these may be poor candidates for use with older populations. However, additional research will be needed before we can be confident about the nature of speed and aging on other ability tests. At this point it is an open question as to how much the WAIS-R Performance subtests are influenced by speed (Botwinick, 1977; Salthouse, 1985). Clearly, Digit Symbol Substitution is an excellent psychometric measure of this speed dimension. However, to what extent would performance on other tests (e.g., Block Design) be influenced by speed, and would this influence be caused by slowing in construct-relevant processes or be a performance-related confound? Part of the problem is that Wechsler (1981) assumes that speed is a defining characteristic of intelligence and hence assigns bonus points for fast, correct responses for many subtests.

Some research examining the relative contribution of the visual-perceptual and motor speed components of some speed tests has provided important information about the properties of these tests. This work remains at a research level of investigation, but offers promise that clinical applications may be possible soon. Several years ago, Glosser, Butters, and Kaplan (1977) examined whether deficits on a modified Digit Symbol Substitution Test of the Wechsler Adult Intelligence Scale were related to psychomotor or visuoperceptual factors. They found that while the psychomotor factor was a significant variable in the performance of intact normal subjects, a number of visual processing variables (e.g., visual scanning, contour formation, and origination) were significant in the performance of brain-damaged patients. Recently, Schear and Sato (1989) completed a study that hypothesized that vision, motor speed, and visual-motor speed are related to performance on complex cognitive tests that place a premium on these components' abilities. Schear and Sato (1989) assessed a sample of neuropsychiatric patients and found that near vision acuity did not contribute to the regression model as well as the measure of pure motor speed and a test of higher level visual motor speed and dexterity. Although no age comparisons were made in this study, it is very possible that the data may be different for the older persons based on what we know about motor slowing and aging.

Sensory Deficits and Test Performance

Audition can affect psychological test performance. Hearing loss is common in the elderly, especially for high frequency sounds (Brant, Wood, & Fozard, 1986; Corso, 1977, 1981). Investigators working with the elderly have demonstrated a relationship between hearing loss and performance on auditory-verbal tests of intellectual abilities (Granick, Kleban, & Weiss, 1976). Some researchers have suggested that neuropsychological test norms attempt to compensate for age-related changes. However, the reasons why errors increase with age is not fully understood by clinicians. For example, when one examines norms for the Speech Sounds Perception Test of the Halstead-Reitan Neuropsychological Test Battery, an increase in errors accompanies age (Heaton, Grant, & Matthews, 1986).

Recently, one of the authors of this chapter was involved in a multidisciplinary group of researchers (a neuropsychologist, a speech-language pathologist, and an audiologist) that combined expertise to examine the effect of mild high-frequency hearing loss on two clinical tests commonly used in neuropsychology and speech-language pathology. In these studies, an attempt was made to simulate mild high-frequency hearing loss in young adults. Twenty-four young male and female volunteers with normal hearing sensitivity were recruited from the staff and student population of a university and a VA Medical Center complex to serve as the sample. The assumption was made that mild peripheral hearing loss could be modeled by simple acoustical filtering. The stimulus material was presented to the subjects in a sound-treated chamber through a single loudspeaker. The overall sound pressure level of the unfiltered stimulus material was approximately 70 dB as recorded in the sound field at location of the subject's head. The stimulus material was recorded on tape and filtered through a calibrated audiometer and multifilter. Figure 2 shows the extent to which the spectrum of speech was altered by the two levels of filtering as shown in terms of

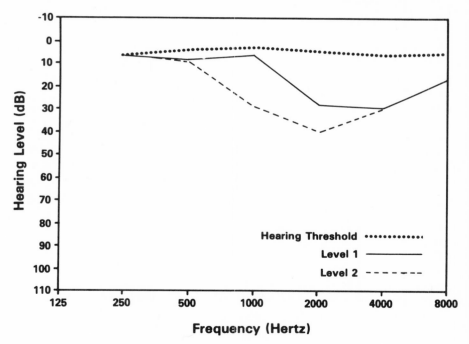

FIGURE 2. Illustration of simulated hearing losses. (From Schear, Skenes, & Larson, 1988. Copyright 1988 by Swets Publishing Service. All rights reserved. Reproduced by permission.)

an audiogram. Level 1 reduced frequency content above 1000 Hz while the filtering began above 500 Hz. As can be seen in Figure 2, there is a systematic reduction in the amount of higher frequency speech energy.

In one study published by this multidisciplinary group, Schear, Skenes, and Larson (1988) examined the effect of two levels of simulated high-frequency hearing loss on the Speech Sounds Perception Test (SSPT) of the Halstead-Reitan Neuropsychological Test Battery. SSPT was selected because it is used clinically to assess speech perception abilities and because a qualitative analysis of the item content shows a high preponderance of high frequency sounds. The results are shown in Figure 3. These findings provide empirical support for the hypothesis that high frequency hearing loss can adversely affect performance on auditory verbal tests. Recognizing that this kind of hearing loss is common in the elderly, hearing loss itself may be one of the causes of age-related increase in errors on auditory verbal tests.

These researchers also examined the hypothesis that there would be a systematic decrease in the number of errors with a systematic decrease in simulated hearing loss on a test of phrase repetition (Skenes, Schear, & Larson, 1987; in press). The Phrase Repetition subtest of the Boston Diagnostic Aphasia Exam (Goodglass & Kaplan, 1983) was presented with the more difficult (more filtered) condition presented first, followed by the less difficult filtered condition, and finally, the normal condition. Subjects wrote their responses instead of repeating them in order to avoid the confounding effects by the examiner when listening to the subjects' repetition. The re-

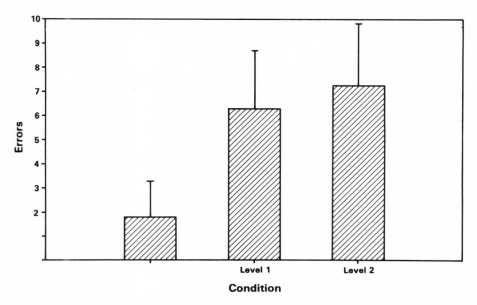

FIGURE 3. Speech Sounds Perception Test errors under normal hearing and under two levels of simulated high-frequency hearing loss. (From Schear, Skenes, & Larson, 1988. Copyright 1988 by Swets Publishing Service. All rights reserved. Reproduced by permission.)

sults are found in Figure 4. The data show a significant difference in the number of errors across conditions. Post-hoc analyses revealed significant differences between the more filtered and less filtered, less filtered and normal, and more filtered and normal conditions ($p < .003$). Qualitative analysis of data revealed that the kind of errors that subjects made could be misinterpreted by clinicians as linguistic (paraphasic) errors (i.e., the substitution of an inappropriate word during the effort to say something specific). Thus, diagnostic specificity may be lost as a function of diminished hearing ability. Furthermore, clinicians may be at risk of attributing errors to a higher central auditory processing deficit when in fact errors are related to hearing loss.

Whereas additional research is required to extend these findings to an elderly subject sample, the data are compelling and consistent with what others have found (Granick et al., 1976; Thomas et al., 1983). These studies raise some interesting questions about some of the reasons why change in performance on aurally presented verbal tests are observed with increasing age.

PRACTICAL ISSUES FOR TEST EXAMINERS

There are a number of practical testing issues that need to be considered by the examiner of an elderly subject. The following discussion will elaborate on some of these that arise from both empirical data, such as that previously described, and clinical experience.

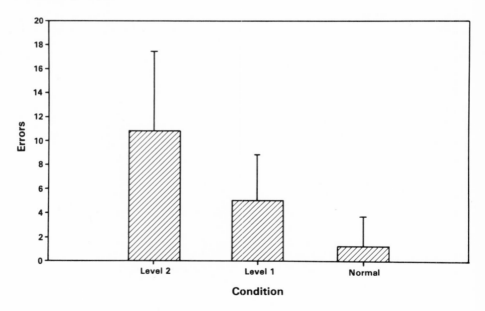

FIGURE 4. Phrase repetition errors under normal hearing and under two levels of simulated high-frequency hearing loss. (From Skenes, Schear, & Larson, 1987. Reproduced by permission of the authors.)

The Testing Environment

The first issue involves the appropriate testing context. Concern for the testing environment is part of ensuring the validity of the test results. From the componential perspective, one is seeking to hold constant any environmental variables that might, under less-than-ideal circumstances, cause variation in test scores independent of the latent variable (construct) the test supposedly measures. It is well known that older persons are more likely than the general population to experience various physical limitations that may limit performance on psychometric tests. For example, sensory deficits may prevent older persons from comprehending test instructions or cause them to miss the signal to begin performance on a timed test. Construction of testing environments must attend to this issue.

In general, the test environment must provide adequate lighting, limit distracting stimuli, and accommodate any physical problems or disabilities of the individuals being tested. Ensuring an optimal testing environment for an older person may be problematic at times. In addition to diminished hearing acuity and slower reaction time, older persons may experience sensitivity to the pacing of the stimulus material, increased sensitivity to glare, the possible need to use larger print stimuli, and so forth. Each of these factors has been demonstrated empirically to have a negative impact on the older adult's ability to perform in the testing situation (see Crook, 1979; Schaie & Schaie, 1977).

The behavior of the examiner is also part of the testing context. Clarity and audibility of instructions interact with sensory problems of older persons. In addition, the older person brings to the test situation a set of beliefs, concerns, and so on about his or her ability to perform. An examiner can unwittingly affect the older person's present or future performance by the nature of his or her communication and interaction style, before, during, and after testing. Good testing procedure requires the use of standard instructions and consistent examiner behavior. Nevertheless, it is necessary to establish good rapport with the older examinee prior to assessment. It may also increase the validity of the test to engage in behaviors that indirectly reassure the older examinee prior to testing, so that test anxiety does not impair performance or adversely affect future testing experience.

Practical Considerations in Testing

Older subjects have problems coping with distraction and interference, and efforts to account for this in testing often are needed. Testing accommodations must include a quiet setting where subjects can be comfortable and feel like they can concentrate.

Fatigue can lower performance, but often only a trained examiner can recognize the signs of fatigue. Frequent rest breaks can offset fatigue and even extend the testing session; however, the examiner may need to consider multiple testing sessions for shorter periods of time.

In clinical settings, the need to describe the reasons for the testing is critical (Schear, 1984). Older persons are often intimidated by tests. Their cautious test-taking set and resistance to performing tasks that they fail to see as relevant can be a major obstacle to testing. Therefore, any good examiner will take considerable care to orient the subject to the assessment process by explaining both the reasons for the assessment as well as something about the test procedures to be employed. Too often test examiners fail to make full use of their time on the front side of the assessment process. It has been suggested that prior to testing the clinician should interview the subject and attempt to explain the testing session and answer any questions. If a psychometrist is going to administer the tests, then that person should be introduced and possibly even sit in on the pretest interview.

An excellent overview of testing the older person was described by Aiken (1980) some years ago. He suggested that test examiners consider eight test procedures when working with older adults:

1) Allow ample time for the subject to respond.

2) Provide sufficient practice on sample items.

3) Consider arranging several short sessions rather than one or two long ones.

4) Be sensitive to examinee fatigue.

5) Be prepared to make provisions for visual, auditory, and other sensory deficits.

6) Keep the testing environment free of distractions.

7) Offer generous amounts of encouragement.

8) Avoid placing undue stress or pressure on a subject when he or she has repeatedly declined.

The discussion to this point has been focused on individual subjects; while the same issues exist for groups, there are distinctively different problems. The test environment may be especially problematic for tests administered to groups of respondents. In such an administration, one must be sure that all individuals comprehend instructions before proceeding. In practice, our research team has found it useful to structure group testing sessions to have multiple professional examiners in a session. One has the responsibility of reading instructions and monitoring group readiness to respond to tests and questionnaires. The other examiners are, in essence, proctors who float among the respondents and monitor participants' pretesting behaviors, ensuring that individuals are in the proper location in a test or questionnaire booklet and that they have completed practice or sample items correctly (or at least have responded to the appropriate items). These individuals encourage and handle individual questions and may even halt the primary examiner if they determine that an individual needs concentrated instructions or tutoring in how to use the test materials prior to the signal to proceed. In our experience, the need for such proctors increases as the number of elderly (greater than 70 years of age) in a group increases.

PSYCHOLOGICAL ASSESSMENT

The Multidimensional Model

In an effort to arrive at acceptable compromises in assessing older adults, some clinicians have recommended using a multidimensional approach (Gallagher et al., 1980; Schear, 1984). Basically, this approach provides a conceptual framework upon which to derive meaningful inferences while seeking to obtain clinically useful information. *Assessment* is differentiated from *testing* in that testing refers to the actual process of administration of tests and deriving scores, whereas assessment refers to the more comprehensive process of clinically evaluating a patient. In clinical psychology, assessment is conducted by the clinical psychologist, who may rely on several sources of information, including interview and results of psychological tests. This clinician may or may not administer the testing; psychometrists or psychology technicians are sometimes employed to do so.

In the multidimensional model of assessment, test results are only one part of the data set; additional important data are obtained from a variety of other sources, such as the patient's self-report, reports of significant others, medical records, and so forth (see Schear, 1984, for a description of the types of data gathered in a comprehensive neuropsychological assessment). Although the multidimensional model often requires both flexibility and creativity (Gallagher et al., 1980), it can yield a much more complete fund of clinically useful information.

In any assessment, the clinician will employ several procedures in combination. The battery approach offers a rich array of data across a variety of elements in the assessment domain. To rely on a single test to cover cognitive or personality domains is foolish, will be incomplete, and often leads to inaccurate conclusions. That is not to say that a battery must be overly redundant to be satisfactory; rather, it should provide information that adequately measures the construct of interest in significant detail.

Adjustments may be made for the given individual with specific limitations and/ or disabilities (e.g., visual acuity impairment, hearing loss, etc.). The domains to be assessed will be guided by the clinician's theoretical orientation and allied test procedures. Each test procedure should have solid empirical data to support its use with older populations. Validity and reliability should be well known. Any test will be weighted by the empirical data to support its utility. The extent to which a test adheres to the psychometric principles described earlier in this chapter will be directly related to the degree it can be confidently employed in interpretation.

Professional Expertise and Consumers of Psychological Tests and Assessment

Non-psychologist health care providers often rely on their psychologist colleagues to conduct psychological assessments and report on psychological test data. Often the psychologist is a consultant to other colleagues. In this case, the allied health care professional may be either a team member or the primary health care provider for the patient. In the hospital setting, the attending is often a physician. Physicians are usually introduced to psychological testing during their residency. Physicians may use some psychological test procedures in their own work, although most often they rely upon mental status procedures. However, any of these professionals should be familiar with the instruments they employ and recognize the limits of their training in these procedures. Just as most neuropsychologists would not attempt to read an EEG or CT scan, nor would a neurologist attempt to interpret a comprehensive neuropsychological test battery. The best division of responsibility is achieved when each provides specific expertise for the good of the patient and works within the interdisciplinary team.

Psychologists should be prepared to provide patients and non-psychologist colleagues with information about their theoretical orientation, a description of tests they employed, and the kind of validity and reliability information previously described that will support the use of these tests with older persons. The better job psychologists do in presenting such information, the better they will be utilized in sharing their data and expertise.

SUMMARY AND CONCLUSIONS

This chapter has reviewed the principles of psychometric theory that are relevant to testing the older person. The issues of test reliability and validity affect procedures for selecting tests as well as afford a basis for valid interpretation of test scores. We strongly recommend that, wherever possible, tests with demonstrated reliability and validity for older persons be selected. Further, it is important that test users appreciate the many kinds of norms and that classification of elderly persons on the basis of test norms involve a number of issues (e.g., whether the norm ought to be for the entire population or a specific age group, whether norms are based upon large, representative samples, and, if cross-sectional norms are used, whether the construct being assessed is sensitive to generational differences as well as age changes).

The problems of measurement equivalence with aging can be understood in terms of age changes in the importance of different components of test score performance for the overall test score. A test may be valid for old and young, yet still be differentially influenced by different components of performance, making simple quantitative comparison of test scores (e.g., use of cross-sectional norms) hazardous. Normative and nonnormative aging are two sources of possible age-related influences on test score components. Given age changes in speed of basic information processing and its relationship within age differences in intelligence test scores, care must be given in how age changes in performance are interpreted. Slowed or inefficient thinking is not necessarily impaired thinking. Sensory changes can result in poor performance by the elderly, which might be misinterpreted as cognitive deficits.

Psychologists are armed with a plethora of tests for assessing older persons. However, this chapter suggests that consumers of psychological tests ought to maintain a healthy respect for the limits of our current information regarding the tests we use. Clinicians should exercise prudence in test interpretation and may be assisted by conceptual models that employ multidimensional data in assessment.

REFERENCES

Aiken, L.R. (1980). Problems in testing the elderly. *Educational Gerontology, 5,* 119-124.

Albert, M.S. (1981). Geriatric neuropsychology. *Journal of Consulting and Clinical Psychology, 49,* 835-850.

Albert, M.S., & Kaplan, E. (1980). Organic implication of neuropsychological deficits in the elderly. In L.W. Poon, J.L. Fozard, D. Arenberg, L.S. Cermak, & L.W. Thompson (Eds.), *New directions in memory and aging: Proceedings of the George A. Tallard Memorial Conference* (pp. 403-432). Hillsdale, NJ: Lawrence Erlbaum.

Allen, M.J., & Yen, W.M. (1979). *Introduction to measurement theory.* Monterey, CA: Brooks/Cole.

American Educational Research Association, American Psychological Association, & National Council on Measurement in Education (1985). *Standards for educational and psychological testing.* Washington, DC: American Psychological Association.

Anastasi, A. (1982). *Psychological testing* (5th ed.). New York: Macmillan.

Baltes, P.B., & Nesselroade, J.R. (1970). Multivariate longitudinal and cross-sectional sequences for analyzing ontogentic and behavioral change: Methodological note. *Developmental Psychology, 1,* 162-168.

Baltes, P.B., & Nesselroade, J.R. (1973). The developmental analysis of individual differences of multiple measures. In J.R. Nesselroade & H.W. Reese (Eds.), *Life span developmental psychology: Methodological issues* (pp. 219-252). New York: Academic Press.

Baltes, P.B., Reese, H.W., & Nesselroade, J.R. (1977). *Life-span development psychology: Introduction to research methods.* Monterey, CA: Brooks/Cole.

Baltes, P.B., & Willis, S.L. (1977). Towards psychological theories of aging and development. In J.E. Birren & K.W. Schaie (Eds.), *Handbook of the psychology of aging* (2nd ed., pp. 128-154). New York: Van Nostrand Reinhold.

Bentler, P.H. (1978). The interdependence of theory, methodology, and empirical data: Causal modeling as an approach to construct validation. In D.B. Kandel (Ed.), *Longitudinal research on drug abuse, empirical findings and methodological issues* (pp. 267-302). Washington, DC: Hemisphere.

Birren, J.E. (1964). *The psychology of aging.* Englewood Cliffs, NJ: Prentice-Hall.

Birren, J.E. (1965). Age changes in the speed of behavior: Its central nature and physiological correlates. In A.T. Welford & J.E. Birren (Eds.), *Handbook of aging, behavior, and the nervous system* (pp. 191-216). Springfield, IL: Charles C. Thomas.

Birren, J.E., Woods, A.M., & Williams, M.V. (1980). Behavioral slowing with age: Causes, organization, and consequences. In L.W. Poon (Ed.), *Aging in the 1980's: Psychological issues* (pp. 293-308). Washington, DC: American Psychological Association.

Blalock, H.M. (1982). *Conceptualization and measurement in the social sciences.* Beverly Hills, CA: Sage.

Blalock, H.M. (Ed.). (1985). *Causal models in the social sciences* (2nd ed.). Chicago: Aldine.

Botwinick, J. (1977). Intellectual abilities. In J.E. Birren & K.W. Schaie (Eds.), *Handbook of the psychology of aging* (pp. 580-605). New York: Van Nostrand Reinhold.

Brant, L., Wood, J., & Fozard, J. (1986, November). *Age changes in hearing thresholds.* Paper presented at the annual meeting of the Gerontological Society of America, Chicago.

Campbell, D.T., & Fiske, D.W. (1959). Convergent and discriminant validation by the multitrait-multimethod matrix. *Psychological Bulletin, 56,* 81-105.

Carroll, J.B. (1980). *Individual difference relations in psychometric and experimental cognitive tasks* (Final Report No. 163). Chapel Hill: L.L. Thurstone Psychometric Laboratory, University of North Carolina.

Cook, T.D., & Campbell, D.T. (1979). *Quasi-experimentation: Design and analysis issues for field settings.* Chicago: Rand McNally.

Corso, J.F. (1977). Auditory perception and communication. In J.E. Birren & K.W. Schaie (Eds.), *Handbook of the psychology of aging* (pp. 535-553). New York: Van Nostrand Reinhold.

Corso, J.F. (1981). *Aging sensory system and perception.* New York: Praeger.

Cronbach, L.J. (1970). *The essentials of psychological testing* (3rd ed.). New York: Harper & Row.

Cronbach, L.J., & Meehl, P.E. (1955). Construct validity in psychological tests. *Psychological Bulletin, 52,* 281-302.

Crook, T.H. (1979). Psychometric assessment in the elderly. In A. Raskin & L.F. Jarvik (Eds.), *Psychiatric symptoms and cognitive loss in the elderly: Evaluation and assessment techniques* (pp. 207-220). Washington, DC: Hemisphere.

Crook, T., Bartus, R.T., Ferris, S.H., Whitehouse, P., Cohen, G.D., & Gershon, S. (1986). Age-associated memory impairment: Proposed diagnostic criteria and measures of clinical change—Report of a National Institute of Mental Health work group. *Developmental Neuropsychology, 2,* 261-276.

Cunningham, W.R. (1981). Ability factor structure differences in adulthood and old age. *Multivariate Behavioral Research, 16,* 3- 22.

Curran, J.P., & Cattell, R.B. (1976). *Handbook for the 8-State Questionnaire.* Champaign, IL: Institute for Personality and Ability Testing.

Dwyer, J.H. (1983). *Statistical models for the social and behavioral sciences.* New York: Oxford University Press.

Embretson, S. (1983). Construct validity: Construct representation versus nomothetic span. *Psychological Bulletin, 93,* 179-197.

Embretson, S. (Ed.). (1985). *Test design: Developments in psychology and psychometrics.* New York: Academic Press.

Gallagher, D., Thompson, L.W., & Levy, S.M. (1980). Clinical psychological assessment of older adults. In L.W. Poon (Ed.), *Aging in the 1980's: Psychological issues* (pp. 19-40). Washington, DC: American Psychological Association.

Glosser, G., Butters, N., & Kaplan, E. (1977). Visuoperceptual processes in brain damaged patients on the digit symbol substitution test. *International Journal of Neuroscience, 7,* 59- 66.

Goodglass, H., & Kaplan, E. (1983). *The assessment of aphasia and related disorders.* Philadelphia: Lea & Febiger.

Granick, S., Kleban, M.H., & Weiss, A.D. (1976). Relationship between hearing loss and cognition in normally hearing aged persons. *Journal of Gerontology, 31,* 434-440.

Heaton, R.K., Grant, I., & Matthews, C.A. (1986). Differences in neuropsychological test performance associated with age, education, and sex. In I. Grant & K.M. Adams (Eds.), *Neuropsychological assessment of neuropsychiatric disorders* (pp. 100-120). New York: Oxford University Press.

Hertzog, C. (1987). Applications of structural equation models in gerontological research. In K.W. Schaie (Ed.), *Annual review of gerontology and geriatrics* (Vol. 7, pp. 265-293). New York: Springer.

Hertzog, C. (1989). Using confirmatory factor analysis for scale development and validation. In M.P. Lawton & A.R. Herzog (Eds.), *Special research methods for gerontology* (pp. 281-306). Amityville, NY: Baywood.

Hertzog, C. (in press). Influences of cognitive slowing on age differences in intelligence. *Developmental Psychology.*

Hertzog, C., Hultsch, D.F., & Dixon, R.A. (1987, August). *What do metamemory questionnaires measure? A construct validation study.* Paper presented at the Annual Meeting of the American Psychological Association, New York.

Hertzog, C., & Nesselroade, J.R. (1987). Beyond autoregressive models: Some implications of the trait-state distinction for the structural modeling of developmental change. *Child Development, 58,* 93-109.

Hertzog, C., & Schaie, K.W. (1986). Stability and change in adult intelligence: 1. Analysis of longitudinal covariance structures. *Psychology and Aging, 1,* 159-171.

Hertzog, C., & Schaie, K.W. (1988). Stability and change in adult intelligence: 2. Simultaneous analysis of longitudinal means and covariance structures. *Psychology and Aging, 3,* 122-130.

Horn, J.L., Donaldson, G., & Engstrom, R. (1981). Apprehension, memory, and fluid intelligence decline in adulthood. *Research on Aging, 3*(1), 33-84.

Kaplan, O.J. (1979). Psychological testing of seniles. In O.J. Kaplan (Ed.), *Psychopathology of aging* (pp. 45-77). New York: Academic Press.

Kaszniak, A.W. (in press). Psychological assessment of the aging individual. In J.E. Birren &

K.W. Schaie (Eds.), *Handbook of the psychology of aging* (3rd ed.). New York: Academic Press.

Keyser, D.J., & Sweetland, R.C. (Eds.). (1985-1988). *Test critiques (Vols. 1-7)*. Kansas City, MO: Test Corporation.

Kramer, N.A., & Jarvik, L.F. (1979). Assessment of intellectual changes in the elderly. In A. Raskin & L.F. Jarvik (Eds.), *Psychiatric symptoms and cognitive loss in the elderly: Evaluation and assessment techniques* (pp. 221-271). Washington, DC: Hemisphere.

Liang, J. (1984). Dimensions of the Life Satisfaction Index A: A structural formulation. *Journal of Gerontology, 39,* 613-622.

Liang, J. (1985). A structural integration of the Affect Balance Scale and the Life Satisfaction Index A. *Journal of Gerontology, 40,* 552-561.

Lorge, I. (1936). The influence of the test upon the nature of mental decline as a function of age. *Journal of Educational Psychology, 27,* 100-110.

Matarazzo, J.D. (1972). *Wechsler's measurement and appraisal of adult intelligence* (5th ed.). Baltimore: Williams & Wilkins.

McDonald, R.P. (1978). A simple comprehensive model for the analysis of covariance structures. *British Journal of Mathematical and Statistical Psychology, 31,* 59-72.

McNair, D.M., Lorr, M., & Droppleman, L.F. (1971). *Profile of Mood States.* San Diego: Educational and Industrial Testing Service.

Messick, S. (1981). Constructs and their vicissitudes in educational and psychological measurements. *Psychological Bulletin, 89,* 575- 588.

Nesselroade, J.R., & Labouvie, E.W. (1985). Experimental design in research on aging. In J.E. Birren & K.W. Schaie (Eds.), *Handbook of the psychology of aging* (2nd ed., pp. 35-60). New York: Van Nostrand Reinhold.

Nesselroade, J.R., & Reese, H.W. (Eds.). (1973). *Life-span developmental psychology: Methodological issues.* New York: Academic Press.

Nunnally, J.C. (1978). *Psychometric theory* (2nd ed.). New York: McGraw-Hill.

Poon, L.W. (Ed.). (1980). *Aging in the 1980's: Psychological issues.* Washington, DC: American Psychological Association.

Poon, L.W. (Ed.). (1986). *Handbook for clinical memory assessment in older adults.* Washington, DC: American Psychological Association.

Raskin, A., & Jarvik, L.F. (Eds.). (1979). *Psychiatric symptoms and cognitive loss in the elderly: Evaluation and assessment techniques.* New York: John Wiley.

Reinert, G. (1970). Comparative factor analytic studies of intelligence throughout the human life span. In L.R. Goulet & P.B. Baltes (Eds.), *Life-span developmental psychology: Research and theory* (pp. 467-484). New York: Academic Press.

Rock, D.A., Werts, C.E., & Flaugher, R.L. (1978). The use of analysis of covariance structures for comparing the psychometric properties of multiple variables across populations. *Multivariate Behavioral Research, 13,* 403-418.

Salthouse, T.A. (1985). *A theory of cognitive aging.* Amsterdam: North-Holland.

Schaie, K.W. (1973). Methodological problems in descriptive developmental research in adulthood and aging. In J.R. Nesselroade & H.W. Reese (Eds.), *Life-span developmental psychology: Methodological issues* (pp. 253-280). New York: Academic Press.

Schaie, K.W. (1977). Quasi-experimental research designs in the psychology of aging. In J.E. Birren & K.W. Schaie (Eds.), *Handbook of the psychology of aging* (2nd ed., pp. 39-58). New York: Van Nostrand Reinhold.

Schaie, K.W. (1988). Ageism in psychological research. *American Psychologist, 43,* 179-184.

Schaie, K.W., & Hertzog, C. (1982). Longitudinal methods. In B.B. Wolman (Ed.), *Handbook of developmental psychology* (pp. 91-115). Englewood Cliffs, NJ: Prentice-Hall.

Schaie, K.W., & Hertzog, C. (1985). Measurement in the psychology of adulthood and aging. In J.E. Birren & K.W. Schaie (Eds.), *Handbook of the psychology of aging* (2nd ed., pp. 61-92). New York: Van Nostrand Reinhold.

Schaie, K.W. & Schaie, J.P. (1977). Clinical assessment and aging. In J.E. Birren & K.W. Schaie (Eds.), *Handbook of the psychology of aging* (pp. 692-723). New York: Van Nostrand Reinhold.

Schear, J.M. (1984). Neuropsychological assessment of the elderly in clinical practice. In P.E. Logue & J.M. Schear (Eds.), *Clinical neuropsychology: A multidisciplinary approach* (pp. 199-236). Springfield, IL: Charles C. Thomas.

Schear, J.M., & Sato, S.D. (1989). Effects of visual acuity and visual motor speed and dexterity on cognitive test performance. *Archives of Clinical Neuropsychology, 4,* 25-32.

Schear, J.M., Skenes, L.L., & Larson, V.D. (1988). Effects of simulated hearing loss on speech sounds perception. *Journal of Clinical and Experimental Neuropsychology, 10,* 597-602.

Skenes, L.L., Schear, J.M., & Larson, V.D. (1987, February). *Simulated hearing loss and phrase dictation.* Paper presented at the annual meeting of the International Neuropsychological Society, Washington, DC.

Skenes, L.L., Schear, J.M., & Larson, V.D. (in press). Simulated hearing loss and phrase dictation. *The International Journal of Neuroscience.*

Spieth, W. (1965). Slowness of task performance and cardiovascular diseases. In A.T. Welford & J.E. Birren (Eds.), *Behavior, aging, and the nervous system* (pp. 366-400). Springfield, IL: Charles C. Thomas.

Sternberg, R.J. (1977). *Intelligence, information processing, and analogical reasoning.* Hillsdale, NJ: Lawrence Erlbaum.

Sternberg, R.J. (1985). *Beyond IQ: A triarchic theory of intelligence.* New York: Cambridge University Press.

Storandt, M., Siegler, I.C., & Elias, M.F. (Eds.). (1978). *The clinical psychology of aging.* New York: Plenum.

Thomas, P.D., Hunt, W.C., Garry, P.J., Hood, R.B., Goodwin, J.M., & Goodwin, J.S. (1983). Hearing acuity in a healthy elderly population: Effect on emotional, cognitive, and social status. *Journal of Gerontology, 38,* 321-325.

Thurstone, L.L., & Thurstone, T.G. (1949). *Examiner's manual: SRA Primary Mental Abilities Test (Form 11-17).* Chicago: Science Research Associates.

Wechsler, D. (1981). *WAIS-R manual.* New York: Psychological Corporation.

Zarit, S.H., Eiler, J., & Hassinger, M. (1985). Clinical assessment. In J.E. Birren & K.W. Schaie (Eds.), *Handbook of the psychology of aging* (2nd ed., pp. 725-754). New York: Van Nostrand Reinhold.

4

Neuropsychological Assessment of Older Adults

FREDERICK A. SCHMITT, PH.D., JOHN D. RANSEEN, PH.D.

Neuropsychology, in its study of brain-behavior relationships, spans the artificial gap between psychological, psychiatric, and neuroscientific knowledge. As a branch of clinical and experimental psychology, neuropsychology was born from a tradition of psychometric evaluation—in this case, the quantification of cognition and behavior associated with neurological disease. Consequently, neuropsychological assessment has become increasingly valued as a clinical and research tool for studying the elderly population, whose number is expanding rapidly relative to the general population and in whom neurological disease is quite prevalent. Alzheimer's disease, which alone comprises about 50% of the various conditions that give rise to dementia, is estimated to afflict 3 million older adults. As a result, psychologists frequently are asked to provide neuropsychological assessment and consultation regarding elderly patients experiencing some perceived or actual decline in cognitive and behavioral functioning. The detection and evaluation of disease-related processes in older adults is facilitated by neuropsychological assessment (Albert, 1981), which can assist, for example, in the discrimination between primary degenerative dementias viewed as untreatable (e.g., Alzheimer's disease, Pick's disease) and those that may be the result of potentially reversible conditions (e.g., affective disorders, toxic/metabolic disturbances, other medical illnesses).

Growing interest in the application of neuropsychological techniques to geropsychology has led to a recent proliferation of evaluation procedures, each with its own strengths and weaknesses. Neuropsychological evaluation of the elderly, however, cannot be viewed merely from the narrow perspective of specific test procedures and findings. Geriatric evaluation shares features common to all psychological assessment, including the need to understand test findings in relation to the patient's background and environmental demands, but additional issues and challenges face the psychologist engaged in assessing older adults. For example, the growing literature invariably points to the older adult's particular physical, emotional, and attitudinal states that may interfere with assessment (Herman & Barnes, 1982). In addition, the neuropsychologist must be aware that the effects of normal aging on cognitive functioning have not been fully delineated; consequently, current neuropsychological techniques by and large are better normed for younger adults.

It is a virtual necessity for the neuropsychologist to have some knowledge of common neurological and medical conditions, their relationship to cognitive and psychological functioning, and how these can alter the interpretation of assessment findings. In addition, some understanding of the information derived from physical, neurological, and neuroradiological examinations will likely be necessary to provide an appropriate assessment. Further, the neuropsychologist is commonly faced with providing an evaluation within a limited time period. In sum, the appropriate and timely neuropsychological assessment of an older adult can be a formidable task, requiring a synthesis of diverse information.

PREASSESSMENT CONSIDERATIONS

Clinical neuropsychological assessment traditionally has entailed a battery-oriented approach, based initially on Halstead-Reitan techniques. Although there are strengths to this strategy, most notably the standardization of procedure, it tends to be costly, time-consuming, and all too often geared towards providing redundant information. As a result, the growing emphasis in recent years has turned towards flexible approaches to neuropsychological assessment, tailored to the needs of a given patient within the context of answering specific referral questions. A flexible approach is especially important in the evaluation of older adults, whose limitations often render them unable to complete lengthy batteries of neuropsychological tests. With the goal of flexibility, it is imperative that the neuropsychologist consider a wide range of information prior to formal assessment: the exact nature of the referral question, the patient's background information (with an emphasis on past and present medical conditions), and any physical impairments (motor, visual, auditory) that might alter both test procedures and interpretation.

The clinician must also consider the extent of the older adult's informed consent during preassessment planning. Many older patients face the fear of being labeled "senile" as a result of the evaluation, and thus the professional should take care to explain the nature and purpose of the assessment adequately.

Nature of the Referral

Clarification of the specific referral question is often the most important initial consideration in neuropsychological evaluation. Neuropsychologists frequently encounter generic referrals to "Please evaluate this patient" or vague questions concerning an evaluation of the patient's "status." This is especially true in settings where the majority of referrals come from sources unsophisticated with regard to neuropsychological assessment. Often a generic neuropsychological consult will be requested even though an answer to a specific question is desired. For instance, a consultation may appear to request diagnostic information about a patient's suspected Alzheimer's disease when the unstated issue is actually the patient's competency to manage his own affairs. The specific question needs delineation in advance of formal assessment because it mandates a particular approach to evaluation. Defining referral questions also can help the referring source to formulate the case more appropriately. Within this defining process some feedback should be given about the degree to which a question can be answered. Finally, in the evaluation of older adults one should be aware of hidden agendas on the part of the referral source. It is not uncommon for a referral to request diagnostic information concerning dementia so that the patient can be assigned to an untreatable class, particularly if the case involves a difficult patient with an unsupportive family situation. The hidden agenda thus may be to consign a patient to a nursing home, even though this may not be the optimal placement.

As with all psychological evaluations, neuropsychological referral questions tend to fall into two broad categories: diagnosis and treatment. The use of neuropsychological assessment in diagnostic formulation has been de-emphasized in recent years with the advent of neuroradiological procedures such as the CT and magnetic resonance imagery (MRI) scans, which can accurately localize neurological lesions. The structural and metabolic changes that accompany early-stage dementing conditions often cannot be visualized on neuroradiological procedures, however. The neuropsychological evaluation can detect subtle disturbances in cognitive and behavioral functioning that may help confirm a specific diagnosis.

Perhaps the most common diagnostic issue encountered by the neuropsychologist concerns the elderly patient who has recently shown some change in behavior, cognition, and/or emotional status. The evaluation is requested to shed some light on the possible reasons for this decline, which typically revolves around observations or complaints of impaired memory. When the question of memory impairment is raised, there is invariably a diagnostic issue involved—is this normal age-related decline, age-associated memory impairment, or a sign of a dementing condition? This question can be quite difficult to answer because, even with a complete medical and neuropsychological work-up, a diagnosis of Alzheimer's disease, for instance, can be established with certainty only at autopsy. Although it might be difficult to differentiate the effects of a toxic exposure and an early Alzheimer's-type dementia, particularly as both conditions present a general diffuse pattern of dysfunction, White (1987) has demonstrated that the anomia characteristic of Alzheimer's disease becomes a reliable measure to discriminate between the two groups. Therefore, the clinician who approaches the evaluation of an older adult should be aware of the type of impairment seen for different neurological conditions, be familiar with the pathognomonic signs associated with each disorder, and have some sense of the lateralizing effects of organic lesions. Diagnostic accuracy increases with repeated evaluations over time.

It is often appropriate to reframe this referral question into one of providing a baseline of information. Because cognitive decline in the early stages of dementing conditions can be quite subtle, neuropsychological re-evaluation can help quantify and track any progression of symptoms. Conditions other than senile dementias (e.g., metabolic, vascular) do not necessarily display declines or may even show improving cognitive functioning with treatment. Consequently, a baseline of quantifiable information is essential, not only to assist in diagnosis but to help in understanding the likely prognosis.

Beyond the basic question of whether decline represents a dementing condition lie more specific differential diagnostic considerations. The distinction between organic and functional psychiatric conditions is a question commonly posed to a neuropsychologist, with the most important specific differential being between senile dementia and affective disorder. As both conditions share common symptomatology—decreased memory, apathy, psychomotor slowing, blunting of affect—this can be a very difficult differential diagnosis. Nevertheless, when this is the specific referral question, an assessment oriented towards a full examination of neuropsychological functioning, with emphasis on the patient's affective state, is crucial in establishing diagnosis. Neuropsychologists are asked less frequently to differentiate between neurological conditions and psychiatric disorders such as schizophrenia, mania, or personality disturbance because these conditions are generally more apparent from the individual's history. (Having a preexisting psychiatric disturbance, of course, does not preclude developing a superimposed organic process.) The clinician should be mindful that there are virtually always psychological reactions to perceived decline in physical and cognitive functioning, such that depression and apathy as well as the full spectrum of emotional and behavioral reactions will be observed as sequelae of declining functioning. Psychological reactions may interact with an actual organic process, rendering an exact differentiation between organic and functional psychiatric disturbance both difficult and artificial.

Neuropsychological consultations often are requested to assist in differential diagnosis when it is quite obvious that the patient displays significant cognitive impairment or behavioral disturbance. Such differentiation involves the myriad possibilities that might give rise to cognitive impairment in the elderly. In this regard it is perhaps most important for the neuropsychologist to be aware of the possible treatable dementias versus those viewed as having chronic progressive courses. For instance, it is thought that perhaps 25% of patients referred for neuropsychological evaluation have a treatable affective disorder (Sloane, 1980). Although dementia is viewed as a diffuse impairment in various memory, intellectual, perceptual, and psychomotor functions, neuropsychological evaluation often can assist in the appropriate diagnosis because differing patterns of cognition and behavior change are associated with specific conditions. For instance, toxic encephalopathy may present with symptoms quite similar to Alzheimer's disease, yet the appropriately tailored neuropsychological evaluation may reveal the subtle differences between these disorders in language and memory functions (White, 1987). Other treatable conditions include normal pressure hydrocephalus, subdural hematoma, and delirium caused by medication and/or metabolic conditions.

There are also subtle neuropsychological differences between the various progressive dementias. The neuropsychological evaluation can assist in the differential diagnosis between Alzheimer's disease, Pick's disease, multi-infarct dementia, and subcortical dementias. Although in the long run exact differential diagnosis may not render specific treatment recommendations, the importance of appropriately labeling a disease, especially for family members, should not be overlooked.

Treatment issues form the other large group of referral questions confronting the neuropsychologist. These consultations typically request a prediction of how the individual's changing functional capacities might impact on his or her life. At one end of the spectrum are questions regarding patients who are obviously quite impaired. In these cases, the difficult issue of competency might be raised, in which an evaluation must address the patient's ability to care for him- or herself, manage personal affairs, and live independently. This is closely allied to the question of placement and the most appropriate environment for a patient with cognitive impairment and/or behavioral problems; that is, what is the safest, least restrictive environment in which to manage and care for a patient, or how can the current environment be modified to provide care? These questions dictate that the neuropsychologist pay as much attention to issues of environmental support and available resources as to specific test findings (which may only reveal what is already obvious).

At times the neuropsychologist will address very specific treatment-oriented questions surrounding functional capacities. For instance, does the patient's condition preclude safely operating a motor vehicle (a consultation that would focus on reaction time and visuoperceptual functioning)? Another referral might question a patient's ability to manage a complicated medication regimen (e.g., will he or she remember to take medications appropriately?) or the efficacy of a certain treatment regimen (e.g., assessment pre- and post shunt surgery).

In cases of higher functioning older adults, a detailed description of a patient's strengths and weaknesses following some focal damage, such as a cerebrovascular accident (CVA), might be requested. Ideally, these findings can be employed to devise rehabilitation strategies for facilitating patient functioning to a maximum level of independence. For instance, various strategies in memory retraining have been employed to facilitate recall (Schmitt & Farber, 1987). Although these procedures are largely experimental and studies to date suggest that their effects are palliative (Wilson, 1987), small improvements in functioning may be quite important for both the patient and the family.

Background Information

To evaluate an older adult's test performance accurately and meaningfully, some understanding of the patient's background, current functional status, associated medical conditions, medication regimen, and gross physical impairments will be necessary. This information must be gathered in advance of formal testing, as it should influence the choice of evaluation techniques and may occasionally preclude the need to continue with a formal evaluation. If, for instance, the psychologist can establish in advance of testing that a patient's rapid cognitive decline is secondary to the initiation of a new medication, it may make more sense to deal with this issue prior to any formal evaluation.

Premorbid functioning. It is essential in neuropsychological assessment to establish some idea of the patient's premorbid cognitive and emotional status and functional abilities. Although some of this information can be obtained with reasonable validity from a patient interview, the evaluator must stay acutely aware of how the patient's cognitive and emotional status relates to his or her ability to report historical information accurately. Often, older patients referred for neuropsychological evaluation do not have the memory capacity to provide reasonable background, although they may confabulate a plausible history. Patients with right-hemisphere disease may be verbally intact, masking their limited ability to sequence life events or provide relevant information. Consequently, whenever possible the psychologist should obtain information from the patient's family, who not infrequently provide a dramatically different account of events.

The neuropsychologist establishes premorbid cognitive status quite simply by obtaining information on the patient's highest level of educational and vocational achievement. In a population of older adults, the majority will be retired; therefore, it is quite important to ascertain under what circumstances this occurred. Although mathematical formulas have been developed to estimate premorbid intellectual functioning based on demographic information (Wilson, Rosenbaum, & Brown, 1979), these probably apply less accurately to the older adult. Nevertheless, on most neuropsychological measures one would not expect the same performance from a coal miner with a sixth-grade education who has been on disability for over 20 years and from a successful, self-employed, college-educated insurance agent who recently retired in order to enjoy his leisure time.

Next, information must be gleaned concerning the patient's current functional status at home—that is, what is he or she able to do? This is of particular importance because referral questions often revolve around some recent change in functional status. The exact indicators of decline can give important clues to guide neuropsychological assessment. For example, the patient's family may observe that she has a memory problem, which they describe as situations in which she has gotten lost in a familiar place. Although this observation may signal a memory problem, it also may indicate a primary problem in visual-perceptual functioning. The family might raise concerns about a patient's increased difficulty in walking or a recent episode of incontinence, which would draw immediate attention to the possibility of normal pressure hydrocephalus.

Information on premorbid psychiatric status is important because emotional functioning is frequently at issue in the evaluation of the older adult. One would consider a patient who has had repeated bouts of depression for many years in a much different light than one whose first insidious onset of depression is noted in psychomotor slowing.

Finally, some indication of premorbid neurological risk factors should always be examined. These include such issues as a history of alcoholism/drug use, head injury, developmental problems, and toxic exposure.

Medical condition. Of particular importance in the evaluation of older adults is detailed medical information, with a particular focus on medication regimen, medical conditions that might affect cognitive and behavioral status, and conditions resulting in sensorimotor impairments, which may require alteration of test procedures. A common cause of altered mental functioning in elderly patients is polypharmacy. It is not unusual for a patient referred for neuropsychological evaluation to present with a bag full of various medications, any of which could affect cognitive status—steroids for chronic obstructive pulmonary disease (COPD), beta-blockers for a heart condition, an anxiolytic for anxiety, an antidepressant for pain management, and so on. The presenting problem may be caused by medication noncompliance. Further, older adults experiencing cognitive impairment are unlikely to follow a complex medication regimen as prescribed. Consequently, it is important for the evaluator to attempt a determination of whether these medications are taken in an appropriate fashion, whether they have been changed recently (initiated or withdrawn), and what conditions are being treated. If medications are suspected as a cause of altered mental status, it may be appropriate to employ a brief neuropsychological evaluation to assess medication effects prior to altering a regimen.

Neuropsychology has delineated the adverse cognitive effects of a variety of neurological illnesses: vascular disturbances, strokes, seizure disorders, neoplastic disease, Parkinson's disease, and the like. Obviously, the evaluator must know whether these disorders are present or suspected. In addition, the field of neuropsychology has been more active recently in delineating cognitive impairment associated with non-neurological medical conditions. As a result, evidence exists to implicate a variety of chronic medical diseases in altered mental status, including Type 1 diabetes, COPD, congestive heart failure, and renal insufficiency. Many older adults suffer from one or more of these conditions.

Finally, some understanding of any physical conditions that might require altering test procedures and interpretation is essential. Accompanying the natural aging process are declines in both sensory and motor skills, frequently exacerbated by some disease process in patients referred for evaluation. The most common sensory deficits are visual and hearing impairments, which can frequently be overcome with special glasses and hearing aids. Briefly evaluating a patient's visual acuity by using a Snellen chart or her potential for hearing better by using a simple hearing amplifier (or stethoscope) can alert the examiner to sensory considerations in selecting appropriate assessment tools. The psychologist should attempt evaluation with these impairments corrected, as sensory deprivation secondary to significant reduction in sensory input can present as cognitive impairment. Motor functioning also characteristically declines with age, such that psychomotor slowing is probably the best documented neuropsychological deficit in the elderly. Fatigue often requires abbreviated testing sessions and limits the evaluator to essential testing procedures. A variety of illnesses may serve to exacerbate problems in motor functioning, altering one's approach to the assessment of perceptual motor skills. Arthritis and tremor are quite common and may make fine-motor control and manipulation impossible, leading the evaluator to choose motor-free tests to assess perception. Standard test procedures may also have to be significantly altered when assessing patients with severe hemiparesis or hemiplegia, usually secondary to a CVA.

GENERAL TESTING GUIDELINES

The foregoing considerations for a neurospsychological evaluation of an older adult lead to a final testing approach that can be described as "clinical." As noted previously, this approach attempts to tailor test administration in a flexible manner, one that is responsive to changes in the examinee's motivation, fatigue, and physiological attributes. A similar approach is used in determining the composition of brief neuropsychological batteries for screening. The clinical approach should attempt to provide a profile of impairment and to report which functions remain intact. In general, such an evaluation should attempt to document a patient's orientation, attention, language, motor, visual-spatial, memory, metacognitive, and abstraction abilities, as well as his or her affect and focal skills such as math, reading, and writing. Each of these general areas involve a number of cognitive processes. For example, memory evaluation could focus on remote information, recall and recognition of words, and spatial information. Language evaluation might be accomplished through comprehension of commands, reading, and writing samples. Given the options that are available in test selection, it is important, again, to be aware of the clinical picture of conditions such as Alzheimer's disease, cardiovascular disease, and COPD.

Neuropsychological procedures for assessing older adults range from brief, unstructured mental status exams to fairly lengthy and well-researched batteries such as the Halstead-Reitan. As previously mentioned, aging per se does not create particular problems in the assessment of brain-behavior relationships; however, a number of different problems in test selection, administration, and interpretation appear to be age related. The discussion that follows does not encompass all neuropsychological tests, but rather highlights both short structured mental status exams and screening batteries developed specifically for the initial evaluation of geriatric patients and then the tests often used in more comprehensive evaluations.

Brief Mental Status Exams

The need to conduct quick screenings within inpatient and outpatient settings has prompted the development of numerous screening tests to document cognitive impairment. Screening tests can be used to identify a need for more extensive neuropsychological evaluation and to monitor change in cognitive abilities over time. These tests also can be used in clinical settings to alert the clinician to cognitive problems that will impact on the patient's ability to provide an adequate history. Such problems also may compromise the patient's ability to function independently. Many different mental status exams are used by physicians (e.g., Strub & Black, 1985), and those used predominantly with older adults have been well described and summarized by Kane and Kane (1981). Brief screening instruments have proliferated in the literature, particularly as clinicians have attempted to develop economical devices sensitive to the impact of dementia on cognitive performance. Some of these instruments are modifications of existing mental status exams (e.g., Mental Status Questionnaire [MSQ]; Kahn & Miller, 1978) while others have been derived from the clinical characteristics of particular disorders such as Alzheimer's disease (Mini-Mental State Examination, Alzheimer's Disease Assessment Scale).

The 30-item Mini-Mental State Examination (MMSE; Folstein, Folstein, & McHugh, 1975) is used extensively as a cognitive screening instrument for geriatric evaluation. This 5- to 10-minute exam covers a variety of cognitive tasks, including orientation to time and place, recall of three objects, mental calculation, and basic language tasks. Interrater and test-retest reliability are fairly high, and the MMSE has shown reasonable correlations (in impaired populations) with Wechsler Adult Intelligence Scale IQ scores. The test's shortcomings include its tendency to misclassify normals as impaired (high false-positive rate) and scores that are often sensitive to educational level. The MMSE also may be less sensitive to very early dementia and right-hemisphere lesions.

Another brief mental status exam is Pfeiffer's (1975) Short Portable Mental Status Questionnaire (SPMSQ), a short version of Kahn and Miller's Mental Status Questionnaire. The exam's 10 items, which require 3 to 5 minutes to administer, assess for orientation to time and place, general information, and mental calculation (serial 3's). The strengths of the SPMSQ are its speed and ease of administration, and it can be included readily in an interview format. Further, this measure includes corrections for education and race. The SPMSQ has demonstrated good reliability and discriminative validity (Pfeiffer, 1975; Fillenbaum, 1980), but it tends to be insensitive to deficits in patients with superior premorbid abilities (high false-positive rate).

Other mental status exams that deserve mention include the Extended Mental

Status Questionnaire (Whelihan, Lesher, Kleban, & Granick, 1984), the Philadelphia Geriatric Center Delayed Memory Test (Whelihan et al., 1984), the Cognitive Capacity Screening Examination (Jacobs, Bernhard, Delgado, & Strain, 1977), and the Orientation Questionnaire (Hutzell & Eggert, 1987). In their studies of patients with Alzheimer's disease, Blessed, Tomlinson, and Roth (1968) have developed a test similar to other brief mental status examinations in that it taps such areas as orientation, verbal memory, and concentration, but that also includes ratings of functional ability. The cognitive portion of their evaluation (Information-Memory-Concentration Test) has demonstrated strong correlations with the degree of structural change (number of senile plaques) seen in the brains of Alzheimer's patients. These mental status exams appear to be useful in identifying patients in the early stages of cognitive decline and appear to discriminate reliably between neurological and psychiatric diagnoses.

Extended Mental Status Exams

Extended mental status exams, which generally require 30 to 45 minutes to administer, are designed to evaluate broader areas of cognitive functioning: construction, conceptualization, perseveration, attention, and memory. Three quite useful evaluations are the Mattis Dementia Rating Scale (MDRS; Mattis, 1976), the Neurobehavioral Cognitive Status Examination (NCSE; Kiernan, Mueller, Langston, & Van Dyke, 1987), and the Alzheimer's Disease Assessment Scale (ADAS; Rosen, Motts, & Davis, 1984). The MDRS consists of five subtests, which evaluate attention, initiation and perseveration, constructional ability, conceptualization, and memory. One strength of the MDRS is that items are arranged hierarchically in order of difficulty; therefore, patients with more intact functioning who correctly respond to the most difficult item within an area are assumed to be able to respond correctly to the remaining items. This allows for a more rapid assessment of intact patients while those with greater impairments can demonstrate differing levels of performance within each area. The MDRS discriminates well between dementia and other types of organic injuries, provides a good balance between verbal and figural memory recognition tasks, and appears to be sensitive to language deficits. When used in conjunction with the Boston Naming Test (Goodglass & Kaplan, 1972), MDRS performance has been found associated with functional competence (Vitaliano et al., 1984, 1986) independent of the effects of education. The MDRS exhibits good validity and is useful for evaluating patients who normally would perform at or below WAIS-R floor levels.

The NCSE, a relatively new test, is similar to the MDRS in its hierarchical arrangement of items. The format presents screening items that are considered the most difficult items in each of 10 independent areas. Once the examinee passes the screening item, additional items within that area are not administered. The strengths of this measure include its use of independent tests to evaluate language, constructional ability, calculations, reasoning, and memory functioning, while also assessing the patient's level of consciousness, orientation, and attention. Data are presented in a profile format, and some age-adjusted norms are provided. The standardization data include only 30 patients with documented brain lesions, but the NCSE demonstrates a better false-negative rate than the MMSE (Schwamm, Van Dyke, Kiernan, Merrin, & Mueller, 1987). Further work is needed to examine its validity, however.

Another scale that appears useful in evaluating the progression of cognitive and behavioral dysfunction characteristic of Alzheimer's patients is Rosen et al.'s Alzheimer's Disease Assessment Scale. This scale shows a high interrater reliability and good test-retest reliability. It covers the cognitive areas that are characteristically impaired in Alzheimer's disease while adding a section of ratings to allow the evaluation of general functional ability. We have used this scale successfully in our Memory Disorders Clinic at the University of Kentucky as it appears to be more sensitive to the early stages of cognitive dysfunction than briefer measures such as the MMSE.

Neuropsychological Screening Batteries

Given that time is often a valuable resource in neuropsychological evaluation, it is appropriate to consider a number of short neuropsychological test batteries (e.g., Golden, Purisch, & Hammeke, 1980; Barrett, Wheatley, & La Plant, 1982) that are designed to provide gross differential diagnostic information about the patient and baselines for future comparisons. While providing some behavioral assessment of patients' strengths and weaknesses, these measures are less time-consuming and more cost-effective than extensive adult neuropsychological batteries. As a full review of the different combinations of neuropsychological tests is beyond the scope of this chapter, three approaches that may be useful with older adults are presented.

The first such battery, presented by Filskov (1983), employs standard tests or subtests from different batteries. Filskov suggests using the WAIS or WAIS-R Information, Vocabulary, Digit Symbol, Block Design, and Digit Span subtests to estimate general intellectual functioning. She further suggests that Digit Symbol and Digit Span provide initial tests sensitive to organic impairment. In addition to the WAIS subtests, Filskov recommends the Wechsler Memory Scale (WMS), including delayed recall as modified by Russell (1975). The Paired Associates task from the WMS can be used as a screening item. It is of interest that the Paired Associates task has proven sensitive to the memory decrements associated with Alzheimer's disease (Rosen, 1983), particularly as patients with a memory disorder tend to do reasonably well with the early paired associates (e.g., north-south) but have difficulty learning the more difficult ones (e.g., inch-obey). Additional tests in the Filskov screening are the Wepman Aphasia Screening Test and Associated Examination for Sensory Perceptual Disturbances (Reitan & Davison, 1974), the Halstead Category Test (booklet form), and the Wisconsin Card Sorting Test (the latter two to assess complex problem solving). Filskov provides excellent case illustrations of the usefulness of this type of screening as well as a discussion of how to individualize a screening battery from these tests. The strengths of this screening approach lie in its assessment of the five basic areas of cognitive functioning critical to evaluating older adults: general intelligence, language, visual-spatial abilities, sensory-perceptual functions, and problem solving.

Benton and his colleagues present another extended screening battery with demonstrated utility in the evaluation of dementia (Benton et al., 1983; Eslinger, Damasio, Benton, & Van Allen, 1985). This battery was developed from an ongoing study of dementia at the University of Iowa and was derived from a comprehensive neuropsychological evaluation of persons over 65 years of age. The large battery included tests from the clinical procedures developed by Benton, Hamsher, Varney, and Spreen (1983). Comparisons between normal older persons and patients with dementia revealed that the combination of three fairly brief tests from the overall battery (Visual Retention, Controlled Oral Word Association, and Temporal Orientation) reliably classified cases of dementia (Eslinger et al., 1985). This screening process requires approximately 15 minutes and is well normed for older patients.

The brief neuropsychological battery developed by Barrett, Wheatley, and La Plant (1982), which can be completed in approximately 2 hours, is based on the Halstead-Reitan approach. This battery includes the Shipley-Hartford Scale, the revised Wechsler Memory Scale, a name-writing task, the Reitan-Indiana Aphasia and Sensory-Perceptual Exam, the Constructional Dyspraxia Exam, the Trail Making Test, and the Finger-Tapping Test. The Wechsler Memory Scale is included to provide a detailed evaluation of memory. Barrett et al. also have developed a very brief screening instrument from this neuropsychological battery (Barrett & Gleser, 1987). In general the battery has a high hit rate and reliably classifies patients with definite and suspected organic damage in comparison to nonorganic cases. Its utility, however, as well as that of other short neuropsychological batteries, still needs particular evaluation with regard to older adults.

Neuropsychological Batteries

There are three major neuropsychological batteries employed in all populations: the Halstead-Reitan Neuropsychological Test Battery (HRNTB), Golden et al.'s Luria-Nebraska Neuropsychological Battery, and the collected tests of Benton and his colleagues (Benton et al., 1983). The HRNTB is made up of a number of procedures described in detail by Reitan and Wolfson (1985) and will not be discussed in detail here. The HRNTB has been the most researched of these three neuropsychological batteries, and a number of studies and reviews have documented significant relationships between age and education and HRNTB performance (e.g., Bak & Greene, 1980; Goldstein & Shelly, 1975).

Perhaps the most comprehensive of these studies was completed by Heaton, Grant, and Matthews (1986), who examined the performance of over 500 individuals aged 15 to 81 years. When they divided their subjects into three age and three education categories, they were able to document the effects of age, sex, and education on the WAIS and HRNTB. Heaton et al.'s cross-sectional data demonstrated that age was associated with poorer performance on those HRNTB measures tapping psychomotor speed, flexibility of thought, incidental memory, and conceptual ability. Weak associations with age were found for the Aphasia Screening Test, Sensory-Perceptual Examination, and motor tasks. A strong association between high educational achievement and both the HRNTB and WAIS was found. In the case of the HRNTB, the highest correlations appeared with tests of language, conceptualization, and cognitive flexibility.

Based on these data, Heaton et al. (1986) demonstrated that groups having low educational achievement showed greater cognitive decline between the young (less than 40 years) and middle-age (40-59 years) periods. They also argued that the better educated group tended to show levels of impairment similar to that of the low education group when they entered the later age period (greater than 60 years). These researchers caution that although the reported age-related differences in abilities were documented by the HRNTB and WAIS, their cross-sectional design suffered from the fact that they were unable to measure changes in ability over time. Clearly, more longitudinal data are required documenting change in neuropsychological ability as a result of healthy and disease-related aging.

Although the Luria-Nebraska is a briefer comprehensive battery than the HRNTB, administration still can entail 3-4 hours with an older patient. Goldstein, McCue, and Shelly (1987) have constructed a shortened form of the Luria-Nebraska that includes items sensitive to dementia (Memory and Intellectual Processes scales) and excludes those (Rhythm scale) that might be confounded by "normal" aging processes (e.g., auditory acuity). Their brief version comprises 141 Luria-Nebraska items, as compared to 269 items for the full assessment. Preliminary comparisons of the original battery and the shortened form in older adults revealed a correct diagnostic classification rate of 74% for the original Luria-Nebraska scales. However, Goldstein et al. caution that more work will be required with both test batteries to evaluate their sensitivity and specificity in diagnosing dementia, psychiatric disturbances, and normal aging effects.

The tests compiled by Benton and his colleagues also have demonstrated differential sensitivity to the effects of aging. Even though these tests appear well normed with regard to age, declines in performance are often seen on Benton Visual Retention Test, Facial Recognition, and Serial Digit Learning, which are measures of short-term visual memory. The General Verbal and Visual Perception tests tend to be less sensitive to the effects of age. It is important to note that the Benton tests do contain age adjustments as well as adjustments for education. Based on their study of dementia, Eslinger et al. (1985) have been able to present data on over 150 normal control subjects as well as a fairly large group of demented individuals.

Memory Evaluation

The appropriate evaluation of memory deserves special consideration within a geriatric population, though it has been argued (e.g., Erickson & Scott, 1977) that the clinical assessment of memory functioning is inadequate at the present time. A number of authors have reviewed the strengths and limitations of currently available tests of memory functioning and have made recommendations for the development of an "optimal" memory test (Erickson & Scott, 1977; Erickson, Poon, & Walsh-·Sweeney, 1980). Memory evaluation is, in itself, a very difficult undertaking because of the rapidly developing research in the area and the different conceptual frameworks for the clinician to evaluate. Clearly, an adequate memory evaluation should assess both input and output functions involved in the registration, storage, and retrieval of to-be-remembered information. Ideally a wide variety of spheres, including visual, auditory, and sensorimotor information, should be evaluated. Assessment of verbal and spatial memory should also include recall and recognition tests, plus some measure of incidental memory, metamemory, and the individual's ability to use strategic memory processes. Often, a comprehensive examination of memory functioning requires that the clinician use a full neuropsychological examination and supplement this evaluation with memory scales. Additionally, significant information about functioning on a day-to-day basis, which can be obtained directly from the patient as well as his or her family members, is important in determining the presence or absence of a memory disorder.

The most commonly used memory scale has been the Wechsler Memory Scale. In its original form, the WMS incorporated tests of orientation, mental control, and verbal and spatial memory. Performance on this measure is sensitive to focal neurological disorders; therefore, patients with aphasia will have difficulty on the verbal portions and those who may have a constructional apraxia will have difficulty with the figural aspects. As a result, without additional information regarding basic language and visual-spatial abilities for a given patient, the Wechsler Memory Scale by itself can provide a misleading evaluation of memory functioning. Further, the WMS does not tap remote information, as it focuses primarily on immediate learning and retention of information. This scale underwent some revision by Russell (1975), who added a delayed recall assessment for both the Logical and Figural Memory subtests. In addition, a revision of the original Wechsler Memory Scale also has been released (Wechsler, 1987) that attempts to improve on the original test. As with most memory measures, it is unclear how scores from the Wechsler Memory Scale relate to a patient's ability to function on a day-to-day basis, remembering information necessary for daily living.

A number of other memory tests are available that briefly evaluate either verbal or figural memory. A useful such test of immediate visual recall is the Benton Visual Retention Test (Benton, 1974). This measure is reasonably well normed for persons up to age 64 and involves the presentation of 10 relatively simple geometric figures for immediate recall or recall after a brief delay. The Rey Auditory Verbal Learning Test (Rey, 1964) provides a measure of a subject's ability to learn a list of words after repeated presentation, and a similar procedure, Selective Reminding (developed by Buschke & Fuld, 1974), looks at repeated presentation effects on the ability of a subject to learn a list of words. The Selective Reminding procedure can be supplemented by adding a delayed recall and recognition test (Levin, Grossman, & Kelly, 1977). In theory, the Selective Reminding test measures storage of words into memory and the ability to consistently recall these words once stored. Rey also developed the Rey Complex Figure (Rey, 1941), which can be used to assess a person's ability to copy a complex design (constructional dyspraxia), but also can be used to assess memory by requesting reproduction of the design from memory.

The Randt Memory Test (Randt, Brown, & Osborne, 1980) represents a more extensive battery. The Randt was developed to assess a broader area of memory functioning and includes a brief mental status exam, a selective reminding procedure, a digit span task, a paired associates learning task, verbatim and gist paragraph recall, incidental recall, and picture recognition. The strengths of this test include assessments of delayed recall at approximately 5 minutes and at 24 hours and norms that extend well into the older aged range.

The newly available Denman Neuropsychology Memory Scale (Denman, 1984) is designed to evaluate both verbal and nonverbal memory. The scale includes immediate and delayed recall of a paragraph, paired associates, a digit span task, and a remote verbal information task, which is similar to the WAIS Information subtest. The scale's nonverbal memory subtests incorporate the Rey Complex Figure, recall of nonverbal information, recognition for human faces, and a memory for tones and melodies measure similar to the HRNTB's Seashore Rhythm Test. A relative weakness of the Denman scale is its lack of alternate forms. However, it is a well-standardized measure with norms extending from age 10 to age 89. An additional strength is that a short form of the evaluation can be used and a memory quotient prorated from the memory scale.

A useful and more ecologically valid assessment battery is the Rivermeade Behavioral Memory Test (RBMT) developed by Wilson, Cockburn, and Baddeley (1985). The RBMT includes Paired Associates as well as the Digit Span subtests. The RBMT attempts to bridge the gap between standard laboratory-based experimental measures of memory and more ecologically valid memory activities. In general the test items require that a patient retain information deemed necessary for adequate day-to-day functioning or remember a task sequence. The RBMT items include remembering a name in conjunction with a person's picture, remembering where a personal object has been hidden, remembering an appointment, remembering a paragraph, picture recognition, and facial recognition. Additional subtests involve reproducing a short route that the examiner traces within the room. The patient must reproduce this route immediately and after a delay. Embedded within the short route is an envelope the examiner leaves somewhere in the room. The patient is required to leave the envelope in the same place while retracing the route. This exercise is hypothesized to be analogous to remembering to run an errand. Another interesting task involves new skill learning, in which the patient must learn the steps involved in putting a message into a calculator. The RBMT has been successfully used with closed head injury patients to evaluate level of functioning and to track recovery from injury. The RMBT data have yet to be generalized to an older adult population or compared with other standardized tests documenting organic dysfunction in older adults. Nevertheless, the RBMT, the Wechsler Memory Scale-Revised, and the Denman scale appear to represent a "second generation" of memory evaluations that correct many earlier tests' deficiencies.

Functional Assessment

A critical area in the evaluation of older adults involves the assessment of functional abilities. Perhaps best known are the approaches of Gurland and colleagues (Comprehensive Assessment and Referral Evaluation, 1982) and Lawton (1986) and the Older Americans Resources and Services Questionnaire (OARS) methodology (e.g., Pfeiffer, 1976) developed at Duke University. These approaches generally attempt to objectify the various activities of daily living, covering instrumental areas such as managing money, driving, traveling, using the telephone, and so on, as well as basic physical activities such as grooming, bathing, continence, and performance of transfers (e.g., bed to wheelchair). These scales are particularly useful when standard neuropsychological measures appear inappropriate (e.g., when a patient has less than a grade-school education or is not a native speaker of English). Functional assessment is an important adjunct to cognitive assessment when making appropriate placement decisions for impaired older adults.

INTERPRETATION OF RESULTS

The examiner must be cautious in the interpretation of normative data currently available for older adults. In reviewing tests it is important to assess for potential biases within the "normal" older adult sample. If the normative sample has screened for the absence of any health problems, one may end up using norms that represent an extraordinarily healthy and capable group. On the other hand, if health factors generally are not reported, the norms may represent actual dysfunction based on the presence and/or absence of individuals with known chronic and acute diseases. Interpretation must consider the important issue of what represents normal aging versus disease-related aging. The fact that many test norms actually represent a cross-sectional comparison of the population at any given time may bias interpretations of what represents normal and disease-related impairment. The fact that, in general, tests such as the WAIS and HRNTB on aging populations show strong relationships between poorer performance and increasing age may not actually represent disease-related decline but rather may reflect cohort differences (e.g., Botwinick, 1977). Current norms are also particularly weak for underserved elderly populations, such as those living in rural and inner city communities.

A second critical issue involves the relationship between neuropsychological test scores and actual functioning on a day-to-day basis. As Lawton (1986) has eloquently put it in his Model of Functional Ability, there is an interaction between the demands of the environment and the actual skills of the individual that results in either adequate or inadequate functioning. Until more data are available on the ecological validity of neuropsychological techniques and psychological techniques in general, the best description of a patient's ability with regard to day-to-day living remains an accurate history (corroborated by a caregiver or family members) and actual observation of day-to-day functioning.

It is important to reemphasize that mental status evaluations only provide a *screening* of dysfunction. While these exams can be used as metrics for progressive dysfunction as well as for the efficacy of intervention, MSEs and neuropsychological screenings should be structured to assess a broad variety of cognitive skills and to signal the need for more detailed assessment in areas where dysfunction is seen. The older adult who is able to complete an extensive neuropsychological examination may, by the very fact of having done so, prove to be quite capable, regardless of the actual subtest scores. On the other hand, patients who score in the borderline area of dysfunction may present with a good social facade but be extremely dysfunctional when it comes to day-to-day abilities such as driving a car or balancing a checkbook. It is important therefore for the clinician to correlate test findings with actual day-to-day living skills and to obtain corroboration of these abilities from some significant other.

COMMUNICATION OF RESULTS

The effectiveness of neuropsychological consultation rests heavily on accurate feedback. Assessment results should be framed in such a manner that they not only can be understood but accepted by the referral source. This chapter's model of neuropsychological evaluation and consultation addresses specific referral questions generated from a third party, usually a physician. Consequently, the value of such a neuropsychological evaluation depends on communication with a discipline whose members are trained quite differently than psychologists, both in content and process. Physicians do not necessarily think like psychologists, and this fact should not be overlooked in the communication of test results. First, physicians often do not view the time frame for receiving feedback in the same manner as the psychologist trained to examine a case from many angles. For a physician, speed is often of the essence, such that immediate feedback is not only desired but expected. Consequently, oral communication with the referral source, even of screening results, is advocated whenever possible to expedite the feedback process. This also allows for discussion of issues other than specific referral questions that the evaluation may have raised.

Secondarily, our experience suggests that physicians tend to be decision and action oriented; thus, they may be much more concerned with the "bottom line" of a referral than various extraneous issues. They may wish to know the neuropsychologist's specific diagnostic opinion, whether there has been decline since the previous evaluation, or perhaps what would be the best placement for the patient. Psychologists are often concerned, appropriately, that these evaluations rarely render unequivocal answers. Nevertheless, they will be faced with having to provide specific information on which decisions about older adults are going to be made.

Most psychological evaluations will generate a written report. Here again, psychologists often are trained to write lengthy, well-synthesized reports incorporating a variety of information. Long sections concerning family dynamics and early history may make interesting reading, but the referral source may see them as irrelevant in terms of the reasons for the requested evaluation. If the information in reports has no bearing on the specific referral question or on any important issue in the patient's management, then it only serves to confuse the referral source. In general, particularly in communicating with medical colleagues, a more streamlined, abbreviated approach to a written report will be better accepted. Additional information may then be communicated orally.

Two cautions are in order regarding the communication of results to any referral source. First, the evaluator should be careful when reporting exact test scores within the body of a report. This is of particular note when reporting IQ scores. Medical colleagues and the general public often have some knowledge of intelligence test scores, and it is fair to say that a little knowledge can be a dangerous thing here. A patient who is dementing may retain an intact IQ yet display profound memory impairment. Reporting this score may obscure these other significant problems and mislead someone who puts too much emphasis on intellectual functioning. Second, although it is important for an evaluator to have confidence and certainty in his or her assessment results, one should err on the side of caution in labeling any disease entity unless there is significant evidence warranting such labeling. This is of particular importance in labeling Alzheimer's disease, which should never be done lightly because this diagnosis has numerous implications and negative connotations.

These cautions are even more important when communicating with the older patient and family members who request information about evaluation results. In such communication, the neuropsychologist must deal with issues beyond the bottom line of a referral question. Families, by and large, desire information on test findings in terms of real life behavior—what will be the effect on their lives and what can be done to improve or support functioning? These are difficult issues that require thought and explanation. In discussion with family members, it is imperative to use language commensurate with the family's ability to comprehend.

Additional information on the relationship between neuropsychological tests and actual CNS functioning should come rapidly over the next few years as new imaging techniques are developed and correlated with neuropsychological evaluations. Work being completed now at medical centers with programs specializing in the evaluation of older adults will yield further normative data on the effects of longitudinal changes in healthy and impaired older adults.

REFERENCES

Albert, M. (1981). Geriatric neuropsychology. *Journal of Clinical and Consulting Psychology, 49,* 835-850.

Bak, J.S., & Greene, R.L. (1980). Changes in neuropsychological functioning in an aging population. *Journal of Consulting and Clinical Psychology, 48,* 395-399.

Barrett, E.T., & Gleser, G.C. (1987). Development and validation of the cognitive status examination. *Journal of Consulting and Clinical Psychology, 55,* 877-882.

Barrett, E.T., Wheatley, R.D., & La Plant, R.J. (1983). A brief clinical neuropsychological battery: Clinical classification trails. *Journal of Clinical Psychology, 39,* 980-984.

Benton, A.L. (1974). *The Visual Retention Test* (4th ed.). New York: Psychological Corporation.

Benton, A.L., Hamsher, K. de S., Varney, N.R., & Spreen, O. (1983). *Contributions to neuropsychological assessment: A clinical manual.* New York: Oxford University Press.

Blessed, G., Tomlinson, B.E., & Roth, M. (1968). The association between quantitative measures of dementia and senile change in the cerebral grey matter of elderly subjects. *British Journal of Psychiatry, 114,* 797-811.

Botwinick, J. (1977). Intellectual abilities. In J.E. Birren & K.W. Schaie (Eds.), *Handbook of the psychology of aging* (pp. 580-605). New York: Van Nostrand Reinhold.

Buschke, H., & Fuld, P.A. (1974). Evaluation storage, retention, and retrieval in disordered memory and learning. *Neurology, 11,* 1019-1025.

Denman, S. (1984). *Denman Neuropsychological Memory Scale manual.* Charleston, SC: Author.

Erickson, R.C., & Scott, M.I. (1977). Clinical memory testing: A review. *Psychological Bulletin, 84,* 1130-1149.

Erickson, R.C., Poon, L.W., & Walsh-Sweeney, L. (1980). Clinical memory testing of the elderly. In L.W. Poon, J.L. Fozard, L.S. Cermak, D. Arenberg, & L.W. Thompson (Eds.), *New directions in memory and aging* (pp. 379-402). Hillsdale, NJ: Lawrence Erlbaum.

Eslinger, P.J., Damasio, A.R., Benton, A.L., & Van Allen, M. (1985). Neuropsychologic detection of abnormal mental decline in older persons. *Journal of the American Medical Association, 253,* 670-674.

Fillenbaum, G.G. (1980). Comparison of two brief tests of organic brain impairment, the MSQ and the Short Portable MSQ. *Journal of the American Geriatrics Society, 28,* 381-384.

Filskov, S.B. (1983). Neuropsychological screening. In P.A. Keller & L.G. Writt (Eds.), *Innovations in clinical practice: A sourcebook* (Vol. II, pp. 17-25). Sarasota, FL: Professional Resource Exchange.

Folstein, M.D., Folstein, S.E., & McHugh, P.R. (1975). Mini-Mental State: A practical method for grading the cognitive state of patients for the clinician. *Journal of Psychiatric Research, 12,* 189-198.

Golden, C.J., Purisch, A.D., & Hammeke, T.A. (1980). *Luria-Nebraska Neuropsychological Battery: Manual.* Los Angeles: Western Psychological Services.

Goldstein, G., McCue, M., & Shelly, C. (1987). Use of short form neuropsychological batteries with geriatric patients. *Public Service Psychology, 12,* 16.

Goldstein, G., & Shelly, C.H. (1975). Similarities and differences between psychological deficit in aging and brain damage. *Journal of Gerontology, 30,* 448-455.

Goodglass, H., & Kaplan, E. 1972). *Assessment of aphasia and related disorders.* Philadelphia: Lea & Febiger.

Gurland, B.J., Dean, L.L., Copeland, J., Gurland, R., & Golden, R. (1982). Criteria for diagnosis of dementia in the community elderly. *The Gerontologist, 22,* 180-186.

Heaton, R.K., Grant, E., & Matthews, C.G. (1986). Differences on neuropsychological test performance associated with age, education, and sex. In I. Grant & K.M. Adams (Eds.), *Neuropsychological assessment of neuropsychiatric disorders* (pp. 100-120). New York: Oxford University Press.

Herman, S., & Barnes, D. (1982). Behavioral assessment in geriatrics. In F.J. Keefe & J.A. Blumenthal (Eds.), *Assessment strategies in behavioral medicine* (pp. 473-507). New York: Grune & Stratton.

Hutzell, R.R., & Eggert, M.A. (1987). An orientation questionnaire. *Psychology and Aging, 2,* 211-216.

Jacobs, J.W., Bernhard, M.R., Delgado, A., & Strain, J.J. (1977). Screening for organic mental syndromes in the medically ill. *Annals of Internal Medicine, 86,* 40-46.

Kahn, R.L., & Miller, N.E. (1978). Assessment of altered brain function in the aged. In M. Storandt, I. Siegler, & M. Elias (Eds.), *The clinical psychology of aging* (pp. 43-69). New York: Plenum.

Kane, R.A., & Kane, R.L. (1981). *Assessing the elderly: A practical guide to measurement.* Lexington, MA: D.C. Heath.

Kiernan, R.J., Mueller, J., Langston, J.W., & Van Dyke, C. (1987). The Neurobehavioral Cognitive Status Examination: A brief but differentiated approach to cognitive assessment. *Annals of Internal Medicine, 107,* 481-485.

Lawton, M.P. (1986). Functional assessment. In L. Teri & P.M. Lewinsohn (Eds.), *Geropsychological assessment and treatment* (pp. 39-84). New York: Springer.

Levin, H.S., Grossman, R.G., & Kelly, P.J. (1977). Assessment of long-term memory in brain-damaged patients. *Journal of Consulting and Clinical Psychology, 45,* 684-688.

Mattis, S. (1976). Mental status examination for organic mental syndrome in the elderly patient. In L. Bellak & T.B. Karasu (Eds.), *Geriatric psychiatry* (pp. 77-121). New York: Grune & Stratton.

Pfeiffer, E. (1975). SPMSQ: Short Portable Mental Status Questionnaire. *Journal of the American Geriatric Society, 23,* 433-441.

Pfeiffer, E. (1976). *Multidimension functional assessment: The OARS methodology.* Durham, NC: Duke University Center for the Study of Aging and Human Development.

Randt, C.T., Brown, E.R., & Osborne, D.P., Jr. 1980). A memory test for longitudinal measurement of mild to moderate deficits. *Clinical Neuropsychology, 2,* 184-194.

Reitan, R.M., & Davison, L.A. 1974). *Clinical neuropsychology: Current status and applications.* New York: Hemisphere.

Reitan, R.M., & Wolfson, D. (1985). *The Halstead-Reitan Neuropsychological Test Battery: Theory and clinical interpretation.* Tucson: Neuropsychology Press.

Rey, A. (1941). L'examen psychologique dans les cas d'encephalopathie traumatique. *Archives de Psychologie, 28,* 286-340.

Rey, A. (1964). *L'examen clinique en psychologie.* Paris: Presses Universitaires de France.

Rosen, W.G. (1983). Clinical and neuropsychological assessment of Alzheimer's disease. In R. Mayeux & W.G. Rosen (Eds.), *Advances in neurology: The dementias* (pp. 51-64). New York: Raven.

Rosen, W.G., Motts, R.C., & Davis, K.L. (1984). A new rating scale for Alzheimer's disease. *American Journal of Psychiatry, 141,* 1356-1364.

Russell, E.W. (1975). A multiple scoring method for the assessment of complex memory functions. *Journal of Consulting and Clinical Psychology, 43,* 800-809.

Schmitt, F.A., & Farber, J. (1987). Perspectives in memory retraining of persons with cognitive deficits. In J.A. Blumenthal & D.C. McKee (Eds.), *Applications in behavioral medicine and health psychology.* Sarasota, FL: Professional Resource Exchange.

Schwamm, L.H., Van Dyke, C., Kiernan, R.J., Merrin, E.L., & Mueller, J. (1987). The Neurobehavioral Cognitive Status Examination: Comparison with the Cognitive Capacity Screening Examination and the Mini-Mental State Examination in a neurosurgical population. *Annals of Internal Medicine, 107,* 486-491.

Sloane, R.B. (1980). Organic brain syndrome. In J.E. Birren & R.B. Sloane (Eds.), *Handbook of mental health and aging* (pp. 554-590). Englewood Cliffs, NJ: Prentice-Hall.

Strub, R.L., & Black, F.W. (1985). *The mental status examination in neurology* (2nd ed.). Philadelphia: F.A. Davis.

Vitaliano, P.P., Breen, A.R., Russo, J., Albert, M., Vitiello, M.V., & Prinz, P.N. (1984). The clinical utility of the Dementia Rating Scale for assessing Alzheimer patients. *Journal of Chronic Diseases, 37,* 743-753.

Wechsler, D. (1987). *Wechsler Memory Scale-Revised: Manual.* San Antonio, TX: Psychological Corporation.

Whelihan, W.M., Lesher, E.L., Kleban, M.H., & Granick, S. (1984). Mental status and memory assessment as predictors of dementia. *Journal of Gerontology, 39,* 572-576.

White, R.F. (1987). Differential diagnosis of probable Alzheimer's disease and solvent encephalopathy in older workers. *The Clinical Neuropsychologist, 1,* 153-160.

Wilson, B., Cockburn, J., & Baddeley, A. (1985). *The Rivermeade Behavioral Memory Test: Manual.* Reading, England: Thames Valley Test Co.

Wilson, B.A. (1987). *Rehabilitation of memory.* New York: Guilford.

Wilson, R.S., Rosenbaum, G., & Brown, G. (1979). The problem of premorbid intelligence in neuropsychological assessment. *Journal of Clinical Neuropsychology, 1,* 49-53.

5

Pseudodomentia, Dementia, and Depression: Test Differentiation

BERNICE A. MARCOPULOS, PH.D.

Referrals to clinical psychologists for testing elderly clients with functional or organic problems have increased substantially over the past two decades. Frequently, the referral is to gather information for making a differential diagnosis between depression and dementia. Less often, the referral question seeks a differentiation between types of dementia (e.g., Alzheimer's versus multi-infarct) when the presence of cognitive dysfunction has already been established. Referrals may come from the physician, wanting to know whether there is a functional component to the physical symptoms his or her elderly patient is reporting, as well as from other allied health professionals needing assistance in implementing useful treatment or extended care programs.

The "organic" (i.e., dementia) versus "functional" (i.e., depression) diagnostic question has had a long history in the psychiatric and psychological literature. As early as 1904, the difficulties with differential diagnosis were discussed in the geriatric psychiatry literature. In his study of 269 patients over the age of 60 who were admitted to the "Insane Department" of Philadelphia Hospital, Pickett (1904) wrote:

> The essence of senile dementia is a quantitative change, —a mental loss; but the more obvious change is frequently qualitative—excitement, depression, delusion—so that the disease may appear in a guise simulating one of the pure insanities—mania, melancholia, paranoia, etc. (p. 82)

This seemingly arbitrary distinction between organic and functional disorders appears even more intertwined and difficult to tease out in an elderly population. Relative to younger persons, older persons are at a higher risk for dementia and depression or both in conjunction (Eisdorfer & Cohen, 1978; Roth, 1980). Blazer, Hughes, and George (1987) found that the prevalence of dysphoria in an elderly community population was 19%, and others have estimated that 10 to 20% of the population over the age of 65 has significant cognitive impairment (Kay, 1979). Between 10 and 30% of dementias are potentially treatable (Benson, 1982; Cummings, Benson, & LoVerme, 1980; Freemon, 1976; Rabins, 1981); therefore, it is important to determine the causes and possible interventions for changes in affective and mental status in older patients. Psychological testing has been used as a clinical aid to make these determinations.

70

The Concept of Pseudodementia

Pseudodementia describes depressed persons who have cognitive impairment that abates when the depression is successfully treated (Cummings & Benson, 1983). This term is often misleading and can result in a quest for differential diagnosis between organic and functional disorders in the elderly, when in fact a more integrative strategy emphasizing clarification of the separate, yet interactive, affective and cognitive elements may be more useful.

Currently, several positions exist regarding the syndrome of pseudodementia. Some authors believe in dichotomous diagnosis, determining whether a patient has *either* depression *or* dementia and treating them as mutually exclusive. There are those who argue that the two often coexist. Some authors emphasize the importance of depression as the primary etiology, while others refer to a number of psychiatric syndromes associated with pseudodementia. The term *pseudodepression* has even been coined to emphasize the importance of real dementia in cases considered to be pseudodementia (Morstyn, Hochanadel, Kaplan, & Gutheil, 1982).

The term *pseudodementia* seems to have been introduced in a 1952 paper by Madden, Luhan, Kaplan, and Manfredi. They studied 300 patients over the age of 45 in the psychiatric unit of a general hospital and found that

> In these cases classified as arteriosclerotic in origin, in some depressions in a pre-senile setting, and occasionally in involutional psychoses there may occur symptoms ordinarily considered to indicate dementia (disorientation, and defects in recent memory, retention, calculation, and judgment) which may disappear on alleviation of the psychotic picture by means of short-term intensive therapy. Such pseudodementia was noted in 10% of all our cases. (p. 1569)

However, it was Kiloh's widely cited paper (1961) that first brought this potentially reversible brain syndrome to the attention of clinicians. He presented several cases in which diagnoses of dementia were made, yet the patients did not deteriorate further upon follow-up; in fact, they responded "dramatically" to antidepressants or ECT. Kiloh claimed that these patients had reversible cognitive impairment due to affective disorder, although no formal psychometric testing was done that would have substantiated his claim. Although most of his patients were younger and had a variety of psychiatric diagnoses, he pointed out that the danger of misdiagnosis was greatest in the elderly because they are more likely to be given a diagnosis of dementia simply by virtue of their age. He recommended that every time a diagnosis of dementia is made, the possibility of depression should be seriously entertained.

Since Kiloh's influential paper, there have been several retrospective studies dramatizing the clinical importance of pseudodementia in elderly patient populations (Marsden & Harrison, 1972; Nott & Fleminger, 1975; Ron, Toone, Garralda, & Lishman, 1979). In each of these studies, clinical records of patients diagnosed with dementia were reviewed. The patients were then recontacted 1 to 15 years after initial evaluation to determine the stability of diagnosis. Fifteen to 47% were judged nondemented at follow-up, after psychological testing revealed no memory loss or intellectual impairment. Functional disorders, most often depression, comprised the most common diagnoses. More recently, Rabins, Merchant, and Nestadt (1984) did a 2-year prospective follow-up on patients diagnosed as both depressed and demented (as determined by a Mini-Mental State Examination [Folstein, Folstein, & McHugh, 1975] score of 24 or less). They found that the patients had not progressed to a dementing illness; however, 3 of their 18 patients remained cognitively impaired.

Post (1975) and Folstein and McHugh (1978) also have been influential in promoting the concept of the "dementia syndrome of depression" and have encouraged differential diagnosis as if the two diagnoses were mutually exclusive. Wells (1979) outlined some clinical features that could be useful in differentiating dementia from depression; he based his findings on the observations of 10 patients with pseudodementia from his own practice. His patients, however, were relatively young (ages 33 to 69), so the tendency to diagnose dementia was perhaps not as great in his sample.

McAllister and Price (1982) have presented current research that supports Kiloh's original paper. They describe four case histories of elderly patients with cognitive impairment due to affective disorder that was indistinguishable from dementia. All four had significant past histories of psychiatric illness and all responded dramatically to ECT or antidepressants. McAllister and Price suggest that antidepressant treatment should be given a trial whenever there is insufficient evidence to diagnose dementia, or when clinical presentation or history suggest depression. Interestingly, two of their cases had dementias (normal pressure hydrocephalus and Jakob-Creutzfeld disease), but both showed dramatic, albeit short-lived, response to ECT. These researchers maintained that even in patients with verified brain damage, cognitive impairment was due more to depression.

Pseudodementia is not associated only with depression. Kiloh (1961), Post (1975), and Roth and Meyers (1975) emphasized a depressive etiology, but Wells (1979) pointed out that only three of his patients were primarily depressed. He stressed that pseudodementia lacks diagnostic specificity and can occur in a variety of psychiatric disorders. After reviewing the literature on pseudodementia, Caine (1986) concluded that pseudodementia was more often associated with depression in elderly patients, whereas a variety of psychiatric disorders could cause pseudodementia in younger patients.

All of these studies underscore the importance for clinicians to consider pseudodementia when presented with an elderly patient with cognitive deficits. Kiloh (1961), Nott and Fleminger (1975), and Ron et al. (1979) warn against therapeutic nihilism with a premature diagnosis of dementia because certain cognitive deficits can be reversed with adequate treatment of depression. Considering how common depression is in the elderly, clinicians seem to have taken this advice. Presently, they often attempt to diagnose *either* depression *or* dementia or, when in doubt, give treatment for depression in the hope that the patient will respond and cognitive impairment will abate. This is certainly a more optimistic view of cognitive impairment in the elderly and it has had a positive effect on mental health care—elderly patients are now evaluated more carefully for reversible causes of cognitive impairment. On the other hand, real cognitive impairment may be disregarded because too much emphasis has been placed on depression.

Pseudodementia and Nonprogressive Cognitive Impairment

The studies reviewed up to this point imply that the dementia is truly "pseudo," and that correction of the underlying affective illness (most often depression) leads to complete and dramatic recovery of symptoms. However, pseudodementia may be associated with real, although nonprogressive, cognitive impairment. Caine (1986) suggested a relationship between the clinical syndrome of pseudodementia and underlying brain disorders. He based this on the fact that two of his patients had mild retardation and three others had possible left-hemisphere dysfunction, diffuse cerebral dysfunction, and a history of subarachnoid hemorrhage. Wells (1979) believed that these underlying brain disorders were not enough to explain the *degree* of mental disability displayed by these patients, but that they may have provided a framework upon which dementia symptoms could be elaborated. Perhaps the depressed patients who develop a pseudodementia already have undetected brain damage of unidentified etiology.

McAllister (1983) examined the concept of pseudodementia in a literature review of case reports and studies that he divided into reports of 1) pseudodementia without associated cerebral dysfunction and 2) pseudodementia with co-existing cerebral dysfunction. He pointed out the confusion regarding the term, due in part to the fact that there are no widely accepted diagnostic criteria, and stated that pseudodementia is not a single homogeneous syndrome. In the studies he cited, McAllister showed that the patients with depressive pseudodementia were significantly older and had a higher incidence of past psychiatric illness. He cited evidence (i.e., hypothalamic pituitary adrenal axis dysfunction, decreased cerebral blood flow, disorder of amines) that depression is a "true" organic mental disorder and suggested the descriptive term *depression-induced organic mental disorder.*

No specific neuroanatomical correlates of pseudodementia have been found yet. Jacoby and Levy (1980) found that although elderly patients with affective disorders had lower memory and orientation scores, there were no differences in CT scans in terms of enlarged ventricles, widened sulci, or Evans ratio. They concluded that there was no detectable cerebral basis for depressive pseudodementia. However, they did find a subgroup of nine depressed patients with enlarged ventricles. These patients had late onset depression, were older, and their depression tended to be endogenous. Thus, these authors speculated that there may be a subgroup of elderly depressives who have affective disorders related to cerebral pathology that is not due to coexisting or undiagnosed dementia. However, Parr (1955) reported a case of a man with histologically proven Alzheimer's disease who presented with both depression and cognitive impairment, but did not necessarily deteriorate. Without the biopsy, his most likely diagnosis would have been pseudodementia.

The Coexistence of Depression and Dementia

Perhaps clinicians should not be so anxious to rule out depression or dementia; it may be more prudent to entertain both diagnoses. Caine (1986) admitted that "it may be impossible to determine where a psychiatric disorder leaves off and a neurological disorder begins. Indeed such a distinction may not be necessary as long as one establishes that the course is nonprogressive" (p. 228). Even when mental impairment improves after treatment for psychiatric disorder, coexisting neurological disorders cannot be ruled out. Caine (1981, 1986) theorized that both depression and aging, while separate neurobiological processes, lead to impaired verbal processing, attention, and memory. The two conceivably could interact and cause pseudodementia.

Several authors have questioned the validity of the concept of pseudodementia and believe that this syndrome is better explained as a coexistence of both depression and dementia. Shraberg (1978), in the first clear objection to pseudodementia, described a case study of an 85-year-old man with coexisting depression and dementia whose mood and mental status improved considerably with imipramine, but who was still cognitively impaired enough to warrant a diagnosis of dementia. Shraberg wrote that the concept of pseudodementia oversimplifies the division between cognitive and affective illness. Although the mental status of Shraberg's patient improved after alleviation of depression, he argued that his patient did not have pseudodementia. He argued that

> both depression and dementia are dynamic and fluctuating processes and that what may disable the patient is the severity of one or both together. . . . Therefore the concept of dementia and depression occurring as parallel and interrelated processes in the senium is a more helpful treatment guide. (1978, p. 602)

Authors have begun to reconceptualize the diagnostic problem of pseudodementia in terms of coexistence of depression and dementia. Kral (1983) found that 15% of Alzheimer patients in a geriatric unit of a mental hospital were depressed. He followed 22 patients with depressive pseudodementia (average age = 76.5 years) for 4 to 18 years (mean duration = 8 years) and found that in 20 cases, permanent dementia (i.e., Alzheimer's disease) had developed. Kral put forth four interesting hypotheses regarding this relationship: 1) cognitive impairment with depression predisposes one to later developing dementia; 2) depression can act as a catalyst for manifesting preexisting dementia; 3) endogenous depression itself can be a predisposing factor in dementia; and 4) treatment of depression with antidepressants with anticholinergic properties can lay the groundwork for later development of Alzheimer's disease. Kral stated that Alzheimer patients can suffer from three types of depression: 1) endogenous, which responds to tricyclic antidepressants, 2) reactive, which responds to supportive psychotherapy, and 3) one that is part of the brain degeneration of Alzheimer's characterized by chronic depressive mood, irritability, aggressiveness, and paranoid ideation. This latter type does not respond to antidepressant medications, but will respond to neuroleptics.

Reifler and associates (Reifler, 1982; Reifler, Larson, & Hanley, 1982) are perhaps the most vocal opponents of the concept of pseudodementia, pointing out the prevalence of coexistent dementia and depression in their sample of 88 cognitively impaired patients referred to a geriatric outpatient assessment program. Of 103 patients, 88 were cognitively impaired, and of these, 20 (33%) were depressed. These researchers found that the severity of dementia was inversely related to depression, with the more severely demented patients less likely to show depression. Reifler et al. judged that 3 of their patients had depression only and the remaining 17 (85%) had depression superimposed on dementia. They estimated that in patients brought to a geriatric clinic specializing in behavioral problems, the coexistence of cognitive impairment and depression is between 20 and 25%. However, they also argued that depression is not necessarily more common with dementing illnesses, but instead more closely matches the estimates of depression in a general medical population (Moffic & Paykel, 1975). These researchers agreed with Shraberg (1978) that depression can make cognitive impairment worse and that treatment of depression can improve mental status.

Reifler (1982) puts forth some very convincing arguments for abandoning the term *pseudodementia*. Citing Kiloh's (1961) and Wells's (1979) assertion that this term should be descriptive, not diagnostic, Reifler argued that pseudodementia implies mutually exclusive categories. He criticized the cases presented in the literature as illustrations of pseudodementia because they have not convincingly mimicked dementia. Psychometric evidence and adequate follow-up time were lacking, which would have documented that the patients actually improved or failed to decline.

There has been much recent research that supports Reifler et al.'s and Kral's ideas of coexisting disorders. Devanand and Nelson (1985) presented four cases in which depressive symptoms abated with treatment but dementia persisted. Their cases illustrated that depression can be recurrent or reactive to failing memory, but the severity of cognitive deficits cannot be accurately assessed if depression coexists.

Major depressive disorders can develop in patients with severe dementia, but the "typical" expression of depression in the demented patient is skewed due to the decrease in cognitive capacity (DeMuth & Rand, 1980; Snow & Wells, 1981). Significant symptoms overlap in dementia and depression (i.e., psychomotor retardation, weight loss, fatigue, decreased libido, and insomnia), which may cause an overestimation of the extent of depression in demented patients (Lazarus, Newton, Cohler, Lesser, & Schweon, 1987). Lazarus et al. (1987) found that demented patients had a higher incidence (40%) of depressive symptoms than controls (12%), even when both groups were screened for prior history of psychological disorder. Depression may be overlooked in dementia because depression can exacerbate the already regressed behavior of a demented patient. These depressions can respond to ECT or other treatments and behavior can improve.

Knesevich, Martin, Berg, and Danziger (1983) have argued that depression may be an independent symptom when it coexists with dementia and thus aggressive treatment of depression is warranted. They compared symptoms of depression in a group of mildly demented and normal elderly (mean age = 71). Using the Hamilton Rating Scale for Depression (Hamilton, 1967) and the Zung Self-rating Depression Scale (Zung, 1965), they found significant differences, but both groups were in the nondepressed range.

Since Reifler et al. (1982) reported persistent cognitive deficits in patients initially diagnosed with depression, there have been similar reports from other geriatric clinics. Reding, Haycox, and Blass (1985) examined the prevalence of depression in 225 clinic patients referred for evaluation of cognitive complaints. In 70% of the nondemented patients, a diagnosis of depression was given. These patients were reevaluated approximately 30 months after the initial diagnosis, and 16 of the 28 (57%) recontacted had become demented. This finding contradicts Nott and Fleminger (1975) and Ron, Toone, Garralda, and Lishman (1979). Reding et al.'s patients who had become demented tended to be older and had more neurological abnormalities, but they did not differ on sex, duration of symptoms, percent spontaneously complaining of cognitive deficit, or type of depression. None had initially looked demented according to the Mental Status Questionnaire (Kahn, Goldfarb, Pollack, & Peck, 1960). They found that the Hachinski Ischemic Score (Hachinski et al., 1975) and neurologic exclusion criteria were more useful in predicting dementia in this group. The deterioration score for Alzheimer's patients with depression was slower to decline than for those without. None of the four patients who later turned out to have multi-infarct dementia showed obvious stroke progression. Five out of six depressed patients with cognitive impairment insufficient for a diagnosis of dementia at initial assessment later progressed to frank dementia. Reding et al. concluded that depression may be an early manifestation of dementia caused by Alzheimer's disease, multi-infarct Parkinson's, progressive supranuclear palsy, and spinocerebellar disorders.

Psychodynamic Interpretations

Pseudodementia has also been interpreted psychodynamically as a manifestation of a passive-dependent personality. A marked dependency for emotional and physical care that seems disproportional to measured cognitive impairment has been a striking feature of pseudodementia patients reported by Wells (1979). It has been speculated that pseudodementia might be used as an effective means of communicating a sense of helplessness. Brink (1982) described a patient who initially presented as demented, but further interview revealed that she had a long-standing history of a passive-dependent personality disorder. Kirby and Harper (1987, 1988) have described cases in their geriatric clinic in which hysterical behavior presented as dementia. According to these researchers, hysterical pseudodementia refers to a "false presentation of dementia generated by hysterical behavior in patients who may or may not also have additional underlying true organic pathology" (Kirby & Harper, 1988, p. 260). They emphasize the importance of a multidisciplinary team assessment approach because psychometric testing alone can be misleading.

Diagnostic "Attitudes"

Instead of being overly willing to diagnose organic disease, clinicians may be insufficiently sensitive to organic symptomatology. Morstyn et al. (1982) illustrate how cognitive impairment can be misinterpreted as signs of reactive depressive disorder or "pseudodepression." For instance, a severely demented patient may present as depressed because his or her speech, although stereotyped and perseverative, has depressive content. Empty, vague speech or difficulty with concentration may be misinterpreted psychodynamically as the patient avoiding sensitive issues. Verbal perseveration can be misinterpreted as a preoccupation with affect-laden issues. Affective response could be suggestibility; that is, the demented patient sometimes reacts in a stereotypical fashion to an interviewer's empathic tone. A paper by Good (1981) provides an example of this tendency to interpret what appear to be obviously neurological signs and symptoms in a psychodynamic manner.

It has been reported that organic disorders are diagnosed more frequently in the U.S., where the importance of geriatric psychiatry has historically been neglected compared to Great Britain (Duckworth & Ross, 1975). Duckworth and Ross have even accused "American diagnostic habits" of depriving elderly patients of treatment for curable conditions. This report sensitized North American clinicians, as evidenced by the amount of current literature on pseudodementia and accurate diagnosis. No doubt this report contributed to the popularity of the pseudodementia diagnostic concept.

It would be interesting to study North American "diagnostic habits" presently. As Reding et al. (1985) have intimated, diagnostic attitudes may have changed towards a preponderance of affective disorders. Perhaps this occurrence is in retribution for the depressions and reversible dementias that previously were missed due to ageist stereotypes! One could speculate that recognizing the existence of reversible dementia and dementia associated with severe affective disorder has led to a tendency to overdiagnose these disorders because there is hope for recovery and improvement. Instead of erring in the nihilistic side, clinicians may be reluctant to acknowledge the presence of permanent cognitive dysfunction in many of these patients thought to have pseudodementia. This has already been suggested by Liston (1978), who stated that an antecedent history of signs or symptoms of depressive disorder or previous psychiatric history in patients with presenile dementia is associated with significant delay in reaching a diagnosis. He indirectly blames this delay on the tendency for clinicians to assume that poor concentration and memory and reduced abstraction abilities are related to affective disorder and pseudodementia.

Although the concept of pseudodementia has been enthusiastically accepted as a clinical entity, systematic, well-controlled studies have not been carried out. The authors espousing the pseudodementia concept reported improvements in mental status that were determined by clinical judgment, not psychometrics. None of the studies of pseudodementia have employed pre- and post-neuropsychological testing, which would have provided evidence for the existence of this syndrome. Although it is an appealing concept, Kiloh himself admitted "it is purely descriptive and carries no diagnostic weight" (1961, p. 336). Pseudodementia implies reversibility of cognitive impairment, but as Shraberg (1978) and others have shown, this is often not the case. Perhaps the term itself is too dramatic—if *pseudodementia* actually refers to diminished test performance due to low effort and motivation and poor concentration, as Kiloh (1961) has suggested, then one would not expect the associated cognitive dysfunction to be so severe as to be mistaken for the brain damage associated with dementia.

The pseudodementia literature still has some questions left unanswered. For example, it is not clear if the cognitive impairment is the same type of deficit as that reported in depressed patients who were *not* mistaken for dementia patients. We do not know whether pseudodementia is associated with endogenous depression or only psychotic depression. The syndrome does not appear to occur with any great regularity, nor have its specific neuropsychological brain-behavior relationships been described clearly enough that the clinician has a "cognitive deficit profile" by which to recognize it. Caine (1986) and Cummings and Benson (1983) have suggested that pseudodementia resembles a subcortical type of dementia, but they have not provided adequate case material by which to diagnose this disorder dependably in an individual patient.

EXPERIMENTAL EVIDENCE FOR DEPRESSION-RELATED COGNITIVE
IMPAIRMENT

It is often surmised that any cognitive deficit associated with depression may be more marked in the elderly than in younger depressed patients. In fact, Cole, Branconnier, Salomon, and Dessain (1983) remarked that "older depressives 'should' be more vulnerable than younger depressives to cognitive impairment" (p. 16). As evidence of increased vulnerability, they cited Tomlinson's (1972) findings of an increase in neurofibrillary tangles, neuritic plaques, and granulovacuolar degeneration in the brain with advancing age.

Indeed, what is the evidence that depression causes greater cognitive impairment in older persons? The literature on younger depressed patients is equivocal, with some researchers finding a decrement (e.g., Sternberg & Jarvik, 1976; Weingartner, Cohen, Murphy, Martello, & Geralt, 1981) and others finding no effect (e.g., Friedman, 1964; see Miller [1975] and McAllister [1981] for reviews). It seems widely accepted that the deficit most likely is a nonspecific attentional-motivational factor that is directly related to the severity of depression (Henry, Weingartner, & Murphy, 1973). Cognitive failures appear on tasks that lack obvious structure as well as on those in which the subject must impose structure for successful performance (Weingartner et al., 1982). Unlike demented patients, depressed patients can effectively use provided organizational strategies to improve their performance.

Learning and Memory in Depression versus Dementia

There are few objective studies of cognitive impairment associated with depression in the elderly. Whitehead (1973) investigated the performance of depressed and demented elderly on tests of verbal learning and memory. She found that digit span performance did not differentiate depressed from demented elderly; however, rote learning, logical memory, and recognition memory did. More interesting were the types of errors made by the subjects. At initial assessment, depressed subjects made more errors of omission and false negatives than when retested when the depression was in remission. Demented subjects also made more omission errors, but in addition produced more irrelevant random errors and more false positives. Depressives either failed to respond or made transposition errors that were "misplaced within the task or relevant to it" (Whitehead, 1973, p. 208).

Miller and Lewis (1977) used signal detection analysis to investigate the purported memory deficit in elderly depressives. They found a slight decline in memory scores as compared to controls. Depressives tended to use stricter decision criteria and were reluctant to guess. Miller and Lewis concluded that the memory deficit in elderly depressives is related to decision criteria and is not a true memory deficit.

Gibson (1981) found that elderly depressives (mean age = 70 years) showed no qualitative differences in memory compared to normal controls. On a serial learning task they showed a similar learning curve, but they remembered fewer words. The author concluded that there is a "simple suppression" of memory in depression that is probably temporary.

Raskin, Friedman, and DiMascio (1982) found that depression diminished performance on tasks requiring sustained effort and concentration, perceptual flexibility or fluidity, abstract thinking, motivation, and accuracy. Subjects ranged from 17 to 60 years of age. These authors analyzed the data for age and found that people over 40 performed more poorly than younger subjects on many cognitive tasks, and this may be unrelated to depression.

Weingartner and his colleagues have meticulously outlined the determinants of cognitive failure associated with functional disorders (such as depression) and dementias (such as Alzheimer's disease). Tariot and Weingartner (1986) found that different disorders causing memory and learning impairment can be discriminated by the unique pattern of disturbances in both cognitive and noncognitive processes. For instance, they claim that Alzheimer patients show memory failures because of deficits in both episodic memory (recent memory for contextual material, such as a word list) and knowledge memory (long-term memory for semantic structure, procedures, and skills). In Alzheimer patients, episodic memory is impaired in part because of disturbances in knowledge memory, which inhibits normal organization of incoming to-be-remembered material. Depressed patients show no deficits in knowledge memory, but they have difficulties with automatic versus effortful cognitive operations. If more demands are made on depressed patients' information-processing capacities, such as by presenting a word list that requires organizational strategies for successful recall, these patients tend to perform poorly. However, they do improve if they are provided with structure. Depressed patients also show impairment in noncognitive processes of motivation and obtaining reward, factors that also have an influence on efficiency of information processing.

Testing to Discriminate Functional and Organic Disorders

Because there appear to be differences in learning and memory in functional and organic disorders, researchers and clinicians have looked for tests that will discriminate these disorders accurately and efficiently. Inglis and his associates (Inglis, Shapiro, & Post, 1956; Shapiro, Post, Lofving, & Inglis, 1956) found that tests that measured "memory function" (such as a word learning test) could discriminate between "functional" and "organic" groups of elderly persons. Newcombe and Steinberg (1964) looked at the discriminating ability of several tests used to distinguish between functional and organic disorders in the elderly and speculated that these tests may not be as efficient in classifying older patients into functional and psychiatric disorders (they may tend to produce more false positives over the age of 70). The Inglis Paired-Associate Learning Test (Inglis, 1959) made the best discrimination, especially using the Delayed Recall score.

More recently, LaRue, D'Elia, Clark, Spar, and Jarvik (1986) examined the diagnostic utility of the Benton Visual Retention Test (Benton, 1974), the Inglis Paired-Associate Learning Test, and the Fuld Object-Memory Evaluation (Fuld, 1980) in evaluating depression and dementia. On all three tests, the demented patients scored lower than the depressed, who scored lower than the normal controls. The Fuld test's Consistent Retrieval score was the most powerful predictor and discriminated the best among the three groups. While the Fuld evaluation was very useful in discriminating between depression, dementia, and normal aging, it was not found to be useful in discriminating between Alzheimer's patients and those with other types of dementia.

Reisberg, Ferris, Georgotas, deLeon, and Schneck (1982) found that the Beck Depression Inventory scores for 22 elderly depressed volunteers (mean age = 68.8 years) were not related to psychometric test scores, but that self-assessments of negative mood on the Mood Scale for the Elderly (Raskin & Crook, 1976) were correlated with poor performance on the Wechsler Digit Span-Digits Backward, perceptual speed, reaction time, and finger tapping with the dominant hand.

Cavanaugh and Wettstein (1983) administered the Beck Depression Inventory (Beck, Ward, Mendelson, Mock, & Erbaugh, 1961) and the Mini-Mental State Examination (MMSE; Folstein, Folstein, & McHugh, 1975) to 289 randomly selected medical in-patients aged 17 to 88 years (mean age = 57 years). A nonsignificant trend was found between severity of depression and cognitive dysfunction in patients 65. Because this study used an unselected sample of medical patients, the between-subject variance was probably quite large, possibly obscuring significant differences. Also, a gross mental status measure such as the MMSE is not a very sensitive test of the nature of the cognitive deficit in depression. Moreover, patients in this study with suspected dementia were not excluded, so the relationship between cognitive dysfunction and age may have been exaggerated.

Hart and associates (Hart, Kwentus, Taylor, & Harkins, 1987; Hart, Kwentus, Wade, & Hamer, 1987) have used rate of forgetting and the Digit Symbol test from the Wechsler Adult Intelligence Scale-Revised for effectively differentiating between demented and depressed individuals. Both demented and depressed subjects performed more slowly on Digit Symbol; thus, standard administration is not helpful in differential diagnosis. They found that an additional incidental learning component, in which patients were immediately given empty symbol boxes to fill in, could accurately discriminate between depressed and demented subjects. Rates of forgetting line drawings of common objects could also discriminate. Depressed patients had difficulty with acquisition but not consolidation, which agrees with an attentional-motivational hypothesis regarding cognitive impairment in depression (Cohen, Weingartner, Smallberg, Pickar, & Murphy, 1982; Weingartner, 1984; Weingartner et al., 1981). Also, the depressed patients did not show a rapid rate of forgetting like the demented subjects.

Thus, there is some evidence that depression is associated with poor performance on cognitive tasks, and it is possible that this is more frequent in an elderly population. None of these studies reported memory impairment so severe that dementia was suspected. The studies looking at depressed (not pseudodementia) patients have found impairments in information processing, but these impairments are quite different from the "organic" impairments one sees on the testing protocols of patients with Alzheimer's disease and multi-infarct dementia (e.g., intrusion errors, rapid rate of forgetting). Despite this, clinicians do have difficulties evaluating these elderly patients.

One source of confusion when assessing aged clients is that depressed elderly tend to complain more about their memory (Brink, 1981; Kahn, Zarit, Hilbert, & Niederehe, 1975; Popkin, Gallagher, Thompson, & Moore, 1982). This subjective report of failing memory may not be corroborated by objective memory testing. When depression is alleviated, the memory complaint tends to diminish (Popkin et al., 1982; Zarit, Cole, & Guider, 1981). Thus, part of the fuel for the pseudodementia syndrome may come from the patients themselves.

Assessing the Elderly Client for Depression and Dementia

A multidisciplinary approach to assessment of the elderly patient has been recommended by numerous authors (e.g., Kirby & Harper, 1988; Thompson, Gong, Haskins, & Gallagher 1987). The assessment must include 1) a careful medical history and physical examination, including drug inventory and evaluation of the sensorium; 2) a neurological evaluation; 3) a comprehensive cognitive assessment, including examination for aphasia; 4) a psychiatric interview, including a mental status examination; 5) a psychosocial assessment of the patient's environment; 6) laboratory tests, including clinical chemistries, hematology, urinalysis, serology; 7) a chest x-ray, and 8) a CT scan (Cummings & Benson, 1983; Eisdorfer & Cohen, 1980). The elderly are prone to numerous physical disorders that may cause dementia (see Cummings & Benson [1983] and Haase [1977] for reviews).

Physiological Considerations

Neurological disorders that are common in the elderly often present as functional symptoms (Lishman, 1978; Marsden, 1984). Depression is listed as one of the features of multi-infarct dementia on the Hachinski Ischemic Score (Hachinski et al., 1975), which is used to aid in the distinction between Alzheimer's disease and multi-infarct dementia. Hallucinations, delusions, and illusions can be present in both functional and organic disorders (Cummings & Benson, 1983, p. 312). For instance, paraphrenia, or late onset paranoid disorder, is relatively common in older adults (Bridge & Wyatt, 1980). Miller, Benson, Cummings, and Neshkes (1986) discovered significant brain disorder, most often cerebral infarctions ("silent strokes"), in their patients with late-life onset of schizophrenic symptomatology.

Headache, dizziness, fatigue, and weakness may accurately describe physiological symptoms, or they may be a patient's somatic interpretation of depression and anxiety (Pincus & Tucker, 1978). There is evidence that the elderly tend to somatize and see their physician when they are suffering from depression and anxiety. However, the presence of anxiety symptoms or depression does not automatically rule out nonfunctional explanations for patients symptoms (Lipowski, 1978; Lishman, 1978; Post, 1975). Hall, Popkin, DeVaul, Faillace, and Stickney (1978) found that 9% of their patients had medical causes for their psychiatric symptoms and were most often given diagnoses of psychoneurotic depression, organic brain syndrome, or anxiety neurosis. Cardiovascular, endocrine, infectious, and pulmonary disorders were the most frequent causes for psychiatric symptoms in their sample of 658 consecutive psychiatric outpatients.

Patient History

Establishing a patient's history is of utmost importance in making a diagnosis of depression or dementia in the elderly patient. History of psychiatric disturbance; psychomotor retardation; depressed mood or agitation; impaired immediate memory and learning abilities; defective attention, concentration, and tracking; impaired orientation; listlessness; loss of interest; and poor self-care are all clinical factors that confuse dementia and depression (Gainotti, Caltagirone, Masullo, & Miceli, 1980; Lishman, 1978; Wells, 1979). However, history of affective disorder is a strong indicator of a depressive component in a case of suspected cognitive impairment (Ron et al., 1979).

The clinical presentation of depression in the elderly involves autonomic symptoms, such as appetite and sleep disturbance, weakness, dry mouth, constipation, and cognitive deterioration with psychomotor retardation (Shraberg, 1978). In dementia, by contrast, the vegetative symptoms of depression, such as lowered appetite, insomnia, and constipation are less likely to occur (Kaszniak et al., 1981). Depressives tend to be more aware of their cognitive deficits and complain of them (Kahn et al., 1975; Wells, 1979). Subacute onset of a vegetative withdrawal is unlikely in dementia or vascular insult. Dementia supposedly has a slow, insidious onset, whereas depression can evolve over several weeks' time (Folstein & McHugh, 1978). However, history of affective disorder, persistent dysphoria, history of poor appetite and weight loss, and delusions of self-blame, hopelessness, or physical ill health suggest that a patient has an affective disorder (Rabins et al., 1984).

Obtaining a social history is also very important. Retirement, a death in the family, or a sudden change in residence should alert the clinician to the possibility of depression. On the other hand, loss of a job might herald the onset of cognitive impairment, serving as a consequence of brain dysfunction rather than an antecedent for a reactive depression. One should be cautious when using social history to date the onset of symptoms with family reports. An onset may sound acute as the family describes it, occurring suddenly during a family vacation, for example. Actually the disease process could have been progressing insidiously for quite some time when a sudden change in routine brought it to the family's attention rather abruptly, due to the patient's inability to adapt to a new situation.

Obtaining social history from the patient him- or herself is often very revealing. Large gaps in memory for important biographical events (e.g., date of retirement, date of spouse's death) are more indicative of dementia than depression. Depressives may find it difficult to attend to the interview and may be very psychomotorically slowed, but when pressed, they will remember important life events correctly.

Psychometric Testing

Kiloh (1961) claimed that psychometric testing is not helpful in making the depression versus dementia differential diagnosis. It is true that tests of orientation alone are of limited value in "diagnosing" organicity in an elderly patient (Reding et al., 1985; Eisdorfer & Cohen, 1980), but more extensive neuropsychological testing is very helpful in identifying brain damage. Wells (1979) claimed that inconsistencies in testing performance can give evidence for pseudodementia. For instance, Nott and Fleminger (1975) found that only their demented patients had difficulties with naming, writing, calculation, or motor praxis. Defects in language (e.g., dysnomia, paraphasias) are commonly noted in patients with Alzheimer's disease (Cummings, Benson, Hill, & Read, 1985; Rosen, 1980; Schwartz, Marin, & Saffran, 1979) and are not considered associated with depression. Cummings et al. (1985) believe the aphasic defect in Alzheimer's disease is similar to transcortical sensory aphasia.

Demented patients have impaired auditory comprehension, impaired narrative writing, and abnormal writing to dictation, but repetition is relatively unimpaired.

Lezak (1983) has given valuable guidelines for interpreting test performance. The qualitative, non-scored elements in a patient's protocol are often more helpful in identifying organicity or presence of brain damage. This has been called the "process approach" to assessment, in which a patient's test strategy is examined (Kaplan, 1983). The end result (i.e., score) on a particular test provides less information than the manner in which the patient arrived at that score. This approach is particularly useful given the research showing that while depressed subjects may not use information-processing or problem-solving strategies effectively, demented patients often use no strategies at all or ones that are profoundly disorganized or concrete. For example, on a word-generating task a demented patient may look around the room for objects that begin with the letter c.

According to Lezak (1983), there are patterns of neuropsychological test performance that suggest organicity regardless of how much the patient's problem appears purely functional in nature. Some of these "organic" indicators are rotation on a visuoconstructional task, perseverative writing, inexplicable low scores or a few low scores on the same function, and a pattern of test performance that makes anatomical sense, such as a consistently slow or clumsy right hand relative to left hand in a right-hander. On the Wechsler scale, demented patients tend to perform within normal range on overlearned verbal tests, such as Information, Vocabulary, Comprehension, Similarities, and Digit Span-Digits Forward. Unfamiliar, abstract, or speeded tests, such as Block Design, Digit Symbol, and Digit Span-Digits Backward, tend to be impaired. Object Assembly tends to be low, but it is often higher than Block Design and Digit Symbol. On Block Design, a depressed patient may give up or not complete the design within the time limit, while a brain-impaired patient might put the blocks on top of the design or lack appreciation for the gestalt, placing blocks randomly or rotating the design. A patient who is purely depressed would not be expected to make such errors. Lezak (1983) cites an unpublished study by Coolidge, Brown, and Harsch that suggests a Vocabulary test score twice as high as Block Design is an indicator of dementia and rarely occurs among depressed patients.

Albert and Kaplan (1980) have analyzed drawing performance in normal aging and dementia. Early in the disease, Alzheimer patients show constructional apraxia, such as in drawing a clock or completing the Wechsler Block Design subtest. Depressed drawing performance tends to be "shabby" and carelessly executed, presumably because of apathy. "Organic" signs of rotation, perseveration, "closing in," or segmentation are not apparent. With encouragement, the depressed patient may be able to improve his or her performance.

Intrusion errors, a type of perseveration in which a response that was appropriate for an earlier test item is given for a later one, are common in Alzheimer patients (Butters, Granholm, Salmon, Grant, & Wolfe, 1987; Fuld, 1980; Fuld, Katzman, Davies, & Terry, 1982) but uncommon in those who are depressed (Marcopulos & Graves, 1987). Fuld et al. (1982) found an association between intrusion errors and the neuropathology of Alzheimer's disease (i.e., senile plaques and reduced choline acetyltransferase). Fuld (1980) developed a modification of the Buschke-Fuld (1974) procedure of selective reminding that she uses in her research on cholinergic behavioral markers in dementia. LaRue et al. (1986) found this test most helpful in distinguishing among demented, depressed, and normal older persons.

The Fuld Object-Memory Evaluation (1981), which promises "guaranteed initial stimulus-processing" for older persons who may have sensory impairments, tests storage, retrieval, and retention for 10 common objects. In addition, it incorporates a verbal fluency task between the memory trials to measure the ability to retrieve words rapidly from familiar semantic categories. Fuld also uses the evaluation, especially its rapid semantic retrieval aspect, for quantifying intrusion errors during the test protocol. This instrument also provides information about tactile recognition, object naming, and left-right orientation. Norms for storage, retrieval, consistency of retrieval, and response to reminders are provided for community-residing and institutionalized 70- to 79-year-olds and 80- to 89-year-olds.

There seem to be qualitative differences in intrusion errors, perhaps related to severity of memory disorder and presence of dementia. Intrusions in which the subject recalls an item that was not in the Fuld memory item bag (e.g., saying *apple,* which was an item produced during rapid semantic retrieval) were extremely rare in a sample of depressed elderly. Marcopulos and Graves (1987) found that the most common type of intrusion in their sample of nondemented elderly subjects occurred on the Wechsler Vocabulary subtest, in which a definition that was appropriate for a previous word was given for a later item. This type of error seems similar to Whitehead's (1973) "transpositional error." It appears to be a form of guessing, with perseverative features, in which the subject uses previous definitions or parts of a previous definition for the harder words. In these cases, subjects did not give any indications that they were repeating a definition or parts of a previous definition, nor did they say that they did not know the definition.

The California Verbal Learning Test (Delis, Kramer, Kaplan, & Ober, 1983) is also a good test to give to a patient with possible dementia and/or depression. The 16-word list is organized into four categories (fruit, clothing, spices and herbs, and tools) that could aid recall if the patient utilizes these categories for semantic organization. This measure tests for some of the cognitive processes that Weingartner and associates have stated are disturbed in dementia and depression. Blau (1986) found differences between depressed and normal elderly in the number of words produced on trial 1, but by trial 5, depressive subjects performed as well as the nondepressed.

When a full neuropsychological battery is not possible, there are several extended mental status tests that can provide a quick index of most higher cortical functions likely to be compromised in many dementing processes. Thompson et al. (1987) provide a good overview of the mental status examinations available to the clinician for brief cognitive screening. The Mattis Dementia Rating Scale (MDRS; Coblentz, Mattis, Zingesser, Kasoff, Wisniewski, & Katzman, 1973; Mattis, 1976) is an extended mental status examination used to quantify degree of dementia, good for moderately to severely impaired patients and those who cannot cooperate or otherwise tolerate lengthy testing. The MDRS includes measures of attention, initiation and perseveration, construction, conceptualization, and memory. Mattis claims that it is sensitive to both focal and diffuse brain damage and has reported a test-retest reliability of .97 over a 1-week period. Litjmaer, Fuld, and Katzman (1976) found change in a patient's clinical status reflected in Mattis scores, and the scale's internal reliability has been reported quite high (Gardner, Oliver-Munoz, Fisher, & Empting, 1981; Hersch, 1979). According to Mattis (1976), normal elderly with WAIS scores greater than 85 and a Wechsler Memory Quotient within one standard deviation of IQ score had MDRS scores greater than 140 (total is 144). Normative data for the elderly are available and a cutoff score of 123 has been established (Montgomery & Costa, 1983a, 1983b). Administration takes from 15 minutes (for non-impaired elderly) to 45 minutes (for impaired). Recently, Vitaliano, Breen, Albert, Russo, and Prinz (1984) found that the MDRS was useful in rating severity of dementia and that it correlated with functional impairment in demented persons. However, it was not found to be helpful in distinguishing controls from mildly demented patients.

CONCLUSION

Even after extensive neuropsychological testing and careful interviewing for affective disorder, the clinician may still feel unsure of the diagnosis. If so, it is best simply to report, very descriptively, the kinds of cognitive problems found rather than proceeding with a diagnosis of dementia. It is always a good idea to recommend that the patient return for retesting in 3 or 6 months to document any progressive impairment that would support a diagnosis of dementia.

An untreated, severely depressed person certainly might appear cognitively impaired because psychomotor retardation, agitation, persistent ruminations, or psychotic symptoms may interfere with concentration and attention to testing. But if the results of neuropsychological testing suggest dementia, one should not disregard this potential diagnosis just because depression is the most prominent symptom. As the foregoing studies have indicated, depression can be successfully treated in the elderly.

Regardless of the presence or absence of cognitive deficit, clinicians should continue to look for treatable affective symptoms in their older patients, a message that Kiloh and successors have been effective in communicating. However, one should not assume, as perhaps did the early promoters of pseudodementia, that the patient who appears markedly brighter, with improvements in mood and energy, will show an improvement in neuropsychological test scores. Rather than making a differential diagnosis, psychological testing of older patients with suspected dementia or depression can be most helpful in identifying affective or other psychiatric disorders and thoroughly describing a patient's current level intellectual functioning.

REFERENCES

Albert, M.S., & Kaplan, E. (1980). Organic implications of neuropsychological deficit in the elderly. In L.W. Poon, J.L. Fozard, L.S. Cermak, D. Arenberg, & L.W. Thompson (Eds.), *New directions in memory and aging* (pp. 401-431). Hillsdale, NJ: Lawrence Erlbaum.

Beck, A.T., Ward, C.H., Mendelson, M., Mock, J., & Erbaugh, J. (1961). An inventory for measuring depression. *Archives of General Psychiatry, 4,* 561-571.

Benson, D.F. (1982). The treatable dementias. In D.F. Benson & D. Blumer (Eds.), *Psychiatric aspects of neurologic disease* (Vol. 2, pp. 281-287). New York: Grune & Stratton.

Benton, A.L. (1974). *Revised Visual Retention Test* (4th ed.). New York: Psychological Corporation.

Blau, E. (1986). The effect of depression on memory performance and memory complaint in older adults. *Dissertation Abstracts International, 47,* 4294B.

Blazer, D., Hughes, D.C., & George, L.K. (1987). The epidemiology of depression in an elderly community population. *The Gerontologist, 27,* 281-287.

Bridge, T.P., & Wyatt, R.J. (1980). Paraphrenia: Paranoid states of late life. I. European research. *Journal of the American Geriatrics Society, 28,* 193-200.

Brink, T.L. (1981). Self-ratings of memory versus psychometric ratings of memory and hypochondriasis. *Journal of the American Geriatrics Society, 29,* 537-538.

Brink, T.L. (1982). Passive-dependent personality and pseudodementia [Letter to the editor]. *Clinical Gerontologist, 1*(2), 83-85.

Buschke, H., & Fuld, P.A. (1974). Evaluating storage, retention, and retrieval in disordered memory and learning. *Neurology, 24,* 1019-1025.

Butters, N., Granholm, E., Salmon, D.P., Grant, I., & Wolfe, J. (1987). Episodic and semantic memory: A comparison of amnesic and demented patients. *Journal of Clinical and Experimental Neuropsychology, 9,* 479-497.

Caine, E.D. (1981). Pseudodementia. *Archives of General Psychiatry, 38,* 1359-1364.

Caine, E.D. (1986). The neuropsychology of depression: The pseudodementia syndrome. In I. Grant & K.M. Adams (Eds.), *Neuropsychological assessment of neuropsychiatric disorders* (pp. 221-243). New York: Oxford University Press.

Cavanaugh, S.V., & Wettstein, R.M. (1983). The relationship between severity of depression, cognitive dysfunction, and age in medical inpatients. *American Journal of Psychiatry, 140,* 495-496.

Coblentz, S.M., Mattis, S., Zingesser, L.H., Kasoff, S.S., Wisniewski, H.M., & Katzman, R. (1973). Presenile dementia: Clinical aspects and evaluation of cerebrospinal fluid dynamics. *Archives of Neurology, 29,* 299-308.

Cohen, R.M., Weingartner, H., Smallberg, S.A., Pickar, D., & Murphy, D.L. (1982). Effort and cognition in depression. *Archives of General Psychiatry, 39,* 593-597.

Cole, J.O., Branconnier, R., Salomon, M., & Dessain, E. (1983). Tricyclic use in the cognitively impaired elderly. *Journal of Clinical Psychiatry, 44,* 14-19.

Cummings, J., Benson, D.F., & LoVerme, S. (1980). Reversible dementia: Illustrative cases, definition, and review. *Journal of the American Medical Association, 243*(23), 2434-2439.

Cummings, J.L., & Benson, D.F. (1983). *Dementia: A clinical approach.* Boston: Butterworth.

Cummings, J.L., Benson, D.F., Hill, M.A., & Read, S. (1985). Aphasia in dementia of the Alzheimer type. *Neurology, 35,* 394-397.

Delis, D.C., Kramer, J., Kaplan, E., & Ober, B.A. (1983). *California Verbal Learning Test.* San Antonio, TX: Psychological Corporation.

DeMuth, G.W., & Rand, B.S. (1980). Atypical major depression in a patient with severe primary degenerative dementia. *Journal of Psychiatry, 137,* 1609-1610.

Devanand, D.P., & Nelson, J.C. (1985). Concurrent depression and dementia: Implications for diagnosis and treatment. *Journal of Clinical Psychiatry, 46,* 389-392.

Duckworth, G.S., & Ross, H. (1975). Diagnostic differences in psychiatric patients in Toronto, New York and London, England. *Canadian Medical Association Journal, 112,* 847-851.

Eisdorfer, C., & Cohen, D. (1978). Differential diagnosis of the cognitively impaired elderly. In M. Storandt, I. Siegler, & M.F. Elias (Eds.), *Clinical psychology of aging* (pp. 7-42). New York: Plenum.

Eisdorfer, C., & Cohen, D. (1980). Diagnostic criteria for primary neuronal degeneration of the Alzheimer's type. *Journal of Family Practice, 11,* 553-557.

Folstein, M.F., Folstein, S.E., & McHugh, P.R. (1975). Mini-Mental State: A practical method for grading the cognitive state of patients for the clinician. *Journal of Psychiatric Research, 12,* 189-198.

Folstein, M.F., & McHugh, P.R. (1978). Dementia syndrome of depression. In R. Katzman, R.D. Terry, & K.L. Bick (Eds.), *Alzheimer's disease, senile dementia and related disorders.* New York: Raven.

Freemon, F.R. (1976). Evaluation of patients with progressive intellectual deterioration. *Archives of Neurology, 33,* 658-659.

Friedman, A.S. (1964). Minimal effects of severe depression on cognitive functioning. *Journal of Abnormal and Social Psychology, 69,* 237-243.

Fuld, P.A. (1980). Guaranteed stimulus processing in the evaluation of memory and learning. *Cortex, 16,* 255-271.

Fuld, P.A. (1981). *The Fuld Object-Memory Evaluation.* Chicago: Stoelting.

Fuld, P.A., Katzman, R., Davies, P., & Terry, R.D. (1982). Intrusions as a sign of Alzheimer dementia: Chemical and pathological verification. *Annals of Neurology, 11,* 155-159.

Gainotti, G., Caltagirone, C., Masullo, C., & Miceli, G. (1980). Patterns of neuropsychologic impairment in various diagnostic groups of dementia. In L. Amaducci, A.N. Davison, & P. Antuono (Eds.), *Aging of the brain and dementia* (pp. 245-250). New York: Raven.

Gardner, R., Oliver-Munoz, S., Fisher, L., & Empting, L. (1981). Mattis Dementia Rating Scale: Internal reliability study using a diffusely impaired population. *Journal of Clinical Neuropsychology, 3,* 271-275.

Gibson, A.J. (1981). A further analysis of memory loss in dementia and depression in the elderly. *British Journal of Clinical Psychology, 20,* 179-185.

Good, M.I. (1981). Pseudodementia and physical findings masking significant psychopathology. *American Journal of Psychiatry, 136,* 811-814.

Haase, G.R. (1977). Diseases presenting as dementia. In C.E. Wells (Ed.), *Dementia* (2nd ed., pp. 27-67). Philadelphia: F.A. Davis.

Hachinski, V.C., Iliff, L.D., Zhilka, E., duBoulay, G.H.D., McAllister, V.C., Marshall, J., Russell, R.W.R., & Symon, L. (1975). Cerebral blood flow in dementia. *Archives of Neurology, 32,* 632-637.

Hall, R.C., Popkin, M.K., DeVaul, R.A., Faillace, L.A., & Stickney, S.K. (1978). Physical illness presenting as psychiatric disease. *Archives of General Psychiatry, 35,* 1315-1320.

Hamilton, M. (1967). Development of a rating scale for primary depressive illness. *British Journal of Social and Clinical Psychology, 6,* 278-296.

Hart, R.P., Kwentus, J.A., Taylor, J.R., & Harkins, S.W. (1987). Rate of forgetting in dementia and depression. *Journal of Consulting and Clinical Psychology, 55,* 101-105.

Hart, R.P., Kwentus J.A., Wade, J.B., & Hamer, R.M. (1987). Digit symbol performance in mild dementia and depression. *Journal of Consulting and Clinical Psychology, 55,* 236-238.

Henry, G.M., Weingartner, H., & Murphy, D.L. (1973). Influence of affective states and psychoactive drugs on verbal learning and memory. *American Journal of Psychiatry, 130,* 966-971.

Hersch, E.L. (1979). Development of the extended scale for dementia. *Journal of the American Geriatrics Society, 27,* 348-354.

Inglis, J. (1959). A paired-associate learning test for use with elderly psychiatric patients. *Journal of Mental Science, 105,* 440-443.

Inglis, J., Shapiro, M.B., & Post, F. (1956). "Memory function" in psychiatric patients over sixty, the role of memory in tests discriminating between "functional" and "organic" groups. *Journal of Mental Science, 102,* 589-598.

Jacoby, R.J., & Levy, R. (1980). Computed tomography in the elderly. 3. Affective disorder. *British Journal of Psychiatry, 136,* 270-275.

Kahn, R.L., Goldfarb, A.I., Pollack, M., & Peck, A. (1960). Brief objective measures for the determination of mental status in the aged. *American Journal of Psychiatry, 117,* 326-328.

Kahn, R.L., Zarit, S.H., Hilbert, N.M., & Niederehe, M.A. (1975). Memory complaint and impairment in the aged: The effect of depression and altered brain function. *Archives of General Psychiatry, 32,* 1569-1573.

Kaplan, E. (1983). Process and achievement revisited. In S. Wapner & B. Kaplan (Eds.), *Toward a holistic developmental psychology* (pp. 143-156). Hillsdale, NJ: Lawrence Erlbaum.

Kaszniak, A.W., Wilson, R.S., Lazarus, L., et al. (1981, February). *Memory and depression in dementia.* Paper presented at the Ninth Annual Meeting of the International Neuropsychological Society, Atlanta.

Kay, D.W.K. (1979). The epidemiology and identification of brain deficit in the elderly. In C. Eisdorfer & R.O. Friedel (Eds.), *Cognitive and emotional disturbance in the elderly: Clinical issues* (pp. 11-26). Chicago: Year Book Medical.

Kiloh, L.G. (1961). Pseudo-dementia. *Acta Psychiatrica Scandinavica, 37,* 336-361.

Kirby, H.B., & Harper, R.G. (1987). Team assessment of geriatric mental patients: The care of functional dementia produced by hysterical behavior. *The Gerontologist, 27,* 573-576.

Kirby, H.B., & Harper, R.G. (1988). Team assessment of geriatric mental patients (II): Behavioral dynamics and psychometric testing in the diagnosis of functional dementia due to hysterical behavior. *The Gerontologist, 28,* 260-262.

Knesevich, J.W., Martin, R.L., Berg, L., & Danziger, W. (1983). Preliminary report on affective symptoms in the early stages of senile dementia of the Alzheimer type. *American Journal of Psychiatry, 140,* 233-235.

Kral, V.A. (1983). The relationship between senile dementia (Alzheimer type) and depression. *Canadian Journal of Psychiatry, 28,* 304-306.

LaRue, A., D'Elia, L.F., Clark, E.O., Spar, J.E., & Jarvik, L.F. (1986). Clinical tests of memory in dementia, depression, and healthy aging. *Journal of Psychology and Aging, 1,* 69-77.

Lazarus, L.W., Newton, N., Cohler, B., Lesser, J., & Schweon, C. (1987). Frequency and presentation of depressive symptoms in patients with primary degenerative dementia. *American Journal of Psychiatry, 144,* 41-45.

Lezak, M. (1983). *Neuropsychological assessment* (2nd ed.). New York: Oxford University Press.

Lipowski, Z.J. (1978). Organic brain syndromes: A reformulation. *Comprehensive Psychiatry, 19,* 309-322.

Lishman, W.A. (1978). *Organic psychiatry.* Oxford: Blackwell Scientific.

Liston, E.H. (1978). Diagnostic delay in presenile dementia. *Journal of Clinical Psychiatry, 39,* 599-603.

Litjmaer, H., Fuld, P.A., & Katzman, R. (1976). Prevalence and malignancy of Alzheimer's disease. *Archives of Neurology, 33,* 304.

Madden, J.J., Luhan, J.A., Kaplan, L.A., & Manfredi, H.M. (1952). Nondementing psychoses in older persons. *Journal of the American Medical Association, 150,* 1567-1572.

Marcopulos, B.A., & Graves, R. (1987, February). *Effect of antidepressants on cognitive test performance in the elderly.* Paper presented at the 15th Annual International Neuropsychological Society Meeting, Washington, DC.

Marsden, C.D. (1984). Neurological causes of dementia other than Alzheimer's disease. In D.W.K. Kay & G.D. Burrows (Eds.), *Handbook of studies on psychiatry and old age* (pp. 145-167). New York: Elsevier.

Marsden, C.D., & Harrison, M.J.G. (1972). Outcome of investigation of patients with presenile dementia. *British Medical Journal, 29,* 249-252.

Mattis, S. (1976). Mental status examination for organic mental syndrome in the elderly patient. In L. Bellak & T.B. Karasu, *Geriatric psychiatry* (pp. 77-121). New York: Grune & Stratton.

McAllister, T.W. (1981). Cognitive functioning in the affective disorders. *Comprehensive Psychiatry, 22,* 572-586.

McAllister, T.W. (1983). Overview: Pseudodementia. *American Journal of Psychiatry, 140,* 528-533.

McAllister, T.W., & Price, T.R.P. (1982). Severe depressive pseudodementia with and without dementia. *American Journal of Psychiatry, 139,* 626-629.

Miller, B.L., Benson, D.F., Cummings, J.L., & Neshkes, R. (1986). Late-life paraphrenia: An organic delusional syndrome. *Journal of Clinical Psychiatry, 47,* 204-207.

Miller, E., & Lewis, P. (1977). Recognition memory in elderly patients with depression and dementia: A signal detection analysis. *Journal of Abnormal Psychology, 86,* 44-46.

Miller, W.R. (1975). Psychological deficit in depression. *Psychological Bulletin, 82,* 238-260.

Moffic, H.S., & Paykel, E.S. (1975). Depression in medical in-patients. *British Journal of Psychiatry, 126,* 346-353.

Montgomery, K., & Costa, L. (1983a, February). *Neuropsychological test performance of a normal elderly sample.* Paper presented at the 11th Annual Meeting of the International Neuropsychological Society, Mexico City, Mexico.

Montgomery, K., & Costa, L.D. (1983b, June). *Concurrent validity of the Mattis Dementia Rating Scale.* Paper presented at the International Neuropsychological Society, Lisbon, Portugal.

Morstyn, R., Hochanadel, G., Kaplan, E., & Gutheil, T.G. (1982). Depression vs. pseudodepression in dementia. *Journal of Clinical Psychiatry, 43,* 197-199.

Newcombe, F., & Steinberg, B. (1964). Some aspects of learning and memory function in older psychiatric patients. *Journal of Gerontology, 19,* 490-493.

Nott, P.N., & Fleminger, J.J. (1975). Pre-senile dementia: The difficulty of early diagnosis. *Acta Psychiatrica Scandinavica, 41,* 210-217.

Parr, D. (1955). Diagnostic problems in presenile dementia illustrated by a case of Alzheimer's disease proven histologically during life. *Journal of Mental Science, 101,* 387-390.

Pickett, W. (1904). Senile dementia; a clinical study of two hundred cases with particular regard to types of the disease. *Journal of Nervous and Mental Disease, 31,* 81-88.

Pincus, J.H., & Tucker, G. (1978). *Behavioral neurology* (2nd ed.). New York: Oxford University Press.

Popkin, S.J., Gallagher, D., Thompson, L.W., & Moore, M. (1982). Memory complaint and performance in normal and depressed older adults. *Experimental Aging Research, 8,* 141-145.

Post, F. (1975). Dementia, depression, and pseudodementia. In D.F. Benson & D. Blumer (Eds.), *Psychiatric aspects of neurologic disease* (pp.99-120). New York: Grune & Stratton.

Rabins, P.V. (1981). The prevalence of reversible dementia in a psychiatric hospital. *Hospital and Community Psychiatry, 32,* 490-492.

Rabins, P.V., Merchant, A., & Nestadt, G. (1984). Criteria for diagnosing reversible dementia caused by depression: Validation by a 2-year follow-up. *British Journal of Psychiatry, 144,* 488-492.

Raskin, A., & Crook, T.H. (1976). *NIMH Mood Scales—Elderly (MS-E)* (ADM-523-5, Rev. 9-76). Washington: National Institute of Mental Health, Psychopharmacology Research Branch.

Raskin, A., Friedman, A.S., & DiMascio, A. (1982). Cognitive and performance deficits in depression. *Psychopharmacology Bulletin, 18,* 196-202.

Reding, M., Haycox, J., & Blass, J. (1985). Depression in patients referred to a dementia clinic. A three year prospective study. *Archives of Neurology, 42,* 894-896.

Reifler, B.V. (1982). Arguments for abandoning the term pseudodementia. *Journal of the American Geriatrics Society, 30,* 665-668.

Reifler, B.V., Larson, E., & Hanley, R. (1982). Coexistence of cognitive impairment and depression in geriatric outpatients. *American Journal of Psychiatry, 139,* 623-626.

Reisberg, B., Ferris, S.H., Georgotas, A., deLeon, M.J., & Schneck, M.K. (1982). Relationship between cognition and mood in geriatric depression. *Psychopharmacology Bulletin, 18,* 191-193.

Ron, M.A., Toone, B.K., Garralda, M.E., & Lishman, W.A. (1979). Diagnostic accuracy in presenile dementia. *British Journal of Psychiatry, 134,* 161-168.

Rosen, W.G. (1980). Verbal fluency in aging and dementia. *Journal of Clinical Neuropsychology, 2,* 135-146.

Roth, M. (1980). Senile dementia and its borderlands. In J.O. Cole & J.E. Barrett (Eds.), *Psychopathology in the aged* (pp. 205-232). New York: Raven.

Roth, M., & Meyers, D.H. (1975). The diagnosis of dementia [special issue]. *British Journal of Psychiatry, 9,* 87-99.

Schwartz, M.F., Marin, O.S.M., & Saffran, E.M. (1979). Dissociations of language function in dementia: A case study. *Brain and Language, 7,* 277-306.

Shapiro, M.B., Post, F., Lofving, B., & Inglis, J. (1956). "Memory function" in psychiatric patients over 60, some methodological and diagnostic implications. *Journal of Mental Science, 102,* 233-246.

Shraberg, D. (1978). The myth of pseudodementia: Depression and the aging brain. *American Journal of Psychiatry, 135,* 601-613.

Snow, S.S., & Wells, C. (1981). Case studies in neuropsychiatry: Diagnosis and treatment of coexistent dementia and depression. *Journal of Clinical Psychiatry, 42,* 439-442.

Sternberg, D.E., & Jarvik, M.E. (1976). Memory function in depression. *Archives of General Psychiatry, 33,* 219-224.

Tariot, P.N., & Weingartner, H. (1986). A psychobiologic analysis of cognitive failures. *Archives of General Psychiatry, 43,* 1183-1188.

Thompson, L.W., Gong, V., Haskins, E., & Gallagher, D. (1987). Assessment of depression and dementia during the late years. In K.W. Schaie (Ed.), *Annual review of gerontology and geriatrics* (Vol. 7, pp. 295-324). New York: Springer.

Tomlinson, B.E. (1972). Morphological brain changes in nondemented old people. In H.M. Van Praag & A.F. Kalverboer (Eds.), *Aging of the central nervous system: Biological and psychological aspects.* Haarlem, The Netherlands: Bonn.

Vitaliano, P.P., Breen, A.R., Albert, M.S., Russo, J., & Prinz, P.N. (1984). Memory, attention, and functional status in community-residing Alzheimer type dementia patients and optimally healthy aged individuals. *Journal of Gerontology, 39,* 58-64.

Weingartner, H. (1984). Psychobiological determinants of memory failures. In L. Squire & N. Butters (Eds.), *Neuropsychology of memory* (pp. 203-212). Hillsdale, NJ: LEA Press.

Weingartner, H., Cohen, R.M., Murphy, D.L., Martello, J., & Geralt, C. (1981). Cognitive processes in depression. *Archives of General Psychiatry, 38,* 42-47.

Weingartner, H., Kaye, W., Smallberg, S., Cohen, R.M., Ebert, M.H., Gillin, J.C., & Gold, P. (1982). Determinants of memory failures in dementia. In S. Corkin, K. Davis, J. Growdon, E. Usdin, & R. Wurtman (Eds.), *Alzheimer's disease: A report of progress* (pp. 171-176). New York: Raven.

Wells, C.E. (1979). Pseudodementia. *American Journal of Psychiatry, 136,* 895-900.

Whitehead, A. (1973). Verbal learning and memory in elderly depressives. *British Journal of Psychiatry, 123,* 203-208.

Zarit, S.H., Cole, K.D., & Guider, R.L. (1981). Memory training strategies and subjective complaints of memory in the aged. *The Gerontologist, 21,* 158-164.

Zung, W.W.K. (1965). A self-rating depression scale. *Archives of General Psychiatry, 12,* 63-70.

6

Assessing Depression in Older Adults

MARLA HASSINGER, PH.D., GLENN SMITH, PH.D.,
ASENATH LA RUE, PH.D..

"Feelings of sadness and disappointment are part of the human condition that all people experience at some point in their lives, whether or not they are clinically depressed. The boundary between normal and abnormal symptoms remains undefined. Intense, pervasive, and persistent symptoms that interfere with normal functioning are usually considered pathological, but an incompletely defined gradient exists between normal mood and the clinical state. Thus, persons with depressive symptoms may have an affective disorder, another psychiatric disorder, a medical disorder, or no diagnosable disorder" (Boyd & Weissman, 1981, p. 1040).

Although written a number of years ago, these lines still provide an excellent synopsis of the problems that clinicians face in evaluating a person for possible depression. The shades of gray that differentiate normal and abnormal mood in a young adult still exist, and they may even be amplified in an older person. People who are currently old must face medical problems and bereavement more often than young adults, and many have few economic or social resources to assuage the ill effects of these experiences. In evaluating aged people, therefore, it is easy to come to expect some degree of depression and, perhaps, to underestimate the worth of formal evaluation.

This chapter is written with the assumption that meaningful distinctions can be made within the broad set of depressive feelings and behaviors observed in older people, and that arriving at these distinctions can sometimes point the way toward helpful interventions. Criteria for diagnosing depression are considered first, followed by a discussion of specific features that may be amplified or diminished in old age. Prevalence of the disorder is described, as are specific assessment procedures and instruments. Special issues in assessing old age depression are considered, and three case examples are offered where evaluation of depression played an important role in diagnosis and treatment decisions.

DIAGNOSTIC CRITERIA FOR DEPRESSIVE DISORDERS

Many geropsychologists minimize the use of a medical model in assessing emotional and behavioral problems, particularly when dealing with older people in community settings (cf. Knight, 1986; Zarit, 1980). However, it is important to be familiar with neuropsychiatric diagnostic criteria because much of the research literature and all insurance transactions make use of medical nomenclature.

The most recent set of standards for diagnosing depressive disorder are those provided by the revised third edition of the *Diagnostic and Statistical Manual of Mental Disorders* (DSM-III-R; American Psychiatric Association, 1987); summarized below are criteria for Major Depressive Syndrome, that is, a group of mood and associated symptoms that occur together for at least a 2-week period and that represent a change from the person's normal state of well-being. Either symptom 1 or 2 listed below must be present, and a total of five or more of the following nine symptoms must be present during the same 2-week period: 1) depressed mood almost daily as indicated by self-report or observation; 2) greatly reduced interest or pleasure in almost all activities, most of the day, nearly every day; 3) decrease or increase in appetite nearly daily or weight change of 5% of body weight in a month (when not dieting); 4) insomnia or hypersomnia almost daily; 5) psychomotor agitation or retardation that is observable to others; 6) almost daily fatigue or loss of energy; 7) feelings of worthlessness or excessive or inappropriate guilt almost daily (may be delusional); 8) diminished ability to think, concentrate, or make decisions almost daily; or 9) recurrent thoughts of death (not just fear of dying), suicidal ideation with or without a plan, or a suicide attempt (see DSM-III-R, pp. 222-223). An individual is diagnosed as having a Major Depressive Disorder if he or she talks and behaves in a manner consistent with this syndrome *and* if organic causes, uncomplicated bereavement, and nonmood psychotic disorders (e.g., schizophrenia) have been considered and ruled out.

If the episode of major depression occurs in a person who also has a clear history of one or more manic episodes, the appropriate DSM-III-R diagnosis is Bipolar Disorder, Depressed (296.5x). If there is no history of either manic or hypomanic episodes, the appropriate diagnosis would be Major Depression, Single Episode (296.2x) or Recurrent (296.3x). Fifth-digit code numbers are used to specify severity (e.g., 296.23 represents single Major Depressive Episode, severe, without psychotic features). "Seasonal Pattern" is a new classification to be included along with diagnoses of bipolar disorder or major depression when a regular temporal relationship is observed over at least a 3-year period between the onset of symptoms and a particular 60-day period of the year. For individuals who have had numerous periods of depressed mood or loss of interest or pleasure for at least 2 years, alternating with numerous hypomanic episodes, the most appropriate classification is Cyclothymia (301.13); in this disorder, depressive symptoms are not as extensive or severe as those in a Major Depressive Episode. This is also the case in the DSM-III-R diagnosis of Dysthymia (300.40); this condition is characterized by a chronic mild depressive syndrome of at least 2 years' duration. Depressive symptoms are also coded as an associated feature for many other DSM-III-R diagnoses, as in Dementia with depression (290.21) and Adjustment Disorder with depressed mood (309.00), and are included in the diagnostic criteria for Uncomplicated Bereavement (V62.82) and Schizoaffective Disorder (295.70). Table 1 lists and organizes all of the principal DSM-III-R diagnoses that should be considered in a diagnostic evaluation of a person with depressive complaints or behaviors.

Age Differences in Depressive Symptoms

DSM-III-R does not provide separate diagnostic criteria for older adults. Under the heading of age-specific features of mood disorders, the manual notes only, "In

TABLE 1

DSM-III-R DIAGNOSES TO CONSIDER IN ASSESSMENT OF DEPRESSIVE COMPLAINTS
OR BEHAVIORS

Mood Disorders
  Major Depressive Episode, Single (296.2x)
  Major Depressive Episode, Recurrent (296.3x)
  Bipolar Disorder, Depressed (296.5x)
  Bipolar Disorder, Mixed (296.6x)
  Dysthymia (300.40)
  Cyclothymia (301.13)

Psychotic Disorders
  Schizoaffective Disorder (295.70)

Adjustment Disorder
  Adjustment Disorder with Depressed Mood (309.00)

Organic Mental Syndromes and Disorders
  Primary Degenerative Dementia of the Alzheimer Type, Senile Onset, with
    Depression (290.21)
  Multi-infarct Dementia with Depression (290.43)
  Other or Psychoactive Substance Mood Disorder (292.84)
  Organic Mood Disorder, specify Depressed or Mixed (293.83)

Codes for Conditions not Attributable to a Mental Disorder That Are a Focus of Attention or Treatment
  Uncomplicated Bereavement (V62.82)

---

elderly adults some of the symptoms of depression, e.g., disorientation, memory loss, and distractibility, may suggest Dementia" (p. 220). Brief as it is, this comment does serve to forewarn a clinician that older people who are severely depressed may exhibit serious cognitive deficits, referred to as "pseudodementia" (p. 220). Many young depressed patients also have problems with concentration and possibly with memory and logical thinking; therefore, the presence of cognitive difficulties in depression is not strictly age specific. However, the combination of age-related and depression-related impairments can result in such strikingly lowered performances that the possibility of dementia must be entertained. Some guidelines for differentiation are described later in the chapter, but even at this point it is important to note that about one in every five older depressed patients will have significant cognitive problems (cf. La Rue, Spar, & Hill, 1986, for references) and that these problems often improve substantially with treatment or over time (cf. La Rue et al., 1986, for references).

There is also a substantial literature suggesting that somatic complaints are likely to be more prominent in older depressed patients than in younger ones. In part, this seems to result from the higher rates of actual illness in the aged; that is, complaints of pain, disability, and fatigue or lack of energy may be realistic reflections of physical state and not depressive symptoms. Disentangling the sources of somatic complaints in older patients is one of the most difficult aspects of assessment. In attempting to do so, it is important to keep in mind that somatic complaints may serve as depressive equivalents, taking the place of mood disturbance, and that complaints may be amplified out of proportion to the underlying physical state. In both of these circumstances, a diagnosis of depression may be appropriate even if actual medical illness complicates the picture.

Some geriatric practitioners (cf. La Rue, Dessonville, & Jarvik, 1985, for references) believe that "masked depressions," where dysphoric affect is minimal and somatic complaints predominate, are more common in aged patients than in younger individuals. The increase in medical illness that occurs with advancing age provides most older people with a convenient and socially acceptable language for conveying discomfort and distress. Moreover, many older people have negative attitudes about mental illness, considering emotional problems to be a negative reflection on one's character or strength. Still, as discussed below, there is little systematic information about "masked depression" in any age group.

Currently, there is no consensus about whether depression in the elderly is the same entity as in younger people. La Rue et al. (1985), in their review of aging and mental disorders, indicate that depressive illness seems both to affect elderly individuals and younger adults in similar ways and to respond to similar treatments in both age groups. However, it is suggested that depression may often develop in the elderly in reaction to age-associated stresses, such as losses, and that the aging process itself may influence both the older person's susceptibility to depression and pattern of depressive symptomatology.

PREVALENCE OF DEPRESSION IN OLDER ADULTS

There is widespread agreement that depressive illness is a major public health problem, as well as a growing acknowledgement that depression can develop or recur late in life. Epidemiologic studies have defined and assessed depression in many different ways, making it difficult to compare results and to arrive at a consensus about prevalence. However, in a review of English language studies on the epidemiology of affective disorders, Boyd and Weissman (1981) observed fair agreement on several points. In industrialized nations, for every 100 individuals living in the community, 1.8 to 3.2 men and 2.0 to 9.3 women were found to meet psychiatric diagnostic criteria for nonbipolar depression at any given point in time. By contrast, 6-16% of men and 11-24% of women obtained elevated scores on depression rating scales. Both measurement approaches show that a substantial minority of the population is afflicted with depression and that the disorder is more common in women than men; however, for every person who meets criteria for depressive illness, there are likely to be several others with milder depressive symptoms.

Gurland (1976) has reviewed the literature on age-specific prevalence rates for depression and has discussed methodological factors that may influence age distributions. *As diagnosed by psychiatrists,* depression occurs most often between the ages of 25 and 65 years; however, the highest rates of depressive symptoms have been found in groups above the age of 65 years. Gurland argued that there may be significant age biases in psychiatrists' criteria for diagnosing depression: in one large-scale investigation, even when the clinical condition of patients was held constant across age groups, public hospital psychiatrists in both the United States and the United Kingdom tended to diagnose affective disorders most often in the middle age range and organic disorders most often in the older age group (Fleiss, Gurland, Simon, & Sharpe, 1973). Symptom surveys of nonpatient samples also suffer from measurement difficulties; for example, it may be especially difficult to distinguish between physical and psychiatric symptoms in aged individuals, or to distinguish depression from realistic responses to adverse social situations.

One of the most comprehensive recent studies of depression in late life was conducted by Blazer and Williams (1980). Subjects were drawn from a stratified random sample of people aged 65 and older who were living in Durham, North Carolina; about 85% of the people contacted agreed to participate, yielding a total sample of 997 individuals. Depression was assessed with a self-rated instrument, the Depression scale of the Duke Older Americans Resources and Services (OARS) Multidimensional Functional Assessment Questionnaire. Seven of the 18 items assessed dysphoric mood and the other 11 tapped additional symptom criteria of major depression as defined by DSM-III (APA, 1980). Almost 15% (14.7%) of the sample were found to have "substantial depressive symptomatology"; that is, they answered more than half of the items about dysphoric mood affirmatively. About one quarter of these subjects (3.7% of the total sample) met DSM-III criteria for major depression, about 30% were simply dysphoric (i.e., they had depressed mood but did not have associated features required for DSM-III diagnosis), and for the remainder, depressive symptoms were judged to be related to medical illnesses. Only about 1% of the total sample were in therapy at the time of the study and the percentage with a history of psychiatric treatment was also very low.

Blazer and Williams (1980) concluded that "much of what is called 'depression' in the elderly may actually represent decreased life satisfaction and periodic episodes of grief secondary to the physical, social, and economic difficulties encountered by aging individuals in the community" (p. 442). Gurland (1976) made a similar point, noting that older people may be especially prone to transient depressions that are "distressing" but not "incapacitating" (p. 290). Nonetheless, both urged appreciation for the fact that severe depressions have a high prevalence in the aged (e.g., compare the 3.7% rate of major depression that Blazer and Williams reported to the overall point prevalence rates summarized above), and for the fact that few older people are receiving any treatment for depressive symptoms.

Depression in older people has rarely been studied longitudinally. This is an important omission in view of the fact that depression is believed to remit with time and also to recur. In addition, longitudinal studies are needed to define the circumstances and conditions that predispose an older person to episodes of depression. A recent study by Phifer and Murrell (1986) has begun to address the latter question. Their sample of 1,233 subjects was taken from a larger study using stratified area probability sampling of adults in Kentucky over the age of 55. Depressive symptoms were assessed initially and at a 6-month follow-up using the 20-item Center for Epidemiologic Studies–Depression Scale (CES-D). Using hierarchical discriminant analyses, the investigators examined factors that differentiated 1,167 subjects who remained healthy over the follow-up interval from the 66 individuals who developed significant depressive symptoms. The subjects who became depressed were found to have had higher initial depression scores; this is despite the fact that people with very high initial scores above the mean had been excluded from follow-up analyses. People who became depressed also had poorer initial health and more new health problems in the interim than those who stayed well emotionally. Limited social supports also proved predictive of depression; the absence of social supports interacted with health and loss events, potentiating the already negative effects of illness or bereavement. Status factors such as intelligence and social and economic status did not relate to the development of depression over this short time interval, and the overall rate of stressful events (except for loss and health events) was not predictive of depression.

Clinicians who treat older people are all too aware of the corrosive effects of health problems, loss of loved ones, and dwindling support systems (cf. Epstein, 1976; Jarvik, 1976; Silverman, 1968). Nonetheless, Phifer and Murrell (1986) document these effects in a carefully controlled investigation and underscore the potential for preventive interventions. Their findings suggest that it is important to take even mild depressive complaints in older persons seriously over time as many of the low-level problems progress. It is also important to appreciate that medically ill older people, and those who have lost significant others, are at risk for depressive illness—although sadness and discouragement are normal reactions under these circumstances, such symptoms always warrant careful clinical evaluation. Finally, this study and many others suggest that professionals working with older people need to be willing to serve as an involved and persistent supporter, helping to buffer the effects of illness and loss for those whose friends and family are no longer available.

PROCEDURES FOR ASSESSING DEPRESSION

Structured Interviews

Structured interviews offer one approach to assessing depression in the elderly. Such interviews offer the advantage of standard administration so that important areas for exploration are not overlooked. A number of structured clinical interviews, developed in a variety of contexts, are available. Among the most widely used are the Schedule for Affective Disorders and Schizophrenia (SADS; Spitzer & Endicott, 1977), the Structured Clinical Interview for DSM-III (SCID; Spitzer & Williams, 1985), and the Comprehensive Assessment and Referral Evaluation (CARE) series (Gurland et al., 1977; Gurland, Golden, Teresi, & Challop, 1984; Golden, Teresi, & Gurland, 1984).

The Schedule for Affective Disorders and Schizophrenia was developed in concert with Spitzer, Endicott, and Robbins's (1978) Research Diagnostic Criteria (RDC). The latter were developed "to enable research investigators to apply a consistent set of criteria for the description or selection of subjects with functional psychiatric illness" (Spitzer & Endicott, 1977, p. 1). When used in its entirety, the SADS involves over 78 pages of questions or ratings. It is also possible to use only parts of the Schedule, such as those pertaining to Major Depressive Disorder or Minor Depressive Disorder. However, this would seem to run counter to the purpose and strength of the SADS-RDC, which is differential diagnosis. It would seem the most appropriate use for this interview is as intended by its authors; that is, for research where differential diagnosis can be pursued without typical clinical constraints.

The Structured Clinical Interview for DSM-III (Spitzer & Williams, 1985) was developed as an assessment device to parallel precisely the DSM-III (APA, 1980). The SCID is to DSM-III what SADS is to RDC. To date, there is little published information about use of the SCID with older adults.

The Comprehensive Assessment and Referral Evaluation (Gurland et al., 1977) was developed for use in the United States/United Kingdom Cross-national Geriatric Community Study. This structured interview was developed specifically for use with the elderly residing in the community. Development of CARE drew from the Present State Evaluation (Wing, Birley, Cooper, Graham, & Isaacs, 1967) and Mental Status Schedule (Spitzer, Fleiss, Burdock, & Hardesty, 1964), two interviews designed to assess psychiatric variables in the general public. CARE, however, was broadened to assess functioning in a variety of areas not traditionally considered in psychiatric diagnosis (e.g., physical and social/environmental problems). Moreover, the interview addresses etiological considerations, personal and social impact of problems, presence and utilization of support systems, changes in the problem over time, and risk factors for institutionalization or mortality. Consequently, the original CARE involved 1,500 items and required a lengthy interview. The authors suggest that even experienced interviewers should train for approximately 1 month before administering CARE clinically.

Gurland et al. (1984) reduced the semi-structured interview into SHORT-CARE, designed to focus on two main issues in geriatric psychiatry, depression and dementia. SHORT-CARE contains 143 items within the following six scales: Disability, Dementia, Depression, Sleep Disorder, Somatic Problems, and Subjective Memory (Gurland & Wilder, 1984). In addition, the SHORT-CARE contains additional items included for the purpose of diagnosis of pervasive depression, pervasive dementia, and/or disability. However, the authors note that diagnoses obtained from SHORT-CARE do not correspond to specific disorders or conditions but are useful in identifying areas needing further investigation or intervention.

Projective Tests

Projective tests utilize patients' responses to ambiguous stimuli in order to make inferences about psychological status.

The Thematic Apperception Test (TAT) is a well-known projective measure of personality and adjustment in which the subject is shown pictures susceptible to many different interpretations and asked to make up stories about them. The test is felt to reveal covert features of personality, such as unsatisfied desires, suppressed anxieties, and preferred pattern for perceiving the world and the social environment. Lawton, Whelihan, and Belsky (1980) provide an excellent review of TAT use in the elderly. The Gerontological Apperception Test (GAT), developed in 1971 by Wolk and Wolk, is based upon the same principles as the TAT and lends itself specifically to the issues of the aged, such as isolation, physical changes, sexuality, and reversal of dependency and parental roles, as well as the more pragmatic concerns of health, financing, and housing. All 14 stimulus cards depict at least one elderly subject in diverse situations. We have found the apperception tests to be useful clinical assessment aids with which our patients generally identify and become actively involved. The interested reader is referred to Bellak (1986) for a detailed review of the clinical use of the TAT and GAT.

The Rorschach Inkblot Test, another traditional and widely used projective test, incorporates ambiguous inkblot patterns and asks the subjects what they might be. Although literature on the use of the Rorschach with older subjects is limited, a review by Lawton et al. (1980) concluded that Rorschach responses of older people are constricted, stereotyped, and lacking in clarity, relative to younger subjects. They warned, however, that most studies have not used community-residing subjects, but rather institutionalized subjects. Ames, Metraux, Rodell, and Walker (1973) indicate that healthy community-residing elderly often give rich and varied answers, responding as would "a vigorous healthy younger person" (p. 203). Depression is indicated on the Rorschach by the presence of several types of responses, such as use of achromatic color, a low number of responses, shading responses, and morbid content. One of our concerns regarding use of this test with the elderly is that several classes of responses may be affected by visual changes in the aging eye, as the ability to make relatively fine visual discriminations is prerequisite to the Rorschach. All in all, use of the Rorschach can be valuable with the elderly, but the tool must be interpreted with caution because of the lack of both meaningful norms and external correlates to validate inferences with elderly subjects.

The Incomplete Sentences Blank developed by Rotter and Rafferty (1953) has also been used with the elderly and is relatively undemanding of the older patient. As its title suggests, this test requires the subject to provide the endings to phrases beginning each of several sentences. Most clinicians interpret responses informally, looking for patterns of response, areas of conflict, and attitudes toward specific persons.

Machover's (1949) Draw-A-Person Test has been recommended by Butler and Lewis (1982) for diagnostic use with elderly patients. They suggest that, barring severe tremor and visual problems, self-drawings provide valuable clues to the feelings of older people. Elements of interpretation include such factors as size and placement of the drawing, amount and kind of detail, underemphasis or overemphasis of body parts, omissions, posture and facial expression, activity or inactivity, and the general emotional quality of the picture. We advise that one pay special attention to any physical and visual limitations of the patient, as these will strongly influence performance (e.g., a Parkinsonian patient may evidence micrographia).

Kahana (1978) provides an excellent review of projective personality assessment with older subjects. He suggests that the greatest problem with projective measures is the poverty of convincing data to validate various test data as reflections of specific personality dimensions or dynamics. However, he suggests that such tests may be especially well suited to elderly patients, as these measures do not depend on a high vocabulary level, do not require complex discrimination, and can be readily adapted by clinicians (e.g., change length of protocol) to meet the demands/limitations of a particular patient. We generally agree with Kahana's viewpoint, with the exception of our concerns raised earlier about the Rorschach Inkblot Test.

Objective Scales

The Minnesota Multiphasic Personality Inventory, a 550-item true/false self-report symptom inventory, has become the most widely used "objective" test of personality. The MMPI consists of 10 clinical scales and 4 validity scales, the latter of which correct for response styles that either inflate or deflate clinical scale scores. In assessment of depression, the *relationship* between scores on the Depression scale and other scales is used to clarify the nature and severity of overt and covert (e.g., somatic equivalents) depressive symptoms.

One major criticism of use of the MMPI with the elderly has been the dearth of elderly subjects in the original normative sample. A more general concern about use of the MMPI has been the recognized need to renorm the instrument to correct for changes in societal mores, educational attainment, and so on over the past four decades.

Colligan, Osborne, Swenson, and Offord (1984), in response to these concerns, have developed contemporary norms comprised of seven age ranges, including 60-69 and 70 and above. In the general population today, scores on some scales are more elevated than in the original sample. Additionally, significant relationships between age and scale scores for both sexes are noted, with correlation coefficients ranging from .11 to .44. These relationships are summarized as follows:

> scores on L, for both men and women, increased with age, a finding that suggests greater feelings of conservatism among older age groups. Expressions of somatic concern and dysphoric emotional tone also increased with age for both sexes. Scores on scale 4 [Psychopathic Deviate] decreased with age for both sexes, a reflection of fewer feelings of impulsivity and rebelliousness. For women, scores on scale 5 [Masculinity-Femininity] increased with age; this result suggests a wider range of interests among younger women than was observed in the original standardization sample. Scores on scale 5 for men decreased with age, probably a reflection of somewhat lower educational levels in older age groups. Scores on scale 9 [Hypomania] decreased with age for both sexes, an indication of gradually decreasing energy levels after adolescence and young adulthood. (pp. 383-384)

Although these findings are not yet incorporated into most MMPI scoring systems, we recommend that one take this information into consideration and exercise conservatism when interpreting an older person's MMPI profile.

Much of the interest in use of the MMPI with the elderly has focused on orally administered short forms (Fillenbaum & Pfeiffer, 1976); MMPI short forms are summarized in Faschingbauer (1978). A recent comparison of four of the short versions (Hileman, 1981) suggests that the Mini-Mult (Kincannon, 1968) and Maxi-Mult (McLachlan, 1974) best match the profiles of the long form when used with elderly patients. We have found oral administration of MMPI short forms useful with many of our patients, in particular those with low stamina, visual deficits, deficits of expressive speech, attentional deficits, or physical handicaps. The short forms can be administered in about 1 hour, although they need not be completed in one sitting. They offer the clinician valuable behavioral data as well. Sbordone and Caldwell (1979), for example, recommend that the clinician evaluate the patient's responses to determine whether he or she correctly understood the question, and they encourage the clinician to repeat or rephrase questions when in doubt as to whether a question was understood. We have found an additional advantage to oral administration in terms of offering the patient personal contact and building rapport.

Millon (1983) has developed and psychometrically validated a self-report inven tory anchored to the DSM-III personality disorders. The Millon Clinical Multiaxial Inventory (MCMI) is composed of a taxonomic schema that includes eight categories of clinical attributes: behavioral presentation, interpersonal conduct, cognitive style, expressive mood, unconscious mechanism, self-image, internalized content, and intrapsychic organization. The MCMI specifies a defining feature on every attribute for each of the 13 DSM-III personality disorders and yields cumulative scores across multiple clinical attributes; thus, it may yield mixed diagnostic assignments. Millon (1986) suggests that the MCMI is informative in identifying which clinical attributes should constitute the initial focus of patient care (i.e., it may pinpoint a feature of mood expression that may be especially responsive to pharmacological treatment or identify a character and level of intrapsychic organization conducive to psychodynamic therapy). To our knowledge, the MCMI has not been used extensively with the elderly, but it seems to be a promising instrument deserving of research utilizing geriatric subjects.

Depression Rating Scales

For purposes of examining the extent or severity of depression, a number of depression rating scales have been developed. These may be categorized as observer rating scales and self-rating scales. Observer rating scales offer the advantage of avoiding social desirability effects or, conversely, the pervasive negative cognitive set often observed in depression. Considering observable behavior avoids response set bias, but may fail to capture the phenomenological state of the subject accurately. Self-ratings offer just the reverse with respect to strengths and weaknesses.

Possibly the best known observer rating scale is the Hamilton Rating Scale for Depression (HAM-D; Hamilton, 1960). The HAM-D is completed by a clinician following approximately 30 minutes of interviewing the patient. It was originally designed as an outcome measure for drug studies in the general population. As such, it is weighted for the type of variables medications are able to alter; thus, sleep, appetite, weight change, psychomotor speed, and other biological concerns are well represented on this rating. The 23 items of the HAM-D also include depressive mood, anxiety, guilt, loss of libido, general somatic symptoms, gastrointestinal symptoms, hypochondriasis, paranoia, obsessional symptoms, and suicidal ideation.

Adequate reliability and validity of the scale appear dependent on adequate training of the raters (Guy, 1976). In a personal communication (1980), Gallagher has suggested that in elderly populations validity may also depend on distinguishing bases of somatic complaints. Because complaints may arise from age-related illness as well as depression per se, she suggests that the interviewer should expand beyond the confines of the survey to query about physical bases for sleep disturbance, somatic complaints, lack of appetite, etc. She suggests that a guideline for determining the bases for the complaints is to get the patients' perception of their onset and cause. Gallagher also suggests dispensing with libido questions with widowed or unattached patients. Even with these adaptations, Kochansky (1979) has suggested that this and most depression rating scales suffer from failure to differentiate depression from dementia symptoms. He also noted the lack of a normative study with the HAM-D in an elderly population. However, the work of Yesavage, Brink, Rose, and Adey (1983) has provided some descriptive statistics for elderly populations assessed with this instrument. These authors suggest a main consideration with respect to utilizing this instrument versus self-report formats is the greater investment in clinician time necessary to complete the HAM-D.

The Zung Self-rating Depression Scale (SDS; Zung, 1965) is a 20-item survey that may be largely self-administered. It was designed with the intention that it should "be all inclusive with respect to symptoms of the illness [depression], it should be short and simple, it should quantitate rather than qualitate, and it should be self-administered" (p. 63). McGarvey, Gallagher, Thompson, and Zelinski (1982) performed confirmatory factor analysis with the SDS and found it to tap three factors: well-being/optimism, somatic symptoms, and depression/anxiety. Four items that appear consistent with vegetative symptoms of depression did not load on any of these factors.

Although not developed specifically for the elderly, Zung first utilized the scale with older subjects only 2 years after its initial publication (Zung, 1967). He suggests (1983) the scale has been employed rather extensively with the elderly. Among studies employing the SDS with aged populations are Zung et al. (1974), Heidell and Kidd (1975), Morris, Wolf, and Klerman (1975), Salzman, Shader, Harmatz, and Robertson (1975), Yesavage et al. (1983), and Maiden (1987). While the SDS might not be criticized for lacking a "track record" with aged populations, some researchers have expressed concern regarding validity of this instrument with older adults. Gallagher, Thompson, and Levy (1980) note that in elderly populations, the somatic items may have a greater contribution to total score than affective items. The somatic items may have different meaning for old versus young as reflected in their poor correlation with the other items of scale in the former group. Also, Gallagher, McGarvey, Zelinski, and Thompson (1978) found the SDS to have unacceptably poor reliability in an "old-old" population.

The Beck Depression Inventory (Beck, Ward, Mendelson, Mock, & Erbaugh, 1961) is a 21-item, multiple-choice self-report survey that taps mood, sense of pessimism and guilt, social withdrawal, sleep disturbance, loss of energy, and weight and appetite, among other features. It was developed with the goal of quantifying depression, especially for research purposes; however, it has been used quite extensively in clinical settings. Gallagher, Nies, and Thompson (1982) examined the reliability of the survey in an elderly sample of both normal and depressed subjects and obtained values of .90, .84, and .91, respectively, for test-retest, split-half, and alpha reliabilities. These researchers also observed the BDI to display satisfactory validity relative to SADS-rated RDC (Gallagher, Breckenridge, Steinmeitz, & Thompson, 1983).

A 13-item short form of the BDI (BDI-SF) was developed especially for clinical use (Beck & Beck, 1972). Scogin, Beutler, Corbishley, and Hamblin (1987) investigated the reliability and validity of the short form in a sample of depressed and nonpatient older adults. Spearman-Brown split-half and alpha coefficient reliabilities were .84 and .90, respectively. Using a cutoff score of 5, these authors found the BDI-SF to have correctly identified 97% of the depressed sample and 77% of the nonpatient group. Poelker, Shewchuk, and Niederehe (1987) completed confirmatory factor analysis of the BDI-SF administered to an elderly population and developed three factors, which they labeled self-esteem, anergy, and dysphoria. The similarity in factor structure of the BDI and the Zung SDS is notable.

In response to problems noted above in applying general depression scales to elderly populations, Yesavage et al. (1983) developed the self-rating Geriatric Depression Scale. To maintain simplicity, the authors used a yes/no format. From an initial item pool of 100, these authors selected 30 items (based on their appropriateness and performance with the aged population) that best predicted total score for depression (based on the 100 items). The GDS is virtually devoid of somatic items ("Do you often get restless and fidgety?" and "Do you feel full of energy?" are the closest approximations). Items assess cognitive complaints and social behavior, and mood is most extensively surveyed.

Yesavage et al. (1983) compared the GDS with the SDS and the HAM-D for reliability and validity in a stratified sample of elderly subjects. The sample included nondepressed, mildly depressed, and severely depressed subjects (based on number of RDC symptoms observed). However, the subject pool was not stratified by age. Within the pilot sample, the authors found the GDS to have a test-retest reliability of .85, an internal consistency alpha of .94, and a split-half reliability of .94.

Scores on each of the three scales were correlated with subjects' scores on the criterion variable (RDC). Correlations were .83, .82, and .69 for HAM-D, GDS, and SDS, respectively. However, when cutoff scores were set to hold constant the rate of correct identification of normals, hit rates for depressed cases were .90, .86, and .82, respectively, for GDS, HAM-D, and SDS. As the GDS can be self-administered and still provide validity commensurate with the HAM-D, it is a promising depression scale.

Norris, Gallagher, Wilson, and Winograd (1987) recently validated the BDI and GDS against RDC and DSM-III diagnoses of depressive disorders in a geriatric medical outpatient population. The accuracy of diagnosis using the BDI was .84 for both a conservative and a more lenient BDI cutoff score. Accuracy of diagnosis using the SDS was .77 and .84 for lenient and more conservative cutoff scores, respectively. The data thus suggest that both self-report measures have utility as screening instruments with this population.

All in all, it seems that the GDS and BDI are perhaps the most appropriate self-report measures for use with geriatric groups, and the GDS is perhaps the easiest to respond to because of its multiple-choice format.

SPECIAL ISSUES

Somatic Complaints in Depression

Because a high proportion of aged people have medical illnesses that result in such problems as weight loss, insomnia, psychomotor slowing, or fatigue, there is a possibility that depression will be overdiagnosed in old age, particularly when classification is based on quantitative measures.

As noted, some geriatric specialists either have expressed concern that depression rating scales may be invalid for older people or have attempted to develop new instruments that minimize somatic items (e.g., Yesavage et al., 1983). However, in one careful investigation comparing older (aged 55 to 91 years) depressed outpatients to normal elderly persons on the SADS, highly significant group differences were obtained on each scale, and even very old, physically ill control subjects had demonstrably lower scores than clinically depressed individuals (Zemore & Eames, 1979). This finding, combined with others (e.g., Berry, Storandt, & Coyne, 1984; Dessonville, Gallagher, Thompson, Finnell, & Lewinsohn, 1982), suggests that the bias resulting from somatic items is relatively small and that the odds are low that emotionally healthy older people will be mistakenly identified as depressed. This risk is further reduced when rating scale findings are interpreted by a skilled clinician (cf. Gaitz & Scott, 1972); that is, in practice such scores are integrated with other medical, social, and clinical data in arriving at a diagnosis.

There is an opposing risk regarding somatic complaints in older patients—that major depression will go unrecognized if the patient focuses primarily on physical as opposed to affective symptoms. Many middle-aged patients seen in general medical settings have significant symptoms of depression that are not detected or treated by primary care physicians (e.g., Katon, Berg, Robins, & Risse, 1986). Current cohorts of older people are believed to be at even greater risk for misdiagnosis, as they may be especially predisposed to view affective illness in somatic terms (e.g., Epstein, 1976; Gerner, 1979; Goldfarb, 1975; Katon, Kleinman, & Rosen, 1982; Lehmann, 1982; Lesse, 1974). Research evidence for an age bias toward somatization is less extensive than clinical lore, but the prima facie argument is a plausible one: namely, 1) that historically somatization of depression has been the norm in Western culture, 2) that talking about subjective states such as self-depreciation, hopelessness, and helplessness with one's physician is a recent development, prevalent only in urbanized cultures, and 3) that the aged, socialized at an earlier time, are less likely than younger people to think about or talk about their problems in psychological terms.

A recent study with aged, medically ill veterans gives some indication of the magnitude of underrecognition of depression in geriatric patients (Rapp, Parisi, & Wallace, 1987). The SADS and several self-report scales of depression were administered to 150 elderly patients over age 65 who were randomly selected from consecutive admissions to medical/surgical units. After discharge, medical charts were reviewed for indications of depression as recognized by the treating physicians (e.g., diagnosis of depression, use of the word "depressed" or related words such as "despondent," or orders for psychiatric treatment or consultation). Based on data obtained from the SADS and application of Research Diagnostic Criteria, 15.3% were found to have depression. *None* of these patients were assigned a psychiatric diagnosis by house staff; only 2 of 23 were described in terms suggestive of depression, and there were 6 false positives observed, most of whom had some notation about depression in their chart from previous admissions. Thus, there were only 6 patients identified by house staff as showing signs of depression in old or current records who did meet SADS or RDC criteria for depression.

Rather than ignoring somatic complaints or assuming they are age consistent, we strongly encourage psychologists who examine older clients to solicit, interpret, and integrate data about physical function, keeping in mind that somatization may signal the presence of major depression. For patients who somaticize without discernible medical abnormality, the possibility of masked depression should be considered.

More often, however, one will encounter individuals who amplify physical symptoms and overutilize medical services instead of seeking psychological help. Treatment of depression cannot eliminate disability or pain in these cases, but it can enable older patients to cope more effectively and to avoid unnecessary medical interventions.

Cognitive Deficits Caused by Depression: "Pseudodementia"

Differential diagnosis of depression and progressive dementia syndrome has received much attention, as misdiagnosis can occur with disturbing frequency. Severe cognitive deficits have been well established in cases of depression, although most depressed elderly do not appear demented; likewise, depressed affect is not uncommon in organic dementia syndromes. Larson, Reifler, Sumi, Canfield, and Chinn (1985) found, in a study of 200 consecutive outpatients with suspected dementia, that 5% evidenced depression or what has been dubbed by Kiloh (1961) the "pseudodementia" of depression.

A brief summary of longitudinal studies (La Rue et al., 1985) indicates that many elderly patients may present with major cognitive deficits that later remit or improve with treatment for depression, and it further suggests that at least 30% of "dementia cases" may be due to pseudodementia and other treatable conditions. Unfortunately, many practitioners still equate cognitive impairment in and of itself as diagnostic of progressive dementia.

La Rue, Spar, and Hill (1986), studying depressed elderly inpatients, found that those with low scores on a mental status examination were less well educated and more likely to be delusional, anxious, and globally impaired than high-scoring patients. However, perhaps the most important result of this study was the finding that both groups attained similar levels of recovery. The authors note, however, that the low scores required more intensive treatment, including a lengthier hospital stay and use of neuroleptic medications; they conclude by advising the clinician to "anticipate the need for somewhat longer and more aggressive inpatient treatment for elderly patients with major depression accompanied by cognitive impairment" (p. 184).

Although no simple methods are available to guarantee that depression is not overlooked in a patient appearing demented, Wells (1983) has suggested a broad set of guidelines to assess in diagnosis of pseudodementia (see Table 2). It must be cautioned, however, that no one feature is diagnostic, or, for that matter, invariant. Thus, these guidelines tend to hold up better in distinguishing groups of depressed and demented individuals rather than individual cases. Wells (1983) concludes that the "best precaution is . . . to maintain a high index of suspicion for depression, and to pursue the possibility of depression vigorously whenever historical, observational, or ancillary diagnostic features are at variance with those usually present in Alzheimer's disease" (p. 198). He stresses that the observational skills of the clinician are unequaled in few other areas of medicine and that the well-trained clinician's *subjective* response to interaction with the patient is an important component of diagnosis.

Neuropsychological testing has also come to serve an important function as an ancillary tool in differential diagnosis, with attention to both cutting scores and qualitative features of performance. Research in the usage of neuropsychological tests, for example, has rendered useful distinctions between cognitive failures in depression and in progressive dementia (La Rue, D'Elia, Clark, Spar, & Jarvik, 1986). Detailed

TABLE 2

RECOMMENDATIONS FOR DIFFERENTIAL DIAGNOSIS OF PROGRESSIVE DEMENTIA
AND PSEUDODEMENTIA

	Pseudodementia	*Dementia*
Medical History		
Onset	Generally abrupt	Generally gradual
Progression	Rapid (patient may appear severely demented within 2-3 months	Generally slow
History of depression	Consider pseudo-dementia if patient has a history of depression	Not diagnostic
Clinical Observations		
Mental status exam	Tends to show impairment of only some spheres of cognition	Generally global impairment
Behavior	Incongruence between status examination and daily functioning (i.e., poor memory testing, but quickly learns names of staff)	Consistent with mental status examination
Ancillary Procedures		
EEG	Normal	Typically abnormal, especially when progression of symptoms is fast or cognitive impairment is severe
Dexamethasone suppression test	Abnormal	?
Amytal interview	Leads to vocal expression of depressed symptomatology	?

Note: Adapted from Wells, C.E. (1983). Differential diagnosis of Alzheimer's dementia: Affective disorder. In B. Reisberg (Ed.), *Alzheimer's disease: The standard reference* (pp. 193-198). New York: Free Press.

reporting of these distinctions is beyond the scope of this chapter, but the interested reader is referred to Weingartner and Silberman (1982), who provide an excellent review.

Depression in Brain Damage

In the United States, a signficant number of people are living and coping with various types of brain injury; the National Institute of Neurological and Communicative Diseases and Stroke (1983) estimates that over 2 million people presently experience disability from stroke alone. Brain-injured individuals frequently have mental health needs, and many are at risk for depression.

Ross and Rush (1981) discuss the difficulty of recognizing depression in brain-injured individuals. They suggest the need to monitor four processes to detect depression: verbal-cognitive set, affect, vegetative behaviors, and mood. Verbal-cognitive set refers to the patient's potential for and actual use of propositional speech, the content of which has emotional referents. The terms *affect, vegetative behavior,* and *mood* are utilized by these authors in traditional fashion.

Brain insult may selectively impair any one of the first three processes listed, thereby reducing the ability of the patient to express mood. These authors suggest that when some modalities for expression are impaired, the clinician should give greater weight to information presented in the preserved modalities. In the case of global speech impairment, the evaluator/clinician must be attentive to behavior and prosody (the variations in rhythm, accentuation, and pitch) of vocal output. If the patient looks and sounds sad, depression might be assumed, despite his or her unresponsiveness to questions about depression (which they are not likely to be understanding). In cases of aprosodic speech, attention must be turned to propositional speech and behavior. Though a patient's statements regarding depression may seem unbelievable when stated in a monotone with expressionless face, speech content should be taken to reflect mood. Global impairment of vocalization may leave only nonverbal behavior from which to draw inferences, making this the most difficult case in which to assess depression. In each case "depression" is taken to be essentially defined by the putative mood or subjective experience of the patient.

Prigatano (1986) has delineated hypotheses regarding substrates when depression is clearly present in brain injury. His delineation includes the long-held presumptions of reactive depression following insult (e.g., catastrophic reaction described by Goldstein, 1948). This explanation assumes that the patient retains the capabilities to assess the nature of his or her physical and social losses and reacts strongly to these. Loss of regulation of emotional expression may exacerbate emotional display in these cases. As a second etiology Prigatano implicates neurophysiological processes. A considerable amount of research has been devoted to explicating models in this area (Robinson & Steleza, 1981; Davidson, 1984; Flor-Henry, 1976). Although this research has yet to produce a definitive model, it seems to document clearly the importance of neurophysiology in producing depression in many cases. Prigatano also points to the need to consider premorbid factors. Here, loss of emotional regulation may "uncover" dysthymic personality traits, making long-standing mood tendencies more evident.

The importance of considering etiologic processes resides in their relevance to treatment choices and outcome. Psychotherapy may be indicated in reactive depressions to facilitate long-term adjustment to persisting functional loss, but it may be ineffective in cases where lesions have disrupted noradrenergic pathways in the brain. Premorbid factors may suggest psychotherapy to be effective only if the focus is expanded beyond adjustment to immediate functional loss. These dispositional issues reflect the need to move beyond attributing depression solely to neurophysiology. On a case by case basis, there is a need to consider the patient's history and the nature of social role losses. Clinicians need, when possible, to talk to patients about the subjective meaning of their losses. Family must be interviewed to determine if losses outside of neurological insult are present.

Having discussed ways to avoid diagnostic misses with respect to depression in brain damage, there is also a need to consider potential for false positives. Lezak (1983) discusses three types of emotional lability following neurological insult. The first type results from reduced emotional control and low tolerance for frustration. Both the expression and experience of emotion are congruent in these cases, and this lability could be viewed as an exaggeration of typical experience. The second lability is pronounced loss of emotional control, such that any environmental stimuli elicits emotional expression. The third lability is termed *pseudobulbar state*. In this instance, pronounced displays of emotion are unelicited as well as uncontrolled. In each of the latter cases, one cannot assume that subjective experience is congruent with emotional expression. Thus, to the extent that phenomenology is being utilized as the essential determinant of depression, the latter two labilities may not represent depression. Many times, problems of lability alarm signifiant others, who assume depression after observing emotional displays. In this case, there may be greater need to educate the family rather than to "fix" the patient. However, the patient may also benefit by greater insight into the etiology of his or her behavior.

Medical Illnesses That Can Cause Depressive Symptoms

Medical depressions take three forms: 1) adjustment disorder, 2) exacerbation of preexisting mood disorder, and 3) organic focuses upon organic affective syndromes.

Symptoms of depression are often manifest in association with a variety of chronic and acute medical conditions in the elderly patient. Table 3, based on articles by Lehmann (1982), Ouslander (1982), Gerner (1979), and Salzman and Shader (1979), lists medical illnesses felt to exert primary biological depressive effects. Because of the relatively high frequency of medical illnesses in the elderly population, it is crucial that mental health practitioners be aware of the medical care and status of their patients and encourage, when needed, evaluation to rule out treatable medical conditions contributing to depressive symptoms. This need is highlighted by studies finding that at least one third of psychiatric inpatients have undiagnosed medical illnesses that worsen their psychiatric symptoms (Hall, Popkin, DeVaul, Faillace, & Stickney, 1978; Jacobs, Bernhard, Delgado, & Strain, 1977). When depressive symptoms result from a medical condition, organic mood disorder (DSM-III-R code 293.83) should be diagnosed.

Iatrogenically induced depressive symptoms are sometimes a side effect of medications (see Table 4) commonly prescribed in the elderly and on a long-term maintenance basis. Of patients taking antihypertensives, for example, 50-70% experience

TABLE 3

MEDICAL ILLNESSES WITH PROMINENT DEPRESSIVE FEATURES

Alcohol dependence
Amyotrophic lateral sclerosis
Bacterial infection (e.g., acute bacterial endocarditis)
Benign intracranial hypertension
Brain injury
Chronic subdural hematoma
Congestive heart failure
Coronary bypass
Folate deficiency
Heart attack
Hypercalcemia
Hyperparathyroidism
Hyperprolactinemia
Hyperthyroidism
Hyponatremia
Hypothyroidism
Menopause
Multiple sclerosis
Neoplasm (i.e., cerebral metastasis, glioma)
Normal pressure hydrocephalus
Pancreatic disease
Parkinson's disease
Pernicious anemia
Systemic lupus erythematosus
Urinary tract disease
Viral illnesses (i.e., viral encephalitis, Epstein-Barr virus)
Vitamin B^{12} deficiency

depressive features of sadness, weakness, apathy, and agitation (Lewis, 1971). Elderly patients tend to be particularly sensitive to depression-inducing medications. In assessing patients taking such medications, it is especially important to evaluate the relationship between onset and intensity of depressive symptoms, the onset of medication usage, and dosage changes. Psychotropic drugs including stimulants, alcohol, anxiolytics, and neuroleptics can also produce depressive features (see Salzman & Shader, 1979, for review).

Bereavement

Uncomplicated Bereavement is defined in DSM-III-R as the normal reaction to the death of a loved one. Generally, uncomplicated bereavement will set in during the first 3 months of loss, but the duration and nature of griefwork varies among different cultural groups and is quite individualized. A full depressive syndrome is considered a normal reaction to the loss of a loved one, and feelings of guilt, anger, and thoughts of death are not unusual in the bereaved. Approximately 15% of individuals are still

TABLE 4

MEDICAL DRUGS THAT CAN CAUSE DEPRESSIVE SYMPTOMS

Antihypertensives
    Reserpine
    Methyldopa
    Propranolol
    Clonidine
    Hydralazine
    Guanethidine
    Diuretics

Non-narcotic Analgesics
    Indomethacin

Antiparkinsonian
    L Dopa
    Carbidopa
    Bromocriptine
    Trihexyphenidyl

Antimicrobials
    Gentamicin
    Ipruniazid
    Cycloserine

Steroids
    Glucocorticoids

Female Hormones
    Estrogen

Digitalis

Anticancer Drugs
    Vincristine vinblastine
    5-flarodacil
    1-asparaginase

Note: Adapted from Ouslander, J.G. (1982). Illness and psychopathology in the elderly. *Psychiatric Clinics of North America, 5,* 145-158; and from Salzman, C., & Shader, R.I. (1979). Clinical evaluation of depression in the elderly. In A. Raskin & L.F. Jarvik (Eds.), *Psychiatric symptoms and cognitive loss in the elderly* (pp. 39-72). New York: Halstead.

clinically depressed 1 year after their loss (Ziscook & Schucter, 1986); affective distress is usually greatest the first few months after the loss, diminishes significantly during the first year, and then more slowly thereafter, with some depressive symptoms lasting even 4 years after the loss.

How does one distinguish uncomplicated bereavement from poor adjustment and pathological mourning, given the natural variability in the process of uncomplicated bereavement? DSM-III-R indicates that several symptoms suggest pathological bereavement and indicate a need for aggressive treatment: preoccupation with worthlessness, prolonged and marked functional impairment, and marked psychomotor retardation. Belitsky and Jacobs (1986) suggest two main forms of pathological grief. One, delayed grief, occurs when the usual manifestations of grief are absent during the initial months or even for years following the loss. Sometimes somatic "depressive equivalents" develop. An acute grief reaction and major depression may then develop suddenly, often precipitated by an important calendar date (marriage anniversary, anniversary of deceased's death) or some other triggering event. The second type of pathological grief reaction is an unusually intense expression of grief from the onset of loss, often accompanied by a prolonged course; criteria for a Major Depressive Episode are fully met.

Variables that may predispose one to pathological grief are both intrapersonal and situational. Consideration of these variables, a list of which follows, can be potentially important in the differential diagnosis of normal and pathological grief reactions:

1) Obsessive personality disorder (Lindemann, 1974);

2) Prior history of depression (Clayton & Darvish, 1979);

3) Relationship with deceased involving dependency, ambivalence, or unexpressed hostility (Shanfield, 1983);

4) Lack of available social supports (Dimond, Lund, & Caserata, 1987);

5) Early traumatic loss in childhood (Bowlby, 1970) or no previous exposure to death (Bornstein, Clayton, & Halikas, 1973); and

6) Unnatural or sudden death, such as homicide, suicide, or accident (Rynearson, 1986).

Personality Disorders

The topic of personality disorders in late life has only recently gained significant attention (Gurland, 1984; Verwoerdt, 1980). At this point it is helpful to address the interaction between aging, personality disorder, and the development of depression.

Personality disorder is identified far less often in elderly psychiatric inpatients' first admissions than in those of younger adults. However, whether clinicians focus upon assessing for personality disorder with geriatric patients is questionable; it may indeed be underdiagnosed, especially when a patient has prominent Axis I (DSM-III-R) symptoms, or when hospital stays are relatively brief. Additionally, many people are "well adjusted" to their personality disorder (e.g., the prototypical excessively dependent wife who suffers no discomfort because her husband shelters her and makes decisions for her). Such individuals may not come to the attention of health professionals unless their life situation changes dramatically. How does aging influence life-long patterns of personality disorder, given the common developmental tasks of adapting to decreasing stamina, illness, bereavement, retirement, decreased social supports, loss of a future dimension, and the approach of death?

Verwoerdt (1980, 1981) offers several insights into outcomes for particular types of personality disorders. He identifies, for example, several personality disorders for which the core coping patterns require little energy (i.e., dependent, schizoid) and suggests that these individuals may do relatively well with aging. The functioning of a schizoid type may improve after retirement because the stress of work and competitive or demanding personal relationships has been alleviated. Personality types using "high energy" coping modes such as mastery and control and exclusion from awareness are generally felt to have a poorer prognosis with aging. These would include histrionic, compulsive, and paranoid personality types. An example might be the compulsive worker who develops a physical illness and cannot maintain normal tempo. Unable to keep up the pace, he or she may be confronted with unacceptable losses and be likely to become depressed. Verwoerdt suggests that in personality disorder involving poor impulse control (i.e., borderline, antisocial), aging may reduce the strength of drives that previously "got the person into trouble." He cautions that one may see anxiety, depression, or regressive behavior as a result.

It seems Verwoerdt also identifies "the running out of the time clock" as a major psychological force. Whereas some younger individuals with personality disorder might alleviate distress through anticipation that things will work out in the future, the elderly individual may feel bitter disappointment and frustration when he or she has not accomplished desired goals and recognizes that such opportunity is lost.

Diagnosis of personality disorder is often deferred in assessment; however, understanding an underlying personality disorder may be very important in treatment planning. The SCID and MCMI are specifically geared toward diagnosis of DSM-III and DSM-III-R personality disorders and might be especially useful in identification of personality disorder early in the assessment process; the MMPI also provides data regarding characterological adaptation. We strongly feel that the influence of characterological factors as they affect the detection and treatment of geriatric depression is an area deserving of systematic study.

CASE EXAMPLES

Three case examples conclude this chapter. Each is chosen to highlight one or more important issues in geriatric assessment of depression and to illustrate the significance of assessment in influencing a positive treatment outcome.

Example A

Case A underscores the value of formal neuropsychological and personality assessment in the accurate diagnosis of pseudodementia.

Background and presenting problem. This patient was a Caucasian female in her late 60s, referred for neuropsychological evaluation of dementia. She had been admitted to a geriatric psychiatry hospital ward with complaints of jamais vu, incontinence, and personality change. The patient was dehydrated and had evidenced significant weight loss. She had received a diagnosis of breast cancer 5 years earlier, which resulted in two surgeries and a series of radiation treatments. She had appeared stable on anticancer medications for 3 years prior to admission. However, several months prior to admission she began to refuse chemotherapy and quit visiting her internist.

Psychological evaluation. The patient was oriented to person and place, but not year, date, or day. She was given a series of neuropsychological tests and was initially cooperative with assessment, but this cooperativeness waned relatively quickly. She frequently gave "I can't say" responses and even refused to guess on multiple-choice items. The patient displayed flattened affect throughout the assessment. Prominent psychomotor retardation and frequent loss of task demands were observed. The patient denied hallucinations and rumination. Importantly, she also denied experiencing significant depression or anxiety.

The quantitative results of testing were generally low and might initially suggest the presence of a significantly progressed dementia syndrome. For example, she could only remember one unit of information during immediate recall of a short paragraph read to her (Wechsler Memory Scale, Logical Memory Test) and required 289 seconds to complete a number connection task (Trail Making Test) that normally takes an individual her age about one fifth the time to complete.

Qualitative analysis of errors reflected a significant "effort problem" on the part of the patient. This was especially evident in the increase of trial refusals with increasing task complexity. Other features in qualitative error analysis were the frequency of errors attributable to lapses in attention and concentration and errors resulting from psychomotor retardation. By including consideration of the qualitative data, the question of pseudodementia secondary to major depression evolved.

A potentially misleading feature with respect to hypothesizing pseudodementia in this case was the patient's denial of depressed mood. In this regard, MMPI testing was informative. The patient provided an invalid profile with a significantly elevated L scale. She also gave "can't say" responses to items with face valid relevance to her current situation. This approach to the MMPI suggested the patient to be employing significant denial or avoidant strategies in attempting to deal with her situation. The denial of depression was taken to be an instance of this defense style.

Conclusions and implications. The patient was treated with antidepressant medication and subsequently displayed steady and significant improvement in orientation, cognitive function, and self-care skills. During treatment, detection of further metastasis produced re-emergence of psychiatric and cognitive symptoms. More aggressive treatment with antidepressants and psychotherapy appeared to improve the relapse. The course of treatment in this case provided a naturally occurring single baseline reversal process, further suggesting that the cognitive impairments evidenced were secondary to mood disorder.

The valuable outcome of this case was the accurate diagnosis and aggressive treatment of depression of both cognitive and affective symptoms. Additionally, this case illustrates the need to take into consideration qualitative aspects of performance when comparing test scores to normative data.

Example B

Case B illustrates the utility of the MMPI in revising the treatment plan for an inpatient who was unresponsive to medications.

Background and presenting problems. This patient was a 68-year-old Caucasian woman who was admitted to a geropsychiatric inpatient unit because of feelings of depression, anxiety, insomnia, decreased appetite, and loss of energy, which had gradually worsened over the preceding 4 to 5 months. She reported that her anxiety exacerbated a familial tremor, and she had become increasingly socially isolated because of her embarrassment about the tremor.

The patient was a high-school graduate who had retired about 5 years earlier from her job as a cashier. She had been living with and caring for her aged mother for more than 20 years, but her mother died about 6 months prior to admission. The patient had been married twice for brief periods of time, with both marriages ending in divorce. Her only son had died in a motor vehicle accident 12 years earlier. Current medical problems included glossopharyngeal neuralgia, from which she experienced occasional pain, and a recent episode of gastritis.

The patient had no history of psychiatric problems or treatment until a month before this admission. At that time, she entered another psychiatric hospital for treatment of the depressive symptoms described above. She received brief trials of two antidepressant medications, but developed side effects to each and left this facility abruptly after a stay of only a few days. Her family physician then prescribed an antidepressant medication, which was also discontinued due to side effects. At this physician's advice, the patient sought help at our hospital, which offered specialized geropsychiatric evaluation.

Psychodiagnostic evaluation. The patient was referred for psychodiagnostic assessment about 2 weeks following admission. The referral was prompted by the fact that she had again been complaining of side effects to the new antidepressant medication, and no subjective or objective alleviation of the depression had been observed.

Clinical interview indicated that the patient was well oriented to her situation. Her thought processes were logical and goal directed, and her attention, language, memory, and visuoconstructional abilities were all intact on brief mental status testing. Because of her well-preserved cognitive status and her willingness to describe her background and complaints, the MMPI was considered an appropriate instrument for evaluating personality and current psychological state. The patient completed the standard booklet form promptly, answered all items, and did not request clarification of any of the questions.

Scores on the validity scales indicated that she completed the inventory in an accurate and straightforward manner and that the profile was likely to be valid for clinical use. Significant elevations were observed on Depression and Social Introversion, with modest elevations on the Hypochondriasis and Psychasthenia scales (Welsh code: 2"01'7 3 68-49/5:F/LK:). Individuals with this pattern are typically shy, introverted, and inhibited, and may have had problems throughout their lives in forming and maintaining close relationships. They tend to be worriers, and many have come to accept a mild amount of unhappiness as normal. Feelings of inadequacy are usually seen, and insomnia may be a problem. Others may see them as distant, aloof, or unassuming. Women with this profile tend to prefer companions who are gentle and sensitive and who can relate to the complexity of their feelings.

The DSM-III diagnoses most appropriate to this profile are Dysthymic Disorder or Adjustment Disorder with Depressed Mood. This profile is also associated with poor response to antidepressant medication. Recommended interventions include psychotherapeutic approaches such as cognitive-behavioral therapy, desensitization, and social-skills training.

Conclusions and implications. The patient requested feedback on MMPI findings and readily asserted the appropriateness of many aspects of the interpretation. She reported that she had always been troubled by shyness and had the insight to conclude that recent life events (retirement from a very structured job, then recently the death of her mother and the ending of her role as attendant and caregiver) had disrupted her habitual means of achieving social contact. Nonetheless, she continued to maintain that her mother's death could not be the cause of her depression ("I'd known for a long time that her health was poor, and that one day she would die, so how could that be upsetting me now?"). Also, she still felt extremely uncomfortable about her tremor and felt frustrated when staff and other patients told her that the shaking was so slight that they could hardly notice it.

Based on the MMPI findings and accumulated clinical observation, the patient's antidepressant medication was discontinued and arrangements were made for her to see a psychotherapist in her home town. The patient was relieved about not having to take medications and reported that she looked forward to trying therapy as an alternative. She had also generated some ideas about living arrangements (e.g., taking in another older person as a boarder in her home) and activities (volunteering in the local hospital) that would bring her in contact with other people and were well suited to her background and social preferences.

There were several valuable outcomes of formal assessment in this case: 1) it lead to a revised treatment plan, minimizing medication and maximizing psychotherapeutic interventions; 2) it provided a picture of the patient's current symptoms and characteristic means of coping that can be used as a starting point for therapy; and 3) it increased the patient's hope that her habits and her viewpoint could be understood by mental health professionals.

Example C

Case C illustrates the influence of personality disorder in the assessment and treatment of geriatric depression as well as the potential benefit of long-term therapy for individuals with personality disorder and depression.

Background and presenting problem. The patient, a 65-year-old divorced Caucasian woman, was self-referred to a day-treatment program because of symptoms of depression, including sleep disturbance, depressed mood, suicidal ideation, poor concentration, decreased energy, and episodes of acute anxiety. The symptoms had gradually worsened over a 1-year period and were precipitated by her increasing recognition that her financial resources were "running out."

The patient was treated at the day-treatment program with therapy and socialization groups, and was also prescribed antidepressant medications. She showed a modest decrease in depressive symptoms, but was noted not to utilize the group activities well, remaining superficially friendly but avoiding self-disclosure. Because of her difficulty utilizing the program, she was referred for supplemental individual therapy.

Psychodiagnostic evaluation. Psychiatric history revealed two previous therapies, once at age 21 when the patient experienced "an identity crisis" and again at age 42 during and following divorce proceedings that she had initiated. History-taking revealed that the patient had unhappy recollections of childhood; she recalled her father, a successful dentist, as strict and perfectionistic. She remembered her mother as subjugated and emotionally unavailable to the patient. The patient has one younger sister, who she felt was "favored" and more attractive. The patient achieved high grades, but felt her performance "was never good enough"; she resented demands being placed on her and took jobs that were below her abilities. To achieve status, she married a wealthy but sickly man whom she did not love. Shortly after their marriage, he became ill with tuberculosis. Her husband developed an alcohol problem and eventually became physically abusive; she divorced him after 15 years of marriage.

The patient then began a 10-year affair with a married man, in which they would "jet-set and meet in romantic places a few times a year." Her relationship with her sister was poor, and she had a few superficial friendships, based upon "keeping her disguise" as a rich, witty divorcée. She felt she was suffering no emotional distress after the divorce, until she became aware of her dwindling financial resources.

The patient's life-style changed dramatically over the next several years. She moved to a small apartment, maintained few social ties, and worked part-time as a travel agent. She never invited friends to her apartment and virtually severed family ties because of shame over her changed circumstances. Fantasies of "somehow being rescued" and "given recognition" helped her to cope.

After carefully reviewing the patient's history and behaviors, Narcissistic Personality Disorder was diagnosed; the patient evidenced grandiosity (in fantasy), was hypersensitive to the evaluations of others, believed her problems to be unique and misunderstood by others, was preoccupied by feelings of envy, indirectly sought validation and admiration, and evidenced a sense of unreasonable entitlement.

Conclusions and implications. The patient began therapy with great ambivalence and had difficulty expressing her feelings. Initially she described her altered financial circumstances and her feelings of envy towards others who "had what she should have had." She expressed a patronizing attitude toward the other day-treatment program patients, stating that her problems were more complicated than those of the other patients and beyond their comprehension. The main emphases in therapy were to provide the patient with a "corrective emotional experience" and cognitive-behavioral interventions.

It took several months to gain the patient's trust, as she "viewed everyone as a critical parent." However, she gradually began to drop her facade and express honest feelings of hurt and mourning over personal deprivations and the unfulfilling relationships in her life, including those relationships with members of her family of origin. She began to clearly identify her own role in keeping herself emotionally isolated from others and developed optimism about changing the quality of her interactions.

After about 10 months of treatment, the patient began to accept that "she would not be magically rescued" and to take responsible actions toward her own welfare; she actively renewed past friendships (e.g., inviting people to her home for the first time in 15 years) and also became less anxious about contacts with her sister. Of note, she was surprised by the emergence of some positive memories of her parents.

Major changes occurred after 1½ years of treatment. The patient learned to reevaluate and change much of her overt behavior, as well as her attitudes and beliefs about herself and her future. Currently, she feels more genuine and enjoys and values her friendships. She continues working on feelings of loss at not having the life-style that her friends do and fears that she could "slip back into depression," although recent episodes of blue mood have been much briefer, less intense, and less easily induced. The patient is still faced with realistic concerns about her financial security and is now actively exploring income options. Her overall level of functioning has improved dramatically, and therapy continues to be an important source of feedback and support for her.

Diagnosis of Narcissistic Personality Disorder had important implications for the focus and course of treatment in this older adult with major depression. While the detailed focus on the background and treatment of this individual may seem somewhat beyond the scope of a chapter on assessment of geriatric depression, the material was included to illustrate the potential of older adults to benefit from intensive psychotherapeutic interventions, both in terms of acute depressive symptomatology and maladaptive characterological patterns.

REFERENCES

American Psychiatric Association. (1980). *Diagnostic and statistical manual of mental disorders* (3rd ed.). Washington, DC: Author.

American Psychiatric Association. (1987). *Diagnostic and statistical manual of mental disorders* (3rd ed., revised). Washington, DC: Author.

Ames, L.B., Metraux, R.W., Rodell, J.L., & Walker, R.N. (1973). *Rorschach responses in old age.* New York: Brunner/Mazel.

Beck, A.T., & Beck, R.W. (1972). Screening depressed patients in family practice: A rapid technique. *Postgraduate Medicine, 52,* 81-85.

Beck, A.T., Ward, C.H., Mendelson, M., Mock, J., & Erbaugh, J. (1961). An inventory for measuring depression. *Archives of General Psychiatry, 4,* 561-571.

Belitsky, R., & Jacobs, S. (1986). Bereavement, attachment theory, and mental disorders. *Psychiatric Annals, 16,* 276-280.

Bellak, L. (1986). *The TAT, CAT, and SAT in clinical use* (4th ed.). New York: Grune & Stratton.

Berry, J.M., Storandt, M., & Coyne, A. (1984). Age and sex differences in somatic complaints associated with depression. *Journal of Gerontology, 39,* 465-467.

Blazer, D., & Williams, C.D. (1980). Epidemiology of dysphoria and depression in the elderly population. *American Journal of Psychiatry, 137,* 439-444.

Bornstein, P.E., Clayton, P.J., & Halikas, J.A. (1973). The depression of widowhood after 13 months. *British Journal of Psychiatry, 122,* 561- 566.

Bowlby, J. (1970). Separation and loss within the family. In E.J. Anthony & C. Koupernik (Eds.), *The child and his family* (Vol. 1, pp. 197-216). New York: John Wiley.

Boyd, J.H., & Weissman, M.M. (1981). Epidemiology of affective disorders. *Archives of General Psychiatry, 38,* 1039-1046.

Butler, R.N., & Lewis, M.I. (1982). *Aging and mental health* (3rd ed.). St. Louis: C.V. Mosby.

Clayton, P., & Darvish, H. (1979). Course of depressive symptoms following the stress of bereavement. In J.E. Barnett (Ed.), *Stress and mental disorder* (pp. 121-136). New York: Raven.

Colligan, R.C., Osborne, D., Swenson, W.M., & Offord, K.P. (1984). The aging MMPI: Development of contemporary norms. *Mayo Clinic Proceedings, 59,* 377-390.

Davidson, R.J. (1984). Affect, cognition, and hemispheric specialization. In C. Izard, J. Kagan, & R. Zajonc (Eds.), *Emotions, cognitions, and behavior* (pp. 57-73). New York: Cambridge University Press.

Dessonville, C., Gallagher, D., Thompson, L.W., Finnell, K., & Lewinsohn, P.M. (1982). Relation of age and health status to depression symptoms in normal and depressed older adults. *Essence, 5,* 99-117.

Dimond, R.N., Lund, D.A., & Caserata, M.S. (1987). The role of social support in the first two years of bereavement in an elderly sample. *Gerontologist, 27,* 599-604.

Epstein, L.J. (1976). Symposium on age differentiation in depressive illness. Depression in the elderly. *Journal of Gerontology, 31,* 278-282.

Faschingbauer, N. (1978). *Short forms of the MMPI.* Lexington, MA: Lexington Books.

Fillenbaum, G.G., & Pfeiffer, E. (1976). The Mini-Mult: A cautionary note. *Journal of Consulting and Clinical Psychology, 44,* 698-703.

Fleiss, J.L., Gurland, B.J., Simon, R.J., & Sharpe, L. (1973). Cross-national study of diagnosis of the mental disorders: Some demographic correlates of hospital diagnosis in New York and London. *International Journal of Social Psychiatry, 19,* 180-186.

Flor-Henry, P. (1976). Lateralized temporal-limbic dysfunction and psychopathology. *Annals of New York Academy of Science, 280,* 777-779.

Gaitz, C., & Scott, J. (1972). Age and the measurement of mental health. *Journal of Health and Social Behavior, 13,* 55-67.

Gallagher, D., Breckenridge, J., Steinmeitz, J., & Thompson, L. (1983). The Beck Depression Inventory and Research Diagnostic Criteria: Congruence in an older population. *Journal of Clinical and Consulting Psychology, 51,* 945-946.

Gallagher, D., McGarvey, W., Zelinski, E.M., & Thompson, L.W. (1978, November). *Age and factor structure of the Zung Depression Scale.* Paper presented at the 31st Annual Meeting of the Gerontological Society, Dallas.

Gallagher, D., Nies, G., & Thompson, L. (1982). Reliability of the Beck Depression Inventory with older adults. *Journal of Consulting and Clinical Psychology, 50,* 152-153.

Gallagher, D., Thompson, L.W., & Levy, S.A. (1980). Clinical psychological assessment of older adults. In L.W. Poon (Ed.), *Aging in the 1980's* (pp. 19-40). Washington, DC: American Psychological Association.

Gerner, R.H. (1979). Depression in the elderly. In O.J. Kaplan (Ed.), *Psychopathology of aging* (pp. 97-148). New York: Academic Press.

Golden, R.R., Teresi, J.A., & Gurland, B.J. (1984). Development of indicator scales for the Comprehensive Assessment and Referral Evaluation (CARE) interview schedule. *Journal of Gerontology, 2,* 138-146.

Goldfarb, A.I. (1975). Depression in the old and aged. In F.F. Flach (Ed.), *The nature and treatment of depression* (pp.119-144). New York: John Wiley.

Goldstein, K. (1948). *Language and language disorders.* New York: Grune & Stratton.

Gurland, B.J. (1976). The comparative frequency of depression in various adult age groups. *Journal of Gerontology, 31,* 283-292.

Gurland, B.J. (1984). Personality disorders in old age. In D.W.K. Kay & G.D. Burrows (Eds.), *Handbook of studies on psychiatry and old age* (pp. 303-318). New York: Elsevier.

Gurland, B.J., Golden, R.R., Teresi, J.A., & Challop, J. (1984). The SHORT-CARE: An efficient instrument for the assessment of depression, dementia and disability. *Journal of Gerontology, 2,* 166-169.

Gurland, B.J., Kuriansky, J.B., Sharpe, L., Simon, R., Stiller, P., & Birkett, P. (1977). The Comprehensive Assessment and Referral Evaluation (CARE)—Rationale, development and reliability. *International Journal of Aging and Human Development, 8,* 9-42.

Gurland, B.J., & Wilder, D.E. (1984). The CARE interview revisited: Development of an efficient, systematic clinical assessment. *Journal of Gerontology, 2,* 129-137.

Guy, W. (1976). *ECDEU assessment manual for psychopharmacology* (rev. ed., DHEW Publication No. ADM 76-338). Washington, DC: U.S. Department of Health, Education, and Welfare.

Hall, R.C.W., Popkin, M.K., DeVaul, R.A., Faillace, L.A., & Stickney, S.K. (1978). Physical illness presenting as psychiatric disease. *Archives of General Psychiatry, 35,* 1315-1320.

Hamilton, M. (1960). A rating scale for depression. *Journal of Neurology, Neurosurgery and Psychiatry, 23,* 56-62.

Heidell, E.D., & Kidd, A.H. (1975). Depression and senility. *Journal of Clinical Psychology, 31,* 643-645.

Hileman, C. (1981). *The concurrent validity of four abbreviated forms of the MMPI with elderly psychiatric inpatients: A comparative investigation.* Unpublished master's thesis, University of Southern California, Los Angeles.

Jacobs, J.W., Bernhard, M.R., Delgado, A., & Strain, J.J. (1977). Screening for organic mental syndromes in the medically ill. *Annals of Internal Medicine, 86,* 40-46.

Jarvik, L.F. (1976). Aging and depression: Some unanswered questions. *Journal of Gerontology, 31,* 324-326.

Kahana, B. (1978). The use of projective techniques in personality assessment of the aged. In M. Storandt, I.C. Siegler, & M.F. Elias (Eds.), *The clinical psychology of aging* (pp. 145-180). New York: Plenum.

Katon, W., Berg, A.O., Robins, A.J., & Risse, S. (1986). Depression—Medical utilization and somatization. *The Western Journal of Medicine, 144,* 564-568.

Katon, W., Kleinman, A., & Rosen, G. (1982). Depression and somatization: A review. Part II. *The American Journal of Medicine, 72,* 241-247.

Kiloh, L.G. (1961). Pseudo-dementia. *Acta Psychiatrica Scandinavica, 37,* 336-351.

Kincannon, J.C. (1968). Prediction of the standard MMPI scale scores from 71 items: The Mini-Mult. *Journal of Consulting and Clinical Psychology, 32,* 319-325.

Knight, B. (1986). *Psychotherapy with older adults.* Beverly Hills, CA: Sage.

Kochansky, G.E. (1979). Psychiatric rating scales for assessing psychopathology in the elderly: A critical review. In A. Raskin & L. Jarvik (Eds.), *Psychiatric symptoms and cognitive loss in the elderly* (pp. 73-118). Washington, DC: Hemisphere.

Larson, E.B., Reifler, B.V., Sumi, S.M., Canfield, C.G., & Chinn, N.M. (1985). Diagnostic evaluation of 200 elderly outpatients with suspected dementia. *Journal of Gerontology, 40,* 536-543.

La Rue, A., D'Elia, L.F., Clark, E.O., Spar, J., & Jarvik, L.F. (1986). Clinical tests of memory in dementia, depression, and healthy aging. *Psychology and Aging, 1,* 69-77.

La Rue, A., Dessonville, C., & Jarvik, L.F. (1985). Aging and mental disorders. In J.E. Birren & K.W. Schaie (Eds.), *Handbook of the psychology of aging* (2nd ed., pp. 664-702). New York: Van Nostrand Reinhold.

La Rue, A., Spar, J., & Hill, C. (1986). Cognitive impairment in late-life depression. *Journal of Affective Disorders, 11,* 179- 184.

Lawton, M.P., Whelihan, W.M., & Belsky, J.M. (1980). Personality tests and their uses with older adults. In J.E. Birren & R.B. Sloane (Eds.), *Handbook of mental health and aging.* Englewood Cliffs, NJ: Prentice-Hall.

Lehmann, H.E. (1982). Affective disorders in the aged. In L.F. Jarvik & G.W. Small (Eds.), *Psychiatric clinics of North America* (pp. 27-44). Philadelphia: W.B. Saunders.

Lesse, S. (1974). Depressive equivalents and the multivariant masks of depression. In S. Lesse (Ed.), *Masked depression* (pp. 3-23). New York: Jason Aronson.

Lewis, W.H. (1971). Iatrogenic psychotic depressive reaction in hypertensive patients. *American Journal of Psychiatry, 127,* 1416-1417.

Lezak, M.D. (1983). *Neuropsychological assessment* (2nd ed.). New York: Oxford University Press.

Lindemann, E. (1974). Symptomatology and management of acute grief. *American Journal of Psychiatry, 101,* 141-148.

Machover, K. (1949). *Personality projection in the drawing of a human figure.* Springfield, IL: Charles C. Thomas.

Maiden, R.J. (1987). Learned helplessness and depression: A test of the reformulated model. *Journal of Gerontology, 42,* 60-64.

McGarvey, B., Gallagher, D., Thompson, L.W., & Zelinski, E. (1982). Reliability and factor structure of the Zung Self-rating Depression Scale in three age groups. *Essence, 5,* 141-153.

McLachlan, J.F.C. (1974). Test-retest stability of long and short form MMPI scales over two years. *Journal of Consulting Psychology, 30,* 189-191.

Millon, T. (1983). *Millon Clinical Multiaxial Inventory manual* (3rd ed.). Minneapolis, MN: National Computer Systems.

Millon, T. (1986). Personality prototypes and their diagnostic criteria. In T. Millon & G. Klerman (Eds.), *Contemporary directions in psychopathology: Toward the DSM-IV.* New York: Guilford.

Morris, J.N., Wolf, R.S., & Klerman, L.V. (1975). Common themes among morale and depression scales. *Journal of Gerontology, 30,* 209- 215.

National Institute of Neurological and Communicative Diseases and Stroke (NINCDS). (1983). *Stroke: Hope through research.* Bethesda, MD: National Institute of Health.

Norris, J.T., Gallagher, D., Wilson, A., & Winograd, C.H. (1987). Assessment of depression in geriatric medical outpatients: The validity of two screening measures. *Journal of the American Geriatric Society, 35,* 989-995.

Ouslander, J.G. (1982). Illness and psychopathology in the elderly. *Psychiatric Clinics of North America, 5,* 145-158.

Phifer, J.F., & Murrell, S.A. (1986). Etiologic factors in the onset of depressive symptoms in older adults. *Journal of Abnormal Psychology, 95,* 282-291.

Poelker, G.A., Shewchuk, R.M., & Niederehe, G. (1987). Confirmatory factor analysis of the short form Beck Depression Inventory in elderly community samples. *Journal of Clinical Psychology, 43,* 111-118.

Prigatano, G.P. (1986). *Neuropsychological rehabilitation following brain injury.* Baltimore: Johns Hopkins University Press.

Rapp, S.R., Parisi, S.A., & Wallace, C.E. (1987, November). *Detection of depression in elderly medical patients.* Paper presented at a meeting of the Gerontological Society of America, Washington, DC.

Robinson, R.G., & Steleza, B. (1981). Mood change following left hemispheric brain injury. *Annals of Neurology, 9,* 447-453.

Ross, E.D., & Rush, J. (1981). Diagnosis and neuroanatomical correlates of depression in brain-damaged patients. *Archives of General Psychiatry, 38,* 1344-1354.

Rotter, J.B., & Rafferty, J.E. (1953). Rotter Incomplete Sentence Blank. In A. Weider (Ed.), *Contributions toward medical psychology* (Vol. 2, pp. 590-598). New York: Ronald.

Rynearson, E.K. (1986). Psychological effects of unnatural dying on bereavement. *Psychiatric Annals, 16,* 272-275.

Salzman, C., & Shader, R.I. (1979). Clinical evaluation of depression in the elderly. In A. Raskin & L.F. Jarvik (Eds.), *Psychiatric symptoms and cognitive loss in the elderly* (pp. 39-72). New York: Halstead.

Salzman, C., Shader, R.I., Harmatz, J., & Robertson, L. (1975). Psychopharmacological investigations in elderly volunteers: Effects of diazepam in males. *Journal of the American Geriatrics Society, 23,* 451-457.

Sbordone, R.J., & Caldwell, A. (1979). OBD-168. *Clinical Neuropsychology, 4,* 38-41.

Scogin, F., Beutler, L., Corbishley, A., & Hamblin, D. (1987, November). *Reliability and validity of the Short Form Beck Depression Inventory with older adults.* Paper presented at the Annual Convention of the Gerontological Society of America, Washington, DC.

Shanfield, S.B. (1983). Predicting bereavement outcome: Marital factors. *Family Systems Medicine, 1,* 20-26.

Silverman, C. (1968). *The epidemiology of depression.* Baltimore: Johns Hopkins University Press.

Spitzer, R.L., & Endicott, J. (1977). *Schedule for Affective Disorders and Schizophrenia— Life-Time Version (SADS-L).* New York: New York State Psychiatric Institute.

Spitzer, R.L., Endicott, J., & Robbins, E. (1978). Research diagnostic criteria: Rationale and reliability. *Archives of General Psychiatry, 35,* 773-782.

Spitzer, R.L., Fleiss, J.L., Burdock, E.I., & Hardesty, A.S. (1964). The Mental Status Schedule: Rationale reliability and validity. *Comprehensive Psychiatry, 5*, 384-395.

Spitzer, R.L., & Williams, J.B.W. (1985). *Structured Clinical Interview for DSM-III—Patient Version (SCID-P)*. New York: New York State Psychiatric Institute.

Verwoerdt, A. (1980). Anxiety, dissociative and personality disorders in the elderly. In E.W. Busse & D.G. Blazer (Eds.), *Handbook of geriatric psychiatry* (pp. 368-380). New York: Van Nostrand Reinhold.

Verwoerdt, A. (1981). *Clinical geropsychiatry* (2nd ed.). Baltimore: Williams & Wilkins.

Weingartner, H., & Silberman, E. (1982). Models of cognitive impairment: Cognitive changes in depression. *Psychopharmacological Bulletin, 18*, 27-42.

Wells, C.E. (1983). Differential diagnosis of Alzheimer's dementia: Affective disorder. In B. Reisberg (Ed.), *Alzheimer's disease: The standard reference* (pp. 193-198). New York: Free Press.

Wing, J.K., Birley, J.L.T., Cooper, J.E., Graham, P., & Isaacs, A.D. (1967). Reliability of a procedure for measuring present psychiatric state. *British Journal of Psychiatry, 113*, 499-515.

Wolk, R.L., & Wolk, R.V. (1971). *Manual for the Geriatric Apperception Test*. New York: Behavioral Publications.

Yesavage, J.A., Brink, T.L., Rose, T.L., & Adey, M.A. (1983). The Geriatric Depression Rating Scale: Comparison with other self- report and psychiatric rating scales. In T. Crook, S. Ferris, & R. Bartus (Eds.), *Assessment in geriatric psychopharmacology* (pp. 153-168). New Canaan, CT: Mark Powley.

Zarit, S.H. (1980). *Aging and mental disorders: Psychological approaches to assessment and treatment*. New York: Free Press.

Zemore, R., & Eames, N. (1979). Psychic and somatic symptoms of depression among young adults, institutionalized aged and noninstitutionalized aged. *Journal of Gerontology, 34*, 716-722.

Ziscook, S., & Schucter, S.R. (1986). The first four years of widowhood. *Psychiatric Annals, 16*, 288-294.

Zung, W.W.K. (1965). A self-rating depression scale. *Archives of General Psychiatry, 12*, 63-70.

Zung, W.W.K. (1967). Depression in the normal aged. *Psychosomatic Medicine, 8*, 287-292.

Zung, W.W.K. (1983). Self-rating scales for psychopathology. In T. Crook, S. Ferris, & R. Bartus (Eds.), *Assessment in geriatric psychopharmacology* (pp. 145-152). New Canaan, CT: Mark Powley.

Zung, W.W.K., Gianturco, D., Pfeiffer, E., Wang, H.S., Whanger, A., Bridge, T.P., & Potkin, S.G. (1974). Pharmacology of depression in the aged: Evaluation of Gerovital-H3 as an antidepressant drug. *Psychosomatics, 15*, 127-131.

7

Assessment of Persons with Motor Disabilities

DAVID SCHLENOFF, ED.D.

Though most clinicians are adequately trained to evaluate able-bodied adults and perhaps children, many are minimally trained or experienced in the evaluation of motor-impaired elderly persons. The special and distinctive psychological circumstances of this ever-growing group of patients warrant attention if the psychologist expects to obtain a valid sample of behavior upon which to base conclusions. An understanding of the aging process as well as the process of adjusting to physical disability is very important. The diagnostician must fully appreciate the physical limitations of an elderly motor-impaired person and adjust the psychologist/patient relationship and the testing situation itself accordingly. This adjustment will facilitate both maximum performance on the psychological tests and openness in the interview, thus preventing the loss of much valuable information.

Physical and psychological functions are interrelated with cultural attitudes and social factors; therefore, it behooves the psychologist to assess all of these factors during the testing process in order to view the individual's gestalt. Testing an older motor-impaired adult must go beyond pointing out mental impairment and illness; it must uncover the individual's potential (Storandt, Siegler, & Elias, 1978). Also of importance in this assessment is separating out the normal effects of aging from the effects of illness (Storandt et al., 1978). Schaie and Schaie (1977) have cited the major objectives of testing the elderly as 1) assessment of adjustment to changes in role, 2) determination of a baseline level of functioning, and 3) diagnosis of psychopathology. The method of approach to this task when evaluating an elderly person who is also motor impaired must be carefully planned.

DEVELOPMENT AND MOTOR IMPAIRMENT

Personality development apparently continues throughout the life span. Although research indicates that personality remains relatively stable throughout the adult years, observed changes can usually be partialled out into those due to changes in physical condition, cultural changes and age-related effects, or those changes due to the process of maturation (Storandt et al., 1978). Havighurst (1972) cites the developmental tasks facing older adults as 1) accepting the fact of one's own aging and that of others, 2) adjusting to the stresses of decreased mobility and those from the occupational and social realms, 3) accepting responsibility for good health habits and practices, and 4) evolving a periodic assessment of one's life goals.

Along these lines, Butler and Lewis (1982) have claimed that the primary task of old age involves clarifying, deepening, and discovering use for that which has been experienced throughout the life span. If impairment is present in the realm of motor functioning, this task becomes more complex. The examiner cannot assume that the shared, basic underlying experiences of the elderly population are similar among the able bodied and the physically impaired. Normal developmental experiences, both motoric and social, usually are encountered later in the lives of disabled or incapacitated persons.

The type, severity, and duration of disability have pronounced effects on life experiences (Schlenoff, 1974). Motor disability ranging from mild to severe can result from traumatic injury, amputation, cerebrovascular accident, insidious disease entities, or more usual concomitants of aging. The examiner must bear in mind that traumatic changes in an individual's functioning and self-image involve that person in a process of accepting and integrating the disabling condition into his or her self-image (Schlenoff, 1975). This reintegration typically progresses through a series of stages similar to the mourning process; this is experienced in an individual way, with various degrees of acceptance occurring at variable points over time. The more serious the impairment, the more likely that a strong psychological reaction to it will exist.

Serious physical disability is replete with far-reaching problems, psychosocial as well as personal, which seem to be woven into the very fabric of life for the motor-impaired elderly person. Research (Safilios-Rothschild, 1972) indicates that change to one's body image encounters considerable resistance, and the recency of this change and onset should be taken into account for prognostic purposes. The elderly person who has been motor impaired for quite some time may have had time to "work through" the process of integrating the disability into his or her self-image. On the other hand, he or she also may have long been exposed to societal percepts of the disabled person as different, deviant, or abnormal. The way in which the motor-impaired, aged individual comes to view him- or herself will certainly be influenced by the person's subculture, beliefs, values, social class, degree of family support, modes of interpersonal relationships, and stereotypes (Safilios-Rothschild, 1972). Further, the examiner must remember that severely disabled persons who are accustomed to being labeled by society as deviant may approach any interaction with an able-bodied person (let alone in a testing situation) with great apprehension. All of these factors are important enough to deserve attention in the assessment of older persons with motor impairments. Unfortunately, most of the literature to date reflects an interest in the cognitive problems rather than the emotional life of the elderly (Zarit, 1980).

COMMON MOTOR DISORDERS OF THE AGED

The more common motor disorders of the elderly may involve a manifestation of generalized brain-cell loss, but more frequently they are associated with small, circumscribed losses of brain tissue (Reichel, 1983). The examiner is responsible for becoming familiar with the nature of the illness in question, its ramifications, prognosis, and characteristic types of impairment; this aids in partialling out other age-related impairments and establishing differential diagnosis. An overview of some of the more prevalent motor impairments affecting the elderly will follow. This is by no means meant to represent an all-inclusive survey, but rather is intended to offer a basic review of those conditions seen commonly by the clinician that might affect test administration and interpretation.

Parkinsonism is characterized by bradykinesia (extremely slow movements), tremor resembling a "pill-rolling" motion of the thumb and forefinger, a posture of flexion, and jerking muscle movements when pressure is applied to limbs (cogwheel rigidity).

Essential familial or senile tremor, a motor disorder of late life, is distinguished by a side-to-side or up-and-down tremor of the head and lateral motion of the fingers, which is aggravated by action. This impairment becomes most apparent when the patient is manipulating an object such as a cup or pencil.

Senile chorea may be manifested by a constant succession of writhing and involuntary movements of the fingers and hands (athetosis). This movement disorder of later life often becomes intensified by activity.

Apraxia is a disorder of voluntary movement in which the person is able to name and recognize an object and its use, such as a pen, but is unable to apply its use. This bilateral disorder usually results from a unilateral lesion in the dominant hemisphere. It may affect grasp or gait as well.

Peripheral neuropathies, which commonly result from diabetes, represent diseases of the peripheral nerves. They are seen in the testing setting as sensory loss in the affected areas (such as the hands) along with possible weakness and loss of reflex.

Muscle weakness (myopathy) also is seen frequently in patients over the age of 63 (Reichel, 1983). Cerebrovascular accidents often produce weakness or even paralysis of arms, legs, and other parts of the body.

Effects of medications may present side effects that mimic motor impairments in older adults. Clinicians should have a cursory knowledge of the more common medications and their frequently seen side effects. Such an understanding helps the psychologist to avoid confounding issues in the testing situation and possibly to identify the source of the motor disturbance more accurately. Many elderly patients who are referred for testing have been taking prescribed psychotropic medication to help in abating what has been perceived as an emotional disturbance. Such medication can cause extrapyramidal symptoms such as involuntary motor restlessness, constant pacing, and difficulty sitting still. This syndrome could easily be confused with agitation in psychotic patients (Storandt et al., 1978). A slowing of movements, possibly resulting in tremor and rigidity, may also be apparent. Spasmodic, uncoordinated movements of the arms and legs are not uncommon upon initiation of antipsychotic drug therapy, while tardive dyskinesia, a neurological syndrome resulting in purposeless quick movements of the extremities, may occur from long-term use of psychotropic medication (Goodman & Goodman, 1975). When lithium, a drug commonly used for treatment of bipolar disorder, reaches toxic levels within the body, fine tremor can result, progressing to coarse tremor and possibly even to drowsiness or confusion. Insulin usage can produce slurred speech, somnambulance, and confusion, all related to hypoglycemia (Hollister, 1977).

In addition, medications can *mask* motor problems, such as in the tranquilization of hypomania or psychogenic tremors. Thus, the importance of asking the patient about medication usage and side effects is obvious. The psychologist should not hesitate to involve a physician should any question arise within this domain.

THE TESTING SITUATION

Referral Questions

Of primary concern in approaching the testing situation is the all important "reason for referral," which determines what techniques should be used and what slant the interpretation of data should take. Common referral questions for elderly motor-impaired patients include determining adjustment to physical disability, assessing cognitive abilities and/or deficits, identifying suicidal indications, eliciting potential for vocational or avocational rehabilitation (Schlenoff, 1983), and assessing emotional problems that are material to placement planning (i.e., into or out of institutions). Competency to manage finances and other personal affairs as well as differential diagnosis of functional depression versus organicity are also fairly common reasons for testing.

Physical Setting

With the reason for referral established, attention turns to the physical aspects of the testing situation. If the patient is wheelchair bound, is the testing room wheelchair accessible? Is the patient's desk usable for a person confined to a wheelchair or is it too low? Are railings available? Is lighting adequate for the all-too-often failing eyesight of the elderly? Scatter rugs can prove lethal for persons who use crutches, walkers, or canes, or who are otherwise unsteady on their feet (Reichel, 1983).

Outside stimulation, such as noise, may be particularly distracting to persons whose motor dysfunction results from CNS impairment, and, in addition to a quiet setting, such persons may require much structure, encouragement, and repetition. The physically disabled tire more easily than the non-impaired, perhaps requiring frequent rest periods, multiple testing sessions, and administration of longer, more complex instruments toward the end of the battery (Storandt et al., 1978). While the aging process tends to slow down motor skills, traumatic physical disability may tend to do so to an even greater extent. Accordingly, timed tests should be avoided unless the main factor being measured is speed. Patience and flexibility on the part of the examiner are of utmost importance.

Occasionally, an elderly motor-impaired patient may require testing at bedside. This actually can be advantageous, as older persons typically function best within familiar surroundings. The examiner should be prepared to offer the bedridden patient a clipboard or similar device on which to write and rest testing materials. In addition, one must consider that the less-than-optimal writing position of the recumbent may affect the motor coordination required for writing, manipulation of test materials, and the like.

Modifications of Procedures

When approaching the challenge of testing an older person, it may become necessary, due to perceptual-motor problems, to modify testing procedures. For example, it may be warranted on occasion to administer written tests orally. The clinician must consider that altering the manner in which the material is presented and in which results are collected also can affect interpretation; however, this trade-off may be necessary for the patient who otherwise would not be amenable to testing at all (Storandt et al., 1978). Moses and Patterson (1973) claim that the usefulness of many tests could be enhanced if the examiner would assume a more "imaginative and less stereotyped approach" to administration. This sort of departure from standardized test administration has long been the norm when assessing blind persons, and Bauman (1972) adds that paper-and-pencil tests invariably should be adapted by employing tape recorders or reading aloud for those who would otherwise be unable to take the test.

Occasionally, a motor-impaired examinee may have other correlates of illness superimposed upon the motor dysfunction. Not infrequently, persons who have suffered a cerebrovascular accident (CVA) have a serious speech impairment in addition to motor impairment. In this instance, the patient may be able to write answers to questions asked while unable to verbalize intelligible responses. If the person is unable to speak at all (as is the case with many recently diagnosed CVA patients), the examiner can resort to asking "yes" and "no" questions exclusively.

Currently, numerous devices are available with which to adapt a computer keyboard for an individual who is motor impaired. Some can be operated with the slightest of movements, and some even by blowing one's breath or using a sipping/sucking motion. In one study, Wilson, Thompson, and Wylie (1982) compared disabled patients' scores from automated forms of three well-known psychological tests with those from standard forms. They found that correlations between the two formats were acceptably high for clinical use. Thus, in addition to the typical computerized versions available for tests such as the Minnesota Multiphasic Personality Inventory, the Sixteen Personality Factor Questionnaire, and the usual battery of objective tests, projective techniques such as the Incomplete Sentences Blank can be computer administered (e.g., by using a switch that can be operated by an unimpaired part of the body) to subjects who cannot use a writing implement.

The primary problem for this unique population appears to be the means by which the patient communicates with the computer (Wilson et al., 1982); in addition to a "tailor-made" test battery, the elderly motor-impaired examinees may also require a "tailor-made" mode of administration. The clinician must rely on his or her judgment regarding this issue. At present, the average examiner may not have access to sophisticated, adaptive computer devices and must make do with available resources. Accordingly, one may consider recording responses for patients who are unable to execute the necessary fine-motor skills for writing. This approach may also be useful for less severely motor-impaired examinees who are capable of recording their own responses, but require an inordinately long period of time in which to do so.

The Assessment Procedure

Clinical Interview

When working with an older adult who has motor problems, the importance of the clinical interview as a tool for obtaining a great breadth of valuable information cannot be overestimated (Schlenoff, 1974). The interview as an assessment vehicle must merge data from the physical examination and from the patient's history for interpretation within the dual developmental framework of "elderly" and "physically impaired."

Of foremost concern in this setting is the degree or severity of impairment. The patient's current level of functioning can be explored by inquiring how the individual perceives the motor impairment as impinging upon his or her life. Questions concerning adaptation to the disabling condition can provide much information on how well the patient has integrated the problem into his or her psychosocial functioning. The astute examiner establishes a feel for the affect surrounding the impairment and might focus on related issues centering around loss, such as loss of mobility, job status, significant others, living conditions, material possessions, and the like. Feelings of hopelessness and helplessness, which are possible adverse reactions along with fear of death, might be elicited as well (Storandt et al., 1978). The clinician also should pursue some understanding of the patient's premorbid personality and sense of body image.

The clinical interview should attempt to examine in depth the physical, sociocultural, emotional, leisure, vocational, financial, and spiritual world in which the motor-impaired elderly person resides (Gress & Bahr, 1984). The examiner might ask the patient what he or she sees as the most pressing problems in each area, and what are the history of and plans for dealing with these problems. This may provide insight into resources as well as resourcefulness. Once again, questions concerning use of prescribed and non-prescribed drugs as well as alcohol can yield information with a profound bearing on diminished motor functions.

Observing the patient's grammar and vocabulary during questioning can provide information on ability, and educational achievement should be determined as well. Wilson et al. (1982) claim that frequently motor-impaired persons are assumed (erroneously) to be impaired in the cognitive realm as well, and consequently they may be frustrated and depressed. The diagnostician must be vigilant against applying this stereotype. Questions that address physical and emotional complaints along with compiling a history of surgical procedures, traumatic injuries, institutionalizations, and a description of what the patient considers a "typical day" can supply the interviewer with dramatic insight into physical and emotional limitations (Reichel, 1983). Transportation, for example, often proves problematic for persons with severely limited motor functioning, and those with diminished mobility seem to be at higher risk for physical assault and related experiences, which threatens the maintenance of their sense of well-being. Other questions material to a more generic sort of clinical interview (regarding mental status, diet, marital issues, etc.) should, of course, be included as well.

With an understanding of developmental issues affecting the geriatric patient as well as knowledge of the confounding effects of motor impairment, the clinician must begin the task of assembling a test battery to obtain additional data on personality and cognition. In sum, physical disability may necessitate a departure from standardized test administration procedures. Although one must bear in mind that age-appropriate norms for older persons are scarce, the valid psychological assessment of a geriatric patient with diminished motor function is limited primarily by the thoroughness and skill of the psychologist (Reichel, 1983).

Intelligence Testing

Operationally defined, intelligence is the "aggregate or global capacity of the individual to act purposefully, think rationally, and to deal effectively with the environment" (Wechsler, 1958). Typically, this function is measured by standardized tests that assess crystallized, informational abilities along with perceptual-motor skills. However, when assessing aged and physically impaired persons, certain questions arise concerning the applicability of conventional intelligence tests. First, as a person ages, the notion of intelligence changes from that of crystallized, specific information to a more socially oriented, practical, everyday problem-solving ability (Rybash, Hoyer, & Roodin, 1986). This conceptualization of intelligence versus the more common "irreversible decrement" model (wherein the aged person is thought to be on active intellectual decline) may not be amenable to testing by conventional IQ measures such as the Wechsler Adult Intelligence Scale-Revised (WAIS-R), which is based on the latter premise (Rybash et al., 1986). However, an altered model, which takes into account the modified style of thinking and reasoning that typifies an older population, may provide a more realistic concept of intelligence in the later stages of the human life cycle (Rybash et al., 1986). Standardized tests may fail to tap these underlying intellectual resources.

Tests must suit the physical condition of the individual in order to secure a behavior sample sufficient for reaching a valid conclusion (Schlenoff, 1974). A person whose motor impairment involves either upper extremities or central nervous system might obtain a rating on a verbally loaded measure that would represent a more accurate assessment of intelligence than would an IQ score derived from a test dependent upon psychomotor skills. If, due to motor impairment, a person's ability to perform in any of these areas is diminished, the question arises whether the score on the test reflects intelligence or merely the degree of physical impairment in a specific instance (Schlenoff, 1974).

Typically, a measure such as the WAIS-R Verbal scale can be used to obtain some estimate of intelligence-related abilities in the older motor-impaired population. Based on the degree of motor impairment, the examiner must make a judgment about how useful data from the WAIS-R timed tests of psychomotor skills would be in assessing intelligence. An IQ test requiring the execution of any significant amount of psychomotor tasks (such as the Revised Beta Examination) should be avoided. Cull and Colvin (1970) found that when administered to 30 severely handicapped persons, there was no significant difference between mean IQ scores of the brief Quick Test (QT) and the WAIS Verbal scale. Thus, the QT might be used to assess a motor-impaired elderly individual, although the WAIS has proven to be the most widely accepted tool for prediction and assessment with motor-disabled persons (Cull & Colvin, 1970).

Data from any intelligence measure can be corroborated with impressions gleaned from the interview and from suggestions of intelligence reflected in projective testing. To avoid errors in assessment, examiners using IQ tests must determine if the patient is performing in accordance with his or her capacities, and if not, why. Here, projective testing can supplement information on intellectual potential. If the degree of motor dysfunction is minimal enough to allow administration of the Human

Figure Drawing Test, a resulting estimate of IQ might be derived from the Good-enough-Harris scoring system (Machover, 1952). When dealing with the motor impaired, projective tests may provide more useful data than standardized intelligence tests by assessing the "fluid" type of cognition.

Instruments such as the Rorschach Inkblot Test are virtually immune to the limitations that paper-and-pencil tests impose on the disabled (Sattler, 1982). Most notably, responses on Rorschach protocols can provide some index of intelligence. Exner (1974) claims that Whole (W) responses are related to intellect, as does tendency to give Blend responses (the ability to generate responses that employ multiple scored determinants, such as human movement combined with form-dominated color). Klopfer, Ainsworth, Klopfer, and Holt (1954) cite as significant both number and form level of human movement responses as well as original responses. Phillips and Smith (1953) state that intelligence can be estimated reliably from the vocabulary observed in responses. However, Exner (1974) cautions that no individual factor or array of Rorschach responses correlates significantly with IQ. Once again, the variables of clinical skill and experience prove indispensable in making sound determinations.

In light of the fact that many standardized intelligence measures, despite their widespread use, are poorly suited for this unique population, results from such tests should be viewed only as guidelines or estimates concerning intelligence (Schlenoff, 1974). If broad discrepancies in ratings occur (e.g., a low score on the WAIS-R Verbal scale and indications of high intelligence on projective testing), then the examiner must question the appropriateness of the test yielding the lower score. Only after resolving these considerations can the examiner make valid predictions on the basis of IQ testing and obtain a better understanding of the individual (Schlenoff, 1974).

Personality Testing

Projective personality instruments, typically less structured than other types of tests, are very appropriate for elderly examinees with diminished motor skills. Typically, these measures do not require a form of administration that penalizes persons with declining speed and coordination, do not involve short-term memory or complex verbal discrimination, and do not rely on culturally related symbols or complex instructions. Further, as they are not extremely dependent upon standardization, the examiner may even vary the length of the test in accordance with the demands of the particular situation. Additionally, because projective tests are administered in an intimate, face-to-face setting, the trained clinician is afforded an opportunity to observe any special difficulties experienced by the elderly debilitated patient. Even partially completed projective test protocols can provide invaluable personality information on the motor-impaired elderly examinee (Storandt et al., 1978). Storandt et al. (1978) add that older persons seem prone to giving socially desirable responses, but even this phenomenon may be minimized through the use of projective techniques. Kahana and Kahana (1976) found that in a population of 200 institutionalized and 50 community-placed aged subjects (a large number of whom had some motor problems), the majority were able to complete Bender Visual Motor Gestalt Test designs (94%) and human figure drawings (76%).

With projective techniques, the examiner frequently observes a certain degree of regularity (that is, reliability) across tasks with regard to coping styles, goals, self-concept, conflicts, and intrapsychic problems (Storandt et al., 1978). Such information can be most useful in identifying an individual's creative capacities, potentials, and hidden resources, as well as whether to use a "mental health" rather than a "mental illness" paradigm. That is, overall style of adaptation can be measured readily via projective techniques (Oberleder, 1967). Along these lines, Kahana and Kiyak (1976) employed the Incomplete Sentences Blank, Bender Visual Motor Gestalt Test, and human figure drawings to measure long-term adaptation to institutional living. These researchers judged that behaviors such as rotation of the page, requests for further instructions, and latencies of responses on the Incomplete Sentences Blank provided valid data regarding adaptation, as did response content on these projective techniques.

The commonly used projective techniques for older persons are the Rorschach, human figure drawings, Bender Visual Motor Gestalt Test, Incomplete Sentences Blank, and Thematic Apperception Test (Storandt et al., 1978). Among these the Rorschach appears uniquely well suited for holistically assessing perceptual, affective, and cognitive functioning and is routinely employed by most psychologists in their assessment batteries (Klopfer, 1974). Virtually all motor-impaired elderly persons (except for those whose impairment also involves other functions, such as speech, sight, or hearing) seem capable of providing responses to this technique. It allows the psychologist to recognize the broad range of characteristics among the aged and to focus on the dynamics of the individual (Storandt et al., 1978), as it readily provides data on inner strengths as well as liabilities.

Although Exner has developed a comprehensive scoring system (including a useful index of suicidal potential, a valid concern with the elderly), one should note that no formal data have been reported yet regarding use with an elderly population. Kahana and Kiyak (1976) have observed, however, that the elderly typically emit fewer responses per card, and this appears consistent with the lessened verbal output of the elderly on other projective techniques such as the Thematic Apperception Test (Storandt et al., 1978). Further, the more seriously disabled person who has not yet accepted his or her disability may have a tendency to see persons or objects that are disfigured, incomplete, or otherwise somewhat damaged (Ogdon, 1967). (This theme may be repeated throughout the administration of other techniques, especially on human figure drawings).

It is generally understood that the product of the Human Figure Drawing Test is a representation of a patient's self-perception (Ogdon, 1967). If degree of motor impairment allows administration of this test, the disabled person typically will portray the part of the body affected by the impairment and will indicate the conflictual area of the body via exaggeration of size, omission of the body part, or poor line quality for the part in question. Machover (1952) indicates that even blind subjects have been known to produce figure drawings that reflect an articulated body image on this quick, nonverbal measure of personality and cognitive functioning. Sensory and motor problems that are not readily apparent may surface during administration, and conversely, perceptual-motor strengths can be uncovered in those experiencing obvious motor impairments (Storandt et al., 1978).

However, the clinician must use caution in interpreting human figure drawings for elderly patients, as poor line quality, difficulty in coordination, and poorly executed contours may be the result of arthritis rather than functional disorders. Accordingly, dynamic interpretations must integrate the existence of conditions involving motor dysfunction. Despite these factors, Lakin (1956) claims that variables such as centeredness of the figure, height, and area covered by the drawing are not easily affected by motor impairment in the elderly.

The Bender Visual Motor Gestalt Test, another useful projective instrument, requires the patient to copy nine designs, one at a time, onto a sheet of paper. Assuming that the existing motor impairment allows the examinee to execute this test, it can provide the examiner a measure of underlying dynamics as well as perceptual-motor strengths or dysfunctions. The Pascal-Suttel (1951) scoring system has been used widely with an elderly population in both research and clinical settings (Storandt et al., 1978), and while the Bender has not been validated for the elderly, it has been recommended for use with this population (Storandt et al., 1978). A greater number of errors generated by perceptual-motor dysfunction should probably be expected and incorporated into the interpretation. Accordingly, the examiner should be mindful of the neurological concomitants of aging, such as increased rigidity of response, fixed response patterns, distractability, and difficulty in ignoring irrelevant details. These phenomena, along with a possible repetitive response pattern, appear to be adaptive for the elderly in terms of decreasing demands on memory and providing stability in new environmental conditions (Reichel, 1983). If any of these clues to functioning emerge, they are certainly germane to the process of establishing a well-integrated, complete picture of the individual.

The Incomplete Sentences Blank, a projective technique wherein the examiner reads aloud statement stems and records subject's completions, has proven to be methodologically as well as theoretically valid for tapping unconscious motivations and indexing mental health and adaptation (Storandt et al., 1978). Virtually any elderly person whose speech and hearing are relatively intact is capable of completing this test despite motor impairment. The clinician should be aware that responses on this short, easily administered technique often reflect a social desirability bias, a tendency to which, as previously noted, the elderly seem particularly prone. Carp (1967) has developed an objective scoring system that measures adjustment in an aged population, which renders the Incomplete Sentences Blank a most useful instrument in assessing motor-impaired elderly.

The Thematic Apperception Test (TAT) typically presents little difficulty to the aged patient with diminished motor ability. The examiner chooses a series of pictures portrayed on the stimulus cards, asks the patient to tell a story about the card, including a distinct beginning, middle, and end, and then records these responses. Examiners must base qualitative assessment on clinical experience, as norms do not exist for this technique. Despite this shortcoming, the TAT has been credited as one of the best indices of attitude toward dying and of mode for coping with the environment (active, passive, and magical) (Shrut, 1958; Storandt et al., 1978). Britton (1963) found that elderly subjects who were viewed positively by their peers portrayed competence and self-assurance on the TAT; Britton thus suggests that adjustment in the aged may be measured by TAT responses.

In administering this technique, the clinician should be aware that TAT responses from an elderly person typically reflect a degree of concreteness and lack of verbal productivity. Not infrequently, the patient who continues to struggle with physical disability will project that disability onto a character in the story; thus, attitudes centered around the impairment can once again be glimpsed by the examiner.

Two attempts to modify the TAT into a more relevant instrument for the elderly are represented by Bellak's (1975) Senior Apperception Test and Wolk and Wolk's (1971) Gerontological Apperception Test (which, at the time of this writing, was no longer in print). These instruments depict older persons engaged in situations that are common to the elderly and/or require change and adaptation. The administration and interpretation for both of these measures is conducted in a manner similar to that of the TAT. Research, however, has not supported the conclusions that cards designed specifically for the aged are more useful than the traditional Thematic Apperception Test (Storandt et al., 1978).

Similarly, the Hand Test, a technique in which the patient explains the meaning of hands depicted in different positions on cards, seems well suited to the motor-impaired older person, as debilitated motor functions do not interfere. Panek, Sterns, and Wagner (1976) recommend this device for use with the aged, as it requires only 10 minutes to administer and subjects seem to find the stimulus pictures meaningful. These researchers are attempting to validate this instrument on a large sample of elderly persons; however, their findings suggest constriction of personality when compared to protocols of younger subjects (Panek et al., 1976).

SUMMARY

Research and clinical observations indicate that motor-impaired persons can be accurately and validly assessed for intellectual as well as vocational and social personality functions. However, methods of administration and interpretation may require alteration so that the patient will be amenable to assessment. An understanding of the developmental tasks involved in both aging and adjusting to impairment is essential, as is an assurance that one is assessing a factor or dimension other than the degree of intervening motor impairment. The marked variability in levels of functioning in this population requires a careful, holistic examination of behavior and a flexible attitude toward the patient. Only then can one attempt to fulfill the responsibility for sound judgments and recommendations that may have far-reaching effects on an elderly motor-impaired individual.

REFERENCES

Bauman, M. (1972). *Psychological testing and blindness—A retrospect.* Washington, DC: American Association of Workers for the Blind.

Bellak, L. (1975). *The T.A.T., C.A.T., and S.A.T. in clinical use.* New York: Grune & Stratton.

Britton, J. (1963). Dimensions of adjustment of older adults. *Journal of Gerontology, 18,* 60-65.

Butler R., & Lewis, M. (1982). *Aging and mental health: Positive psychosocial and biomedical approaches.* St. Louis: C.V. Mosby.

Carp, F. (1967). The application of an empirical scoring standard for a sentence completion test administered. *Journal of Gerontology, 22,* 301-307.

Cull, J., & Colvin C. (1970). Correlation between the Quick Test (QT) and the WAIS Verbal scale in the rehabilitation setting. *Psychological Reports, 27,* 105-106.

Exner, J. (1974). *The Rorschach: A comprehensive system.* New York: John Wiley.

Goodman, L., & Goodman, A. (1975). *The pharmacological basis of therapeutics*. New York: Macmillan.

Gress, L., & Bahr, R. (1984). *The aging person: A holistic perspective*. St. Louis: C.V. Mosby.

Havighurst, R. (1972). *Developmental tasks and education*. New York: David McKay.

Hollister, L. (1977). Mental disorders in the elderly. *Drug Therapy, 7,* 128-135.

Kahana, E., & Kahana, B. (1976). *Strategies of coping in institutional environments* (Progress Report). Washington, DC: National Institute of Mental Health.

Kahana, B., & Kiyak, A. (1976, May). *The use of projective techniques as an aid to assessing coping behavior and coping styles among the aged*. Paper presented at the 29th Annual Meeting of the Gerontological Society, New York.

Klopfer, W. (1974). The Rorschach and old age. *Journal of Personality Assessment, 38,* 420-422.

Klopfer, B., Ainsworth, M., Klopfer, W., & Holt, R. (1954). *Rorschach technique*. New York: Harcourt, Brace, World.

Lakin, M. (1956). Formal characteristics of human figure drawings by institutionalized aged and by normal children. *Journal of Consulting Psychology, 20,* 471-474.

Machover, K. (1952). *Personality projection in the drawing of the human figure*. Springfield, IL: Charles C. Thomas.

Moses, H., & Patterson, D. (1973). *Research readings in rehabilitation counseling*. Urbana, IL: Stipes.

Ogdon, D. (1967). *Psychodiagnostics and personality assessment: A handbook*. Beverly Hills: Western Psychological Services.

Oberleder, M. (1967). Adapting current psychological techniques for use in testing the aged. *Gerontologist, 7,* 188-191.

Panek, P., Sterns, H., & Wagner, E. (1976). An exploratory investigation of the personality correlates of aging using the Hand Test. *Perceptual and Motor Skills, 43,* 331-336.

Pascal, G., & Suttell, B. (1951). *The Bender Gestalt Test: Quantification and validity for adults*. New York: Grune & Stratton.

Phillips, L., & Smith, J. (1953). *Rorschach interpretation: Advanced technique*. New York: Grune & Stratton.

Reichel, W. (1983). *Clinical aspects of aging*. Baltimore: Williams & Wilkins.

Rybash, J., Hoyer, W., & Roodin, P. (1986). *Adult cognition and aging*. New York: Pergamon.

Safilios-Rothschild, C. (1972). *The sociology and social psychology of disability and rehabilitation*. New York: Random House.

Sattler, J. (1982). *Assessment of childrens' intelligence and special abilities* (2nd ed.). Boston: Allyn & Bacon.

Schaie, K. W., & Schaie, J. (1977). Clinical assessment and aging. In J.E. Birren & K.W. Schaie (Eds.), *Handbook of the psychology of aging* (pp. 692-716). New York: Van Nostrand Reinhold.

Schlenoff, D. (1974). Considerations in administering intelligence tests to the physically disabled. *Rehabilitation Literature, 35*(12), 362-363.

Schlenoff, D. (1975). A theory of career development for the quadriplegic. *Journal of Applied Rehabilitation Counseling, 6*(1), 3-11.

Schlenoff, D. (1983). Rehabilitation of the unemployable mentally restored person: The avocational alternative. *Rehabilitation Literature, 44*(1), 27-28.

Shrut, S. (1958). Attitudes toward old age and death. *Mental Hygiene, 42,* 259-266.

Storandt, M., Siegler, I., & Elias, M. (Eds.). (1978). *The Clinical Psychology of Aging*. New York: Plenum.

Wechsler, D. (1958). *The measurement and appraisal of adult intelligence.* Baltimore: Williams & Wilkins.

Wilson, S., Thompson, J., & Wylie, G. (1982). Automated psychological testing for the severely physically handicapped. *International Journal of Man-Machine Studies, 17,* 291-296.

Wolk, R.L., & Wolk, R.B. (1971). *The Gerontological Apperception Test.* New York: Behavioral Publications.

Zarit, S.H. (1980). *Aging and mental disorders.* New York: Macmillan.

8

Assessing the Visually Impaired Older Adult

STEVE SHINDELL, PH.D.

The assessment of older adults with visual impairments is one of the more complex tasks that can befall the average clinician. Ignorance, combined with an inability to utilize many common instruments, causes havoc with the standardized testing procedure. Recent government guidelines critically outline the dilemma a psychologist faces when testing people with disabilities in a variety of settings (Sherman & Robinson, 1982). Freedman (1975) specifically reviews the extensive information needed from a variety of sources to assess a visually impaired older person accurately. He shows that, due to the inability of clinicians to utilize comprehensive normative data, the actual scores obtained from assessment devices are often less useful than the examiner's own interpretation of the client's characteristic style.

Several key terms require definition before a discussion of the effects of visual impairment can ensue. *Legal blindness* is defined in the United States as a best corrected visual acuity of 20/200 or less in the better eye or a visual field of 20 degrees or less. The term *severe visual impairment* means best corrected visual acuity of 20/70 or less in the better eye. The first number in the ratio relates to what the person can see at 20 feet, the second to the distance at which a fully sighted individual can see the same object. That is, a person with 20/70 vision can see at 20 feet what an individual with no visual disability sees at 70 feet. These numbers by themselves are only approximations, as they vary depending on available lighting, glare, whether the task utilizes near or far focusing, and so forth. The definition of legal blindness also varies geographically. Many countries employ a more stringent cutoff (e.g., 20/400), and some, such as Switzerland, simply have no definition. Rather, they employ a functional approach to service delivery (e.g., a watchmaker with 20/40 vision may be more vocationally disabled than a bricklayer with vision assessed at 20/200).

STEREOTYPES VERSUS REALITY FOR THE VISUALLY IMPAIRED PERSON

The media image of the lives of people with a visual impairment offers a very distorted view. The picture of a young, totally blind male walking with his guide dog to his place of employment, where he utilizes braille, talking computers, and other technological wonders, is a false portrayal. The first misconception here is that people with visual impairments are typically young, or at least match the age stratification of the general population. The majority of visually impaired people in developed countries acquire this disability as a result of aging. Roughly half of those who are legally blind in the United States are over 65. According to census bureau projections,

135

there are currently 26 million people in the U.S. over the age of 65, and this number is expected to rise to almost 32 million by the year 2000 (Lowman & Kirchner, 1979). Various data sources estimate the following figures on the subsection of the population that is visually impaired:

1) 73% of the legally blind are over the age of 45
2) 46% of the legally blind are over the age of 65
3) 91% of the severely visually impaired are over the age of 45
4) 68% of the severely visually impaired are over the age of 65

The most recent estimates indicate there are 2 million adults over age 65 currently severely visually impaired, and that figure is projected to rise to 2.5 million by the year 2000 (Nelson, 1987). The chance of becoming visually impaired increases virtually exponentially as one ages, and severe visual impairment is found in approximately 25% of the U.S. population that is over age 85 (Nelson, 1987).

A second popular myth is that most people with a vision loss see nothing but blackness. Actually, approximately 80-90% of legally blind persons have usable sight. Visual characteristics, measured by Snellen acuities, can range from moderate loss to total blindness. With partial sight, one can experience predominantly central or predominantly peripheral field loss. An individual may suffer from night blindness, color blindness, decreased spatial contrast sensitivity, increased sensitivity to glare, or prolonged recovery from the effects of glare. Additionally, the extent of the problem created by a visual disorder depends not only on the nature and extent of the actual loss but also on the needs, aspirations, attitudes, and general physical abilities of the affected individual. That is, there is not a perfect positive correlation between the results of a physical sensory examination and a person's performance on perceptual tasks, nor is there a perfect positive correlation between these perceptual task results and the person's performance in various real-world settings. Individual differences in motivation, perceptual tracking skill, contrast sensitivity, and skills in perceptual estimations and risk taking all contribute to this variance.

The next myth in the media scenario deals with sex. Because the majority of people with visual impairments are older and the majority of older people are female, there are more women than men who are visually impaired. The concerns of an elderly woman with a visual impairment and little out-of-home vocational experience and income present several clinical (and assessment) challenges. Issues of safety, work role, and self-value, along with a high potential for additional, concomitant sensory disabilities, make the possibility of vision loss a frightening prospect. Many individuals rely on their sense of vision to maintain vigilance in a potentially hazardous environment, and the loss of this ability to control, anticipate, and react to the environment can be very detrimental, increasing feelings of learned helplessness.

A fourth common misconception relates to the use of guide dogs. While these dogs can have a profoundly positive impact on the lives of many visually impaired individuals, their use is not warranted or appropriate for the majority for several reasons. First, dogs require grooming, trips to the veterinarian, places to defecate, and several long walks per day. Many elderly people do not have the consistently good health that would allow such an undertaking. Secondly, guide dogs are useful for people who wish to travel rapidly and safely over long distances of familiar, learned terrain. It is a mistake to think that travel with a dog is "easier" or requires less thought and reaction time than cane travel. In fact, dog and owner work as a team and together perform tasks more quickly by relying on each other's strengths. For example, a dog can easily weave in and out of stationary and moving obstacles, avoid overhangs, and detect certain dangerous situations; however, it only knows the routes it has been taught and cannot respond to "Fifth and Main—and hurry!" Guide dogs have no color perception and rely on their owners to tell them (by the surge of traffic) when to step off a curb. Many elderly people have no need to travel at this pace and to this extent and, further, do not possess the physical or mental attributes necessary for the task. Guide dogs would not provide more useful information to most people who have residual sight, and they do require skilled masters who have been trained in their care and are committed to ongoing care and training. As a result, less than 1% of people with legal blindness utilize a guide dog.

The notion that most people with visual impairments are employed is a fifth myth. As previously noted, 68% of the visually impaired population is over 65. Of those between the ages of 18-65, approximately 70% are unemployed. Of those who are employed, only 25% have full-time jobs (Taylor, Kagay, & Leichenko, 1986). Many disincentives keep people with visual impairments unemployed, such as the lack of alternative affordable medical coverage and the long delays in reentering the Social Security system if they lose their job for any reason, including a reduction in sight. Many visually impaired workers are underemployed (based on skill and background) because they lack the vocational mobility of non-disabled individuals. Given the difficulty of securing employment, many people with a visual impairment opt to stay with one employer over considerable time in spite of dissatisfaction with pay or advancement.

Mobility and communication, the main challenges to people with visual impairment disorders, necessitate significant adaptation and commitment to achieve most vocational and avocational pursuits. Very few people with a visual impairment use braille (approximately 4%). While this and other labeling schemes are helpful to some, most people with adventitious sight loss rely on cassette tapes, large print, and other alternatives. Braille is cumbersome and difficult to master, and even expert users tend to be exceedingly slow (40-80 words a minute, without the ability to scan for information). Fancy technology such as talking computers, lasercanes, and reading machines is accessible and beneficial to a small subset of people with vision loss rather than the population in general. Thus most people with a visual impairment are also faced with economic disability. Few have adequate health insurance, and most live below the poverty line.

Another often-expressed stereotype is that of a "blind personality," typified by frequent depression, chronic adjustment problems related to the disability, and a higher incidence of suicide, substance abuse, and divorce. No study in the literature supports this stereotype. On the contrary, the literature shows that 1) adaptation to sight loss normally occurs without professional intervention and 2) few long-term differences are found between groups of visually impaired and unimpaired individuals on measures of life satisfaction (Shindell, Goodrich, & Dunn, 1986). Rehabilitation research (e.g., Brown, 1987) suggests that severe depression is a relatively infrequent phenomenon on rehabilitation wards, but one that is greatly overi-dentified by staff members, perhaps as a response to their own anxiety toward interacting with disabled people. Also, many studies have noted that adaptation to disability is not negatively correlated with the amount of disability (Kemp & Vash, 1971; Bauman, 1954; VanderKolk, 1987; Shindell, Muray, & Needham, 1987).

People with partial sight do not "have it easier" than those with little or no visual ability. The process of rehabilitation brings forth unique feelings and situations for the person with a partial sight loss, many related to having a hidden disability that may fluctuate or progress over time. Unlike incapacitating disabilities, low vision does not lend itself to an easy understanding or empathy from other people. Others may feel that the person thus impaired does not have a "real disability" or that he or she should feel "lucky" for not being totally blind. In fact, the individual coping with low vision may feel devalued, less in control of his or her own life, and uncomfort-able utilizing supports in either the fully sighted or blind arenas. This "marginal" status can cause significant stress and concern, and the person may consider the prospect of more visual loss with ambivalent feelings (Mehr & Mehr, 1969; Shin-dell, in press).

The preceding discussion has shown that a much more accurate portrayal of vision loss would involve an elderly, widowed female with adventitiously acquired and deteriorating partial sight due to age-related maculopathy, cataracts, or glau-coma, who spends most of her day within her home environment due to economic, communication, and/or mobility difficulties. In general, this person functions well psychologically, although she may rate her quality of life slightly lower than her peers. This slight decline in quality of life may be due to concomitant disabling condi-tions, such as economic decline, loss of customary societal roles, lack of security due to loss of medical insurance, and so forth. The assessment difficulties that this person presents will be covered in the remainder of the chapter.

GENERAL ASSESSMENT ENVIRONMENT AND EXAMINER CONSIDERATIONS

In any assessment situation, the competent psychologist relies on three main sets of information: the behavioral observations of the subject in the testing situation, the clinical interview, and the formal test scores derived from standardized tests. The clinician uses both formal and informal means to assess an individual's behavior and attitudes as compared to a reference group. Many behaviors unique to a person with visual impairment may cause confusion even for a seasoned clinician in assessing the frequency or "normalcy" of the behaviors in the person's reference group. For exam-ple, a visually impaired client may arrive several hours early for the assessment inter-view or may have very rigid requirements concerning its scheduling and length. Often this is more a function of coordinating available transportation than a sign of resistance.

Giving a visually impaired client general information about the nature of the assessment, the presence of other people in the room, and environmental data usually gathered through informal visual scanning is helpful. This kind of interchange allows the clinician both to differentiate a lack of knowledge of the situation from the per-son's normal behavior and to assess the client's social skills and assertiveness in exploring the environment. Such an approach signals that it is safe and appropriate to explore and ask questions, and thus it builds rapport.

As with all elderly individuals, those with visual impairments also may have other deficits, such as in hearing, and the clinician should ask about these problems before proceeding. In most cases, normal voice volume is adequate; persons with visual impairments often speak of annoying encounters in which it is assumed that because they have problems seeing they also must be hard of hearing. Although this is generally a misconception, it should not be discounted with older clients. First, as noted previously, elderly people in general are more likely to be hard of hearing. Second, 10-15% of auditory information comes from a combination of lipreading and visual cues, so often people with visual impairment complain of problems with auditory discrimination.

Some general rules in assessing people with visual impairment follow:

1) Don't assume that the person has a hearing impairment. Speak in a clear, normal tone of voice.

2) Always ask before rendering assistance.

3) To guide someone who is visually impaired, ask first, then place the person's hand on your arm just above the elbow (her right hand on your left arm or her left hand on your right arm). Take the lead and guide the person around obstacles, noting the presence and location of restrooms and stairs for emergencies. Walk in front, as if to lead, and don't push or pull. A person with a visual impairment does not "count steps"; rather, he or she develops a visual map based on auditory and kinesthetic cues. Define locations in terms of carpet changes, doorway openings, and so on.

4) To seat a person with a visual impairment, either guide his or her hand to the chair back or give an auditory cue, such as gently patting the chair seat. Don't push the person into the chair.

5) Explain any changes in environment. For example, tell the person if you are leaving the room, if you have refilled his or her coffee cup, and so on.

6) Inquire about the examinee's preferred means of communication. For example, if he or she is bilingual, establishing the language of preference (vis-à-vis the clinician's abilities, training, and usage of that language) is essential. Asking whether braille or large print is utilized, for how long, and with what proficiency, speed, and duration is crucial in determining the assessment vehicle. Ask how long it has been since the client has read print, because many language-based tasks, such as spelling, rapidly deteriorate with lack of use.

7) Ask the person to describe his or her vision (such as any idiosyncrasies that involve color, contrast, or field deficits) and to tell you if there is any problem with glare or lighting in the room.

8) Limit attempts at direction and encouragement to verbal or kinesthetic cuing. Nonverbal behavior is likely to be either misunderstood or missed entirely.

9) Feel free to use common expressions such as "I see what you are saying."

TEST SELECTION AND ADMINISTRATION

When assessing a person with visual impairment, consider carefully beforehand what is to be assessed. For example, if the question involves a client's suitability for occupations that require speed, visual scanning, and similar skills, preparing the testing materials to be presented only verbally is inappropriate. Similarly, if the presentation of materials in alternative forms is unwieldy, cumbersome, and creates fatigue in the examinee, the validity of using norms based on sighted subjects is questionable regardless of how closely the individual items match on the alternative presentation. Many individual items make no sense when translated into verbal form (e.g., describing several objects and asking an examinee to tell which ones are different).

The process of assessing someone with visual impairment goes beyond giving a test "translated" for their use. Rather, it requires the psychologist to examine the process that was used in developing each test, the types of items used to test each skill domain, the evidence that the items validly meet their intended purpose, and the populations on which norms have been based. Most often, no single, appropriate group exists for a given measure to which the visually impaired elderly person can be compared. In most cases the examiner must use a variety of normative samples based on age, vision loss, and other demographic characteristics as confidence intervals. Data from these various sources act as template overlays that define the boundaries in which the clinician could expect each individual population to perform.

Given these caveats, most tests appropriate for the non-visually impaired population can be administered to a portion of those with a visual impairment. For example, this author has administered instruments such as the Rorschach Inkblot Test to clients who were legally blind due to field restrictions but who, under special lighting conditions, were able to complete the task effectively. Further, numerous articles appear in the literature regarding appropriate tests to be used with people with visual disabilities (Bauman, 1973, 1974; Bauman & Kropf, 1979; Coveny, 1976; Klig & Perlman, 1976; Scholl & Schnur, 1976; Swallow, 1981). Clinicians are urged not to limit themselves to a specific group of tests for "the blind," but rather to assess each situation individually in order to determine what means will provide information useful to the referral question. Several categories of tests (intelligence, personality, etc.) either have norms reported for the blind and partially sighted population or have substantial numbers of non-visual or easily read items.

Intelligence Tests

When choosing an intelligence test for someone with a visual impairment, it is important to pay close attention to the appropriateness of individual test items as well as the generalizability of the normative group scores for the examinee at hand. Information regarding the norm group's visual functioning, the length of time since their visual impairment, and whether they acquired this impairment congenitally, within their formative years, or late in life is crucial in deciding the usefulness of the test. While differences have not been found between congenital and adventitiously blinded adults on measures of intelligence, it is important to realize that the experiencing of the environment can differ drastically for these two groups. For example, Smith (1987) describes a congenitally blind professional woman with advanced degrees who, having never flown before, made the assumption that airplanes flap their wings like birds to be come airborne because airplane flight has been explained to her as "flying like a bird." Similarly, Foulke and Uhde (1974) reported a case of a congenitally blind male who, after a sex education class, accurately described intercourse but thought that the vagina was located somewhere near the armpit. Individual gaps in learning need to be explored by the clinician in order to determine the effect of previous experience and learning on test performance.

The Wechsler Adult Intelligence Scale-Revised (WAIS-R) is a well-known multi-task intelligence test that has been normed on fully sighted individuals aged 16-74. Numerous studies have shown that, in general, the WAIS-R Verbal subtests are appropriate for the visually impaired population and the age-based norms given in the test manual are complete and appropriate for this use (VanderKolk, 1977; Smits & Mommers, 1976; Rich & Anderson, 1968; Jordan & Felty, 1968; Bauman & Kropf, 1979). Items #7 and #10 of the Comprehension subtest need to be given with additional instructions to have the person answer as if fully sighted. There is some evidence (Bauman & Kropf, 1979) that the variance is greater on Digit Span, but this may be due to external factors such as greater reliance on concentration and short-term memory or the negative effects of anxiety and environmental deprivation found in many of the hospitals and rehabilitation centers where the testing was undertaken. No significant differences have been found in Wechsler Verbal scores between adventitiously and congenitally blinded individuals (VanderKolk, 1982) or the partially sighted and totally blind (Jordan & Felty, 1968).

The administration of all of the WAIS-R Performance subtests is inappropriate for the general population of people with visual impairments. However, individual performance on any of the tasks may provide answers regarding the examinee's efficiency in using his or her remaining sight. Scores derived from these subtests are, of course, measurements of a completely different phenomenon and cannot be directly compared to the norms in the test manual. Alternative measures of Performance IQ (work samples, observation, etc.) have been used with some success in answering some diagnostic questions (Bauman, 1973, 1974; Rusalem, 1972), but normative information extends only up to age 74 and may not be as useful for the large number of elderly people past this age.

The Haptic Intelligence Scale for Adult Blind is a tactile performance test designed to mimic the Performance subtests of the WAIS and WAIS-R for people with no usable vision. Each of its six subtests (Digit Symbol, Block Design, Object Assembly, Object Completion, Pattern Board, Bead Arithmetic) parallels a WAIS Performance subtest and requires the subject to make tactile discriminations to discover relationships or to evaluate missing parts from the whole. The total test takes approximately 2 hours to administer and does not provide normative information for adults over age 64. Partially sighted subjects are blindfolded during the entire administration. Test-retest reliability coefficients for the sum of five of the six tests (Arithmetic was omitted) was .91. Split-half reliability was .95. The test is so similar to the WAIS that the clinician may be tempted to see it as a replacement for WAIS subtests that a visually impaired client is unable to perform. However, as the authors state in their manual,

> Any implication that the Haptic Intelligence Scale tests measure in the blind the same factors that the WAIS Performance tests measure in the sighted is not intended. They may or may not. It seems reasonable to suppose that the two scales do assess to some extent the same abilities, but to what extent can never be

determined with precision, for the blind cannot take the WAIS Performance Scale. (Shurrager & Shurrager, 1964, p.3)

The authors report a correlation of .65 between the Haptic Intelligence Scale and the WAIS Verbal scale. Streitfeld and Avery (1968) indicated in their study that the WAIS Verbal and the Haptic scales were equally good at predicting grades in totally blind children at a residential school, but the Haptic was less useful with partially sighted individuals of the same age. The normative data relate only to 700 subjects that have varying degrees of residual sight, experiences, and training (Shurrager, 1961; Shurrager & Shurrager, 1964). As stated by Jordan and Felty (1968) and Bauman (1974), the development of the Haptic Intelligence Scale is flawed by its lack of control over each of these variables as well as its inability to show cross-validity accurately with other measures. Although an interesting assessment device, used widely as a measure of intelligence in the field of visual impairment, the Haptic appears to have little direct utility for a clinician who only occasionally sees elderly visually impaired clients for assessment.

Originally developed in 1923 as a nonverbal measure of problem solving, the Kohs Block Design is familiar to most psychologists because one form of it is given in both the WAIS-R and in the Wechsler Intelligence Scale for Children-Revised. Ohwaki (1960) adapted this test for use with people with visual impairment. The blocks were originally covered with cloths of varying textures, but an adaptation by Suinn and Dauterman (1966) enlarged the blocks and replaced the cloth with two surfaces, smooth white and rough black. Subjects are blindfolded during administration, which takes approximately 40 to 80 minutes. The correlations between the two adaptations is .87 (Suinn & Dauterman, 1966). The authors report that test-retest reliability of the Stanford-Ohwaki-Kohs Block Design Test is .86, and norms are available for both blind and low vision clients above age 16. Unfortunately, no work has been done to test this instrument's ability to differentiate between various populations (e.g., brain injured vs. normal) to address whether it would have the same utility as the WAIS-R subtest. As with virtually all the tests used with visually impaired people, more research needs to be done, but the clinician may find this block design test useful in making gross assessments and observing problem-solving style.

Personality Tests

In many cases, the measurement of personality characteristics in clients with visual impairment is done by reading the test items aloud to the examinee or using audiotaped, large-print, or braille versions of existing tests. The examiner should be aware, however, that each of these methods will greatly extend the time needed to take the test, and thus tests should be chosen with care so as not to confuse or fatigue the client. Clients who are visually impaired cannot efficiently scan material, nor can they deal effectively with multiple-choice questions that require a great deal of mental comparisons and manipulations. They cannot scan their answers to determine patterns in a way that often influences fully sighted individuals. Lastly, there is always the concern that examinees may vary in their performance when an examiner is present recording their answers. Preliminary pilot data from McKinley (1987) indicate the potential for subjects to present themselves in a more positive light when given the

Profile of Mood States by a reader rather than in written form or by computer-generated synthetic speech. Adrian, Miller, and Del'Aune (1982) found similar findings using the California Psychological Inventory.

Research by Cross (1947), Klimasinski (1972), and Adrian et al. (1982) indicates success in adapting the Minnesota Multiphasic Personality Inventory (MMPI) for subjects who are visually impaired. However, their study shows that elevations on many of the scaled scores may reflect adaptive processes of persons who experience visual impairment rather than individual pathology. Each of these samples utilized either a specifically congenitally blind sample or an unreported mixture of congenitally and adventitiously blinded individuals. These two groups have drastically different experiences both from each other as well as the general population, and it is not unrealistic to postulate that variance would be found in MMPI scores. This does not suggest a "blind personality"; rather, it indicates that the experiences of people with visual impairment are often dissimilar to the average population. Given this situation, the clinician should be conservative in drawing conclusions from individual personality test data.

While space does not allow a review of the other common psychological tests adapted for use with people with visual impairment, a partial list includes the Sixteen Personality Factor Questionnaire (Jones, 1983); Adjective Check List (Domino, 1968); California Psychological Inventory (Adrian et al., 1982; Bast, 1971; Hayes, 1949; Sommers, 1944); Taylor Manifest Anxiety Scale (Hardy, 1966, 1968a; Weiner, 1967); MMPI (Adrian et al., 1982; Cross, 1947; Klimasinski, 1972); and Rotter Incomplete Sentences Blank (Dean, 1968).

The personality tests that have been designed specifically for people with visual impairment can be organized into two groups: measures of general personality and measures of adaptation to visual impairment. As with intelligence tests for this population, most measures of personality designed for people with visual impairment are attempts to develop analogous forms of existing tests used with people who have full vision. An example of this is the Auditory Apperception Test (Ball & Bernadoni, 1953), in which the subject is given 10 sets of sound situations (a train crash, a typewriter, wind, etc.) and asked to make up a story. While this is an interesting process, it is not currently used in the field of visual impairment due to the lack of appropriate norms. Similarly, tests such as the Auditory Projective Test (Braverman & Chevigny, 1955, 1964), the Bas-Relief Projective Test (Harris, 1948), the Draw-A-Person Test (Chase & Rapaport, 1968), the Smith-Madan Projective Test (Smith & Madan, 1953), the Sound Test (Palacios, 1964), and the Twitchell-Allen Three Dimensional Apperception Test (Twitchell-Allen, 1947) all enjoy the same disuse, supporting the notion that the biggest limitation to projective testing in people with visual impairment is not investigator creativity. Rather, it is the fact that the visually impaired population is small but very heterogeneous, making it extremely difficult to simply "translate" a test into another sensory mode and expect it to assess the same phenomena.

Tests involving the assessment of adaptation and adjustment to visual impairment come in many forms. The 43-item Teare Sentence Completion Test (Teare, 1966) presents incomplete sentences related to problem areas associated with blindness. These include relationships, individual adjustment, and reactions toward becoming visually impaired. It is a face valid scale that is easily administered and interpreted by the clinician. However, no norms exist concerning its interpretation.

The Belief About Blindness Scale (Ehmer & Needham, 1979) is a 40-item instrument that expresses irrational and limiting beliefs about blindness in a 5-point Likert-scale format. These belief statements are either frankly erroneous or inconsistent with the survival value or happiness of the person maintaining them. This is an empirically derived scale that has been given both to people with visual impairment as well as to professionals in the field of blind rehabilitation. It has been shown that scores on the Belief About Blindness Scale correspond to staff ratings of improvement in patients involved in rehabilitation (Needham & Ehmer, 1980), and significant differences were found between various health and rehabilitation care professionals (Ehmer, Needham, Del'Aune, & Carr, 1982; Shindell et al., 1987). The scale is easily administered within 10 minutes and yields specific information about the person's attitude toward visual impairment. Normative information is available both for people entering rehabilitation and upon its completion as well as for samples of various occupational groups. The Belief About Blindness Scale is appropriate for adults of any age, although norms based on age are not provided.

The Anxiety Scale for the Blind (Hardy, 1966, 1967, 1968a, 1968b), which is similar to the Taylor Manifest Anxiety Scale (Hardy, 1968a), consists of 78 true/false items judged a priori by psychologists to be symptoms of anxiety in people with visual impairment. Norms are available for high school age individuals only; however, the scale's content and format make it applicable for other contexts, and the clinician should not hesitate using it qualitatively to derive useful information.

The Emotional Factors Inventory (Bauman, 1950, 1968) measures attitudes (such as distrust), sensitivity, somatic symptoms, and depression in visually impaired subjects. This measure consists of 170 true/false items and yields a total of eight scales, including a validation scale. The normative sample comprises totally blind and partially sighted individuals (males and females, age range unspecified).

Neuropsychological Tests

The ability to administer neuropsychological tests to older people who are visually impaired is of critical importance, yet it unfortunately has not received the scientific attention and study it deserves. Few studies exist in the literature regarding the use of neuropsychological tests with this population; most often, tests with norms derived from fully sighted populations are administered. Further, a phenomenon important to people with visual impairment but rarely addressed in neuropsychological batteries is the ability to utilize mental imagery in problem solving.

To confound matters, older people are more prone to auditory and tactile decrements that can influence neuropsychological test data obtained through these channels, so redundancy of test characteristics applied through a variety of perceptual channels is of critical importance in any measure selected. Thus, the Roughness Discrimination Test (Nolan & Morris, 1965), for example, originally developed to predict success in ninth-grade blind children at reading braille, is useful for determining whether tactile sensitivity will present a problem. Similarly, a complete audiological examination will address whether auditory impairment could influence test results.

The clinician thus is faced with a severe deficit in his or her library of available tests and instruments and must proceed cautiously to address the referral question, using a multitude of measures developed for fully sighted persons combined with astute behavioral observations. Unfortunately, many longstanding skill deficits may become evidenced only after sight loss. For example, a person who has always had a very poor auditory memory may have compensated for this by outstanding visual memory and imagery. After the onset of a visual impairment, he or she is left with no outlet for the positive skills and, hence, must rely on an undeveloped auditory memory. This person may appear to have deteriorated suddenly, behaviorally as well as on standardized measures, when in fact his or her cognitive abilities have not significantly changed. Neuropsychological assessment of people with visual impairments thus should include some measurement of their imagery skills so as to address some of these issues.

Measures such as the Wechsler Memory Scale (Wechsler, 1945; Loring & Papanicolaou, 1987) and the Rey Auditory Verbal Learning Test (Rey, 1964) offer some data about general memory and concentration but fall short of providing a comprehensive picture of the pattern of results necessary to make a clear neuropsychological assessment. Many of the subtests of the Halstead-Reitan Neuropsychological Test Battery—Tactual Performance Test, Finger Tapping Test, WAIS-R Verbal subtests, Strength of Grip Test, Reitan-Klove Sensation-Perceptual Examination (Reitan & Davison, 1974)—are directly applicable to the blind and partially sighted population, but unfortunately yield little data concerning significant brain-related tasks, such as cognitive reasoning, sequential analysis, and complex problem solving. In addition, many tasks specific to spatial awareness are inadequately addressed in this model. Some success can be found in giving untimed complex tasks such as the Category Test or the Wisconsin Card Sorting Test (Grant & Berg, 1948) to people with enough remaining sight to observe all the items accurately, but a low score on this test may point to one of several problems, including difficulty in complex problem solving and abstract reasoning and/or difficulty in accurately scanning and discriminating the figures.

The Stanford Multi-Modality Imagery Test (Dauterman, 1970) measures a subject's success in tactile, kinesthetic, and verbal modes. Of special interest is that this test is divided into three parts, the first two being learning phases designed to compensate for the prior learning that some visually impaired people may have acquired. Norms involved over 200 legally blind adults and children who had been blind a minimum of 1 year. Concurrent validity with the Stanford-Ohwaki-Kohs Block Design was .62; however, no studies have been undertaken to develop validity evidence based on other test data or behavioral measures. Although age norms have not been developed for the elderly, the ability to use mental imagery may be a significant portion of the variance seen in the performance of many visually impaired elderly people when administered neuropsychological tests.

CONCLUSION

In this overview of assessment of an older adult with visual impairment, it becomes clear that there are no easy answers to the multitude of problems facing the average clinician. Having few tests specifically designed to address the assessment needs of this population as well as a short supply of appropriate normative data bases for tests one must adapt, the clinician is forced to collect data from a variety of comparable sources so as to best estimate an examinee's abilities. As this population is expected to grow dramatically, specialized testing materials need to be developed for all spheres of psychological assessment. It is hoped that future research will offer assistance to clinicians in answering the pressing needs within this setting.

REFERENCES

Adrian, R.J., Miller, L.R., & Del'Aune, W.R. (1982). Personality assessment of early visually impaired persons using the CPI and MMPI. *Journal of Visual Impairment and Blindness, 76*(5), 172-178.

Ball, T.S., & Bernadoni, L.C. (1953). The application of an auditory apperception test to clinical diagnosis. *Journal of Clinical Psychology, 9,* 54-58.

Bast, B. (1971). A predictive study of employability among the visually impaired with the California Psychological Inventory. *Dissertation Abstracts International, 32,* 1817B-1818B.

Bauman, M.K. (1950). A comparative study of personality factors in blind, other handicapped, and non-handicapped individuals. *American Psychologist, 5*(7), 340-341.

Bauman, M.K. (1954). *Adjustment to blindness: A study reported by the Committee to Study Adjustment to Blindness.* Harrisburg, PA: State Council for the Blind.

Bauman, M.K. (1968). *A report and a reprint: Tests used in the psychological evaluation of blind and visually handicapped persons and a manual for norms for tests used in counseling blind persons.* Washington, DC: American Association of Workers for the Blind.

Bauman, M.K. (1973). An interest inventory for the visually handicapped. *Education of the Visually Handicapped, 3*(10), 78-83.

Bauman, M.K. (1974). Blind and partially sighted. In M. Wisland (Ed.), *Psychoeducational diagnosis of exceptional children* (pp. 159-189). Springfield, IL: Charles C. Thomas.

Bauman, M.K., & Kropf, C.A. (1979). Psychological tests used with blind and visually handicapped persons. *School Psychology Digest, 8*(3), 257-270.

Braverman, S., & Chevigny, H. (1955). *The Auditory Projective Test.* New York: American Foundation for the Blind.

Braverman, S., & Chevigny, H. (1964). *The Braverman-Chevigny Auditory Projective Test: A provisional manual.* New York: American Foundation for the Blind.

Brown, J.C. (1987, November). *Validity of the Beck Depression Inventory and other tests with the SCI population.* Paper presented at the conference of the American Association of SCI Psychologists and Social Workers, Las Vegas.

Chase, J.B., & Rapaport, I.N. (1968). A verbal adaptation of the draw-a-person techniques for use with blind subjects: A preliminary report. *International Journal of Education for the Blind, 18*(12), 113-115.

Coveny, T.E. (1976). Standardized tests for visually handicapped children: A review of research. *The New Outlook for the Blind, 70*(6), 232-236.

Cross, O.H. (1947). Brailled edition of the Minnesota Multiphasic Personality Inventory for use with the blind. *Journal of Applied Psychology, 31,* 189-198.

Dauterman, W.L. (1970). *Manual for the Stanford Multi-Modality Imagery Test.* New York: American Foundation for the Blind.

Dean, S.I. (1968). Some experimental findings about blind adjustment. *The New Outlook for the Blind, 62*(5), 182-185.

Domino, G. (1968). A nonverbal measure of intelligence for the totally blind adults. *The New Outlook for the Blind, 62*(8), 247-252.

Ehmer, M.N., & Needham, W.E. (1979). *The Beliefs About Blindness Scale.* New Haven, CT: Authors.

Ehmer, M.N., Needham, W.E., Del'Aune, W.R., & Carr, R.B. (1982, April). *Experience, expertise, and expectation: Three important factors influencing beliefs about blindness.* Paper presented at the Annual Meeting of the Eastern Psychological Association, Baltimore.

Foulke, E., & Uhde, T. (1974). Do blind children need sex education? *The New Outlook for the Blind, 68*(5), 193-200, 209.

Freedman, S. (1975). The assessment of older visually impaired adults by a psychologist. *Journal of Visual Impairment and Blindness, 69,* 361-364.

Grant, D.A., & Berg, E.A. (1948). A behavioural analysis of degree of reinforcement and ease of shifting to new responses in a Weigl-type card sorting problem. *Journal of Experimental Psychology, 38,* 404-411.

Hardy, R.E. (1966). A study of manifest anxiety among blind residential school students using an experimental instrument constructed for the blind. *Dissertations Abstracts, 27,* 3693.

Hardy, R.E. (1967). Prediction of manifest anxiety levels of blind persons through the use of a multiple regression technique. *International Journal of Education of the Blind, 17,* 51-55.

Hardy, R.E. (1968a). A study of manifest anxiety among blind residential school students. *The New Outlook for the Blind, 62,* 173-180.

Hardy, R.E. (1968b). *The Anxiety Scale for the Blind.* New York: American Foundation for the Blind.

Harris, W.W. (1948). A bas-relief projective technique. *Journal of Psychology, 26,* 3-17.

Hayes, S.P. (1949). What mental tests shall we use? *The New Outlook for the Blind, 43,* 271-279.

Jones, W.P. (1983). Measurement of personality traits of the visually limited. *Education of the Visually Handicapped, 15*(1), 12-19.

Jordan, J.E., & Felty, J. (1968). Factors associated with intellectual variation among visually impaired children. *Research Bulletin of the American Foundation for the Blind, 15,* 61-70.

Kemp, B., & Vash, C. (1971). Productivity after injury in a sample of spinal cord injured persons: A pilot study. *Journal of Chronic Disease, 24,* 259-275.

Klig, S., & Perlman, S. (1976). *The assessment of children with sensory impairments: A selected bibliography.* Washington, DC: Bureau of Education for the Handicapped.

Klimasinski, K. (1972). An attempt to test the personality of the blind using the MMPI. *Research Bulletin of the American Foundation for the Blind, 24,* 65-74.

Loring, D.W., & Papanicolaou, A. (1987). Memory assessment in neuropsychology: Theoretical considerations and practical utility. *Journal of Clinical and Experimental Neuropsychology, 9*(4), 340-358.

Lowman, C., & Kirchner, C. (1979). Elderly blind and visually impaired persons: Projected numbers in the year 2000. *Journal of Visual Impairment and Blindness, 73*(2), 69-73.

McKinley, J. (1987). *The administration of the Profile of Mood States (POMS) via synthetic speech, written, and oral forms.* Unpublished manuscript, Palo Alto VA Medical Center.

Mehr, E.B., & Mehr, H.M. (1969). Psychological factors in working with partially sighted persons. *Journal of the American Optometric Association, 40*(8), 842-846.

Needham, W.E., & Ehmer, M.N. (1980). Irrational thinking and adjustment to loss of vision. *Journal of Visual Impairment and Blindness, 74,* 57-61.

Nelson, K. A. (1987). Visual impairment among elderly Americans: Statistics in transition. *Journal of Visual Impairment and Blindness, 81*(7), 331-334.

Nolan, C.Y., & Morris, J.E. (1965). *Roughness Discrimination Test manual.* Lafayette, IN: Purdue Research Foundation.

Ohwaki, Y. (1960). *Manual of the Ohwaki-Kohs Tactile Block Design Intelligence Test for the Blind.* Tokyo, Japan: Ohwaki Institute of Child Psychology.

Palacios, M.H. (1964). Auditory perception and personality patterns of blind adults. *Journal of Projective Techniques and Personality Assessment, 28*(3), 284-294.

Reitan, R.M., & Davison, L.A. (1974). *Clinical neuropsychology: Current status and applications.* New York: Hemisphere.

Rey, A. (1964). *L'examen clinique en psychologie.* Paris: Presses Universitaires de France.

Rich, C.C., & Anderson, R.P. (1968). A tactile form of the Progressive Matrices for use with blind children. *Research Bulletin of the American Foundation for the Blind, 15,* 49-60.

Rusalem, H. (1972). *Coping with the unseen environment.* New York: Teacher's College Press.

Scholl, G., & Schnur, R. (1976). *Measures of psychological, vocational, and educational functioning in the blind and visually handicapped.* New York: American Foundation for the Blind.

Sherman, S.W., & Robinson, N.M. (Eds.). (1982). *Ability testing of handicapped people: Dilemma for government, science, and the public.* Washington, DC: National Academy Press.

Shindell, S. (in press). Psychological sequelae to diabetic retinopathy. *Journal of the American Optometric Association.*

Shindell, S., Goodrich, G.L., & Dunn, M. (1986). Development of a life satisfaction scale applicable for people with severe disabilities. *Rehabilitation R&D Progress Reports, 22*(4), 341-342.

Shindell, S., Muray, L., & Needham, W.E. (1987, April). *Beliefs about blindness among various types of health care professionals.* Paper presented at the Annual Meeting of the Eastern Psychological Association, Arlington, VA.

Shurrager, H.C. (1961). *Haptic Intelligence Scale for Adult Blind.* Chicago: Psychology Research Technology Center, Illinois Institute of Technology.

Shurrager, H.C., & Shurrager, P.S. (1964). *Manual for the Haptic Intelligence Scale for Adult Blind.* Chicago: Psychology Research Technology Center, Illinois Institute of Technology.

Smith, A. (1987, August). *Training perceptual strategies in patients with visual loss.* Paper presented at the Annual Meeting of the American Psychological Association, New York.

Smith, F.V., & Madan, S. (1953). A projective technique based on the kinesthetic and tactile modalities. *British Journal of Psychology, 44,* 156-163.

Smits, B.W.G.M., & Mommers, M.J.C. (1976). Differences between blind and sighted children on WISC Verbal subtests. *The New Outlook for the Blind, 70,* 240-246.

Sommers, V.S. (1944). *The influence of parental attitudes and social environment on the personality development of the adolescent blind.* New York: American Foundation for the Blind.

Streitfeld, J.W., & Avery, C.D. (1968). The WAIS and HIS tests as predictors of academic achievement in a residential school for the blind. *International Journal of Education of the Blind, 18,* 73-77.

Suinn, R.M., & Dauterman, W.L. (1966). *Manual for the Stanford-Kohs Block Design Test for the Blind.* Washington, DC: Vocational Rehabilitation Administration, Department of Health, Education, & Welfare.

Swallow, R.M. (1981). Fifty assessment instruments commonly used with blind and partially seeing individuals. *Journal of Visual Impairment and Blindness, 75*(2), 65-72.

Taylor, H., Kagay, M.R., & Leichenko, S. (1986). *The ICD survey of disabled Americans: Bringing disabled Americans into the mainstream.* New York: Louis Harris & Assoc.

Teare, R.J. (1966). *The Sentence Completion Test (SC) manual.* McLean, VA: Champion.

Twitchell-Allen, D. (1947). A three-dimensional apperception test: A new projective technique. *American Psychologist, 2,* 271-272.

VanderKolk, C.J. (1977). Intelligence testing for visually impaired persons. *Journal of Visual Impairment and Blindness, 71*(4), 158-163.

VanderKolk, C.J. (1982). A comparison of intelligence test score patterns between visually impaired subgroups and the sighted. *Rehabilitation Psychology, 27*(2), 115-120.

VanderKolk, C.J. (1987). Psychosocial assessment of visually impaired persons. In B. Heller, L. Flohr, & L. Zegans (Eds.), *Psychosocial interventions with sensorially disabled persons.* New York: Grune & Stratton.

Wechsler, D. (1945). A standardized memory scale for clinical use. *Journal of Psychology, 19,* 87-95.

Weiner, B. (1967). A new outlook on assessment. *The New Outlook for the Blind, 61,* 73-78.

9

Assessment of Persons with Hearing Disabilities

McCAY VERNON, PH.D.D.

Hearing deficit is the most prevalent chronic health problem in most scientifically advanced countries of the world, affecting about 1 in 15 people in the U.S. (Schein & Delk, 1974; Vernon, Griffin, & Yoken, 1981). More people suffer from this medical problem than from heart disease, blindness, cancer, tuberculosis, venereal disease, and multiple sclerosis combined. When looking at the elderly population, the prevalence of hearing loss is, of course, even greater than for the population as a whole. Figure 1 shows average hearing loss at different ages; one in every three or four persons over 60 has a significant hearing problem, and the rate is higher for men than

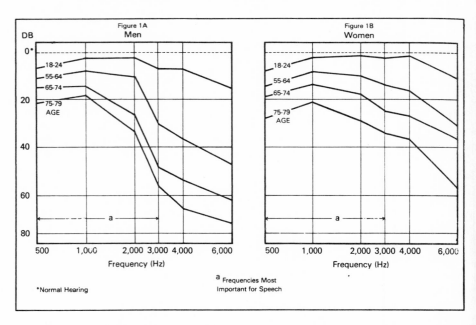

FIGURE 1. Hearing levels by age group. (From Vernon, Griffin, & Yoken, 1981. Copyright 1981 by Appleton & Lange. Reproduced by permission.)

for women (Foster, 1987). It is both sad and astonishing that despite the pervasiveness of hearing loss in the elderly, books on their treatment and care almost never mention it. When hearing loss *is* mentioned, often nothing is said about its implications for the elderly person or what can be done to help him or her.

HEARING LOSS AND AGING

A human being is born with all of the neurons for hearing that he or she will ever have (Marshall, 1981). In other words, from the moment after birth when the newborn hears him- or herself cry, there is a gradual loss of the neurological cells needed for hearing (Marshall, 1981). Children and adolescents can hear a wider range of pitches than adults. They can also hear softer sounds. The teenager who cannot grasp an older parent's difficulty in understanding the lyrics of a rock-and-roll singer exemplifies this overall problem (Foster, 1987). As a human being ages past 44, each decade doubles the probability that a significant hearing loss will emerge (Marshall, 1981). Thus, many people are stricken during the prime years of their careers. This is especially true of professional people because their most productive periods usually occur at an older age than those of the tradesperson or laborer. Hearing loss has tremendous impact on the quality of the lives of elderly people and on their effectiveness as human beings (Vernon, 1984), but little definitive information exists on this impact, how to ameliorate it, or how to treat it.

The kinds of hearing losses most older people have make it especially difficult for them to hear under adverse auditory conditions. For example, when the amount of background noise increases, older hearing-impaired people are disproportionately affected; that is, they have far greater difficulty distinguishing speech sounds from the background noises (Milne, 1977). Technically known as a problem of signal-to-noise ratio or as a figure-ground problem, this phenomenon affects us all to varying degrees. Even those with perfect hearing cannot converse during a rock concert. However, for the hearing-impaired older individual, the presence of relatively low volume background sounds can completely mask the understanding of speech sounds. This is especially true if the hearing loss is sensorineural and if hearing aids are being used. Thus, in crowds, churches, movies, cafeterias, meetings, at parties, or in most places where people gather socially, elderly hearing-impaired individuals are lost; they cannot understand what is being said. Decreased pitch perception is also characteristic of hearing loss in older adults (Milne, 1977). This is related to the figure-ground problem in general and specifically impairs response to music.

A psychologist engaged in assessing older adults should be familiar with the symptoms of hearing loss: 1) tinnitus or history of ear infections; 2) sounds can be heard, but not understood (e.g., *pin* mistaken for *tin, watch* mistaken for *wash*); 3) social withdrawal; 4) asking people to repeat, then blaming them for poor articulation; 5) loud speech; 6) inability to understand in group or social situations, that is, to make figure(speaker's voice)-ground (background sounds) distinctions; 7) turning television and radio up loud; and 8) watching speaker's mouth intently and/or putting on glasses to converse (unconscious dependence on lipreading). In many forms of hearing loss associated with aging, the site of the lesion causing the auditory defect is unknown, as is the role played by other aspects of the aging process on speech discrimination and hearing loss. Thus, the potential for serious psychological implications is obvious.

PSYCHOLOGICAL IMPLICATIONS

Because hearing loss is invisible (i.e., people do not see the handicap), hard-of-hearing or deaf persons tend to get very little understanding or sympathy. The public is inclined to blame them for their problems rather than expressing concern and compassion (Vernon, 1984). Comments such as "She can hear when she wants to," "He doesn't pay attention," or "Grandmother is just stubborn" show the tendency to blame the hard-of-hearing person, not the hearing loss, for communication difficulties that arise. Typically, with blame comes anger and hostility.

Among psychological implications of hearing loss is a reduction of options for leisure activities. Religious services may become frustrating due to difficulty in understanding the speakers. Television may have to be played so loudly that others complain and the set must be turned off. Parties, general socializing, hobbies, and almost every facet of life are affected. Hearing loss also reduces one's ability to identify danger and leads to generalized feelings of insecurity, which may contribute to the aforementioned problem of paranoid reactions. Overall, these psychological implications have a traumatic, chronic, insidious impact on the quality of human life and on mental health and survival; thus, a psychologist cannot afford to ignore hearing loss in the care of elderly people, especially in psychodiagnostic evaluation.

Isolation

Hearing loss isolates a person by reducing interpersonal interactions. The individual who does not hear well finds social interaction stressful (Vernon, 1984). It is exhausting to have to strain to understand every word spoken. It is embarrassing to say the wrong thing or continually ask others to repeat. Most important of all, friends start rejecting the hearing-impaired person, to avoid having to shout and repeat as part of every conversation. Of course, the entire problem of isolation is compounded by the difficulty elderly people have in understanding speech in an environment that includes noisy background or crowds. The end result of all of this is a social withdrawal by the hearing-impaired person coupled with a rejection by others—isolation. This is a problem of major psychological significance.

Depression

Because hearing loss severely isolates elderly people, it contributes significantly to the 15% depression rate found in this population (Solomon, 1982). With 30-60% of elderly people at risk for depression and two thirds of the hospitalizations of elderly people related to depression, the diagnosis and treatment of hearing loss assumes obvious importance (Solomon, 1982). This is especially true with paranoid depressions.

Dementias

In problems of dementia as well as pseudodementia in the elderly, hearing loss assumes major importance. For example, this loss, especially when chronic and of early onset, can lead to the misdiagnosis of dementia when the actual problem is one of communication, not mental retardation (Mindel & Vernon, 1987). The interaction effects of the three major "softening dementias" (Alzheimer's, the Guam form of Parkinson's, and multi-infarct syndrome) on hearing loss and vice versa are not yet fully understood. Regardless, it is important in psychological testing to pick up the behavioral symptoms of these kinds of conditions and to make appropriate referrals.

Cognitive Input

One of the most obvious effects of hearing loss is reduced cognitive input (Drachman & Sahakian, 1980). Hearing-impaired individuals are denied information. They cannot understand their peers. Television, radio, lectures, and almost all of the ways we learn, except for reading, are denied or reduced by hearing loss. This lack of information input may be a major factor in the broadly defined intellectual decline that apparently occurs as a function of aging.

Paranoid Reaction

A person who cannot hear well tends to misinterpret communication. When this occurs in someone who is somewhat suspicious anyway, the end result can be a rather pronounced paranoid-type reaction often seen in conjunction with depression (Zimbardo & Anderson, 1981).

Denial

There are some psychological aspects of hearing loss that make it extremely difficult to diagnose in adults. First, the average person with a significant hearing loss goes for 5 years before ever seeking help or reporting it to his or her physician (Vernon et al., 1981). There is an intense psychological need to deny the problem, which has to do, in part, with denial of the aging process itself, for which a hearing aid is seen as symbolic. Another factor that impedes diagnosis is the aforementioned invisibility of deafness. Sensorineural deafness cannot be seen even by a doctor who looks into the ear, and if only routine diagnostic techniques are used, even middle-ear conditions are often invisible and undiagnosable.

Thus, the psychologist is frequently oblivious to the hearing loss and proceeds as if it did not exist (Sullivan & Vernon, 1979), the results of which can be disastrous for the patient—IQs 20 or more points below that which validly reflects the individual's intelligence, misdiagnoses of mental disorders, and other invalid psychodiagnostic findings (Vernon & Ottinger, 1981). The point is that with older patients, the psychologist must be alert to the possible existence of a hearing deficit even if denied or not mentioned by the patient.

CAUSES OF HEARING LOSS IN THE ELDERLY

In general, the value of knowing the etiology of a hearing loss is that these data can alert a psychologist to the presence of cognitive defects due to brain damage. In some cases, knowing the cause of the auditory deficit can give clues to the specific location of central nervous system lesions and related behavioral manifestations (Vernon, 1988). Thus, identifying these factors is fundamental to comprehensive psychodiagnostics.

Presbycusis

Presbycusis (loss of hearing associated with aging) is the most common cause of hearing loss in the elderly (Gordon-Salant, 1987). However, the exact pathological changes involved in this condition are not well known. For example, some authorities argue that presbycusis has a large genetic component, but there are few data to prove or disprove this (Ruben, 1981). In general, the condition takes one of four forms or some combinations therein (Foster, 1987; Gordon-Salant, 1987): 1) a conductive hearing loss due to aging of tissue of the middle ear; 2) a loss of sensory units in the basal turn (cochlea); 3) a chemical or metabolic abnormality following changes in the vascular system; or 4) a loss of neurons in the central nervous system. In the latter two forms of presbycusis, one could expect other psychological processes to be involved as well. Comprehensive psychological testing is needed to detect and describe these processes and related behaviors when they are present. For example, if a hearing deficit is due to blocking of the vascular system occurring during bypass surgery, the psychologist should be alert to other manifestations of anoxia such as memory loss.

Drugs and Allergens

Certain antibiotics (e.g., kanamycin or neomycin) and medicines such as aspirin and quinine termed *ototoxic* can cause deafness (Goin, 1976). Alcohol, tobacco, and carbon monoxide are known to result in hearing loss, as are some diuretics, such as ethaconic acid (Vernon & Andrews, in press). As with presbycusis, some of these ototoxic substances also increase the probability of brain damage and related behavioral changes when used in sufficient excess to cause hearing loss.

Circulatory Disorders

Although poor circulation is infrequently mentioned as a cause of hearing loss, it is used to explain some cases of Ménière's disease and some sudden onset of deafness (Foster, 1987). Circulatory disorders may be a part of a pervasive problem such as arteriosclerosis, which may have degenerative effects on brain function.

Noise

Noise primarily damages the hearing for high frequency tones. Such losses are often work related. Rock musicians, heavy equipment operators, boilermakers, pilots, and others whose occupations expose them to loud noises for extended periods of time are often hearing impaired by middle or old age (Vernon & Andrews, in press). A history that includes such an occupation should alert a psychologist to the possibility of hearing loss.

Central Organic Impairments

Acoustic neuromas, cardiovascular accidents, syphilis, multiple sclerosis, Alzheimer's disease, and an entire host of diseases and other traumas can cause brain damage (Vernon & Andrews, in press). In many cases the processing of auditory information is affected. Thus, the psychological evaluation must take into account multiple factors, and when the condition is progressive, re-evaluations should be scheduled to check changes over time.

MAJOR GROUPINGS OF OLDER HEARING-IMPAIRED PEOPLE

It is helpful for psychologists to know that there are groupings (i.e., early and late onset) of older hearing-impaired people. Familiarity with these groupings will help to determine, in large part, which tests are appropriate and which means of communication should be used.

Congenital and Early Onset

Deaf persons in this group are born without sufficient hearing to understand speech or have lost their hearing before having learned language (by approximately 3 years of age). In considering the needs of hearing-impaired examinees, it is the pre-lingually deafened client who is likely to be the greatest challenge to the psychologist. In fact, psychologists who rarely see early-onset deaf clients generally feel lost when called upon to provide psychological testing services for them. This reaction is understandable—it reflects an honest, realistic sensitivity to the situation and to the complexity of this kind of deafness. Without a knowledge of the psychological, educational, communicational, and vocational ramifications of profound hearing loss, plus an understanding of the techniques with which to address them, professionals often are unable to do full justice to deaf clients. Although early-onset deafness is rare, the task of evaluating such persons is extremely complex. Sign language is often crucially important.

Late Onset

By far the largest number of hearing-impaired people are those who are hard of hearing or deaf as a consequence of the aging process (Marshall, 1981). These individuals have functioned most of their lives with normal hearing and are now experiencing an increasing difficulty in understanding conversational speech, television, group discussions, church sermons, and, in general, the speech of social and professional interaction. For example, 52-year-old Mr. "A," suffering from a progressive hearing loss, came to a psychologist to ask for help. After years of successful business experience, he had reached a position of prominence. He sat on the boards of several major corporations, headed key civic organizations, and was the president of his own company. Mr. "A" saw all of this slipping away and a lifetime of striving wasted. In addition to a thorough psychological evaluation, he needed extensive services to cope with what must become a fundamentally different life-style. His situation illustrates the seriousness of a late onset hearing loss.

With this population there are three key issues in psychological testing. The first is to maximize the client's ability to understand oral communication via techniques such as the following:

1) Do psychological testing in a quiet setting. Background noises are the worst of all blocks to the hard-of-hearing person's understanding of speech.

2) Be sure there is good lighting on your (the speaker's) face. The worst situation is a window behind you or any shadow on your face.

3) Face the client and speak slowly and distinctly. Do not over-exaggerate your mouth movements.

4) When it is necessary to repeat, try to rephrase the concept being expressed.

5) Position yourself close to the patient.

6) If possible, provide the test questions in writing as well as orally. For example, in administering the Wechsler Adult Intelligence Scale-Revised (WAIS-R) to hard-of-hearing patients, it is helpful to have the questions and directions typed on individual index cards.

7) If communication breaks down, feel free to write out key words or sentences.

8) Assistive devices such as audio loops, F.M. listening aids, amplifiers, and so on should be used if available and desired by the patient.

9) Be patient. If the client does not understand, help him or her by writing, speaking slower, and so on. Do not show anger or frustration; the client cannot help being hard of hearing.

10) Take frequent breaks. It is a stressful, demanding task for an older hearing-impaired person to lipread a psychologist for an entire psychological evaluation.

While techniques such as these help, the psychologist must be especially perceptive in detecting a breakdown in communication. Hearing-impaired people are masters at concealing the fact that they do not understand. Intuitively they become skilled users of the neutral response (pseudo-Rogerian therapists), smiling rather than answering, nodding, giving vague responses, and in general conveying understanding when none has taken place. This is a natural effort on their part not to appear stupid, to conceal their hearing loss, and to reduce the frustration of the person speaking. Unfortunately, people, psychologists included, are often sufficiently egocentric to misinterpret head nods, "hmmms," yeses, and related efforts at hiding a failure to hear as evidence of their own wisdom rather than as attempts to convey understanding when none has taken place. It is surprising how often the result is a total breakdown of communication. Even worse, gross psychological misdiagnoses are a frequent consequence.

The second issue with late-onset hearing impairment relates to neuropsychological testing. Because sensorineural hearing loss is often associated with other neurological dysfunctions, the psychologist must be especially sensitive to the presence of these other problems (Vernon, 1988). Full neuropsychological evaluations cannot and should not be done on all older hearing-impaired patients. However, complete medical histories, astute clinical observation, and careful interpretation of WAIS-R subtests, Bender Visual Motor Gestalt protocols (including recall of designs), and other commonly used psychological tests can aid in detecting the possibility of organic brain syndromes and degenerative neurological disorders. Appropriate referrals and/or neuropsychological testing can follow.

Finally, psychologists will find that almost none of those who lose their hearing late in life use sign language or fingerspelling. Thus, these skills have no applicability.

GENERAL PRINCIPLES FOR PSYCHOLOGICAL EVALUATION

The purpose of this section is to recommend and review tests and techniques for the psychological evaluation of early-onset elderly deaf adults, thereby assisting in psychologists' selection of appropriate tests. The considerations discussed should substantially increase the probability of obtaining meaningful evaluations of older early-onset deaf clients and facilitate the difficult task of doing justice to their needs. This section is intended as a useful reference for psychologists and others who are occasionally faced with the responsibility of testing or interpreting test results of deaf clients.

A complete psychological evaluation should comprise a measure of intelligence, an evaluation of personality structure, an appraisal of communication skills, and case history data. In some cases, the data can be obtained in part from records or sources other than the psychological examination. Four basic concepts underlie effective psychological examinations of older deaf clients:

1) Psychological tests that involve the use of verbal language to measure intelligence, personality, and aptitude are generally not valid with this population because they measure the older deaf person's language limitations due to his or her deafness. They do not measure how bright the person is, what the person can do, or the person's emotional stability.

2) Tests given by psychologists not experienced with deaf or hard-of-hearing clients are subject to appreciably greater error than when administered by examiners familiar with individuals who are deaf.

3) Group testing with deaf and hard-of-hearing clients is a highly dubious procedure and should at best be regarded as only a screening technique.

4) Often the older congenitally hard-of-hearing client is, from a psychodiagnostic point of view, much more like a congenitally deaf client than his or her speech and gross response to sound would suggest. It is, therefore, crucial in a psychological evaluation that such a client be given tests appropriate for a person with a profound (almost total) hearing loss, as well as tests for one with normal hearing. Where large differences appear between the sets of test responses, they often show that the client did better on the non-language tests appropriate for the deaf person. It is these findings that should be considered to be valid.

5) A general issue with older hearing-impaired patients relates to medication. Most older persons are taking some sort of medicine, many of which dramatically affect behavior. Some possible consequences are drowsiness, loss of memory, impaired motor function, and a wide range of atypical behaviors. Thus, the psychologist must know what medications the patient is taking and their side effects. Otherwise psychological test scores and responses cannot be meaningfully interpreted.

Intelligence Testing

To be valid with a great majority of older early-onset deaf clients, an intelligence test must be a nonverbal performance measure. Drastic and tragic consequences have resulted when verbal tests have been given to deaf people. There have been cases of deaf persons of above-average intelligence being put in hospitals for the retarded (Vernon et al., 1981), and there have been many cases of deaf people denied proper rehabilitation because inappropriate tests were employed. As stated earlier, a verbal test of intelligence usually does not measure the intelligence of an older early-onset deaf person; it measures the language handicap that results from the client's hearing loss. However, performance IQ tests *do* measure an older early-onset deaf person's

TABLE 1

EVALUATION OF SOME OF THE INTELLIGENCE TESTS MOST COMMONLY
USED WITH EARLY-ONSET DEAF AND HARD-OF-HEARING ADULTS

Tests	Appropriate Age Range Covered by the Test	Comments
WAIS-R Performance scale	16 to 70 years	The WAIS-R Performance scale is at present the best test for deaf adults. It yields a relatively valid IQ score and offers opportunities for qualitative interpretation of factors such as brain injury or emotional disturbance. It has good interest appeal, is relatively easy to administer, and is reasonable in cost.
Raven's Progressive Matrices	9 years to adult	Raven's Progressive Matrices are appropriate to substantiate another more comprehensive intelligence test. The advantage of the matrices is that they are extremely easy to administer and score, take relatively little of the examiner's time, and are very inexpensive. Invalid test scores are yielded for impulsive deaf subjects who tend to respond randomly rather than with accuracy and care. For this reason, the examiner should observe the client carefully to assure that he or she is making a genuine effort.
Revised Beta Examination	Adult	The Revised Beta Examination is a non-language test involving mazes, spatial relations, matching, and similar performance type items. It provides an adequate measure of the intelligence of adults who are deaf.

intelligence. For example, it is possible for such a person to score at the genius level on a performance IQ test and at the retarded level on a verbal IQ test, or even on the verbal scale of the same tests.

A valid appraisal of intelligence is most important. Verbal tests may be used in those few cases where an older deaf or hard-of-hearing client has exceptional language achievement. However, when this is not the case, it is indicative of a poor psychological evaluation when results on an older deaf client include verbal IQ scores, especially if these results are not carefully qualified. Table 1 describes three IQ tests recommended for use with early-onset deaf and hard-of-hearing clients.

Personality Evaluation

Personality evaluation of older early-onset deaf and hard-of-hearing individuals presents a far more complex task than does IQ testing. For this reason, test findings should be carefully interpreted in light of case history data and personal experiences with the client. In fact, it is often wise for psychologists with sophistication and long experience in the field of deafness to view skeptically results reported by examiners who are unfamiliar with deafness when these findings sharply contradict their own impressions of a deaf client.

Due to communication problems inherent in severe hearing loss, personality tests are more difficult to use with deaf subjects than with the general population (Graham & Kendall, 1960; Myklebust, 1962; Levine, 1974; Sullivan & Vernon, 1979). Not only do these tests depend on extensive verbal interchange or reading skill, they also presuppose a rapport and confidence on the part of the subject that is difficult to achieve when he or she does not fully understand what is being said or written. Paper-and-pencil personality measures are perhaps suitable for hearing-impaired persons with well-developed expressive and receptive language ability; however, such individuals are the exception among elderly people whose onset of hearing loss was prelingual. Even with those whose hearing loss is postlingual, the problems of test administration and interpretation make the meaningfulness of results highly fallible (Graham & Kendall, 1960; Myklebust, 1962; Levine, 1974; Sullivan & Vernon, 1979). If projective measures like the Rorschach Inkblot Test or the Thematic Apperception Test are used, fluency in manual communication (the language of signs) by the examiner is mandatory if the client's fluency is in sign language.

There is some question as to whether the norms for the personality structure of hearing people are appropriate for elderly early-onset deaf and hard-of-hearing subjects (Sullivan & Vernon, 1979). Conceivably deafness alters the perceived environment sufficiently to bring about an essentially different organization of personality, in which normality differs from what it is for a person with unimpaired hearing. Although at present this is an unanswered question, it is frequently raised by scholars in the field of deafness and should be considered in any discussion of the personality of someone with severe hearing loss (Vernon & Andrews, in press).

The use of interpreters to express the psychologist's directions in fingerspelling and sign language is a questionable procedure. What is required is an interpreter fluent not only in manual communication but also in psychology and testing (Vernon & Andrews, in press); obviously, such an individual would be doing the examining him- or herself and not interpreting it for another. Therefore, results reported where an interpreter is involved are not likely to meet high standards of validity.

It is important to note that the confusion and disassociation reflected in the writing of early-onset deaf and hard-of-hearing clients with low-level verbal skills rarely indicate a deranged thought process. This is usually only the result of the language deficiency growing out of prelingual hearing loss. Psychologists unaware of this phenomenon have been known to equate the written language of semiliterate deaf persons with that of schizophrenics, and unfortunate diagnoses have been made based in large part on this confusion.

Few personality tests have had wide successful application with early-onset deaf or hard-of-hearing elderly adults because of the difficulties described above. Five of the more commonly and effectively used personality tests are synopsized in Table 2.

Appraising Communication Skills

A formal evaluation of communication skills is best done by a speech and language pathologist or an audiologist. However, a psychologist evaluating a hearing-

TABLE 2

PERSONALITY TESTS USED WITH OLDER EARLY-ONSET
DEAF AND HARD-OF-HEARING ADULTS

Test	Appropriate Subjects	Comments
Draw-A-Person	9 years through adult	This is a good screening device for detecting severe emotional problems. It is relatively nonverbal and is probably the most practical projective personality test for use with deaf subjects. Its interpretation is highly subjective and in the hands of a poor psychologist it can result in rather extreme diagnostic statements about deaf clients.
Thematic Apperception Test	Those who can communicate well manually or are skillful in written language	This is a test of great potential, if the psychologist giving it and the deaf subject taking it can both communicate with fluency in manual communication. Otherwise, it is of very limited value unless the deaf subject has an exceptional command of language. The test could be given through an interpreter by an exceptionally perceptive psychologist, although it is more desirable if the psychologist can do his or her own communicating.
Rorschach Inkblot Test	Those who are able to communicate fluently manually or with exceptional skill orally	In order for the Rorschach to be used, it is absolutely necessary that the psychologist giving it and the deaf subject taking it be fluent in manual communication. Even under these circumstances it is debatable whether it has great value unless the subject is of above-average intelligence. With a very bright deaf subject who had a remarkable proficiency in English, it would be possible to give a Rorschach through writing, but this would be a dubious procedure.
House-Tree-Person Technique	School age through adult	This is a procedure similar to the Draw-a-Person test. It requires little verbal communication and affords the competent clinician some valuable insight into the subject's basic personality dynamics.
Bender Visual Motor Gestalt Test	12 years through adult	This is a useful projective test for personality assessment and also for the detection of brain damage. Because of the rather high prevalence of brain damage among people who are deaf, it is often valuable to administer a Bender-Gestalt to clients who have severe learning problems or who give evidence of bizarre behavior.

impaired client should provide a cursory evaluation, including elements such as the following:

1) Is the client's speech intelligible? Approximately what percent of what he or she says can be understood under ordinary circumstances?

2) How much speech can the client understand in a conversation in a quiet one-to-one situation? What percent of speech is grasped against noisy backgrounds and/or in groups?

3) In general, how well does the client lipread?

In congenitally or prelingually hearing-impaired clients, some estimate of English language competence is important. Further, if the individual is competent in American Sign Language, it is imperative to indicate this.

Case History Data

The past is still the one best predictor of the future. Vernon and Andrews (in press) have found that with any patient (hearing or deaf) the best psychiatric and psychological evaluations are often based 70% upon background information. For this reason, complete background information on a client is of extreme importance, especially if he or she is deaf and cannot be accurately evaluated with regular psychological procedures. Some factors to consider are the client's performance on past jobs, whether he or she has habitually demonstrated any particular problems or assets, what kinds of circumstances have led to his or her successes or failures, and what specific educational and vocational skills he or she has mastered.

SUMMARY

The psychological testing of elderly hearing-impaired persons necessitates an understanding of the communication issues involved in hearing loss and their implications for psychodiagnostics, as well as an awareness of other conditions associated with aging that affect cognitive process and overall psychological functioning. It is with the small minority of older persons whose onset of hearing loss was prelingual and severe that there arises the greatest probability of misdiagnosis. With these persons, sign-language skills and a full understanding of the relationship of early onset hearing loss to linguistic competence (especially in English) are absolutely essential. As such specialized skills are needed, the general psychologist would do well to refer such clients to a colleague experienced with this population.

REFERENCES

Drachman, D.A., & Sahakian, B.J. (1980). Memory and cognitive function in the elderly. *Archives of Neurology, 37,* 674-675.

Foster, N.L. (1987). Age-related changes in the human nervous system. In H.G. Mueller & V.C. Geoffrey (Eds.), *Communication disorders in aging: Assessment and management* (pp. 3-35). Washington, DC: Gallaudet University Press.

Goin, D.W. (1976). Trauma of the middle and inner ear. In G.M. English (Ed.), *Otolaryngology: A textbook* (pp. 189-199). New York: Harper & Row.

Gordon-Salant, S. (1987). Basic hearing evaluation. In H.C. Mueller & V.C. Geoffrey (Eds.),

Communication disorders in aging: Assessment and management (pp. 301-333). Washington, DC: Gallaudet University Press.

Graham, F.K., & Kendall, B.C. (1960). Memory for Designs Test: Revised general manual. *Perceptual and Motor Skills Monograph Supplement 2*(7).

Levine, E.S. (1974). Psychological tests and practices with the deaf: A survey of the state of the art. *Volta Review, 76,* 298-319.

Marshall, L. (1981). Auditory processing in aging listeners. *Journal of Speech and Hearing Disorders, 46*(3), 226-240.

Milne, J.S. (1977). A longitudinal study of hearing loss in older people. *British Journal of Audiology, 11,* 7-14.

Mindel, E., & Vernon, M. (1987). *They grow in silence* (2nd ed.). San Diego: College-Hill.

Myklebust, H. (1962). Guidance and counseling for the deaf. *American Annals of the Deaf, 107,* 370-415.

Ruben, R.J. (1981). Genetics of hearing loss in the elderly. *Shhh, 2*(3), 3-5.

Schein, J.D., & Delk, M.T., Jr. (1974). *The deaf population.* Silver Spring, MD: National Association of the Deaf.

Solomon, A. (1982). [In-service lecture, Taylor Manor Hospital, Elliott City, MD]. Unpublished data.

Sullivan, P.M., & Vernon, M. (1979). Psychological assessment of hearing impaired children. *School Psychology Digest, 8,* 271-290.

Vernon, M. (1984). Psychological stress and hearing loss. *Shhh, 5*(4), 3-6.

Vernon, M. (1988). The primary causes of deafness. In E.D. Mindel & M. Vernon (Eds.), *They grow in silence* (pp. 31-38). Boston: College-Hill.

Vernon, M., & Andrews, J.F. (in press). *Understanding deaf and hard of hearing people.* White Plains, NY: Longman.

Vernon, M., Griffin, D.H., & Yoken, C. (1981). Hearing loss: Problems in family practice. *Journal of Family Practice, 12,* 1053-1058.

Vernon, M., & Ottinger, P. (1981). Psychological evaluation of the deaf and hard of hearing. In L.K. Mindel & T. Jabaley (Eds.), *Deafness and mental health* (pp. 49-64). New York: Grune & Stratton.

Zimbardo, P.G., & Anderson, S.M. (1981). Induced hearing deficit generates experimental paranoia. *Science, 212,* 1529-1531.

10

Assessment in Behavior Management Programs for Older Adults

CAROL J. DYE, PH.D.

Assessment is an integral part of the process of planning, developing, and applying behavior management programs with older adults. Assessment takes place at the very beginning of the process of developing a behavior management program as the behavior to be managed is defined and baseline information is gathered. An important part of assessment at this point is gathering data about the environment within which the modification of behavior is to take place. Assessment can occur in the evaluation of the older adults who will participate in the program to determine both if they are suitable for it and if the reinforcers included as part of the program are optimal for them.

Many times the assessments that occur at any of these points in the development of behavior management programs are accomplished by clinical observation. The contingencies in the environment that maintain the behavior to be managed and the potential of older adults for participation and change of behavior also are evaluated by this process of careful observation. In addition, however, some behavior management programs assessments are made by using paper-pencil tests or other standardized procedures. This chapter will focus on each of these areas and methods of assessment in behavior management programs for older adults and will discuss the bases for an expanded role for assessment in these programs.

DEFINING BEHAVIOR MANAGEMENT

In the broadest sense, behavior management could include the control, management, direction, and/or guidance, systematic or not, of any behavior (continence, memory , etc.) in any group (nursing home, community-based, etc.) or for any individual. Behavior management can be a program directed by someone other than the persons whose behaviors are to be modified or it can be self-directed in some instances. In a self-directed program, older adults identify a need by self-evaluation, seek out a program to address the need, and work toward modification of their own behavior. In this context, behavior management usually is directed toward enhancement or improvement in the quality of life. Self-directed programs hold great promise for the older adults involved because of their potential generalization to other problems (Burgio & Burgio, 1986). For the most part, however, behavior management programs for older adults are developed and directed by persons other than the older adults themselves. The behavior to be managed usually has some negative connotations indicating deterioration from some previous level of function. Either this is negative behavior to be reduced in frequency, such as hostility, constant calling out, or repetitive behavior, or it is behavior to be re-elicited, such as self-feeding, toileting, or social verbalizations.

The reasons for managing behavior vary. Richards and Thorpe (1978) indicate there are *socially significant* behaviors (self-feeding, incontinence, aggression) and *clinically significant* behaviors (depression, anxiety) to be managed. Usually older adults do not complain of the presence of socially significant behaviors in themselves. These become the focus of behavior management programs because caretakers or others in the environment complain about them. The reason for management of these behaviors, then, is to reduce interpersonal conflicts, annoyance, or the need for care. On the other hand, clinically significant behaviors are likely to be perceived as discomforting by the older adult who experiences them. Older adults complain of clinical symptoms and may seek ways to gain relief from them. The reason for management of clinical symptoms, then, is to reduce the perceived discomfort of the older adult. The preponderance of the studies in behavior management concern socially significant behaviors.

The behavioral management programs described in the gerontological literature vary in a number of significant ways. Some assist in the recovery of an old skill that has been lost, such as continence, others focus on learning new skills, such as progressive muscle relaxation. The program might focus on very specific behaviors, such as telephone conversational skills, or on more generalized behaviors, such as the control of aggression or agitation. Behavioral management programs also differ in the population addressed, which might be the older adult, the staff of a congregate setting for older adults, or family caretakers. The programs differ in the settings in which they occur—the community, a hospital, or a nursing home. Behavior management programs differ in the method that is used to modify behavior, applying, for example, biofeedback, operant conditioning, or educational approaches. The reports of these programs in the literature differ in that some are individual case studies, while others are reports of group trials of a procedure. Finally, the reports of behavior management programs differ as to whether they are self-managed or managed by a caretaker. Some of the available studies in this area are shown in Table 1, which reflects the wide variety of problems addressed.

Models of Behavior Management Programs

Usually behavior management programs are developed in keeping with the principles of behavior modification. Some are educational in their method. In the behavior modification process, the management program begins with a careful definition of the behavior that will be the focus of the program. Instead of using general descriptions such as "training for continence" or "reducing hypochondriacal behavior," the behavior is carefully and concretely described so that there can be satisfactory reliability from person to person in understanding the behavior to be managed. After the behavior is defined, baseline data are gathered to determine the actual amount of the behavior that may already be evident, when it occurs, and so on. These

TABLE 1

SELECTED REPORTS OF BEHAVIOR MANAGEMENT PROGRAMS

Problem addressed	*Reference*
Agitation/aggression	Haley, 1983; Rosberger & MacLean, 1983
Ambulation	MacDonald & Butler, 1974; Wiggam, French, & Henderson, 1986
Anxiety/depression/paranoia	Sallis, Lichstein, Clarkson, Stalgaitis, & Campbell, 1983; Zeiss & Lewisohn, 1986; Hussian & Lawrence, 1981; Reaven & Peterson, 1985-86; Power & McCarron, 1975; Carstensen & Fremouw, 1981
Caretaker training	Eyde & Rich, 1982; Breckenridge, Zeiss, & Thompson, 1987; Sperbeck & Whitbourne, 1981
Continence	Whitehead, Burgio, & Engel, 1985; Chanfreau-Rona, Bellwood, & Wylie, 1984; Long, 1985; Grosicki, 1968
Disorientation	Hanley, 1981
General well-being	Klein, Frank, & Jacobs, 1980; Yesavage, 1984; Garrison, 1978; Welden & Yesavage, 1982; Perlmutter & Langer, 1983; Dapcich-Miura & Hovell, 1979; Tauber, 1982
Headaches	Linoff & West, 1982
Memory training	Yesavage & Rose, 1983
Pain control	Boczkowski, 1984
Participation in activities	Bunck & Iwata, 1978; MacDonald, Davidowitz, Gimbel, & Foley, 1982
Self-feeding	Baltes & Zerbe, 1976; Rinke, Williams, Lloyd, & Smith-Scott, 1978
Sleep regulation	Alperson & Biglan, 1979; Kolko, 1984
Sociability/interpersonal skills	MacDonald, 1978; Hoyer, Kafer, Simpson, & Hoyer, 1974; Blackman, Howe, & Pinkston, 1976; Thralow & Watson, 1974; O'Quin, O'Dell, & Burnett, 1982; Lopez, 1980; Williamson, 1984; Nigl & Jackson, 1981; Berger, 1979
Spatial orientation/inductive reasoning	Willis & Schaie, 1986
Tardive dyskinesia	Jackson & Schonfeld, 1982
Telephone skills	Praderas & MacDonald, 1986
Weight loss	Perkins & Rapp, 1985-86

two processes, defining the behavior that will be managed and gathering baseline data, may be the same operation. Also at this beginning stage careful assessments are made of the environment to determine the ways that the interpersonal or physical characteristics of the milieu influence behavior. With behavior modification approaches, a good deal of emphasis is given to the reinforcing properties of the interpersonal behavior within the environment in initiating, enhancing, or perpetuating behavior.

The next step in the behavior management program using behavior modification procedures is to assign the older adult(s) to the program and to do any assessments of the subject group that are thought necessary. One of the functions of evaluations at this point is to screen out individuals who might not benefit from the program. For example, in depression management, individuals scoring in the non-depressed range on a test of depression would not likely be included. Another function of evaluation at this point would be to provide additional baseline data for the variables important to the training. Finally, evaluation would occur again after the program is completed to reassess the targeted behaviors. If an educational approach is used in a behavior management program, the same process of evaluation would be followed except that the evaluations would likely be more objective and not involve the clinical observations inherent in the behavior modification approach.

Self-monitored behavior management programs tend to follow the educational method. In these cases an older adult perceives a need for behavior management, then seeks out a program to meet that need. The role of assessment in these self-managed programs varies widely. For example, a frequently perceived problem by older adults is memory functioning. There are many programs available that seek to enhance memory functioning, ranging widely in structure, organization, amount of time and practice required, and so on. In the less formally organized programs, such as some of those more popularly available, there may or may not be an evaluation of the memory deficit before the training begins or after it is completed. On the other hand, memory training programs for community-based elderly adults that are conducted within university or clinical settings tend to be more formally organized, with pre- and post-testings included.

As can be seen, there are at least two models that behavior management programs can follow with differing models of assessment. In the following pages, the roles of assessment in these programs will be discussed more fully with suggestions for the expansion and further development of the evaluation process.

ASSESSMENT OF PARTICIPANTS IN BEHAVIOR MANAGEMENT PROGRAMS

Assessments may be made of the older adults who participate in behavior management programs for a number of reasons: to provide baseline data against which progress in the subsequent program may be judged, to provide information about concomitant variables that might be relevant to progress in the program, or to determine the ability of older adults to participate in the program. Additionally, these older adults may be assessed to determine their motivational level or the reinforcements that would be efficacious for their achievement in the program. Data may be gathered by clinical observation, by interview, or by direct assessment utilizing standardized scales. As will be seen, the amount of assessment performed in the studies, though adequate, could be greatly enhanced to provide much more useful information about the subject population and on the concomitant variables that may affect performance. This will be discussed further after reviewing the evaluation procedures for the subject populations already found in the literature.

Clinical Observation

A study by Wiggam et al. (1986) offers one example of the application of the clinical observation method in defining the behavior to be managed and in gathering baseline data. These investigators sought to increase the ambulation of four older residents of a retirement center. They initially observed the daily walking habits of these individuals (i.e., the distance walked under certain conditions), gathering information over a 14-day period. The walking observed and recorded during this baseline period was defined as that occurring during normal waking hours along four known pathways from the front door of the residence. In another behavior management program, this one designed to reduce hostile behavior in a single individual, Rosberger and MacLean (1983) had as their first task to define the behavior(s) that were of concern to the staff in the nursing home in which that individual was housed. Six of these were pinpointed by the staff—kicking, throwing objects, exposing self, banging dishes on siderails of bed, pushing self and things at staff, patients, or visitors, and smearing feces. During the baseline period, staff members were asked to record the occurrence of any of these behaviors, the time of occurrence, and the antecedent and consequent conditions.

The observation of behavior for baseline assessments may occur for various periods of time depending on the behavior addressed. In the two studies just described in which the target behaviors did not occur with great frequency per unit time, observation took place over a number of days. For other behaviors, however, observation may take place for much smaller segments of time. In assessing the level of spontaneous verbalizations occurring during mealtimes, O'Quin et al. (1982) observed nursing home residents at 6-second intervals over the period of their evening mealtime counting the number of times they spoke.

This careful definition of the behavior to be managed and the assessment of its incidence are very important to the development of a successful intervention. In some cases this step may be all that is needed to help manage behavior. This was demonstrated in a study by Donat (1984) that took place in a congregate setting. The presenting problem was that of the wandering of a resident, a common problem in such settings. This older woman entered other residents' rooms and caused a good deal of annoyance and some altercations. On careful assessment and evaluation of this woman's wandering, it was determined that she entered certain rooms with much greater frequency than others and spent much of her time while in these rooms looking out of the windows, which provided a different view than those in her own room. The solution to the wandering problem was to change the room of the wanderer to one of those with the view that she continually sought. This change accomplished, the number of intrusions into other residents' rooms was reduced by 84%. In this case study, then, the process of establishing baseline data led directly to intervention and effective management.

Behavioral Rating Scales and Interviews

Observations of the behavior of the older adult may be made more systematic or standardized by the use of some type of a behavioral rating scale. These scales range in the number and type of behaviors (activities of daily living, psychiatric symptoms, etc.) sampled. One of these that has been used in behavior management programs is the 32-item Nurses' Observation Scale for Inpatient Evaluation (NOSIE; Honigfeld & Klett, 1965), which yields ratings of six psychiatric symptoms: social competence and interest, personal neatness, cooperation and irritability, manifest psychosis, and psychotic depression. Others that have been used to assess older adults in behavior management programs are the Stockton State Hospital Geropsychiatric Profile (Meer & Baker, 1966), the Hospital Adjustment Scale (Hussian & Lawrence, 1981), and the Clifton Assessment Procedures for the Elderly (Pattie & Gilleard, 1979). For the clinician or researcher interested in using these scales, several reviews of the issues and instruments are available (Salzman, Shader, Kochansky, & Cronin, 1972; Ernst & Ernst, 1984; Lawton, 1986; Kane & Kane, 1981).

Another way that the clinical process is applied to gather baseline data is by individual interview. Interviewing may be especially useful in the evaluation of clinical symptoms. The interview can result in an overall impression of functioning or a more systematic rating of symptomatology by the use of a rating scale. One scale that has been used with older adults in behavior management is the Hamilton Rating Scale for Depression (Hamilton, 1967), which consists of 23 items that are completed by a trained interviewer. The behavior management study in which this scale was used was one that taught older adults to concentrate and learn more efficiently (Yesavage & Rose, 1983). In this study, depression was assessed as a concomitant variable affecting cognitive functioning.

In a few behavior management studies focused on cognitive functioning or including cognitively impaired subjects, mental status exams have been used to group subjects for baseline measurement or to screen out older adults who would be ineligible for the study (Yesavage, 1984; Yesavage & Rose, 1983; Lopez, 1980). Mental status exams require individual interviewing and testing but are reasonably short procedures. Among those that have been used in behavior management programs are the Mini-Mental State Exam (Folstein, Folstein, & McHugh, 1975); the Kahn-Goldfarb Mental Status Examination (Kahn, Goldfarb, Pollack, & Gerber, 1960), and the Short Portable Mental Status Questionnaire (Pfeiffer, 1975).

Self-report Measures

In some behavior management programs, assessment may proceed through the use of paper-pencil questionnaires completed by the older adults themselves. As with interviewing, this method is more often seen in the evaluation of clinical symptoms simply because of the availability of tests in those areas. A number of tests of depression have been used in behavior management studies, including the Zung Self-rating Depression Scale (SRDS; Zung, 1965, 1967), the Beck Depression Inventory (BDI; Beck, Ward, Mendelson, Mock, & Erbaugh, 1961), the Center for Epidemiologic Studies–Depression Scale (CES-D Scale; Radloff, 1977), the Depression Adjective Check List (Lubin, 1981), and the Geriatric Depression Scale (Yesavage et al., 1983;

Sheikh & Yesavage, 1986). Most of these scales were originally developed to determine levels of depression in younger populations and then were borrowed to evaluate depression in older adults. Some are symptom scales (BDI and SRDS) and as such may exaggerate the levels of depression in older adult populations because of the similarities between the manifestation of normal aging and the symptoms of depression. On the other hand, most of the scales have been used widely with older adults in behavior management and for other purposes, and there is a considerable literature about them. Among the depression scales listed, the Geriatric Depression Scale is one that has been developed specifically for older adults. This 30-item scale has a yes/no response format and has been studied for validity against the Research Diagnostic Criteria (Spitzer, Endicott, & Robbins, 1978) as well as two of the other depression scales indicated above (Hamilton Rating Scale for Depression and SRDS). The items on this scale are short and to the point, making it easy to administer even to frail older adults. (A discussion of the issues and problems of the utilization of depression scales with older adults is found in another chapter in this book.)

Another scale developed for older adult populations that has been used in behavior management programs assessing a variable akin to depression is the Philadelphia Geriatric Center Morale Scale (PGCMS; Lawton, 1972, 1975). A revised version of this scale contains 17 items that are easily understood by older adults and answered by a simple "yes" or "no." Three factors seem to be reliable on this scale—agitation, attitude toward own aging, and lonely dissatisfaction (Liang & Bollen, 1983; Morris & Sherwood, 1975; Lawton, 1975). The construct of morale has received a good deal of attention in gerontological research; reviews may be found in Nydegger (1977) and Sauer and Warland (1982).

A recent addition to the scales available for self-administration in an area receiving increasing attention is the Geriatric Behavioral Self-Assessment Scale developed by Yesavage, Adey, and Werner (1981). This scale was designed to assess mild to moderate symptoms of dementia. What makes this scale worthy of special mention to the individual working in the area of behavior management is that it is a self-assessment and does not require individual administration by a trained evaluator.

Only one test of anxiety, the State-Trait Anxiety Inventory (Spielberger, Gorsuch, & Lushene, 1970), is mentioned in the behavior management literature and then only with minimal frequency. It seems unusual that the variable of anxiety is not studied or assessed with greater frequency in behavior management programs for older adults. Studies indicate that the aged experience more anxiety than other age groups (Sallis & Lichstein, 1982; Zung & Green, 1973) and that anxiety exerts a powerful influence in the process of learning (Elias & Elias, 1977). Therefore, it would seem to be important to control this variable in studies of behavior management with older adults. Not only is there a need for assessment of this variable within older populations, there is also a need to develop behavior management programs to reduce anxiety for this population.

Differentiating Subject Populations

Taking a closer look at the number and type of assessments made of older adults in behavior management programs as discussed above, one can see that much more information could be provided through more extensive evaluation. More extensive evaluation should be performed for two reasons: to provide a more detailed description of the subject population and to provide more information on concomitant variables that may modify the learning process in the behavior management program. In many of the previously cited studies, the subject group is described only minimally. Mean age and the setting from which participants were drawn are usually indicated, and subjects are described in blanket terms such as "a group of psychogeriatric patients," "Alzheimer patients," or "nursing home residents." Beyond this very basic information, however, other important knowledge about the participants in the program is generally lacking.

In behavior management studies, older adults are expected to learn a new skill or relearn an old one. It would seem important, therefore, to determine something about those variables that relate to the ability to learn, such as level of concentration and attention, persistence, ability to understand abstractions, ability to follow commands, and so on. Behavior management programs are complex sequences of learning involving many of these basic operations repeated within any one program. Without information about the ability to perform these basic operations of learning or about other related processes (level of anxiety, educational level, etc.), it becomes problematic to interpret the results of trials in a behavior management program, especially if there is only partial success. In only a few studies have subjects actually been assessed to determine their ability to learn previous to the trials in the behavior management program. In one such study of 18 fecally incontinent patients, Whitehead et al. (1985) tried participants on a habit-training regimen that could have been considered an assessment of the subject population's ability to learn before beginning the main study. This was done in addition to gathering data from a number of physical tests that assessed their physiological capacity to become continent. A few other studies have used mental status exams for screening and grouping subjects as a way to gain some information about subjects' ability to perform at the learning tasks involved in behavior management programs.

The need for more comprehensive information on the subject group as was gathered by Whitehead et al. (1985) has been supported by several other researchers. They point out that the amount of variability in the older adult group makes it almost imperative to know more about the subject group included. Schaie (1984) discussed this variability in regard to normally aging older adults. He indicated that as aging proceeds, most adults experience declines in various specific abilities, making for greater heterogeneity in functioning within any one group of aged persons than with younger persons. Consequently, rather than there being a global or catastrophic decline to some minimal level of functioning across all functions, there is a great deal of intra- and interindividual variation.

Alperson and Biglan (1979) reflected on the practical problems that arise because of the variability of groups of older adults who are subjects in behavior management studies. In their study of sleep onset insomnia, two older adult subjects dropped out part way through the study because their health had worsened, and the older adult group showed less improvement generally than the comparison younger group. The authors hypothesized that health status may have been the reason for the discrepancy in achievement. There was no way to test this hypothesis, however, because there was no assessment of the subject groups for health status.

Chanfreau-Rona et al. (1984) reinforced the need for more assessment to provide information on variability within the subject population. They emphasized learning more about how behavior management programs might be successful and under what conditions; for example, *how much* memory function is necessary for adequate performance in behavior management programs? Rather than describing subjects by diagnostic labels that convey only limited information about memory function, these investigators suggest direct assessment of learning and other variables important to the program. Reflecting on the variability within even a group of Alzheimer's patients, Cameron and Gambert (1987) support this notion. This need for more evaluation and description among both healthy and demented aged was also indicated by Vitaliano, Breen, Albert, Russo, and Prinz (1984), who demonstrated significant intra- and intersubject variability in attention and memory functioning in two groups of older adults (healthy and demented).

An example of the usefulness of differentiating the subject population, even very simply, was demonstrated in a study by MacDonald et al. (1982). Three behavioral treatments were tested to determine their differential effectiveness in increasing the activity level of older adult residents in a psychiatric hospital. The results showed that those with higher initial baseline activity scores reacted positively to the stimulated environment condition (enriched programming of dayroom activities). Additional prompting by the staff, another condition, did not make significant improvement in their behavior beyond that shown as a result of the stimulating environment. However, those older adults who showed low initial baseline activity improved their level of activity only as a result of prompting and encouragement by the staff. The stimulating environment and reinforcements by the staff did not further improve their activity level. In this study, then, gathering one bit of baseline data that differentiated the subject group led to greater usefulness of results for future application in this area.

It is obvious that two things need to be accomplished in future behavior management studies with older adults. Subject populations should be described to a greater extent, and they should also be assessed for some of the functions important to the study. For a study including Alzheimer patients, the description of the subject group should include at least the stage of the disease present. Then, additional measures should be taken, such as the ability of the subject population to follow commands, the number of trials taken to learn a task relevant to the one in the behavioral program, ability at retention, understanding of abstractions, presence of concomitant emotional symptomatology, and so forth. For a behavior management program involving community-based older adults, the subject group should be described at least by their educational levels and their health status, as these two variables have been found to have a significant relationship to the ability to learn and remember. Additionally, it would be ideal if the subject group could be assessed for basic cognitive abilities, deficits in sensory capacities as they might impact on learning in the program, the presence of emotional symptoms, and other variables.

There are a number of tests that are useful in assessing the areas indicated above. To assess learning ability, the Inglis Paired Associate Learning Test (Inglis, 1959), the Shopping List Test (McCarthy, Ferris, Clark, & Crook, 1981), and the Fuld Object-Memory Evaluation (Fuld, 1981) provide standardized learning materials and procedures. The Paired Associates subtest on the Wechsler Memory Scale also provides a standard learning list containing both easy and hard association pairs. To assess persistence, there are procedures such as the Trail Making Test, Part A, and the Crossing-Off Test (Botwinick & Storandt, 1973), which was developed originally to assess psychomotor speed and requires the individual to make a slash through dashes arranged on an 8½" x 11" sheet of paper. On each of these two tests there is no new learning involved in performance, simply the need to keep at the task. The Digit Span subtest on the Wechsler Memory Scale-Revised or the Wechsler Adult Intelligence Scale-Revised are best for the assessment of attention span. To evaluate the understanding of abstractions, the interpretation of proverbs might be considered, such as those found on the Proverbs Test (Gorham, 1956). The scoring system indicating concrete, functional, or abstract understanding of the proverbs is a useful way to categorize responses.

These reasonably short procedures can be used to expand the knowledge about the subject population in reports of behavior management programs and to help in the generalization of results to other behavior management situations. These points will be given further emphasis in the following section.

ASSESSMENT OF MOTIVATION IN OLDER ADULTS

An important part of the process of developing successful behavior management programs is being able to rearrange contingencies for behavior changes. This is usually accomplished by careful application of the principles of learning and behavior modification. The assessment of the nature of reinforcers that perpetuate the behavior to be modified is part of the initial process of assessment that is very often accomplished by clinical observation, as described previously. The reinforcers in behavior management include a wide variety of tangible and intangible factors, such as the opportunity for greater social interaction, verbal praise, tokens that can be used to obtain other desired items, access to activities, food, and drink, and so on. Some of these are easier to quantify than others; therefore, the exact amount of reinforcement that is given to older adults may be better known in some cases than others.

Because behavior management studies have generally indicated success in modifying behavior, it is assumed that all the operations of the program, including the contingencies, have been planned correctly. Yet, the level of success in these programs is variable. For example, in the previously cited individual case study reported by Rosberger and MacLean (1983), six behaviors were pinpointed for management and all but one (fecal smearing) were successfully managed. For some reason, this one behavior was resistant to the modified contingencies and persisted. In a study by Sperbeck and Whitbourne (1981), in which four patients were encouraged toward increased ambulation, one of the patients showed initial gains, but these dissipated quickly. The authors hypothesized that, for the patient, the benefits of walking did not outweigh the amount of energy expended. They pointed out that this evaluation by the patient of the "worth" of the activity is a consideration often ignored by behavior analysts. In a study by Libb and Clements (1969), four patients were encouraged to exercise and were given the reward of marbles for a certain number of minutes of exercise that could be redeemed for cigarettes, chewing gum, peanuts, and so forth. The value of each marble was about one cent. The first three patients responded positively to the reinforcement but the last one did not.

Other investigations have shown unexpected results. Such was the case in a study by Grosicki (1968) of urinary/fecal continence training with a group of older psychiatric patients, in which the control group showed a decrease in incontinence while the experimental group did not. This was a study utilizing behavior modification procedures for retraining. Patients were given social and then, after a time interval, monetary rewards for being continent at times when regular periodic checks were made by staff. In this study, neither type of reinforcement resulted in greater change toward continency in the experimental group. Behavior modification is a frequently used approach with such patients, though habit training (Long, 1985) and biofeedback approaches (Whitehead et al., 1985) may also be found in the behavior management literature. In another study showing unexpected results, Lopez, Hoyer, Goldstein, Gershaw, and Sprafkin (1980) investigated the effects of monetary reinforcement and overlearning in teaching conversational skills. One half of their subject group received a monetary reward for performance. This group showed less achievement than those who did not receive the monetary reward.

Similarly, in the first of two studies focused on encouraging increased verbalizations in institutionalized older adults, Hoyer et al. (1974) gave a token reinforcer (pennies) for verbalization. These investigators reinforced two of four subjects. Although the two who were systematically reinforced did increase their verbalizations over the trials that were planned, the other two "non-reinforced" subjects did also. Apparently there was some unquantified reinforcement operating for these latter two subjects, such as the factor of attention from the experimenters. In the second study reported by these authors, another set of trials to increase verbalizations were run, again with a group of four subjects. The authors reinforced all four of the subjects with a slightly different schedule of reinforcement than in the previous study, and all of the subjects increased their verbalizations, indicating that the reinforcers were effective. However, two of the subjects did considerably better than the other two.

Clearly, one of the reasons the older adults cited above achieved in the way that they did and with the variation they showed was that the contingencies arranged by the investigators had different meanings than anticipated. Lindsley (1964) has discussed this problem of the saliency of reinforcers for the elderly, indicating that contingencies useful within younger populations may not be so appropriate for older persons. As the adult ages, positively reinforcing factors may lose their salience, neutral ones may gain or decline in importance, and negatively reinforcing factors may become more positive. Solomon (1982) discussed how stereotyping and changed societal expectations for the aged among health care workers results in an increase in negative reinforcers in later life in health care settings. This study indicated that negative and stereotyped attitudes (belief that older adults are less resilient physically, have negative personality traits, are pessimistic and insecure, etc.) as well as a disparity in status between health care workers and older adults can lead to inappropriate or inadequate care (more bedside nursing, slower convalescence, greater affective distance, etc.). This in turn can result in loss of will and the withdrawal of older adults from meaningful interpersonal interaction.

With exchange theory as his basis for explaining aging behaviors, Dowd (1975) has also hypothesized how societal expectations interplay with the aging process to change contingencies for the older adult. Dowd indicated that the lack of power generally experienced by the older adult in interactions with younger persons becomes a negative reinforcer for continuing such interactions. He hypothesized this as an explanation for the observed social withdrawal of older adults and as the basis for their greater social interaction within their own age group where individual levels of power are more equal.

In addition to these broader environmental forces, the cognitive, health, and other changes of aging may work to modify the effectiveness of reinforcers for older adult populations. Whatever the etiologies, the situation is that the optimal kind and amount of reinforcement for older adult populations is relatively unknown at this time. This, then, is an additional problem for behavior managers. Those management studies that allow older adults to choose their own rewards (either by direct choice or through earning tokens that may be redeemed for a variety of things) address this issue of the variability and the individual differences in effective reinforcers among older adults to some extent. Yet, the choices that have been made by the subjects in these studies have not been documented, so that no additional information about this important variable has been gathered even in these studies.

Currently there are relatively few ways available to sample the individual differences in the salience of reinforcers objectively. One way of doing this, of course, would be just to ask older adults what they would like as their reward for achievement and learning. On the other hand, it would seem that this is another place where perhaps more standard and readily available procedures would be helpful. Some years ago, Cautela and Kastenbaum (1967) developed a checklist of reinforcers that could be used to determine the efficacy of the contingencies for older adults in learning programs. This checklist has received relatively little attention despite the need for more information in this area, not only for behavior management purposes but in other areas as well.

In summary, it is unclear at this point in the behavior management literature how much the lack of knowledge about the salience of reinforcers for older adults has affected the results of studies, especially in partially successful ones. Even in the case of successful trials, it might be that more salient reinforcers could have accelerated learning. Certainly much more research needs to be done in this area.

ASSESSING THE ENVIRONMENT IN BEHAVIOR MANAGEMENT STUDIES

Up to this point, the discussion has emphasized the need for a reasonable assessment of the older adult's individual capacities in planning and utilizing behavior management programs. Another area that must be evaluated is the environment (interpersonal and physical) in which the behavior is to occur. This environment must be evaluated for its existing characteristics and for its potential for change. Two issues in the assessment of the environment in behavior management studies are of importance for the discussion here. One is the extent to which the environment is given attention in behavior management studies compared to the amount of attention given the older adult. The second has to do with the method that is used to assess the environment when it does occur.

The environment has long been recognized within the psychological community as a powerful force influencing behavior. Within gerontological psychology, there has been a history of research and clinical work involving the role of the environment in determining behavior. In the first handbooks on aging published in the 1960s, several chapters were devoted to this topic, and since then both theory and research have developed further. Much of the effort has focused on the environment of the congregate setting, probably because of its potential both for greater manageability and consistency as well as for changing and shaping the behavior of the frail elderly adults who reside within it. Additionally, the problem of optimal person-environment fit has been a major interest of researchers because the opportunity for older adults to be instrumental in making housing moves is reduced. Gerontologists have sought ways to understand how care-providing environments impact on health, mood, and functioning and how to manage these environments to enhance effectiveness.

The role of the environment in producing and perpetuating behaviors in older adults is an important issue for behavior management, yet less emphasis is given to this variable in the behavior management literature than to older adults themselves. The question of why this is so may be raised, especially as there is a notable amount of information on the impact of the environment in the gerontological literature. Part of the reason may be an apparent attributional bias among those who are the behavior managers (Karuza, Zevon, Rabinowitz, & Brickman, 1982). This bias (i.e., that the basis of problems lies within the individual) causes helpers to focus on the individual to correct problems. Another reason for neglect of the environment may be that working with the individual is easier than attempting to manage the variables associated with the environment. Further, the individual may appear more salient to the investigator than the more vague environment (Wright & Fletcher, 1982). Additionally, the potential number of variables to be controlled within the environment and so much that is not controllable makes the environment a formidable problem in behavior management.

Defining Environmental Variables

There are many who could be cited here for their work in defining the variables in the environment that impact on behavior and the mechanisms by which that occurs. However, because a full review of this literature is beyond the scope of this chapter, the reader is referred to Carp (1976), Lawton (1977), Lawton and Nahemow (1973), Windley and Ernest (1975), and Kahana (1974), as well as to other appropriate chapters in this book.

When assessments are made of the environment to determine its impact on behavior, those evaluations usually have been accomplished by clinical observation. This is the same effective method that is often used to evaluate older adults in these studies. By comparison, relatively little formal assessment of the environment has been done. When the milieu is emphasized in management studies, the variables that have been given focus are usually the existing contingencies for behavior, especially the actions of caretakers. Sometimes the physical characteristics of the environment have been of interest.

In one such investigation, McClanahan and Risley (1975) observed how, just by changing the availability of materials and encouraging prompts by staff, the amount of recreational activity participation by older adult nursing home residents could be increased. Newkirk, Feldman, Bickett, Gipson, and Lutzker (1976) also found that the spatial arrangements of rooms in which activities were held as well as prompting by staff members were important determinants of resident attendance at recreational and therapeutic activities in an extended care facility. Melin and Gotesdam (1981) discovered that rearranging furniture to stimulate conversation, changing mealtime routines to allow more time to eat, increasing choices of what could be eaten, and providing more pleasant surroundings increased the frequency of interpersonal communication in the residents of a psychogeriatric ward. Quattrochi-Tubin and Jason (1980) showed how a stimulus control procedure (access to free coffee and cookies) increased attendance and social interactions in the lounge area of a residential-setting nursing home.

Rosberger and MacLean (1983) focused on the attitudes of the staff in congregate settings in enhancing and perpetuating the behavior of an aggressive patient. Chanfreau-Rona et al. (1984) also discussed the crucial role of these staffs—their individual personalities, their group dynamics, and the extent to which their full cooperation could be obtained—in the success of any program that might be planned for patients. Sperbeck and Whitbourne (1981) focused exclusively on the role of the staff in perpetuating maladaptive dependency behaviors in residents in a nursing home and developed an educational and experiential training program around behavior modification principles. Their method of evaluating the success of these staff members after training was to observe the presence of dependency behaviors in the patients for whom they cared.

The emphasis on clinical observation to evaluate salient environmental variables can be seen in studies that have addressed the need to optimize the adjustment of older adults in the community as well. These community-based programs have focused on many of the same processes that have been researched within congregate settings. Bunck and Iwata (1978) sought to increase the participation of community-based elders in nutritional programs. In an unusual evaluation of the several ways used to get these community-based older adults into these programs, the investigators calculated the cost of each condition and compared that with the amount of participation that resulted. Interestingly, incentives (choice of a number of activities or services) for attendance was the most economical and the most effective.

Other community studies have concerned individual cases. For example, Kolko (1984) worked with an elderly female toward self-management of excessive daytime sleepiness. Clinical evaluation of the woman and her environment suggested several management procedures that in combination were successful even at 6 and 12 months follow-up. Other studies of insomnia in community-based older adults have been done by Alperson and Biglan (1979) and Davies, Lacks, Storandt, and Bertelson (1986). Eyde and Rich (1982) and Green, Linsk, and Pinkston (1986) developed training programs that focused on the caretakers (spouses, families, etc.) of older adults continuing to reside within the community. Dapcich-Miura and Hovell (1979) studied enhanced compliance to a medical regimen in an elderly male. These investigators performed a thorough clinical evaluation of the environment for its ability to support compliance and then set about to modify those aspects of the environment that were counterproductive for that goal.

Evaluations and broad modifications of this sort are imperative if the benefits of behavior management programs are to last beyond the learning trials. Yesavage and Rose (1983) worked with a group of older adults from senior centers in the community to reduce anxiety leading to enhanced ability at learning and recall. While there was evaluation of the older adults along the various dimensions important to the study, little evaluation was made of existing problems in their environment that might arouse anxiety or retard learning and memory. DeBerry (1981-82) taught 10 anxious elderly women progressive muscle relaxation to reduce psychosocial stress. In this study, a number of assessments were made of the environment for its anxiety-reinforcing properties and so forth.

Standardized Assessment Procedures

In the studies cited above, no standardized assessments were performed on the environmental variables involved. Although the attitudes of the staff might have been indicated as crucial to the success of these programs, no objective assessments were made of staff attitudes or behaviors and no information was gathered as to how these attitudes and behaviors were actually modified as a result of direct training, as in the Sperbeck and Whitbourne study. Neither was information gathered on how staff behaviors and attitudes might have been changed as a result of the modified behavior of these patients. This intricate interaction and interplay of caretaker and older adults needs to be traced and measured. Additionally, no direct standard assessments were used to evaluate the other care procedures or the physical parameters of the environment. It is suggested that this would be particularly useful data to obtain in order to better quantify the variables contributing to behavior. In the same way that the evaluation of the older adults who participate in behavior management studies should be expanded, the environment also warrants more objective evaluation. Such information would further define the success and failure of attempts to enhance the functioning of older adults in that environment.

A variety of assessment procedures can be used to evaluate environmental variables both within congregate settings and within the community. Several assess a number of dimensions at once, combining variables such as satisfaction, quality of life, physical and other atmosphere variables, person-environment fit, general ward or nursing home atmosphere, the availability of services, and the control or constraint exercised in congregate settings. Other procedures focus on just one factor, such as staff attitudes, preferences for privacy, the importance of activities, locus of desired control or extent of control, social interaction, or perceived fear within the environment. Excellent reviews and examples of these measures may be found in Kane and Kane (1981, pp. 189-208), Windley (1982), and Moos (1974).

SUMMARY

Behavior management programs can be thought to fall into two main groups. The first seeks to modify behaviors that are regarded as socially maladaptive. These behaviors may or may not be perceived as discomforting by the older adults involved, and the appropriate programs are usually directed by someone other than the older adults themselves. The second main group of programs deal with clinical symptoms, which *are* most likely perceived as discomforting by the older person. These management programs may or may not be directed by someone other than the older adult, but, regardless of who directs, these are likely to involve greater voluntary participation and more decision making on the part of the older adult. Scanning the behavior management literature indicates most programs focus on managing the behavior of older adults in congregate settings who show socially significant behaviors. This is so even though there is a distinct need for more programs to manage anxiety and other clinical symptoms among older adult populations, both within congregate settings and in the community. The difference in availability of programs of the two types indicated is probably a reflection of the disparity in status between older adults and health care workers in our society and the ability of these two groups to afford the services of behavior managers.

The role of assessment that has developed in behavior management programs has been to evaluate the program participants, to evaluate the contingencies governing behavior, and to assess the environment in which the behavior occurs. However, much more assessment should be done in each one of these areas. It is no longer suitable to gather a group of nursing home residents, community-dwelling older adults, or geropsychiatric patients for a behavior management program without further exploration and description of their level of functioning and suitability for the program under consideration. Greater description is needed within the subject population, and certain evaluation procedures as noted might be useful in providing that description. More attention must be addressed to assessing the contingencies that are so important for modifying behavior; reviewing the results of behavior management studies shows that success in these programs is sometimes less than 100%, suggesting that the reinforcers utilized may not have been salient for some of the participants or that the salience of contingencies was different than expected. The role of reinforcers for the management of behavior among older adults needs much more attention in the literature, both in terms of the method by which these may be determined and in terms of what are the specific things that reinforce behavior in older adults.

Even though gerontologists traditionally have recognized the special impact of the environment on the behavior of older adults, much more attention has been focused on the individual older adult as an independent actor in behavior management programs than on the environment in producing and perpetuating behavior. More research is needed on environmental particulars. Obviously, to develop these assessments fully will take much time and energy; however, the significance of having more information with which to explain the success or failure of any programs and to enhance their generalizability should far outweigh the extra time taken.

REFERENCES

Alperson, J., & Biglan, A. (1979). Self-administered treatment of sleep onset insomnia and the importance of age. *Behavior Therapy, 10,* 347-356.
Baltes, M.M., & Zerbe, M.B. (1976). Independence training in nursing home residents. *The Gerontologist, 16,* 428-432.
Beck, A.T., Ward, C.H., Mendelson, M., Mock, J., & Erbaugh, J. (1961). An inventory for measuring depression. *Archives of General Psychiatry, 4,* 53-65.
Berger, R.M. (1979). Training the institutionalized elderly in interpersonal skills. *Social Work, 24,* 420-423.

Blackman, D.K., Howe, M., & Pinkston, E.M. (1976). Increasing participation in social inter-action of the institutionalized elderly. *The Gerontologist, 16,* 69-76.

Boczkowski, J.A. (1984). Biofeedback training for the treatment of chronic pain in an elderly arthritic female. *Clinical Gerontologist, 2,* 39-46.

Botwinick, J., & Storandt, M. (1973). Speed functions, vocabulary ability, and age. *Perceptual and Motor Skills, 36,* 1123-1128.

Breckenridge, J.S., Zeiss, A.M., & Thompson, L.W. (1987). The life satisfaction course: An intervention for the elderly. In R. Munoz (Ed.), *Depression prevention research: The potential and limits of psychological intervention* (pp. 185-196). New York: Hemisphere.

Bunck, T.J., & Iwata, B.A. (1978). Increasing senior citizen participation in a community-based nutritious meal program. *Journal of Applied Behavior Analysis, 11,* 75-86.

Burgio, L.D., & Burgio, K.L. (1986). Behavioral gerontology: Application of behavioral methods to the problems of older adults. *Journal of Applied Behavior Analysis, 19,* 321-328.

Cameron, D.J., & Gambert, S.R. (1987). Assessing the abilities of institutionalized demented. *The Gerontologist, 27,* 95A-96A.

Carp, F.M. (1976). Housing and living environments of older people. In R.H. Binstock & E. Shanas (Eds.), *Handbook of aging and the social sciences* (pp. 244-271). New York: Van Nostrand Reinhold.

Carstensen, L.L., & Fremouw, W.J. (1981). The demonstration of a behavioral intervention for late life paranoia. *The Gerontologist, 21,* 329-333.

Cautela, J.R., & Kastenbaum, R. (1967). A reinforcement survey schedule for use in therapy, training and research. *Psychological Reports, 20,* 1115-1130.

Chanfreau-Rona, D., Bellwood, S., & Wylie, B. (1984). Assessment of a behavioral pro-gramme to treat incontinent patients in psychogeriatric wards. *British Journal of Clinical Psychology, 23,* 273-279.

Dapcich-Miura, E., & Hovell, M.F. (1979). Contingency management of adherence to a com-plex medical regimen in an elderly heart patient. *Behavior Therapy, 10,* 193-201.

Davies, R., Lacks, P., Storandt, M., & Bertelson, A.D. (1986). Countercontrol treatment of sleep-maintenance insomnia in relation to age. *Psychology and Aging, 1,* 233-238.

DeBerry, S. (1981-82). An evaluation of progressive muscle relaxation on stress related symp-toms in a geriatric population. *International Journal of Aging and Human Development, 14,* 255-269.

Donat, D.C. (1984). Modifying wandering behavior: A case study. *Clinical Gerontologist, 3,* 41-43.

Dowd, J.J. (1975). Aging as exchange. *Journal of Gerontology, 30,* 584-594.

Elias, M.G., & Elias, P.K. (1977). Motivation and activity. In J.E. Birren & K.W. Schaie (Eds.), *Handbook of the psychology of aging* (pp. 357-383). New York: Van Nostrand Reinhold.

Ernst, M., & Ernst, N.S. (1984). Functional capacity. In D.J. Mangen & W.A. Peterson (Eds.), *Research instruments in social gerontology: Vol. 3. Health, program evaluation and demography* (pp. 9-84). Minneapolis: University of Minnesota Press.

Eyde, D.R., & Rich, J.A. (1982). A family centered model for routine management of disturb-ing behaviors in the aged. *Clinical Gerontologist, 1,* 69-86.

Folstein, M.F., Folstein, S.E., & McHugh, P.H. (1975). Mini-Mental State: A practical method for grading the cognitive state of patients for the clinician. *Journal of Psychiatric Research, 12,* 189-198.

Fuld, P.A. (1981). *The Fuld Object-Memory Evaluation.* Chicago: Stoelting.

Garrison, J.E. (1978). Stress management training for the elderly: A psychoeducational approach. *Journal of the American Geriatrics Society, 26,* 397-403.

Gorham, D.R. (1956). A proverbs test for clinical and experimental use. *Psychological Reports Monograph, 2*(1).

Green, G.R., Linsk, N.L., & Pinkston, E.M. (1986). Modification of verbal behavior of the mentally impaired elderly by their spouses. *Journal of Applied Behavior Analysis, 19,* 329-336.

Grosicki, J.P. (1968). Effect of operant conditioning on modification of incontinence in neuropsychiatric geriatric patients. *Nursing Research, 17,* 304-311.

Haley, W.E. (1983). Behavioral self-management: Application to a case of agitation in an elderly chronic psychiatric patient. *Clinical Gerontologist, 1,* 45-52.

Hamilton, M. (1967). Development of a rating scale for primary depressive illness. *British Journal of Social and Clinical Psychology, 6,* 278-296.

Hanley, I.G. (1981). The use of signposts and active training to modify ward disorientation in elderly patients. *Journal of Behavior Therapy and Experimental Psychiatry, 12,* 241-247.

Honigfeld, G., & Klett, C.J. (1965). The Nurses' Observation Scale for Inpatient Evaluation. *Journal of Clinical Psychology, 21,* 65-71.

Hoyer, W.J., Kafer, R.A., Simpson, S.C., & Hoyer, F.W. (1974). Reinstatement of verbal behavior in elderly mental patients using operant procedures. *The Gerontologist, 14,* 149-152.

Hussian, R.A., & Lawrence, P.S. (1981). Social reinforcement of activity and problem solving training in the treatment of depressed institutionalized elderly patients. *Cognitive Therapy Research, 1,* 57-69.

Inglis, J. (1959). A paired associate learning test for use with elderly psychiatric patients. *Journal of Mental Science, 105,* 440-451.

Jackson, G.M., & Schonfeld, L.I. (1982). Comparisons of visual feedback, instructional prompts and discreet prompting in the treatment of orofacial tardive dyskinesia. *International Journal of Behavioral Geriatrics, 1,* 35-46.

Kahana, E.A. (1974). Matching environment to the needs of the aged: A conceptual scheme. In J.F. Gubrium (Ed.), *Late life* (pp. 201-214). Springfield, IL: Charles C. Thomas.

Kahn, R.L., Goldfarb, A.I., Pollack, M., & Gerber, I.E. (1960). The relationship of mental health and physical status in institutionalized aged persons. *American Journal of Psychiatry, 117,* 120-124.

Kane, R.A., & Kane, R.L. (1981). *Assessing the elderly.* Lexington, MA: Lexington Books.

Karuza, J., Jr., Zevon, M.A., Rabinowitz, V.C., & Brickman, P. (1982). Attributions of responsibility by helpers and recipients. In T.A. Wills (Ed.), *Basic processes in helping relationships* (pp. 107-130). New York: Academic Press.

Klein, S., Frank, R., & Jacobs, J. (1980). Token economy program for developing independent living skills in geriatric inpatients. *Psychosocial Rehabilitation Journal, 4,* 1-11.

Kolko, D.J. (1984). Behavioral treatment of excessive daytime sleepiness in an elderly woman with multiple medical problems. *Journal of Behavior Therapy and Experimental Psychiatry, 15,* 341-345.

Lawton, M.P. (1972). The dimensions of morale. In D. Kent, R. Kastenbaum, & S. Sherwood (Eds.), *Research, planning and action for the elderly* (pp. 144-165). New York: Behavioral Publications.

Lawton, M.P. (1975). The Philadelphia Geriatric Center Morale Scale: A revision. *Journal of Gerontology, 30,* 85-89.

Lawton, M.P. (1977). The impact of the environment on aging and behavior. In J.E. Birren & K.W. Schaie (Eds.), *Handbook of the psychology of aging* (pp. 276-301). New York: Van Nostrand Reinhold.

Lawton, M.P. (1986). Functional assessment. In L. Teri & P.M. Lewinsohn (Eds.), *Geropsychological assessment and treatment: Selected topics* (pp. 39-84). New York: Springer.

Lawton, M.P., & Nahemow, L. (1973). Ecology and the aging process. In C. Eisdorfer & M.P. Lawton (Eds.), *The psychology of adult development and aging* (pp. 619-674). Washington, DC: American Psychological Association,

Liang, J., & Bollen, K.A. (1983). The structure of the Philadelphia Geriatric Center Morale Scale: A reinterpretation. *Journal of Gerontology, 38,* 181-189.

Libb, J.W., & Clements, C.B. (1969). Token reinforcement in an exercise program for hospitalized geriatric patients. *Perceptual and Motor Skills, 28,* 957-958.

Linoff, M.G., & West, C.M. (1982). Relaxation training systematically combined with music: Treatment of tension headaches in a geriatric patient. *International Journal of Behavioral Geriatrics, 1,* 11-16.

Lindsley, O.R. (1964). Geriatric behavioral prosthetics. In R. Kastenbaum (Ed.), *New thoughts on old age* (pp. 41-61). New York: Springer.

Long, M.L. (1985). Incontinence: Defining the nursing role. *Journal of Gerontological Nursing, 11,* 30-35.

Lopez, M. (1980). Social-skills training with institutionalized elderly: Effects of precounseling structuring and overlearning on skill acquisition and transfer. *Journal of Counseling Psychology, 27,* 286-293.

Lopez, M.A., Hoyer, W.J., Goldstein, A.P., Gershaw, N.W., & Sprafkin, R.P. (1980). Effects of overlearning and incentive on the acquisition and transfer of interpersonal skills with institutionalized elderly. *Journal of Gerontology, 35,* 403-408.

Lubin, B. (1981). *Manual for the Depression Adjective Check List.* San Diego: Educational and Industrial Testing Service.

MacDonald, M.L. (1978). Programming for the socially isolated aged. *The Gerontologist, 18,* 350-354.

MacDonald, M.L., & Butler, A.K. (1974). Reversal of helplessness: Producing walking behavior in nursing home wheelchair residents using behavior modification procedures. *Journal of Gerontology, 29,* 97-101.

MacDonald, M.L., Davidowitz, J.J., Gimbel, B., & Foley, L.M. (1982). Physical and social environmental reprogramming as treatment for psychogeriatric patients. *International Journal of Behavioral Geriatrics, 1,* 15-32.

McCarthy, M., Ferris, S.H., Clark, E., & Crook, T. (1981). Acquisition and retention of categorized material in normal aging and senile dementia. *Experimental Aging Research, 7,* 127-135.

McClanahan, L.E., & Risley, T.R. (1975). Design of living environments for nursing home residents: Increasing participation in recreation activities. *Journal of Applied Behavior Analysis, 8,* 261-268.

Meer, B., & Baker, J.A. (1966). The Stockton Geriatric Rating Scale. *Journal of Gerontology, 21,* 392-403.

Melin, L., & Gotesdam, J.C. (1981). The effect of rearranging ward routines on communication and eating behaviors of psychogeriatric patients. *Journal of Applied Behavior Analysis, 14,* 47-51.

Moos, R.H. (1974). *Evaluating treatment environments: A social ecological approach.* New York: John Wiley.

Morris, J.N., & Sherwood, S. (1975). A retesting and modification of the Philadelphia Geriatric Center Morale Scale. *Journal of Gerontology, 30,* 77-84.

Newkirk, J.B., Feldman, S., Bickett, A., Gipson, M.T., & Lutzker, J.R. (1976). Increasing extended care facility residents' attendance at recreational activities with convenient locations and personal invitations. *Journal of Applied Behavior Analysis, 9,* 207.

Nigl, A.J., & Jackson, B. (1981). A behavior management program to increase social responses in psychogeriatric patients. *Journal of the American Geriatrics Society, 29,* 92-95.

Nydegger, C. (1977). *Measuring morale: A guide to effective assessment.* Washington, DC: Gerontological Society of America.

O'Quin, J.A., O'Dell, S.L., & Burnett, R.L. (1982). Effects of brief behavioral intervention on verbal interactions of socially inactive nursing home residents. *International Journal of Behavioral Geriatrics, 1,* 3-10.

Parr, J. (1980). Environmental issues. In L.W. Poon (Ed.), *Aging in the 1980's* (pp. 391-434). Washington, DC: American Psychological Association.

Pattie, A.H., & Gilleard, C.J. (1979). *Manual of the Clifton Assessment Procedures for the Elderly.* Seven Oaks, England: Hodder and Stoughton.

Perkins, K.A., & Rapp, S.R. (1985-86). A behavioral weight loss program for a memory-impaired, elderly male. *Clinical Gerontologist, 4,* 32-34.

Perlmutter, L.C., & Langer, E.J. (1983). The effects of behavioral monitoring on the perception of control. *Clinical Gerontologist, 1,* 37-43.

Pfeiffer, E. (1975). A short portable mental status questionnaire for the assessment of organic brain deficit in elderly patients. *Journal of the American Geriatrics Society, 23,* 433-441.

Power, C.A., & McCarron, L.T. (1975). Treatment of depression in persons residing in homes for the aged. *The Gerontologist, 15,* 132-135.

Praderas, K., & MacDonald, M.L. (1986). Telephone conversational skills training with socially isolated, impaired nursing home residents. *Journal of Applied Behavior Analysis, 19,* 337-348.

Quattrochi-Tubin, S., & Jason, L.A. (1980) Enhancing social interactions and activity among the elderly through stimulus control. *Journal of Applied Behavior Analysis, 13,* 159-163.

Radloff, L.W. (1977). The CES-D scale: A self-report depression scale for research in the general population. *Applied Psychological Measurement, 1,* 385-401.

Reaven, J.A., & Peterson, L. (1985-86). The effects of self-monitoring on activity level and mood in elderly nursing home residents. *Clinical Gerontologist, 4,* 38-39.

Richards, W.S., & Thorpe, G.L. (1978). Behavioral approaches to the problems of later life. In M. Storandt, I.C. Siegler, & M.F. Elias (Eds.), *The clinical psychology of aging* (pp. 253-276). New York: Plenum.

Rinke, C.L., Williams, J.C., Lloyd, K.E., & Smith-Scott, W. (1978). The effect of prompting and reinforcement on self-bathing by elderly residents of a nursing home. *Behavior Therapy, 9,* 873-881.

Rosberger, Z., & MacLean, J. (1983). Behavioral assessment and treatment of "organic" behaviors in an institutionalized geriatric patient. *International Journal of Behavioral Geriatrics, 1,* 33-46.

Sallis, J.F., & Lichstein, K.L. (1982). Analysis and management of geriatric anxiety. *International Journal of Aging and Human Development, 15,* 197-211.

Sallis, J.F., Lichstein, K.L., Clarkson, A.D., Stalgaitis, S., & Campbell, M. (1983). Anxiety and depression management for the elderly. *International Journal of Behavioral Geriatrics, 1,* 3-12.

Salzman, C., Shader, R.I., Kochansky, G.E., & Cronin, D.M. (1972). Rating scales for psychotropic drug research with geriatric patients. I. Behavior ratings. *Journal of the American Geriatrics Society, 20,* 209-214.

Sauer, W.J., & Warland, R. (1982). Morale and life satisfaction. In D.J. Mangen & W.A. Peterson (Eds.), *Research instruments in social gerontology: Vol. 1. Clinical and social psychology* (pp. 195-240). Minneapolis: University of Minnesota Press.

Schaie, K.W. (1984). Midlife influences upon intellectual functioning in old age. *International Journal of Behavioral Development, 7,* 463-478.

Sheikh, J.I., & Yesavage, J.A. (1986). Geriatric Depression Scale (GDS): Recent evidence and development of a shorter version. In T.L. Brink (Ed.), *Clinical gerontology: A guide to assessment and intervention* (pp. 165-173). New York: Haworth.

Solomon, K. (1982). Social antecendents of learned helplessness in the health care setting. *The Gerontologist, 22,* 282-287.

Sperbeck, D.J., & Whitbourne, S.K. (1981). Dependency in the institutional setting: A behavioral training program for geriatric staff. *The Gerontologist, 21,* 268-275.

Spielberger, C.D., Gorsuch, R.L., & Lushene, R.E. (1970). *Manual for the State-Trait Anxiety Inventory.* Palo Alto, CA: Consulting Psychologists Press.

Spitzer, R.L., Endicott, J., & Robbins, E. (1978). Research diagnostic criteria: Rationale and reliability. *Archives of General Psychiatry, 35,* 773-782.

Tauber, L. (1982). Biofeedback as an adjunct in treating elders. *Clinical Gerontologist, 1,* 72-73.

Thralow, J.U., & Watson, C.G. (1974). Remotivation for geriatric patients: Using elementary school students. *American Journal of Occupational Therapy, 28,* 469-473.

Vitaliano, P.P., Breen, A.R., Albert, M.S., Russo, J., & Prinz, P.N. (1984). Memory, attention and functional status in community-residing Alzheimer-type dementia patients and optimally healthy aged individuals. *Journal of Gerontology, 39,* 58-64.

Welden, S., & Yesavage, J.A. (1982). Behavioral improvement with relaxation training in senile dementia. *Clinical Gerontologist, 1,* 45-49.

Whitehead, W.E., Burgio, K.L., & Engel, B.T. (1985). Biofeedback treatment of fecal incontinence in geriatric patients. *Journal of the American Geriatrics Society, 33,* 320-324.

Wiggam, J., French, R., & Henderson, H. (1986). The effects of a token economy on distance walked by senior citizens in a retirement center. *American Corrective Therapy Journal, 40,* 6-12.

Williamson, P.N. (1984). An intervention for hypochondriacal complaints. *Clinical Gerontologist, 3,* 64-68.

Willis, S.L., & Schaie, K.W. (1986). Training the elderly on the ability factors of spatial orientation and inductive reasoning. *Psychology and Aging, 1,* 239-247.

Windley, P.G. (1982). Environments. In D.J. Mangen & W.A. Peterson (Eds.), *Research instruments in social gerontology: Vol. 1. Clinical and social psychology* (pp. 383-414). Minneapolis: University of Minnesota Press.

Windley, P.G., & Ernest, G. (Eds.). (1975). *Theory and development in environment and aging.* Washington, DC: Gerontological Society of America.

Wright, B.A., & Fletcher, B.L. (1982). Uncovering hidden resources: A challenge in assessment. *Professional Psychology, 13,* 229-235.

Yesavage, J.A. (1984). Relaxation and memory training in 39 elderly patients. *American Journal of Psychiatry, 141,* 778-781.

Yesavage, J.A., Adey, M., & Werner, P.D. (1981). Development of a geriatric behavioral self-assessment scale. *Journal of the American Geriatrics Society, 29,* 285-288.

Yesavage, J.A., Brink, T.L., Rose, T.L., Lum, O., Huang, V., Adey, M., & Leirer, V.O. (1983). Development and validation of a geriatric depression screening scale: A preliminary report. *Journal of Psychiatric Research, 17,* 37-49.

Yesavage, J.A., & Rose, T.L. (1983). Concentration and mnemonic training in elderly subjects with memory complaints: A study of combined therapy and order effects. *Psychiatry Research, 9,* 157-167.

Zeiss, A.M., & Lewinsohn, P.M. (1986). Adapting behavioral treatment for depression to meet the needs of the elderly. *The Clinical Psychologist, 39,* 98-100.

Zung, W.W.K. (1965). A self-rating depression scale. *Archives of General Psychiatry, 12,* 63-70.

Zung, W.W.K. (1967). Depression in the normal aged. *Psychosomatics, 8,* 287-292.

Zung, W.W.K., & Green, R.L., Jr. (1973). Detection of affective disorders in the aged. In C. Eisdorfer & W.E. Fann (Eds.), *Psychopharmacology and aging* (pp. 213-224). New York: Plenum.

11

Common Adjustment Problems of Older Adults

KENNETH D. COLE, PH.D.

In exploring the psychoanalytic, life-span developmental, and stress and coping literature associated with adjustment in later years, one takes on the task of separating what are normal age changes from the expectancies and myths that surround the coming of age. In brief, it appears that healthy older persons do not lose their tenacity; some have remarkable ability to weather change and loss. What is striking, however, is the variety and profundity of losses that must be absorbed throughout the life span.

As one theorist put it, while the life stresses of younger adults tend to be more of the "challenge" variety, stressors in later years tend to be "threats" (McCrae, 1982). Another way of conceiving this is that older adults tend to be faced with "exit events," while the young tend to encounter "entrance events." Indeed, when one looks at the basic coping strategies of younger and older adults, the similarities of coping styles are more apparent than the differences. The differences that emerge show that elders employ less hostility and escapes into fantasy. Other differences are accounted for by the nature of the stress involved: coping with chronic illness or the death of a spouse naturally demand skills different from starting a family or changing careers (McCrae & Costa, 1985).

Successful aging does not take place through the avoidance of loss; no one can live a full life without commitment and its inherent risk of loss. Rather, effective adaptation rests on assimilating painful losses and maintaining the fortitude and courage to risk again. Separation and loss are of course not new to the older adult (Bloom-Feshbach & Bloom-Feshbach, 1987), and new transitions and losses in late adulthood provide renewed opportunities to work through self-defeating adaptations to earlier losses (Wertheimer, 1983; Mathews, 1979; Cath, 1983).

One of the realizations that many do not attain until the later years is that life is indeed hard. Florida Scott-Maxwell, a fully lived woman who turned to Jungian analysis at the age of 50, wrote in her journal during her later years that she grew more intense as she aged. She added, "I say to Life: you are very hard. . . . suddenly I wonder—is all hardness justified because we are so slow in realizing that life was

The author would like to thank the Library Service, Sepulveda VA Medical Center, for their help in the library research for this chapter.

185

meant to be heroic? Greatness is required of us. That is life's aim and justification" (Scott-Maxwell, 1968, p. 85).

Not only do older adults suffer more loss, but they also are not protected from the "slings of life" by engaging in as many pleasures or duties (Berman, 1986). The sheer profundity of loss, coupled both with expectations that life should be smooth and with poor prior experiences in coping with separation and loss, can render the older adult vulnerable to problems in adjustment. Most commonly this appears as anxiety and depression, which often lead to alcohol and prescription medication abuse. Other times older adults can become irritable, critical, and hostile towards others, further eroding their fragile support system. Indeed, men who were poor adjusters to retirement have been shown to be hostile, intolerant of others, and alert for signs of hostility directed toward them (Richard, Livson, & Peterson, 1962).

The purpose of this chapter is to discuss the major tasks of later adulthood from a life-span development perspective that weaves together some psychoanalytic notions of life tasks with more empirical findings from the field of stress and coping. Severe psychopathology and long-standing mood disorders are reserved for authors of other chapters; the thrust here is to understand and to assess for problems in adapting to common events in later adulthood.

The assessment for adjustment difficulties should include instruments that tap a number of different affects: depression, tension, anxiety, and hostility, as well as positive features of life satisfaction. The goal is to uncover any indicators of "psychological dysequilibrium" by including a broad range of feelings and behaviors. A careful assessment is characterized by a nonjudgmental scrutiny into alcohol and drug use, sleep patterns, somatic preoccupations, eating and elimination habits, and any other change in routine. These behavioral manifestations may be masking considerable psychic distress, and some of them could be missed with simple paper-and-pencil measures.

Major Events of Late Adulthood

Bereavement

Undoubtedly, the most difficult adjustment for most older persons is the loss of a spouse. For many couples this marks the end of a relationship that has spanned several decades, with the spouse having gratified many varied needs. A spouse is a lover, a business partner of sorts, a confidant, an escort, and in other cases a financial manager, homemaker, and cook. No single event in one's life carries with it such loss, ranging from the piercing realization that one is left alone to face the last years of life to the simple frustrations and hassles of managing a checking account or preparing meals for the first time.

The grieving that follows a death can be profound, varying in form and intensity with the depth and quality of the relationship (Worden, 1982). A person also can fail to grieve in a manner that will assimilate the loss and enable moving on with life. Pathological grief reactions inhibit finally coming to terms with the loss and preparing to re-invest in other people. Indications of grief gone awry are chronic or delayed grief reactions or grief masked by physical symptoms, often similar to those displayed by the deceased (Worden, 1982).

How long it takes to regain some equilibrium can vary widely. Some studies have shown that it takes widows 3 to 4 years to reach stability in their lives (Parkes, 1972). "Stability" does not imply getting over the loss, but rather learning to live with it. For many women, the most devastating blow to a subjective sense of well-being is becoming a widow. Reactions can vary from early silent protestations ("How dare he do this to me?") to husband sanctification to introjections of admired features of the late spouse (Bumagin & Hirn, 1982). The double blow for widowed women comes with the loss of some of her friends who are still in intact marriages. The husbands don't want a reminder of their imposing mortality, and the wives shirk away from personifications of their anticipated widowhood. Some couples draw closer together with the threat of impending loss, savoring the time that they still have left together. Others create distance through absence of mind or constant bickering in order to defend against the threatened loss.

Widowerhood, being less common than widowhood in our culture, has not been studied as systematically. However, in the 1980s cohort of older men, many household tasks still are regarded as feminine, so shopping, cooking, and cleaning may be tasks for which widowers are psychologically and behaviorally ill prepared (Solomon, 1984). It is somewhat unusual for this group of older men to label and verbalize their complex feelings of grief and loss. Moreover, the widower may become in demand again sexually, a situation that may be relished from afar but pitted with uncertainty and anxiety when one is "courting" or "being courted" for the first time in 50 years. An elderly man may argue that "just because there's snow on the roof doesn't mean there isn't fire in the furnace" (Sachs, 1983), but with the attendant anxiety and performance concerns surrounding sexuality with a new partner, diseases and medication regimens add to his chances of erectile failure. A few of these experiences may cause the older widower to decide mistakenly that he is "too old for this kind of stuff," thereby avoiding opportunities for sexual encounters and all the other potential growth and healing possible from subsequent relationships.

Retirement

The stress counterpart to widowhood for most males in the current cohort of older adults is retirement. Men vary in their response to retirement, based on the importance of their work, whether retirement was chosen or forced, and the extent of psychological and economic preparation for the event (Cowling & Campbell, 1986; Solomon, 1984). Blue-collar workers typically welcome retirement because it gets them away from boring, repetitive jobs that remain unstimulating and often marked by difficulties with younger co-workers. Men more than women and highly educated people more than lesser educated people tend to prefer tackling a "second career" or cutting down to part-time work as opposed to retirement (Sheppard, 1985). Some studies indicate elevated blood pressure and cholesterol levels among older workers who are unemployed and reversal of these elevations for those who find re-employment (Kasl, Cobb, & Gore, 1972).

Even if the man is ready and willing for retirement, wives sometimes complain that they have "twice his time and half his income." Retirement in a traditional man-works-and-woman-keeps-house marriage can highlight unresolved conflicts and difficulties; their relationship may stand in sharp relief, lacking the diversion of perhaps their single common interest—their children.

This difficulty is frequently played out in rehabilitative and assessment settings. In a common scenario, one spouse suffers a stroke or some other potentially disabling illness and through treatment recovers enough functioning to return home. At this point the caregiving spouse may accuse the treatment team of not doing enough for the patient, an oblique reference to the fact that he or she was finding it quite nice to live alone. Some marriages survive on certain basic principles of labor division, and with the consecutive stressors of children leaving home, retirement, and physical illness, a relationship sustained in a tenuous equilibrium is pushed to its limits. This feeling is unsettling and unbecoming to the partners and thus may be denied, leading to psychiatric or medical symptoms.

Generally speaking, men in the currently retiring cohort have poorer social skills than their wives, and many of their social contacts occur in the work arena (Solomon, 1984). With less facility in striking up friendships, the workplace provides the common purpose and repetitive contact with long-term associates necessary for the establishment of "mateship" (Brooke, 1980). All of these casual contacts can erode after the receipt of the gold watch, and the retiree may become dependent solely on his wife and her relationships for social contacts. Such rolelessness can render an individual full of feelings of isolation and emptiness or, in more alexithymic men, can precipitate self-soothing with increased levels of alcohol and prescription drug ingestion (thereby leaving his wife even lonelier).

Like bereavement, retirement is not only a poignant marker of the transitions through life; it can create stress by adding more daily hassles to a person's life, especially after the honeymoon that follows leaving a boring or difficult work situation is over. For example, in a listing of daily hassles tailored for middle-aged adults (Kanner, Coyne, Schaefer, & Lazarus, 1981), loneliness, insufficient money, and having too much time on one's hands are all encountered in retirement. In many studies the frequency of daily hassles has served as a better predictor of both psychological and physical distress than life events per se (e.g. Holahan, Holahan, & Belk, 1984; Kanner et al., 1981). Perhaps this also accounts for the finding that men retired after a year have lower levels of life satisfaction and self-perceived engagement in physical pursuits than immediate retirees (Ekerdt, Bosse, & Levkoff, 1985).

Again, the counselor or clinician should keep in mind that in the case of retirement, people are faced with more threats than challenges (McCrae, 1982). Both bereavement and retirement force increased loneliness and isolation (Glover, 1979), which often leads to increased focus on both psychological and somatic functioning. Also, isolation and loneliness are risk factors for late-life delusional disorders (Cole, 1987). Overall, older persons in distress will present to the clinician in various ways, so assessors must be astute enough to choose measures that pick up a broad array of concerns as well as sensitive enough to ask the delicate questions. Moreover, when testing the older person on other parameters, such as memory or intelligence, examiners must remain alert to any adjustment problems interfering with the client's performance.

Significant life experiences, such as widowhood, retirement, and medical illness, are more likely to affect life satisfaction than will age per se. In addition, counselors and clinicians must be mindful that elders constantly rate themselves in better emotional and physical health than they actually are (Cath, 1983). At least currently, older American men express psychological distress differently from women. Men are four times more likely to abuse alcohol (but only two times more likely to develop cirrhosis of the liver), and they are more likely to be involved in motor accidents (Cowling & Campbell, 1986). Although women more typically display overt depressive symptomatology, older white males comprise the highest suicide risk group, engaging in self-destruction at a rate five times that of their female counterparts (McIntosh, 1985). One study showed that successful suicides were significantly less likely to have a confidant than those who died of natural causes, and over three quarters of these suicides had visited their physician within a month before the event (Miller, 1976).

Social Isolation and Rolelessness

With the advent of retirement and bereavement comes a constriction of social and interpersonal roles. Schaie (1981) believes that the individual who has options and who can be flexible enough to forge out new roles will be the most resistant to the ravages of time. However, many retired or bereft men and women fail to adopt meaningful, self-perpetuating informal roles, such as that of the neighborhood chauffeur or caretaker, and thus slide into a state of rolelessness. Simply put, everyone needs a reason to get up in the morning. A sense of uselessness or rolelessness can lead to alienation and anomie, both of which have been associated with depressive symptomatology (Solomon, 1984).

As has been noted, the transition from an active work life to retirement is not easy. Even the chairman emeritus of the board may well experience how "hollow" such appointments and functions can be (Solomon, 1984). Often people are encouraged to gradually disengage from work while identifying alternative areas of interest and ways they may be engaged (Cowling & Campbell, 1986). But loss of a spouse and retirement can lead to profound rolelessness and ultimately to social isolation (Sheppard, 1985), accompanied by feelings of loss, mourning, and depression (Solomon, 1984).

Especially for gregarious people, isolation is "social malnutrition" (Glover, 1979). Decreased involvement with the fabric of life leads to fewer diversions to occupy one's attention and more time for concern with physical functions (Henker, 1983). Brooke (1980) feels that loneliness is the most destructive of all the "side effects" of aging, and it leads to cynicism and dejection with regard to the future.

Porcino (1985) speaks of two forms of loneliness: that engendered by separation and loss of loved ones, and the more socially subtle but equally relentless loneliness of being ignored or misunderstood by others. She describes a widow of 20 years, who was respected, smiled at, but never physically touched. Often drugs and alcohol become "people substitutes" (Porcino, 1985; Brooke, 1980), and all too often mental health professionals offer psychopharmaceuticals instead of psychotherapy or community supports. Indeed, perhaps not yet having experienced the piercing chill of loneliness, clinicians tend to diagnose and treat the overt mood disorders rather than exploring and possibly remediating the abject rolelessness and emptiness that older people can feel.

More literature has appeared in the last 5 years on the pivotal role that a confidant can play in the global mental health of the older adult. In an investigation of the tendency towards a heartiness in appraising one's world, more than half of the high cognitive stamina group were currently living with a spouse, while a disproportionately high number of widows were in the group exhibiting low adaptive strength (Colerick, 1985). In her studies of markers of recovery from depression in late life, Murphy (1985) cites the importance of changing relations with confidants in predicting recovery or relapse. In keeping with Porcino (1985), she indicates that many spouses are not necessarily confidants, as many confidants are not necessarily spouses! But she remarked about the resiliency of some recovering depressives in initiating and maintaining new relationships (Murphy, 1985).

Some feel that at least part of this resiliency is a sense of self-efficacy. Holahan and Holahan (1987) measured self-efficacy in dealing with the struggles of everyday life and linked this with higher amounts of social support, which in turn served as a buffer against depression. Others have related loneliness to a variety of maladaptive behavior patterns, such as less planning for old age and less rehearsal of disruptive life events. These authors felt that the ability to maintain or to restore one's personal relationships and to access support networks is important in prolonging health and independence (Hansson, Jones, Carpenter, & Remondet, 1986). Loneliness in widows was also associated with suspicion and hostility towards community mental health and social service personnel, whose assistance might defer dependency and institutionalization. Much earlier Lowenthal (1968) proposed that social isolation may be more a consequence of mental illness, and that physical illness may be the critical incident to both the isolation and the mental illness.

In summary, rolelessness and loneliness can give rise to a host of depressive and anxiety symptoms, foster the abuse of drugs and alcohol, increase interpersonal sensitivity, and create conditions for a higher risk of suspiciousness and delusional thinking. It is all too easy to regard these symptoms and behaviors out of context, without an appreciation for their cause or meaning to the older person. Creative interdisciplinary interventions, such as increasing social interactions in a community setting, encouraging volunteer work, introducing a pet into the household, or training in the proper use of a hearing aid, may sometimes be much more effective than the administration of antidepressants or neuroleptic medications.

Physiological Decline and Chronic Illness

In our very youth-oriented culture, the name of the game of life is to stay as young as possible, both in looks and in deeds, with a kind of "beat the clock" zeal that permeates society (Davidson, 1979; Sachs, 1983). It is difficult to embrace the tasks of middle and later life when everyone is distressed by their wrinkles and graying hair.

While we may have effectively debunked most of the destructive myths that characterized older citizens as "senile and sexless," we have erred towards fostering a denial of the aging process with such slogans as "Use it or lose it" or "The mind is like a muscle." Aging should be that easy—and remediable! Realistically, time marches on and does take a toll on aging bodies. The secret is not to deny the process, but to grow to accept its inevitability while minimizing age-related changes through proper nutrition, adequate and enjoyable exercise, and avoidance of self-destructive habits.

Blau (1979) writes that there are differences in the way that men and women grow older, and Davidson (1979) cynically points out that in all cultures, middle age is the "time when men grow fat and sluggish and women lose their charms" (p. 166). This exemplifies the fears of what growing older means for stereotypical men and women. But this notion is somewhat sexist, as it is based on traditional male and female roles. With the broadening of sex roles, there may be more and more women who are equally distressed by loss of physical vigor and job opportunities as by the appearance of the physical markers of aging.

The passage of youth and the realization in the late 30s or early 40s that life is half over can fill adults with a sense of time urgency, a perception of time left to live rather than time elapsed since birth (Neugarten, 1979). Aptly labeled as the predictable "mid-life crisis" (Levinson, 1977), this tumultuous period is an elusive one to pin down. It appears that the individuals who report distress of crisis proportions have been suffering from inner struggles and conflicts for a number of years (McCrae & Costa, 1985). The persons who suffer mid-life crises are the ones who have made a number of dramatic, impulsive, and often irrevocable changes in their lives, and then live to regret it (Colarusso & Nemiroff, 1981). But the sense of time urgency seems to be a more typical transitional phenomenon of mid-life and it may prove to be quite normative.

Other, more "classic" transitions associated with physical decline include menopause and the "empty nest" syndrome. Despite the fact that women preponderate in epidemiological studies of depression, there is no evidence from community or clinical studies that the incidence of depression increases during the female menopause. Depressed women in their menopausal years do not have a distinct symptom pattern, and they do not exhibit an absence of previous episodes or major life stressors as precipitants (Weissman, 1979).

Similarly, the empty nest syndrome seems to be another media invention. Although morale can drop *before* the launching of children, it seems to soar immediately thereafter (Bumagin & Hirn, 1982). Moreover, anecdotally it has been more common to hear of psychological distress caused by an extended "full nest" syndrome, when grown children for a variety of reasons do not make the transition to independent living arrangements. Parents often feel conflicted about wanting to take care of their grown children with difficulties on the one hand, but being resentful about again sharing their home and spouse with other family members.

Naturally, many people do develop severe adaptive difficulties surrounding the attainment of mid-life, menopause, or children leaving home, but all three events are similar in that the layperson would be likely to list them as common adjustments to aging. However, it seems that there are much more difficult transitions that usually appear later in life. What does cause alarm and considerable adjustment problems is physical illness. Dependency and deterioration, not death, embody the specter of old age (Neugarten, 1979). Diminutions in physical vigor or outright evidence of chronic, potentially debilitating disease are linked to decreased control over one's destiny and the fear of having to depend on others (Cowling & Campbell, 1986). The presence of aches and pains may be a constant remainder of one's vulnerability, which can lead to seemingly inappropriate displays of irritability, anger, and loss of compliance with medical treatment plans (Solomon, 1984).

Contrary to speculations that complaints about somatic symptoms are purely a function of age, recent evidence illustrates that hypochondriacal concerns are related to an individual's level of neuroticism, which does not change across the life span (Costa & McCrae, 1985). It appears that increased complaining is often related to actual increase in medical problems in this age group. High complaints of physical problems in old age could also be characteristic of persons suffering from adjustment difficulties who are using their bodies to communicate psychic distress. Not only on a conscious level are older adults more comfortable with the idea of coming to a medical doctor with their concerns, but this cohort also probably has a greater tendency to translate psychic distress unconsciously into physical disturbance. Unfortunately, many community physicians with extensive geriatric practices are not adept at making accurate psychiatric diagnoses in these clinical presentations (Waxman & Carner, 1984).

A key intervention in the assessment and treatment of adjustment problems in older adulthood is to educate physicians in considering psychosocial histories and their impact on patient reports of somatic distress. In keeping with the work of Waxman and his colleagues (e.g., Waxman & Carner, 1984), we have to assume that primary care providers will be the "first line of defense" in recognizing and treating milder forms of psychopathology in the older adult. Admittedly, physicians are beginning to be trained to think in terms of a masked or atypical depression behind vague physical complaints (Blumenthal, 1980), but this should be extended to include probing for alcohol and drug abuse and other signs of poor coping with the stresses of late life.

Colarusso and Nemiroff (1981) outline a psychoanalytically based life-span developmental progression of individuals' relationship to their bodies. Adolescence and early adulthood are highlighted by the continued development of prowess, a sense of effectiveness in being in the world. As early as the late 30s and 40s comes the awareness of physical limitations and a normal mourning for the body of one's youth, a body that was more resilient and forgiving of physical excesses. The sixth and seventh decades of life are marked by reactions to physical decline and impairment: sensory loss, heart attacks, or even cancer. It appears that sensory disturbances, especially those in the vestibular system, are related to complaints of poor health in several countries (Shanas, Townsend, Wedderburn, Friis, Milhoj, & Stehouwer, 1968). Colarusso and Nemiroff (1981) characterize the major task of later years as maintaining the ability to remain active and outgoing despite frequent physical infirmity. Threading through all of the transitions is the issue of continued care versus neglect of the body.

Increasing physical infirmity brings with it not only the issues of dependency and passivity, but also certain derivative stressors in late life. Coupled with retirement and bereavement, physical decline can mark the final blow in the older adult's continuing isolation from family and friends. Physical and cognitive impairments also can give rise to another stressor in late life: caregiver burden.

Caregiver Strain and Burden

Many middle-age and older adults inevitably will find themselves in a caregiving role with either a physically or cognitively impaired spouse, parent, or in-law. More of the caregiving for a couple's set of parents is likely to be delegated to the wife, regardless of whose parents are involved (Bumagin & Hirn, 1982).

One of the most difficult caregiving scenarios is living independently and caring for a dementing spouse or other close family member. This can be very isolating, as one's needs for affection and intimacy are no longer met (Lezak, 1978). The caregiver's time is consumed by the care of the patient, leaving little time for outside socialization. Mourning may accompany each loss of function in the affected loved one, a process that often feels strange when the person mourned is still alive (Baum & Gallagher, 1985). The burdened caregiver also may utilize considerable denial, not wanting to think ahead or plan for the future, ignoring negative changes in the patient, and continuing to have unrealistic expectations (Barnes, Raskind, Scott, & Murphy, 1981). Some will perseverate in responding to a brain-damaged person as if he or she were intact, apparently with no appreciation for the limits in cognitive functioning. One of the common themes in the successful psychotherapeutic treatment of caregivers is gradual acceptance (Baum & Gallaher, 1985).

Burdened spouses or other family caregivers may suffer from anxiety, depression, feelings of fatigue, anger, resentment, and perhaps guilt on top of it all (Zarit, Orr, & Zarit, 1985). Not only may they feel a lack of social support, but other relatives may criticize them. It appears that how the caregiver manages memory and behavioral problems, along with the level of social support available to him or her and the quality of the relationship before the onset of disease, all predict the extent of burden the caregiver will feel (Zarit et al., 1985). Higher flexibility in the caregiver role, characterized by a willingness to try new approaches, is associated with less burden.

There is no solid data base on the extent of caregivers' psychological burden, so we do not have a good grasp of the prevalence of distinguishable psychiatric disorders in this group. Gallagher (1985) refers to one study suggesting that caregivers' levels of depression on a widely used paper-and-pencil measure were lower than expected, given the interview findings. This is consistent with earlier discussions of the danger of relying too heavily on self-report indices of adjustment difficulties in the absence of a complementary diagnostic interview.

ASSESSMENT OF ADJUSTMENT DISORDERS OF LATE LIFE

The dramatic, threatening events of later adulthood naturally cause major upheaval and problems in adjustment for many older persons. The challenge for the health care professional is two-fold: we do not want to overmedicate older adults who are experiencing loneliness or normal grief reactions, but at the same time we do not want to miss a serious mood disorder masked by physical complaints that could respond to more somatic forms of treatment and lessen the risk of suicide. One aim of psychological assessment with this population is to identify a broad range of psychopathology that may characterize older adults who are coping with severe stressors or whose life-long adaptation has been profoundly compromised by events typically occurring in later years.

As mentioned earlier, measures should be broadly based, tapping a number of affects and concerns. Second, a careful history coupled with a mental status examination should be conducted, to delineate psychosocial stressors and to gain an impression of psychiatric symptoms and behavioral changes that may not be endorsed by the elderly person on self-report measures. Third, a differential diagnosis should be made between adjustment disorders, more serious psychiatric disorders or character pathology that may have been exacerbated by the psychosocial stressors, and organic disorders that may be emerging concomitantly with transitions into late life. A diagnosis based upon a broad array of data will have profound implications for treatment planning.

Personality Functioning

Lawton, Whelihan, and Belsky (1980) report that several investigations found older adults responding well to the Rorschach Inkblot Test, and Cath (1983) maintained that rigidity in the Rorschach is more a function of a decline in intellective capabilities than age per se. However, a revival of research utilizing updated methodologies is necessary before solid conclusions can be drawn about the effectiveness of this instrument with older adult populations (Lawton et al., 1980). These authors also suggest that the Minnesota Multiphasic Personality Inventory (MMPI) can be used with bright, vigorous older people; but this measure, along with the 71-item "Mini-Mult" and its discouraging reliability, should be used as a rough indicator of areas needing exploration and not as an aid in understanding psychodynamic aspects of personality functioning.

The Gerontological Apperception Test (GAT) appears no different from the traditional Thematic Apperception Test (TAT) in eliciting selected themes, and both the GAT and the Senior Apperception Test portray older adults in negatively stereotyped social situations that may pull for more negatively biased material. According to Lawton and his colleagues, the TAT is still the best developed instrument of its kind for use with older adults (Lawton et al., 1980). Also, normal middle-aged and elderly community residents judged high and low on psychological adaptation were differentiated by their responses to ten items on the Rotter Incomplete Sentences Blank.

A full psychological test battery is appropriate for older adults who have protracted psychic strain long after the onset of a serious stressor. For example, the nature of a person's work may have been a "good enough" fit with a particular personality structure, but retirement coupled with adjustment to a chronic illness may cause the person to become overwhelmed with unremitting anxiety and depression. In these cases an "adjustment" model may not be fitting, and more in-depth treatment may be needed. As Cath and Miller (1986) aptly discuss, people over the age of 60 can be as curious, creative, and motivated for psychoanalysis as in any other phase of life. Positive prognostic indicators for psychoanalytic treatment include a relatively low level of defensiveness, a sense of reconciliation to one's level of achievement (to avoid profound despair over what has been accomplished versus what may have been accomplished), and wisdom born of experience in living.

Anxiety and Depression

For a self-report assessment of depressed mood in older persons, the Geriatric Depression Scale (Yesavage, Brink, & Rose, 1983) and the Beck Depression Inventory (Beck, Ward, & Mendelson, 1961) are recommended. Both scales have shown good reliability and validity in several studies, and more recent work indicates that both are specific and sensitive to geriatric depression (Norris, Gallagher,

Wilson, & Winograd, 1987). Probably the Geriatric Depression Scale (GDS) is better for lower functioning patients with physical ailments, while either scale would be useful in healthier and cognitively intact populations. The BDI has the advantage of having scaling for severity of specific symptoms; in particular, it features an item on suicide that can be very helpful in the assessment of older persons suffering from adjustment problems.

The psychometry of anxiety disorders reflects a scant amount of research compared to that on depression. A good deal of work is needed to develop measures that will detect and gauge the severity of anxiety in older adults (Gallagher, 1987). The Brief Symptom Inventory (Derogatis & Spencer, 1982) contains 53 items that factor into nine symptom clusters: anxiety, interpersonal sensitivity, somatization, depression, hostility, obsessive-compulsive behavior, paranoid ideation, psychoticism, and phobic anxiety. The BSI has the advantage of quickly screening for a wide range of psychopathology, including somatization for those patients who may be denying their distress, as well as paranoid ideation and psychoticism for those older persons who may develop late-life delusional disorders in response to losses and social isolation. As with the depression measures, norms for elders on the BSI are available (Hale, Cochran, & Hedgepeth, 1984). Other available omnibus adjective checklists include the Multiple Affect Adjective Check List (Zuckerman & Lubin, 1971). Unfortunately, this instrument has just begun to be used regularly with older adults, so there are no standard scores available for the elderly (Gallagher, 1987).

These indices of anxiety typically correlate highly with measures of depression, suggesting that they are tapping a general "perturbation" characteristic of the mild psychopathology of uncomplicated bereavement and adjustment disorders. In fact, many thinkers in psychopathology currently do not regard anxiety and depression as independent constructs.

Moving away from the more quickly administered self-report measures, there are broad-based inventories that take about 20 minutes for a skilled interviewer to administer. Overall and Gorham (1962) developed the Brief Psychiatric Rating Scale (BPRS) to assess anxiety, tension, somatic concern, emotional withdrawal, conceptual disorganization, guilt feelings, mannerisms and posturing, grandiosity, hostility, suspiciousness, hallucinatory behavior, motor retardation, uncooperativeness, unusual thought content, and blunted affect. Similarly, the Sandoz Clinical Assessment—Geriatric Scale (SCAG), developed by Shader, Harmatz, and Salzman (1974), was designed to assess a wide variety of domains, some of which may help to distinguish between organic deterioration and depression in older adults. Although these two scales typically have not been used for diagnostic purposes with the elderly and have been utilized to assess pharmacotherapeutic outcome (Gallagher, 1987), the attractiveness of both is their global scope and quick administration time (when used by a trained person).

Another potentially useful scale for exploring adjustment concerns is one created recently by Wisocki and her colleagues, aptly called the Worry Scale (Wisocki, in press; Wisocki, Handen, & Morse, 1986). This scale is made up of 35 items that are clustered into three dimensions: finances, health, and social conditions. Correlating in one study with two self-report indices of anxiety (Wisocki, Handen, & Morse, 1986), the responses on the Worry Scale can quickly give the clinician a sense of an elderly person's level of distress over both major life stresses and common daily has-sles. Clusters or themes of worries can help in the diagnosis and treatment of adjust-ment disorders in late life.

Substance Abuse

Increased alcohol and drug abuse is a common maladaptive coping response in the elderly population (Simon, 1980). Although the normative age for alcoholism occurs in mid-life, alcoholism is often seen in the elderly. Facing specific problems associated with retirement or widowhood, elders will sometimes turn to alcohol to self-medicate anxiety, depression, and loneliness (Barnes, 1982). The Michigan Alcoholism Screening Test (MAST; Selzer, 1971), which has been utilized now for almost two decades, is a 25-item self-report measure with weights ranging from 1 to 5. This test also can be scored by dropping the weightings and assigning a unit score for each positive response; this version, dubbed the UMAST, is described in recent work by Willenbring, Christensen, Spring, and Rasmussen (1987). Two shorter forms of the instrument, the Brief Michigan Alcoholism Screening Test (BMAST) and the Short MAST (SMAST), were introduced immediately after the MAST's inception.

Although all four measures have demonstrated validity in younger populations, until very recently none of the measures were validated in elderly populations. How-ever, a recent Minnesota study established the sensitivities and specificities for each of these measures in elderly men. Both the MAST and the UMAST demonstrated excellent sensitivity and specificity, and Willenbring et al. (1987) recommend that clinicians working with older clients feel comfortable using the MAST for alcoholism screening. If greater simplification is desired, it appears better to use the UMAST with its unit scoring rather than one of the shorter forms that demonstrate poorer sensitivities. The minimally longer time to fill out the MAST and UMAST seem to be worth the gain in sensitivity (in not producing many false negatives, for example) in the elderly population. The user should be mindful that psychometric work has not been carried out with these measures specifically on older women, but younger women score similarly to younger men.

With all the paper-and-pencil measures discussed, the goal is to err towards overidentification of distress rather than missing signs of difficulties; it is up to the clinician, of course, to piece the data together to establish a diagnosis or an assess-ment. Naturally, behavioral changes such as medication abuse cannot be discerned by sophisticated psychological testing or the brief screening measures outlined above. These measures should serve as *one step* in the context of a thorough biopsychosocial appraisal of the elderly patient or client. A vital component of this process is the clinician's art in eliciting potentially embarrassing information from the patient. An apparent anxiety disorder may be the short-term withdrawal symptoms from depriva-tion of alcohol or benzodiazepines. Similarly, a depressive-like psychomotor retarda-tion may be from sedative-hypnotic abuse rather than a mood disorder.

The common adjustments of later years—bereavement, retirement, physical decline, rolelessness, isolation, and caregiver burden—produce a myriad of symp-toms and behavioral changes. These depend on the nature of the stressors, their particular meaning to the patient, the extent of social support, the previous coping strategies of the patient, and the biological and psychological predispositions inherent in all of us. The goal of assessment is to identify clusters of symptoms and place them in a context of life-span development and threats to equilibrium. Only then can the clinician conceive of interventions appropriate in scope and intensity.

REFERENCES

Barnes, G.M. (1982). Patterns of alcohol use and abuse among older persons in a household population. In W.G. Wood & M.F. Elias (Eds.), *Alcoholism and aging: Advances in research* (pp.3-15). Boca Raton, FL: CRC Press.

Barnes, R.F., Raskind, M.A., Scott, M., & Murphy, C. (1981). Problems of families caring for Alzheimer patients: Use of a support group. *Journal of the American Geriatrics Society, 29,* 80-85.

Baum, D., & Gallagher, D.E. (1985). Case studies of psychotherapy with depressed caregivers. *Clinical Gerontologist, 4,* 19-29.

Beck, A.T., Ward, C.H., & Mendelson, M. (1961). An inventory for measuring depression. *Archives of General Psychiatry, 4,* 561-571.

Berman, H. J. (1986). To flame with a wild life: Florida Scott-Maxwell's experience of old age. *The Gerontologist, 26,* 321-324.

Blau, D. (1979). On the psychology of the aging woman. *Journal of Geriatric Psychiatry, 12,* 3-8.

Bloom-Feshbach, J., & Bloom-Feshbach, S. (1987). *The psychology of separation and loss.* San Francisco: Jossey-Bass.

Blumenthal, M.D. (1980, April). Depressive illness in old age: Getting behind the mask. *Geriatrics,* pp. 34-43.

Brooke, N. (1980). The effects of retirement. *Australian Family Physician, 9,* 576-578.

Bumagin, V. E., & Hirn, K. F. (1982). Observations on changing relationships for older married women. *The American Journal of Psychoanalysis, 42,* 133-142.

Cath, S. H. (1983). The normal psychology of the aging male: Sex differences in coping and perceptions of life events. *Journal of Geriatric Psychiatry, 16,* 211-222.

Cath, S.H., & Miller, N.E. (1986). The psychoanalysis of the older patient. *Journal of the American Psychoanalytic Association, 34,* 163-177.

Colarusso, C.A., & Nemiroff, R.A. (1981). *Adult development: A new dimension in psychodynamic theory and practice.* New York: Plenum.

Cole, K.D. (1987). Late life paranoid states. *Geriatric Medicine Today, 6,* 77-85.

Colerick, E. J. (1985). Stamina in later life. *Social Science in Medicine, 21,* 997-1006.

Costa, P.T., & McCrae, R.R. (1985). Hypochondriasis, neuroticism, and aging: When are somatic complaints unfounded? *American Psychologist, 40,* 19-28.

Cowling, W. R., & Campbell, V.G. (1986). Health concerns of aging men. *Nursing Clinics of North America, 21,* 75-83.

Davidson, L. (1979). Preventive attitudes toward midlife crisis. *The American Journal of Psychoanalysis, 39,* 165-173.

Derogatis, L. R., & Spencer, P.M. (1982). *The Brief Symptom Inventory (BSI)—Administration, scoring, and procedures manual: I.* Baltimore: Clinical Psychometric Research.

Ekerdt, D. J., Bosse, R., & Levkoff, S. (1985). An empirical test for phases of retirement: Findings from the normative aging study. *Journal of Gerontology, 40,* 95-101.

Gallagher, D. E. (1985). Intervention strategies to assist caregivers of frail elders: Current research status and future research directions. In M.P. Lawton & G.L. Maddox (Eds.), *Annual Review of Gerontology and Geriatrics* (pp. 249-282). New York: Springer.

Gallagher, D. E. (1987). Assessing affect in the elderly. In L.Z. Rubenstein, L.J. Campbell, & R.L. Kane (Eds.), *Clinics in geriatric medicine: Geriatric assessment* (pp. 65-85). Philadelphia: W.B. Saunders.

Glover, B. H. (1979). Psychological needs of the elderly. *Comprehensive Therapy, 5,* 62-67.

Hale, W.D., Cochran, C.D., & Hedgepeth, B.E. (1984). Norms for the elderly on the Brief Symptom Inventory. *Journal of Consulting and Clinical Psychology, 52,* 321-322.

Hansson, R. O., Jones, W.H., Carpenter, B.N., & Remondet, J.H. (1986). Loneliness and adjustment to older age. *International Journal of Aging and Human Development, 24,* 41-53.

Henker, F.O. (1983). All aging is psychosomatic. *Psychosomatics, 24,* 231-233.

Holahan, C.K., & Holahan, C.J. (1987). Self-efficacy, social support, and depression in aging: A longitudinal analysis. *Journal of Gerontology, 42,* 65-68.

Holahan, C.K., Holahan, C.J., & Belk, S.S. (1984). Adjustment in aging: The roles of life stress, hassles, and self-efficacy. *Health Psychology, 3,* 315-328.

Kanner, A.D., Coyne, J.C., Schaefer, C., & Lazarus, R.S. (1981). Comparisons of two modes of stress management: Daily hassles and uplift versus major life events. *Journal of Behavioral Medicine, 4,* 1-39.

Kasl, S.V., Cobb, S., & Gore, S. (1972). Changes in reported illness and illness behavior related to termination of employment: A preliminary report. *International Journal of Epidemiology, 1,* 111-118.

Lawton, M.P., Whelihan, W.M., & Belsky, J.K. (1980). Personality tests and their uses with older adults. In J.E. Birren & R. B. Sloane (Eds.), *Handbook of mental health and aging* (pp. 237-253). Englewood Cliffs, NJ: Prentice-Hall.

Levinson, D. J. (1977). The mid-life transition: A period in adult psychosocial development. *Psychiatry, 40,* 99-112.

Lezak, M.D. (1978). Living with the characterologically altered brain injured patient. *Journal of Clinical Psychiatry, 39,* 592-598.

Lowenthal, M.F. (1968). Social isolation and mutual illness in old age. In B.L. Neugarten (Ed.), *Middle age and aging* (pp. 213-219). Chicago: University of Chicago Press.

Mathews, M.A. (1979). On the psychology of the aging woman: Depression in late mid-life: Change or repetition? Another chance for working through. *Journal of Geriatric Psychiatry, 12,* 37-55.

McCrae, R.R. (1982). Age differences in the use of coping mechanisms. *Journal of Gerontology, 37,* 454-460.

McCrae, R.R., & Costa, P.T. (1985). Personality, stress, and coping processes in aging men and women. In R. Andres, E.L. Bierman, & W.R. Hazzard, (Eds.), *Principles of geriatric medicine* (pp. 141-149). New York: McGraw-Hill.

McCrae, R.R., & Costa, P.T. (1985). *Emerging lives, enduring dispositions: Personality in adulthood.* Boston: Little, Brown.

McIntosh, J.L. (1985). Suicide among the elderly: Levels and trends. *American Journal of Orthopsychiatry, 55,* 288-293.

Miller, M. (1976). Geriatric suicide: The Arizona study. *The Gerontologist, 18,* 488-495.

Murphy, E. (1985). The impact of depression in old age on close social relationships. *American Journal of Psychiatry, 142,* 323-327.

Neugarten, B.L. (1979). Time, age, and the life cycle. *The American Journal of Psychiatry, 136,* 887-894.

Norris, J., Gallagher, D., Wilson, A., & Winograd, C. (1987). Assessment of depression in geriatric medical outpatients: The validity of two screening measures. *Journal of the American Geriatrics Society, 35,* 989-995.

Overall, J.E., & Gorham, D.R. (1962). The Brief Psychiatric Rating Scale. *Psychological Reports, 10,* 799-812.

Parkes, C.M. (1972). *Bereavement: Studies of grief in adult life.* New York: International Universities Press.

Porcino, J. (1985). Psychological aspects of aging in women. *Women and Health, 10,* 115-122.

Richard, S., Livson, F., & Peterson, P.G. (1962). *Aging and personality: A study of 87 older men.* New York: John Wiley.

Sachs, B.C. (1983). Aging well. *Psychosomatics, 24,* 225-230.

Schaie, K.W. (1981). Psychological changes from midlife to early old age: Implications for the maintenance of mental health. *American Journal of Orthopsychiatry, 51,* 199-218.

Scott-Maxwell, F. (1968). *The measure of my days.* New York: Penguin.

Selzer, M.L. (1971). The Michigan Alcoholism Screening Test: The quest for a new diagnostic instrument. *American Journal of Psychiatry, 127,* 1653-1658.

Shader, R.I., Harmatz, J.S., & Salzman, C. (1974). A new scale for clinical assessment in geriatric populations: Sandoz Clinical Assessment-Geriatric (SCAG). *Journal of the American Geriatrics Society, 22,* 107-113.

Shanas, E., Townsend, P., Wedderburn, D., Friis, H., Milhoj, P., & Stehouwer, J. (1968). The psychology of health. In B.L. Neugarten (Ed.), *Middle age and aging* (pp. 213-219). Chicago: University of Chicago Press.

Sheppard, H.L. (1985). Health, work, and retirement. In R. Andres, E.L. Bierman, & W.R. Hazzard, (Eds.), *Principles of geriatric medicine* (pp. 150-153). New York: McGraw-Hill.

Simon, A. (1980). The neuroses, personality disorders, alcoholism, drug use and misuse, and crime in the aged. In J.E. Birren & R.B. Sloane (Eds.), *Handbook of mental health and aging* (pp. 653-670). Englewood Cliffs, NJ: Prentice- Hall.

Solomon, K. (1984). Psychosocial crises of older men. *Hillside Journal of Clinical Psychiatry, 6,* 123-134.

Waxman, M.M., & Carner, E.A. (1984). Physicians' recognition, diagnosis, and treatment of mental disorders in elderly medical patients. *The Gerontologist, 25,* 593-597.

Weissman, M.M. (1979). The myth of involutional melancholia. *Journal of the American Medical Association, 242,* 742-744.

Wertheimer, J. (1983). The mechanisms of permanence: Time: Support for a psychodynamic hypothesis of psychological aging. *Journal of Geriatric Psychiatry, 16,* 245-255.

Willenbring, M.L., Christensen, K.J., Spring, W.D., & Rasmussen, R. (1987). Alcoholism screening in the elderly. *Journal of the American Geriatrics Society, 35,* 864-869.

Wisocki, P. (in press). Worry as a phenomenon relevant to the elderly. *Behavior Therapy.*

Wisocki, P., Handen, B., & Morse, C.K. (1986). The Worry Scale as a measure of anxiety among homebound and community active elderly. *The Behavior Therapist, 5,* 91-95.

Worden, J.W. (1982). *Grief counseling and grief therapy.* New York: Springer.

Yesavage, J., Brink, T., & Rose, T. (1983). Development and validation of a geriatric screening scale: A preliminary report. *Journal of Psychiatric Research, 17,* 37-49.

Zarit, S.H., Orr, N.K., & Zarit, J.M. (1985). *The hidden victims of Alzheimer's disease: Families under stress.* New York: New York University Press.

Zuckerman, M., & Lubin, B. (1965). *Multiple Affect Adjective Check List (manual).* San Diego: Educational and Industrial Testing Service.

12

Assessment of Memory in Older Adults

E. A. ROBERTSON-TCHABO, PH.D., DAVID ARENBERG, PH.D.

Memory involves the capacity to retain information about past events and also to plan and to make projections about future events. Memory problems are probably the most common cognitive complaint that prompts older individuals to seek professional help. Consequently, one of the most frequent questions encountered by clinicians working with the elderly concerns assessment of memory. Perhaps because everyday cognition plays a central role in adaptation to aging, issues related to age differences in mental functioning have become the area most frequently studied by researchers in the psychology of aging (Poon, 1985). Moreover, the research on aging and cognitive performance, especially memory, has been reviewed frequently (Craik, 1977; Craik & Trehub, 1982; Kausler, 1982; Labouvie-Vief & Schell, 1982; Poon, 1980, 1985, 1986; Poon, Fozard, Cermak, Arenberg, & Thompson, 1980; Robertson-Tchabo & Arenberg, 1987; Salthouse, 1982, 1985).

Despite the abundance of research on aging and memory, the current status of memory evaluation of older adults can be characterized as procedure rich but test poor. Practitioners will find many procedures in the aging literature that have been used to assess various aspects of memory, but few of these procedures meet the criteria of a test. Some years ago, Erickson and Scott (1977), in a review of clinical memory testing, contrasted the status of testing in many domains of psychology with that in memory and stated "the important area of memory functioning has been virtually ignored. With the exception of the Wechsler Memory Scale, there are no widely known clinical tests of memory functioning" (p. 1130).

Although much research in memory and aging has been reported since then, progress in test development has lagged far behind. Cunningham (1986) identified several reasons for this state of affairs. Some of the reasons are not specific to aging. One problem is the indeterminate dimensionality of memory. There are many theories/models of memory, and virtually all of them are multidimensional. Although it is generally agreed that there are several aspects and components of memory, unfortunately there is not general agreement about its structure. Without such a structure, it is not surprising that psychometric development of tests to measure components of memory is sparse.

Another problem, also mentioned by Cunningham (1986), is that the procedures developed by memory researchers have been process oriented, with little heed paid to individual differences. Although individual differences are a major concern for practitioners, psychometric properties for the laboratory procedures have rarely been demonstrated, and relevant norms based on large samples are virtually nonexistent. It is especially important to keep in mind that the pattern of age-related differences in cognitive performance is based on group means and that no single pattern is characteristic of all older persons. Within an age group there is always some variability around that mean, and frequently the variability within an older group is greater relative to comparable younger groups. Typically, among the older groups, some performances are found that are indistinguishable from those of young adults. Moreover, some older individuals may give a casual observer the impression that their mental abilities are intact by selectively avoiding settings that would reveal their deficits. Even under closer scrutiny in a laboratory setting, however, many older individuals perform as well as younger individuals. Mean performance measures should not be generalized to all members of an age group. Perhaps group performance should be used as a guideline only in the absence of information about an individual.

Such increased variability makes it difficult to interpret normative data with confidence. In addition, Fozard and Thomas (1975) have reported that within-subject variability appears to increase with age; that is, in general, the test performance of an older individual is less consistent (more variable). Within-subject variability also will decrease the reliability and predictive power of a memory test unless factors contributing to this variability are known and evaluated. Moreover, norms are misleading if extreme scores are due to factors other than memory impairment, such as depression (Kahn & Miller, 1978) or educational level (Birren & Morrison, 1961; Granick & Friedman, 1967).

Erickson, Poon, and Walsh-Sweeney (1980) emphasized that the chief justification of clinical memory tests lies in their ability to provide a better understanding and perhaps remediation of behavioral deficits. They suggested that an instrument should be comprised of tasks with clear analogs that can be validated in terms of everyday behavior and translated into meaningful intervention strategies. Only recently have experimental psychologists acknowledged the importance of issues related to the ecological validity of laboratory measures collected in the controlled environment of an experimental laboratory; that is, age differences in performance in a laboratory also should be obtained in other settings, particularly in everyday, real-life environments. It is important to note that everyday settings may provide compensatory cues that contribute to proficient performance that have no counterparts in laboratory settings (Harris & Morris, 1984). A second concern related to ecological validity is the degree to which test materials are relevant to the everyday environments of elderly individuals. Typically, tests used to assess the cognitive performance of older people have not been developed specifically for use with older populations. Consequently, a test developed and standardized on young adults may be inappropriate to test those behaviors in older individuals, either in terms of content or administration procedure (Schaie, 1977, 1978).

The purpose of this chapter is to outline normal age differences in memory performance and to describe experimental laboratory procedures and psychometric tests frequently used to assess memory of aging individuals.

A GENERAL MODEL OF INFORMATION PROCESSING

Currently, information processing is the dominant and most comprehensive approach to human cognition, and for some time much of the research in memory and aging has investigated various components of information-processing models. Cognitive psychologists who are information-processing oriented are principally interested in the study of higher mental processes, including learning, memory, language, thinking, and problem solving. From an information-processing perspective, cognition refers to the processes by which sensory input is encoded (transformed, reduced, and elaborated), stored, and retrieved. Information-processing models view humans as active seekers and users of information. The cognitive system is seen as constantly active, adding to its environmental input and essentially constructing the mind's view of reality. Information processing concepts have been borrowed from computer science, and terms including *input, output, storage, buffer, executive processor,* and *system architecture* are all used to emphasize the view that the flow of information through the human cognitive system proceeds through active stages that take time.

It is particularly useful to distinguish two major dimensions of the cognitive system, which Atkinson and Shiffrin (1968) termed *structural features* and *control processes.* Structural features refer to permanent features of the system, including both the physical system and the built-in processes that are fixed from one situation to another. Control processes, on the other hand, refer to features that can be modified readily or reprogrammed by the individual and that may vary substantially from one time to another, depending upon such factors as the nature of instructions, the meaningfulness of the information, and the individual's experience. This distinction has important ramifications for research in aging. It is important to evaluate how an individual performs a task in order to distinguish those aspects that an individual can change (improve) from the structural features of the system. The task for the clinician is to evaluate task performance not only under control conditions with no instructional set (spontaneous selection of control processes or usual response) but also under instruction conditions that require subjects to use more efficient strategies (optimal control processes).

It is helpful to describe memory procedures used in research based on information processing by referring to the components of a general model of that kind. For this purpose, the following discussion will use a model with four stores in which information can be held and three information processes. The stores are 1) sensory memory, 2) primary memory, 3) secondary memory, and 4) very long-term storage sometimes referred to as tertiary memory. The processes are 1) encoding, 2) storage, and 3) retrieval. Later the concept of working memory will be introduced, which subsumes some aspects of the stores and processes listed above.

Sensory Memory

Sensory memory is a brief repository of information and is modality specific. Visual sensory memory is referred to as *iconic* memory, and procedures used to investigate age differences in iconic memory involve identification of briefly presented stimuli (e.g., a 3 x 3 matrix of letters displayed for 500 msec). Although small age differences have been reported in iconic memory (Walsh & Prasse, 1980; Cerella, Poon, & Fozard, 1982), and virtually no research has been reported for other sensory memory, it is unlikely that age differences in performance of more usual memory tasks are attributable to differences in sensory memory. Furthermore, we know of no large sample data that can be used for normative comparisons.

Primary Memory

Primary memory is a small-capacity store of information at the focus of attention. It is typically assessed by span tasks such as forward digit span; one measure frequently used is the longest string of digits that can be reproduced in sequence. Age studies almost always report only small differences in forward digit span. Probably the largest body of forward digit span data over the adult age range was collected for the two Wechsler adult intelligence scales (Wechsler, 1955, 1981), but age norms are provided only for a combined measure of both forward and backward digit span. Backward digit span is assumed to involve more than primary memory because the presented information must be transposed before responding. Forward and backward digit span data were reported separately in the Guild Memory Test (Ferris, Crook, Clark, McCarthy, & Rae, 1980), which was developed for diagnostic purposes, but those data do not cover all adult ages. Measures of forward digit span have been collected in the Baltimore Longitudinal Study of Aging (Shock et al., 1984) for the full adult age range, and those data are reported for men and women with and without a college education. Although the participants in this study are not a representative sample of any definable population, these data, especially for the groups with a college degree, may be useful for some purposes. The data in Tables 1-4 are based on four trials of seven strings of digits presented auditorily at a rate of one digit per second. Each trial begins with a 3-digit string and progresses to a 9-digit string. The longest string correctly recalled in sequence on each trial is used to obtain a mean of four trials, and that mean is an individual's score. Each trial serves as the interpolated task for a delayed verbal-memory procedure.

Secondary Memory

Secondary memory is the store of newly acquired information that is more permanent and less vulnerable to interference than information in primary memory. By definition, when the presented information exceeds the capacity of primary memory, that information must enter secondary memory or be forgotten. Typically, in the laboratory, new information is presented that exceeds the capacity of primary memory, and except for the last few items presented, the amount of information that survives is considered to be in secondary memory. Age differences are almost always found with such procedures unless substantial cueing is provided. Much of the research in memory and aging has involved secondary memory, and many procedures have been used to measure it.

Single-trial free recall is one such procedure. Although there is no standard way to administer free recall, typically a string of at least 10 words is presented at a fixed rate, and the task is to recall as many of the words as possible in any order. The words are usually unrelated, and the rate is usually 1-3 seconds per word. Subjects are given as much time as they need to respond with all the words they can recall. The words can be presented visually or auditorily, and the responses can be written or spoken. Currently, the visual modality is more frequently used, in part because visual impairment is more likely to be corrected and also because microprocessors and computers are commonly used in the laboratory.

Recognition is another approach to assessing secondary memory. There are two

TABLE 1

DIGIT SPAN FORWARD, MEAN LONGEST STRING—MEN, NO DEGREE

Score[a]	Age					
	20–29	30–39	40–49	50–59	60–69	70–79
9.0	2	0	0	0	2	0
8.5–8.9	2	3	2	3	1	1
8.0–8.4	2	4	1	4	3	2
7.5–7.9	3	0	4	2	4	2
7.0–7.4	0	2	1	3	1	5
6.5–6.9	5	6	3	3	4	2
6.0–6.4	1	4	4	4	5	1
5.5–5.9	1	1	3	4	1	2
5.0–5.4	2	1	0	1	1	4
4.5–4.9			1	1	0	2
4.0–4.4					1	
Mean	7.14	7.07	6.76	6.90	6.95	6.48
S.D.	1.26	1.01	1.14	1.19	1.23	1.24
N	18	21	19	25	23	21 (127)

[a] Mean of longest correct string on four trials of seven strings (from 3 digits to 9 digits)

general recognition procedures for memory of word lists. One procedure presents the target words (words from the list) one at a time, intermixed with distractor words; the task is to respond "yes" or "no" to each word to indicate whether or not that word was from the list. Another procedure pairs each target word with a distractor, and the task is to select the target word. The advantage of this forced-choice method is that it avoids response bias (i.e., the tendency to respond predominantly "yes" or predominantly "no" when in doubt). Recognition memory is thought to be more sensitive than free recall for assessing what is in secondary memory, and age differences are small or even not found when recognition performance is compared. In order to discuss differences between recall and recognition, however, one must first consider the major processes thought to be operating in information-processing models.

The general model in use here includes encoding, storage, and retrieval. Encod-

TABLE 2

DIGIT SPAN FORWARD, MEAN LONGEST STRING—MEN, COLLEGE DEGREE

Score[a]	Age						
	20–29	30–39	40–49	50–59	60–69	70–79	80–89
9.0	2	3	6	5	8	2	0
8.5–8.9	2	15	10	11	12	7	2
8.0–8.4	5	12	7	13	16	6	6
7.5–7.9	3	8	4	15	11	5	4
7.0–7.4	2	12	7	13	24	19	4
6.5–6.9	3	9	5	13	11	13	7
6.0–6.4	3	4	9	4	17	15	4
5.5–5.9		3	5	8	11	18	5
5.0–5.4		1	1	7	6	6	3
4.5–4.9		1	1	3	2	2	3
4.0–4.4					0	1	1
3.5–3.9					1	1	
Mean	7.55	7.50	7.34	7.14	7.07	6.61	6.58
S.D.	0.94	1.02	1.21	1.22	1.25	1.11	1.23
N	20	68	55	92	119	95	39	(488)

[a] Mean of longest correct string on four trials of seven strings (from 3 digits to 9 digits)

ing involves the active processes that an individual uses to remember information. When the information does not exceed the limited capacity of primary memory, it can be maintained by repetition alone. After finding a telephone number in the directory, in order to remember the number long enough to place the call, repeating the number several times often suffices. (Of course, that assumes that seven digits does not exceed the capacity of one's primary memory.) Sometimes rehearsal is sufficient to store information into secondary memory, but such storage usually requires some associative process. Either the new information is organized in some meaningful way or the information is associated with information already in secondary (or tertiary) memory. Retrieval is the process used to bring stored information to a state that allows the information to be used.

TABLE 3

DIGIT SPAN FORWARD, MEAN LONGEST STRING—WOMEN, NO DEGREE

Score[a]	Age					
	20–29	30–39	40–49	50–59	60–69	70–79
9.0	1	0	1	0	6	0
8.5–8.9	0	3	0	0	4	2
8.0–8.4	1	2	3	1	5	2
7.5–7.9	0	3	1	2	7	2
7.0–7.4	2	4	2	3	6	3
6.5–6.9	5	3	3	5	4	3
6.0–6.4	1	2	3	4	2	6
5.5–5.9	1	0	5	6	2	2
5.0–5.4	1	0	3	4	1	3
4.5–4.9		1		1		2
4.0–4.4				1		1
3.5–3.9						1
Mean	6.77	7.25	6.55	6.17	6.63	6.31
S.D.	1.00	1.03	1.12	0.98	1.08	1.31
N	12	18	21	27	37	27 (142)

[a] Mean of longest correct string on four trials of seven strings (from 3 digits to 9 digits)

No item retrieval is required in recognition memory of word lists; all the words are presented. The fact that large age differences in recognition are not found is evidence that retrieval is an age-related process. Furthermore, recognition memory is thought to be a more sensitive measure of secondary memory than recall because the latter requires accessing items whereas recognition requires accessing only recent information about items (information about whether an item had been presented in the most recent list). List learning is included in the NYU Memory Test. According to Ferris, Crook, Flicker, Reisberg, and Bartus (1986), five alternate forms of the test are available for repetitive administrations, as are detailed norms and an instruction manual.

In recent years, many studies of memory for paragraphs and longer texts have appeared in the literature. Although age differences have not been found as consistently in these studies as in studies of free recall, the focus has usually been on gist

TABLE 4

DIGIT SPAN FORWARD, MEAN LONGEST STRING—WOMEN, COLLEGE DEGREE

Score[a]	Age						
	20–29	30–39	40–49	50–59	60–69	70–79	80–89
9.0	2	3	3	2	0	0	0
8.5–8.9	2	2	3	2	1	1	1
8.0–8.4	3	1	3	2	1	1	1
7.5–7.9	3	8	3	2	8	3	0
7.0–7.4	3	12	6	10	5	4	0
6.5–6.9	4	9	8	5	8	6	2
6.0–6.4	1	6	2	5	4	7	1
5.5–5.9	0	1	1	5	11	7	3
5.0–5.4	1	3	2	1	4	3	2
4.5–4.9	0	2				2	0
4.0–4.4	1	1				1	1
3.5–3.9							1
Mean	7.29	6.83	7.26	6.92	6.52	6.27	5.83
S.D.	1.19	1.12	1.08	1.01	0.96	0.99	1.74
N	20	48	31	34	42	35	12	(222)

[a] Mean of longest correct string on four trials of seven strings (from 3 digits to 9 digits)

recall rather than verbatim recall, and gist recall is the kind of memory individuals are likely to use in everyday contexts. Dixon, Hultsch, and Hertzog (1985) have created 25 structurally equivalent texts, and as their work progresses, their samples are expected to become usable for normative purposes. In addition, paragraph recall is included in the Guild Memory Test (Ferris et al., 1980) and is a subtest of the Wechsler Memory Scale (Wechsler, 1945, 1987).

Tertiary Memory

Tertiary memory is the store of an individual's total knowledge. Unfortunately, there is a severe problem in measuring this kind of memory. Obviously, knowledge can be measured, but knowledge failures cannot be attributed to memory unless it can be demonstrated that the information was well learned at some time in the past. Vocabulary tests are frequently used to assess word knowledge, and substantial age norms are available for psychometric measures of both vocabulary and general information (e.g., Wechsler, 1955, 1981), but these are not truly measures of tertiary memory. Schonfield (1972) proposed that recall of the names of one's school teachers could be used to measure tertiary memory; it is certainly reasonable to assume that such information had been acquired. It would usually be necessary to assume that the responses were correct, however, and such a measure would also confound age with time since the information was acquired. (The latter point would not be a problem for comparisons within age groups.) Questionnaire measures of information about events well identified with respect to calendar time have been used (e.g., Howes & Katz, 1988; Poon, Fozard, Paulshock, & Thomas, 1979), but they all require the assumption that the information had been acquired in order to use such a measure as an assessment of tertiary memory.

It is possible, however, to use such questionnaire performance to measure change in tertiary memory. If it can be demonstrated that information about remote events was part of a person's knowledge base at one point in time but not at a later time, then that is evidence for a decline in tertiary memory. Therefore, although a measure of information about past events is not a measure of tertiary memory, repeated measures of the same information can be used to assess changes in tertiary memory. It would be preferable to assess at the repeat times additional but comparable information about past events to deal with the problem that what is remembered may be enhanced by the previous recall.

Working Memory

Working memory is a store necessary to support higher level integrative processing such as comprehension and inference. Typically, both incoming information as well as information retrieved from secondary or tertiary memory are included in this store. The retrieved information may be pre-experimental knowledge or information previously presented during the current test/experimental session. In some models not only encoding of the incoming information but also the integrative processing are subsumed under working memory as well as the storage function (see, e.g., Hasher & Zacks, in press).

One of the psychometric approaches to working memory is backward digit or letter span (e.g., Horn, Donaldson, & Engstrom, 1981). In a backward span procedure, the incoming information must be stored and transformed (order reversed). Daneman and Carpenter (1980) developed a procedure that has been used as a measure of working memory. Sentences are presented sequentially, and the task is to recall the last word of each sentence. Similar to span tasks, the measure is the longest string of sentences from which all the last words can be recalled.

Salthouse and his colleagues developed a computer-administered procedure to measure working memory that is similar to the procedure of Daneman and Carpenter (1980) but uses simple additions as stimuli. The task, called computational span, is to sum sets of two digits and then to recall the second digit of each set. In a recent application (Salthouse, Mitchell, Skovronek, & Babcock, in press), the score was derived from the convergence of a combined ascending and descending psycho-physical-type series that provided an estimate of the longest stable number of sets with errorless recall. The reliability of that score was .78 in a study of 120 college-educated men ranging in age from 20 to 79, and the correlation with age was -.46.

In Hunt's (1986) presentation of production-activation models of memory, he pointed out that working memory is context specific and that the concept of a general test of working memory is questionable. According to the models, effective cognition requires both "a structural capacity for holding any information and a learned, sub-ject-matter specific capacity for coding information in an efficient way in order to reduce the load on memory structures" (p. 48). Hunt argued that "working memory capacity should be tested in contexts that are important in a person's life" (p. 48).

The results of the study of Salthouse et al. (in press) provide evidence for the context-specific nature of working memory. These researchers attempted to account for the relationship between age and performance on two reasoning tasks using com-putational span as a measure of working memory. Only a small proportion of the variance that age accounted for in the measures of reasoning performance was attributable to computational span. Internal measures of working memory derived from aspects of the reasoning tasks themselves, however, accounted for much more of the age relationships across tasks as well as within tasks. In other words, reasoning measures of working memory, more so than the computational span measure of work-ing memory, accounted for relationships between age and reasoning performance. These findings support Hunt's (1986) conclusion that the quest for a general test of working memory is unlikely to succeed and that multiple measures of working mem-ory may prove too impractical in applied settings.

Nonverbal Memory

All of the examples of laboratory memory procedures described above involve verbal memory. A very large proportion of the research in memory and aging has been in that domain. One of the most studied aspects of nominally nonverbal memory is memory for geometric designs. (The term *nominally nonverbal* is used here because some individuals attempt to encode nonverbal visual information verbally. They convert the visual information into a verbal description, then, when they need to remember the designs, retrieve the stored verbal information and reconvert it back to visual information.) Memory for geometric designs has been studied in aging research with psychometric tests such as the Benton Visual Retention Test (BVRT; Benton, 1974). Design recall is part of the Guild Memory Test (Ferris et al., 1980), and picture recognition is part of the NYU Memory Test (see Ferris et al., 1986).

The most extensive data set of memory for geometric designs and adult age is the BVRT data from the Baltimore Longitudinal Study of Aging (Shock et al., 1984). Some of those data for the men, including longitudinal data, have been published (Arenberg, 1978, 1982, 1987); however, the data for the women in that study and the most recent data for the men have not been published. All of the first test data avail-able at this time are presented in Tables 5-8 for men and women with and without a college degree. The score is the total number of errors on Form C, Administration A (standard administration with 10-second exposure and immediate, untimed reproduc-tion).

TABLE 5

BENTON VISUAL RETENTION TEST—MEN, NO DEGREE

Errors	Age						
	20–29	30–39	40–49	50–59	60–69	70–79	80–89
0	10	7	3	1	0	0	0
1	7	8	8	2	0	1	0
2	11	10	7	4	2	1	0
3	9	8	6	7	2	4	2
4	5	8	9	5	4	2	0
5	3	4	8	6	2	8	0
6		1	4	7	4	7	0
7		5	2	2	6	4	0
8		4	0	3	2	3	1
9		0	3	1	4	2	0
10		1	1	2	1	3	2
11		0		1	1	4	4
12		0		1		1	1
13		0				3	1
14		0				1	1
15		0				1	1
16		1				1	1
17						0	0
18						1	0
19							1
Mean	2.02	3.56	3.75	5.07	6.25	7.72	11.13
S.D.	1.53	3.04	2.46	2.79	2.41	3.92	4.29
N	45	57	51	42	28	47	15

(285)

TABLE 6

BENTON VISUAL RETENTION TEST—MEN, COLLEGE DEGREE

	Age						
Errors	20–29	30–39	40–49	50–59	60–69	70–79	80–89
0	13	23	13	11	3	2	0
1	20	38	23	18	8	3	0
2	21	42	35	33	20	13	0
3	13	30	27	17	15	19	6
4	7	24	25	23	17	14	2
5	13	12	21	26	21	14	4
6	3	6	6	12	12	11	4
7	1	3	2	6	9	22	3
8	1	2	1	3	9	12	4
9		0	1	1	4	11	4
10		1	1	3	0	6	4
11				2	2	4	3
12				0	1	3	0
13				0	0	2	3
14				0	1	1	0
15				0	0	1	1
16				1	1	1	0
17							0
18							1
19							0
20							0
21							0
22							1
Mean	2.47	2.49	2.94	3.67	4.66	6.03	8.15
S.D.	1.87	1.87	1.89	2.57	2.81	3.20	4.25
N	92	181	155	156	123	139	40	(886)

TABLE 7

BENTON VISUAL RETENTION TEST—WOMEN, NO DEGREE

	Age						
Errors	20–29	30–39	40–49	50–59	60–69	70–79	80–89
0	2	3	0	0	1	0	0
1	4	4	2	1	0	0	0
2	4	7	3	3	3	2	0
3	2	3	5	2	4	1	0
4	1	2	7	5	4	1	1
5	3	4	2	11	5	6	1
6	3	2	0	5	6	2	0
7		1	4	6	6	4	1
8		1		1	6	7	2
9				0	4	4	0
10				0	1	1	0
11				1	2	0	0
12						0	0
13						0	3
14						3	1
15						0	
16						1	
Mean	2.90	3.04	3.87	5.11	6.02	7.53	9.44
S.D.	2.08	2.21	1.82	1.95	2.58	3.37	3.84
N	19	27	23	35	42	32	9	(187)

TABLE 8

BENTON VISUAL RETENTION TEST—WOMEN, COLLEGE DEGREE

Errors	Age						
	20–29	30–39	40–49	50–59	60–69	70–79	80–89
0	4	12	3	2	1	0	0
1	7	10	7	2	4	0	0
2	9	16	7	6	4	2	2
3	4	10	4	9	10	4	0
4	4	9	2	7	7	4	2
5	7	7	1	8	12	5	0
6	2	0	3	0	9	8	2
7		4	0	2	4	5	1
8		2	0	1	1	3	0
9			1	1	4	4	3
10						2	1
11						3	0
12						1	0
13						1	0
14						1	1
15							0
16							0
17							1
Mean	2.70	2.67	2.61	3.68	4.57	6.79	7.62
S.D.	1.82	2.11	2.17	1.99	2.17	2.97	4.43
N	37	70	28	38	56	43	13 (285)

Birth-Cohort Differences

A methodological note and a caveat are in order here. Birth-cohort differences in performance can create problems in interpreting cross-sectional age data and in using norms based on data collected many years earlier. Cross-sectional age differences confound age changes with birth-cohort differences, and within-age-group comparisons are affected by birth-cohort differences when data are collected at different times. Potential birth-cohort differences for the BVRT were explored in the Baltimore Longitudinal Study of Aging. A very small increase in errors was found for all age groups of men over a 16-year period, but some unknown part of that difference could be attributed to sampling differences during that period (Arenberg, 1982). Although in this case the differences were very small, the findings call attention to the potential problem. Examiners are vulnerable to unknown but possible birth-cohort differences whenever old norms are used.

MEMORY TESTS

An answer to the question "What diagnostic tests are appropriate to evaluate the memory functioning of the elderly?" is still equivocal. Despite the fact that there is agreement regarding the general features of such an instrument, no single test currently available is adequate. Erickson et al. (1980) outlined 10 points that they believed essential for assessing memory functioning in adults. They suggested that a test battery should include measures of orientation, primary memory, delayed retrieval (secondary memory), and tertiary memory. In addition to assessing the acquisition and retention of verbal information, an evaluation of an individual's ability to learn and to retrieve nonverbal information and motor skills is necessary. Further, the efficiency with which a person is able to process information also should be evaluated (e.g., by learning-to-criterion). Moreover, qualitative analyses of the strategies used by an individual to acquire and to retrieve previously acquired information should be included. The instrument should have alternate procedures to make it possible to test persons unable to make verbal or motor responses, and alternate forms would be desirable for repeated measures (e.g., to quantify improvement following training or therapy). Because older subjects may be slower to adapt to the setting and the testing routine than younger individuals, testing over 2 (or more) days would be preferable. The instrument should include recommendations for further testing and remediation and be structured so that it is brief and relatively easy to administer. Norms for elderly individuals for each of the subtests should be available instead of combining scores as if memory were a unidimensional ability. Finally, and perhaps most critical, the instrument should have established external validity with respect to everyday behaviors. Of course, concomitant information regarding individual differences in education, verbal ability, health status, and emotional states also should be obtained.

It is beyond the scope of this chapter to describe all of the memory batteries that currently are available. Detailed information, however, is available in a number of sources (Erickson & Scott, 1977; Lezak, 1983; Poon, 1986; Raskin & Jarvik, 1979). The Wechsler Memory Scale and its 1987 revision will be described briefly, as it is still the memory battery used most frequently in clinical situations.

Wechsler Memory Scale

Published more than 40 years ago, the Wechsler Memory Scale (WMS) was intended by its author as a rapid, simple, and practical memory examination. The fact that the WMS has maintained its well-entrenched position in the clinical repertoire for so many years is perhaps best attributed to the lag in memory test development. The instrument was designed to measure a number of functions associated with memory and consists of seven subtests: Personal and Current Information, Orientation, Mental Control (sustained attention), Logical Memory, Digit Span, Visual Reproduction, and Associate Learning. Norms were published initially for adults aged up to 64 years (Wechsler, 1945) and extended to include those 80-92 years (Klonoff & Kennedy, 1965, 1966; Meer & Baker, 1965). However, the norms for the WMS are dated and may not reflect contemporary levels of performance. Moreover, scores on all seven subtests are combined into a single summary score, the Memory Quotient, which does not permit comparisons of the various aspects of memory performance.

The WMS also was intended to identify organic problems associated with memory disorders. Unfortunately, the scale does not differentiate among psychotic, neurotic, and organic patients once age and IQ have been controlled (Cohen, 1950). Over the years, other concerns about the limitations of the WMS have been expressed, many of which are summarized by Erickson and Scott (1977) and Prigatano (1978). Issues related to scale content include the preponderance of verbal material (only one of the subtests involves nonverbal stimuli) and the fact that the scale does not measure delayed recall of learned material. Moreover, the scoring rules for two of the subtests, Logical Memory and Visual Reproduction, are too brief and ambiguous to achieve adequate interrater agreement.

Probably the most crucial problem with the WMS is that it is not grounded in a structural theory of memory functioning; that is, issues concerning construct validity remain unresolved. Hulicka (1966) tested subjects 15 to 80 years of age on the WMS and on a name-face test that had both learning and recall components. Correlations between the WMS and the name-face test indicated that four of the WMS subtests (Logical Memory, Digit Span, Visual Reproduction, and Associate Learning) correlated more highly with the learning than with the recall scores. Hulicka suggested that the performance of older persons on the WMS may be more a reflection of willingness to cooperate, ability to understand and follow directions, attention span, and ability (or tolerance) to learn material of little intrinsic value than of ability to recall learned material. In numerous other studies, a significant positive relationship has been found between educational/intellectual level and WMS performance (e.g., Dujovne & Levy, 1971; Piersma, 1986).

Recently, a revised version of the Wechsler Memory Scale was published (Wechsler, 1987). The Wechsler Memory Scale-Revised (WMS-R) is an individually administered, clinical instrument designed to appraise major dimensions of memory functions in adolescents and adults (Herman, 1988). The scale is intended as a diagnostic and screening device for use as part of a general neuropsychological examination or of any other clinical evaluation requiring the assessment of memory functioning. The WMS-R contains 13 subtests. Significant modifications were made in the original subtests, and three nonverbal subtests have been added: a recognition task involving abstract visual forms (Figural Memory), a color-form paired-associate task (Visual Paired Associates), and a nonverbal analog of the familiar digit span task (Visual Memory Span). The WMS-R was standardized on a sample of individuals representative of the nonimpaired United States population aged 16 to 74 years. The sample consisted of approximately 50 subjects in each of six age groups: 16-17, 20-24, 35-44, 55-64, 65-69, and 70-74 years. Each age group included approximately equal numbers of men and women, carefully selected to match the general population with respect to race, geographic region, and educational level.

The first subtest, Information and Orientation Questions, contains 16 items. It combines items from two of the original WMS subtests, Personal and Current Information and Orientation. Seven informational questions and seven orientation-to-time-and-place questions are included, as are two questions concerning the individual's hand preference and whether he or she has any impairments of hearing or vision that could affect performance on some of the subtests. The second subtest, Mental Control, contains three items unchanged from the original scale; however, the scoring rules have been revised to eliminate extra credit for fast, perfect performance. The items include counting backwards, reciting the alphabet, and counting by 3's. The third subtest, Figural Memory, is one of the new subtests. Sets of abstract geometric designs are displayed. After each set has been inspected, the task is to identify the designs previously shown from a larger set of designs.

The fourth subtest, Logical Memory I, is based on the Logical Memory subscale of the original test and consists of two brief (but revised) stories that are read by the examiner. After each story, the task is to recall the story verbatim. The rules for scoring the stories have been made more specific and extensive to improve interscorer agreement. The score is the total number of ideas recalled from both stories. After both stories have been read and responses recorded, the subject is told not to forget the stories because he or she will be asked to tell the stories again later.

The fifth subtest, Visual Paired Associates I, is one of the new subtests and is a visual analog of the Verbal Paired Associates subtest. Six abstract line drawings are paired with a different color and each pair is presented on a card for 3 seconds. After the initial presentation, the same figures are shown again, one at a time in a different order, and the task is to point to the color that goes with each figure. If a subject responds incorrectly or fails to respond within 5 seconds, the examiner points to the correct color. The same set of figure-color pairs is presented and tested two more times. If all six items are answered correctly on the third trial, the subtest is discontinued. If not, the figure-color pairs are presented and tested until all six items are correct or at the end of six trials. After reaching criterion or after the sixth trial, the subject is told to remember which color goes with each figure because he or she will be asked to perform the task later. The score is the total number of correct responses based on the first three test trials.

The sixth subtest, Verbal Paired Associates I, is based on the Associate Learning subtest of the original scale. The examiner reads aloud a set of eight word pairs, then just the first word of each pair; the task is to say the second word from memory. The eight pairs consist of four "easy"-to-associate pairs and four "hard"-to-associate pairs. If a subject gives an incorrect response or does not respond in 5 seconds, the correct associate is supplied by the examiner. As was done in the Visual Paired Associates, the word pairs are presented and tested twice more. If all eight items are correct on the third trial, the subtest is discontinued. If not, a fourth, and if necessary a fifth and sixth, trial is presented. After a subject has reached criterion or after six trials, he or she is told to remember the word pairs for subsequent recall. Separate scores are derived for easy and for hard associations based on the number of correct responses on the first three trials.

The seventh subtest, Visual Reproduction I (Immediate Recall), consists of four geometrical designs. Each design is presented for 10 seconds, and the task is to draw the design from memory. After all four designs are drawn, a subject is told to remember them because he or she will be asked to draw all four designs again later. Detailed criteria for scoring the designs are provided.

The eighth subtest, Digit Span, contains two parts: Digits Forward and Digits Backward. On Digits Forward, digit sequences of increasing length from 3 to 8 digits are read by the examiner, and the task is to repeat each sequence from memory. On Digits Backward, similar sequences of 2 to 7 digits are read, and the task is to repeat the sequence backwards. There are two items for each list length, and the dependent measure is the number of digit sequences recalled correctly on both Digits Forward and Digits Backward.

The ninth subtest, Visual Memory Span, is one of the new subtests and is a visual analog of the Digit Span subtest. Using a card printed with colored squares, the examiner touches the squares in sequences of increasing length. After each sequence, the task is to touch the squares to reproduce the sequence presented by the examiner. This is followed by a backward series in which the task is to repeat the examiner's tapped sequence in reverse.

Following the administration of these nine subtests, the delayed recall measures for Logical Memory, Visual Paired Associates, Verbal Paired Associates, and Visual Reproduction are obtained. Delayed recall measures were not included in the original scale.

Although the original WMS reported a single overall Memory Quotient, an important goal of the revision was to report separate scores for various meaningful components of memory performance. On the WMS-R, information and orientation questions are used for screening purposes and kept separate from the rest of the scale. Two major scores, the General Memory Index and the Attention/Concentration Index, are derived. In addition, the General Memory Index can be subdivided into two subsidiary scores, the Verbal Memory Index and the Visual Memory Index. The Verbal Memory Index is derived from immediate recall scores on Logical Memory and Verbal Paired Associates. The Visual Memory Index is derived from immediate recall scores for the Figural Memory, Visual Paired Associates, and Visual Reproduction subtests. The Attention/Concentration Index is derived from scores on the Mental Control, Digit Span, and Visual Memory Span subtests. The Attention/Concentration Index appears to correspond to the "Freedom from Distractability" factor commonly reported in analyses of Wechsler intelligence scales. In addition, a Delayed Recall Index is derived to summarize performance on the four delayed-recall subtests. Percentile norms also are provided for selected subtests: the forward and backward trials of both Digit Span and Visual Memory Span, and both the immediate- and delayed-recall parts of Logical Memory and Visual Reproduction.

Evidence is accumulating that the WMS-R is far superior to the WMS for assessing memory disorders (Butters et al., 1988; Crossen & Wiens, 1988; Fischer, 1988; Ryan & Lewis, 1988). In a sample of 40 men, Ryan and Lewis (1988) reported that each of the indexes of the WMS-R was significantly and negatively associated with age. The correlation between age and the General Memory Index, the Attention/ Concentration Index, the Verbal Memory Index, the Visual Memory Index, and the Delayed Recall Index were -.60, -.31, -.54, -.39, and -.51, respectively. The correlations between education and the General Memory Index, the Attention/Concentration Index, the Verbal Memory Index, the Visual Memory Index, and the Delayed Recall Index were .53, .53, .55, .32, and .54, respectively (presumably based on age-adjusted index scores provided in the test manual).

Despite the fact that the WMS-R has been improved greatly, it still does not meet several of the criteria proposed by Erickson et al. (1980). No measure of tertiary memory is included, qualitative analyses of the strategies used are not considered, alternate forms are not available, and it is designed to be administered in one session. Moreover, several of the subtests are paced, a condition that is particularly disadvantageous to elderly subjects.

SELF-REPORTED MEMORY FUNCTIONING—METAMEMORY QUESTIONNAIRES

In addition to objective measures of memory performance, clinicians typically want to know how a person assesses his or her memory. The most direct way to find out what a person thinks, values, knows, or believes about his or her mental functioning is to ask directly. Several metamemory questionnaires have been developed to measure a person's subjective assessment of his or her own memory functioning in everyday situations. Scores reflect how a person thinks about his or her memory capacity rather than how well he or she actually performs on objective memory tasks. Questionnaires provide efficient, systematic, and quantified information about self-assessment of memory. Some of these measures can be used as indices of memory complaints; many also provide information about use of memory strategies and knowledge of memory processes. For many older people, questionnaires appear to be less threatening than objective tests. Gilewski and Zelinski (1986) noted that the greater face validity of questionnaires compared with memory tests may increase cooperation during assessment.

Beliefs about memory ability not only may influence an individual's performance on objective memory tests (Poon, Fozard, & Treat, 1978) but also may affect a person's choice or avoidance of intellectual activities in daily life (Sehulster, 1981). Moreover, beliefs about memory ability affect an individual's selection of control processes in performing a memory task; for example, people with poorer impressions of their memory ability report using external aids such as notes (Zelinski, Gilewski, & Thompson, 1980) and rehearsal (Perlmutter, 1978). Furthermore, people who believe that their memory is poor are more susceptible to cognitive failure under stress (Broadbent, Cooper, Fitzgerald, & Parkes, 1982; Reason, 1984).

Selection of an appropriate metamemory questionnaire to assess elderly adults depends upon the questions to be answered. There are many reasons to obtain self-reports of memory functioning, including early detection of cognitive deterioration and differentiation of depression, dementia, and normal aging. Questionnaire content is critical because the interpretation depends on the adequacy of the match between questionnaire items and memory issues of interest. Items should reflect the everyday memory tasks in an individual's usual environment.

Many metamemory questionnaires have been reviewed by Herrmann (1982, 1984), and recently Gilewski and Zelinski (1986) reviewed 10 questionnaires that have been used to assess memory beliefs/complaints in older adults. For several of these questionnaires, no psychometric properties (i.e., reliability, validity, factor structure) have been reported; for others the questionnaire items have not been published, and some were developed for use with younger individuals. The questionnaires that are probably the most applicable for general clinical and research use with older individuals are both the Metamemory Questionnaire and its abbreviated version, the Memory Functioning Questionnaire (Zelinski et al., 1980), and the Metamemory in Adulthood Questionnaire (Dixon & Hultsch, 1983b). Both questionnaires were developed specifically for use with older individuals and both have established reliability and validity.

Metamemory Questionnaire

Zelinski et al. (1980) published a 92-item questionnaire that can be reduced to nine a priori scale scores: General Rating, Reliance on Memory, Retrospective Functioning, Frequency of Forgetting, Frequency of Forgetting When Reading, Remembering Past Events, Seriousness, Mnemonic Usage, and Effort Made to Remember.

The General Rating scale is a global rating measured by the question "How would you rate your memory in terms of the kinds of problems that you have?" The Reliance on Memory scale asks "How often do you need to rely on your memory without the use of remembering techniques such as making lists when you are engaged in: (a) social activities? (b) household chores?" and so on. Retrospective Functioning is measured by the question "How is your memory compared to the way it was: (a) one month ago? (b) one year ago?" and so on.

Frequency of Forgetting is measured by items such as "How often do these present a memory problems for you: (a) names? (b) faces? (c) appointments?" and so on. Frequency of Forgetting When Reading includes items such as "As you are reading a novel, how often do you have trouble remembering what you have read: (a) in the opening chapters once you have finished the book?" and so on. The Remembering Past Events scale asks "How well do you remember things which occurred: (a) last month? (b) between six months and one year ago?" and so on.

The Seriousness scale parallels items rated in the Frequency of Forgetting scale such as "When you actually forget in these situations, how serious of a problem do you consider the memory failure to be: (a) names? (b) faces? (c) appointments?" and so on. The Mnemonics scale includes items such as "How often do you use these techniques to remind yourself about things: (a) keep an appointment book? (b) write yourself reminder notes?" and so on. The Effort Made to Remember scale parallels items rated in the Frequency of Forgetting scale and Seriousness scale such as "How much effort do you usually have to make to remember in these situations: (a) names? (b) faces? (c) appointments?" and so on. All items are rated on 7-point Likert scales, and higher scores indicate a more positive self-assessment.

Using the nine scale scores from the Metamemory Questionnaire, Zelinski et al. (1980) applied cluster analysis to group subjects into three memory evaluation groups: positive, moderate, and negative. They found that the positive and moderate memory evaluation groups consisted primarily of young individuals, while the majority of subjects in the negative evaluation group were elderly. The mean education of the negative evaluation group was significantly lower than that of the positive and moderate group. Moreover, they found reliable memory evaluation group effects for immediate and delayed free recall, recognition, and essay recall. For all tasks, the performance of the positive and moderate memory evaluation groups was superior to that of the negative evaluation group.

Subsequent factor analyses of the 92 items produced three correlated common factors: frequency of forgetting, seriousness, and mnemonics/retrospective functioning. The factor analysis indicated that the number of items could be reduced from 92 to 64, and this abbreviated version is called the Memory Functioning Questionnaire.

These instruments have several advantages. The investigation of their psychometric properties has been as thorough as any other metamemory questionnaire, and adequate norms are available because they have been administered to large samples of elderly adults based on extensive sampling of both clinical and nonclinical populations (Gilewski, 1983; Gilewski, Zelinski, Schaie, & Thompson, 1983; Gilewski & Zelinski, 1986). Despite these important advantages, there may be problems for some purposes. Even the shortened, 64-item Memory Functioning Questionnaire may be too long for some assessment situations, and the absence of a total score also may be a disadvantage. A third problem is that the factor structure may not be the same for all age groups.

Metamemory in Adulthood Questionnaire

An alternate multiple-factor instrument designed to represent a multidimensional construct of metamemory is the Metamemory in Adulthood Questionnaire (Dixon & Hultsch, 1983b, 1984). After content validity was established for a pool of 206 items, this instrument was administered sequentially to three separate samples of adults. Computation of internal consistency estimates (by age and sample) and factorial validity (by sample) resulted in a 120-item instrument. Each item is rated on a 5-point Likert scale, and the items were chosen to reflect eight theoretically meaningful a priori scales: Use of Memory Strategies, Knowledge of Memory Tasks, Knowledge of One's Own Memory Capacity, Perception of Change in Memory, Activities Supportive of Memory, Memory and State Anxiety, Memory and Achievement Motivation, and Locus of Control in Memory Abilities. The first four scales represent knowledge about memory and self-assessment of memory; the remaining scales represent personal or affective components of metamemory.

The first scale, Use of Memory Strategies, contains 18 items such as "Do you keep a list or otherwise note important dates, such as birthdays and anniversaries?" and "Do you post reminders of things you need to do in a prominent place, such as bulletin boards or note boards?" The focus is on the use of memory strategies, and a high score reflects frequent use of memory aids. The second scale, Knowledge of Memory Tasks and Processes, contains 16 items such as "For most people, facts that are interesting are easier to remember than facts that are not" and "For most people, words they have seen or heard before are easier to remember than words that are totally new to them." This dimension refers to fundamental knowledge about memory processes, and a high score is indicative of a high level of understanding of general memory processes.

The third scale, Knowledge of One's Own Memory Capacity, contains 17 items such as "I have no trouble remembering where I put things" and "I am good at remembering names." This scale measures a subject's self-reported memory performance on a variety of everyday memory tasks, and a high score is indicative of a high level of reported memory capacity. The fourth scale, Perception of Change in Memory, contains 18 items such as "My memory has greatly declined in the last ten years" and "My memory for important events has improved over the last ten years." This scale measures the perceived developmental change in memory ability.

The fifth scale, Activities Supportive of Memory, contains 12 items such as "How often do you read non-fiction books?" and "About how much time do you spend writing?" This scale measures the frequency with which a subject regularly engages in intellectual or social activities in which thinking and remembering processes are exercised. A high score reflects a reported high level of such activities. The sixth scale, Memory and State Anxiety, contains 14 items such as "I get upset when I cannot remember something" and "I find it harder to remember things when I am upset." This dimension measures awareness that a person's emotional state can affect memory performance and that a cognitive task can provoke an affective response. A high score indicates a high level of knowledge regarding the reciprocal influence of anxiety and cognitive performance.

The seventh scale, Memory and Achievement Motivation, contains 16 items such as "I think a good memory is something of which to be proud" and "I think it is important to work at sustaining my memory." This scale measures how important it is to a subject to have a good memory and to do well on cognitive tasks. A high score indicates a high level of motivation to perform well. The eighth scale, Locus of Control in Memory Abilities, contains nine items such as "I have little control over my memory ability" and "I know if I keep using my memory I will never lose it." This scale measures an individual's perceived sense of control over remembering abilities. A high score indicates that a person believes that he or she has control over memory ability.

Dixon and Hultsch (1983b) reported significant age differences on the Knowledge of Memory Tasks, Knowledge of One's Own Memory Capacity, Perception of Change in Memory, and Locus of Control in Memory scales. Younger individuals had higher scores for the task, capacity, and change scales than older adults, and younger subjects believed that they had more control of memory performance than older respondents.

The Metamemory in Adulthood Questionnaire is unique in its attempt to measure the affective consequences of age-related changes in memory performance. Information about an individual's use of memory strategies and beliefs concerning perceived control of memory performance would seem central to any consideration of remediation. On the other had, the thoroughness may be a drawback when time constraints do not permit administration of a lengthy questionnaire.

Memory Self-Report Questionnaire

Despite the fact that little technical information concerning psychometric adequacy has been published about the instrument, the 30-item Memory Self-Report Questionnaire (Riege, 1982) has the dual advantage of brevity and of having been developed for use with older people. The major benefit of the Memory Self-Report Questionnaire is that its four categories—short-term, interference-delay, perceptual-spatial, and imaginal—were designed to measure aspects of information processing identified in laboratory tasks that appear to be particularly difficult for older individuals. The questionnaire items are rated on a 4-point scale. Although Riege (1982) did not report the relationship between questionnaire responses and performance of the laboratory memory tasks that match the conceptual organization of the questions (i.e., external validation studies), the approach is promising.

What Metamemory Questionnaires Measure

Because there are several metamemory questionnaires that may be used in a specific assessment situation, it is important to know and to be able to demonstrate what these questionnaires measure. Although criteria such as diaries of memory failures or ratings of memory performance by significant others could be used, the most frequently employed criterion to validate self-reported memory functioning is performance on objective memory tasks. The strongest relationship that has been reported between memory questionnaires and test performance is a canonical correlation of .67 between a set of metamemory scales and a set of objective memory test performance measures (Zelinski et al., 1980). Hulicka (1982) also reported significant negative correlations between memory complaints and logical memory and digit span tests (as measured by the Wechsler Memory Scale) and free recall, but not between memory complaints and performance on a paired-associate task of names and occupations. In addition, Dixon and Hultsch (1983a) reported significant relationships between self-reported memory and text recall.

The inability to demonstrate strong and consistent relationships between subjective memory assessment and objective memory test performance has been, to say the least, disappointing. Currently, the low to moderate validity coefficients preclude the use of metamemory questionnaires as a substitute for actual memory performance. It may be that laboratory memory tests are not the best external validation criteria and that information from naturalistic observation will be needed to improve our understanding of subjective memory.

There are several possible reasons for the lack of correspondence between objective measures of memory performance and subjective measures. It is important to differentiate tasks that are performed frequently and pose no memory problems from tasks that pose no problem because they are performed rarely. If an elderly individual no longer engages in a particular task, such as playing bridge, then the opportunity to experience memory failure is avoided. Active people may have more memory complaints than less active people because their higher activity levels would result in greater opportunities to experience memory failure. In other words, people may have few complaints but poor performance or many complaints and good performance because complaints are relative to the number of tasks attempted.

In addition, the correspondence between complaints and performance in validation studies depends on an individual's relative rank compared to age peers. However, an older individual is likely to make self-comparisons in assessing memory complaints, and even though the objective performance may be average for a particular age group, it seems reasonable that such an individual is accurate when believing that his or her performance was better when he or she was younger.

Another reason may be the lack of congruence between a particular memory complaint and the objective memory test that is used to validate the complaint. For example, a common complaint for people of all ages is the inability to remember names, and typically the specific performance criterion that is employed is recall of novel paired-associate name-face items. However, upon further consideration of the nature of the name recall problem, it appears that the primary difficulty is retrieval of the names of acquaintances who are encountered infrequently. Despite the nominal similarity of the memory tasks (both involve recall of names), the information-processing requirements are clearly different. It is important to evaluate the criterion measure carefully to assure that comparable phenomena are measured.

It should also be noted that, although clearly not a substitute for memory performance, responses to a self-administered metamemory questionnaire can serve as the basis for a more intensive interview concerning the nature of any endorsed memory problems.

MEMORY REMEDIATION AND COMPENSATION

A clinician faced with an older individual who has a memory complaint is expected to provide three kinds of information: diagnostic information—whether any observed deficit is due to the normal aging processes or to a pathological condition; prognostic information—what an individual and his or her family might expect in the future; and treatment plans—remedial action to correct a problem or to teach an individual (and perhaps significant others) to compensate for a problem. In response to this need, psychologists have begun to investigate the efficacy of such procedures (Baltes & Willis, 1982; Rodin, Cashman, & Desiderato, 1987; Treat, Poon, Fozard, & Popkin, 1978; West, 1985; Willis, 1987; Wilson & Moffat, 1984). How much of the normal age differences and age changes in performance can be attributed to biological, structural changes in the nervous system and how much to control processes and environmental contexts that are less than optimal cannot be determined at this time. However, the task for the clinician is to optimize an older individual's use of control processes, as psychologists can do little to modify structural features.

The extensive literature on memory and aging leads us to conclude that normal aging processes do not result in global deterioration of memory performance. It seems reasonable to design memory training techniques to offset apparent age-related deficits in information processing, and most investigators interested in cognitive strategy training identify with an information-processing approach to cognition. In general, two research questions have been addressed: what encoding strategies do older individuals use spontaneously, and if appropriate encoding strategies are taught to older individuals, what is the effect on their memory performance?

The view that older individuals do not use encoding strategies spontaneously, at least for laboratory memory tasks, has been confirmed frequently in the literature (Burke & Light, 1981; Canestrari, 1968; Craik & Simon, 1980; Hulicka & Grossman, 1967). Typically, it is assumed that older individuals had learned the technique at one time but that lack of practice has rendered strategy selection skills somewhat rusty. Of course, it also is possible, and for some older subjects likely, that they had not been taught specific mnemonic techniques (with the possible exception of repetition).

The second important hypothesis is that older individuals can learn or relearn encoding strategies if given appropriate instruction. Procedures that have been shown to improve acquisition and subsequent recall of older individuals include organizing a word list into categories (Hultsch, 1969, 1975) and the use of verbal or visual mediators to make associations between pairs of to-be-remembered words (Canestrari, 1968; Hulicka & Grossman, 1967; Poon, Walsh-Sweeney, & Fozard, 1980; Treat & Reese, 1976). Other studies have shown that when older subjects are taught to use elaborative encoding strategies, their performance improves significantly. Elaboration refers to placing to-be-remembered items of information into an episode, process, or relation involving all of them (Rohwer, 1973). For example, given the paired-associate item *alligator-tree,* a person might imagine an alligator perched in a tree.

Robertson-Tchabo, Hausman, and Arenberg (1976) employed somewhat successfully a mnemonic procedure, the method of loci, to facilitate recall performance of elderly men and women. Using this method, a subject takes a mental trip through his or her residence, stopping in order at 16 places. When learning a list of words, the trip is retraced, visualizing one of the to-be-remembered items in association with each of the locations on the imaginary trip. The intent of personalizing the trip is to capitalize on the familiarity of the stopping places and their natural order, attributes that provide strong retrieval cues that can be applied without adding to the information overload. The explicit selection and conscious execution and monitoring of strategies consume working memory capacity. Strategy selection, execution, and monitoring all become less effortful with practice and require less working memory capacity (Schneider, Dumais, & Shiffrin, 1984). Using familiar spatial locations with elderly individuals capitalizes on self-generated mediators, reduces the interference from dividing attention between input and storage, and reduces search failure as a subject knows where to resume a trip.

Other studies have confirmed the effectiveness of strategy instruction for older individuals. Yesavage, Rose, and Bower (1983) investigated the relative effects of three training conditions on the acquisition of 12 name-face pairs. The image group was taught the standard visual imagery mnemonic technique to learn name-face associations. The image-plus-judgment group received identical mnemonic instructions and were also asked to judge the pleasantness of the image. The non-image group was treated like the image group except that subjects were not instructed to form an image when learning the pairs. The image group and image-plus-judgment group showed higher recall than the no-image control group, and the image-plus-judgment group maintained their recall performance after 48 hours.

Despite the fact that numerous studies have demonstrated the efficacy of memory training for older adults, it would be misleading to conclude that the area is devoid of controversy, and some psychologists question whether the training effects are of sufficient magnitude to warrant the training effort. The raw data, when reported, show large individual variability (Schaffer & Poon, 1982). Most studies have evaluated the effects of strategy instruction on the performance of a single experimental laboratory memory task, and most of the mnemonic techniques are task-limited. It may be that memory training also must include techniques to improve attention and concentration to be maximally effective. A substantial investment in training time does not guarantee that subjects will transfer the training to everyday tasks.

In addition to teaching facilitative strategies, training also must include instruction about when to use these strategies outside of a laboratory setting. The long-term goal of training is to encourage "automatic" use of appropriate strategies. It may be that subjects do not require strategies in everyday settings because their knowledge base is so well developed that new information can be readily and almost automatically assimilated. Alternatively, it may be that subjects routinely employ external memory aids (e.g., writing notes) rather than internal aids (mnemonic strategies) to increase retention of important information. Wilson and Moffat (1984) believe that a goal of alleviation of the problems caused by memory impairment is a more realistic objective rather than restoration of function. In other words, compensation for memory deficits may be possible even for subjects who do not benefit from training in the use of internal memory aids.

Cognitive skill training approaches to memory remediation are only one way to address memory complaints. Perhaps equally effective are interventions designed to reassure older individuals that self-perceived cognitive loss is not necessarily synonymous with the advent of a serious dementing illness. Zarit, Cole, and Guider (1981) noted that training on specific laboratory memory tasks may be less important than changing expectations to help older adults view episodes of forgetfulness in a more balanced way. Everyday memory lapses do not usually represent a barrier to competent functioning in normal adults of any age. Few younger individuals committing a memory error attribute the failure to aging. On the other hand, many older individuals, perhaps especially those with lower levels of formal education, believe that intellectual decline is inevitable and view maintenance of cognitive performance as outside the realm of their personal control (Lachman, 1986). Hulicka (1982) noted that because anxiety affects performance on laboratory tasks of little personal significance, it seems likely that fear of memory impairment could affect general well-being and everyday performance. Clearly, identification and modification of these negative attitudes/beliefs must precede specific cognitive skill training.

SUMMARY AND CONCLUSIONS

There is clearly a demand for memory assessment, but psychologists have not yet designed memory tests that are theoretically sound and clinically feasible. Although investigators generally agree that memory is a multidimensional entity, there is not yet a consensus regarding which memory factors should be included in a memory test. Moreover, although the importance of external validation and the necessity of conducting studies of predictive validity relating memory test performance to everyday memory functioning is acknowledged, little empirical work has addressed these issues.

We have also argued that in addition to memory performance, an individual's perception of his or her memory problems is important. It is probable that an older individual employs retrospective self-comparisons in evaluating memory performance, and as it is unlikely that previous measures of objective performance would be available, self-reported memory functioning is an efficient and necessary part of evaluating change in memory.

The growing literature on memory training suggests that the elderly can benefit from a variety of instructional procedures. In addition, interventions designed to help older individuals to develop realistic expectations of memory performance also have been effective. In order to be more useful to clinical specialists, researchers must study and report in more detail individual differences in the relative effectiveness of various treatments. Moreover, researchers must begin to address the important issue of the generalization of training to everyday memory task performance.

The research questions posed by most cognitive psychologists do not address the issue of memory tests; rather, their concern is the exposition of basic processes of memory performance. Unless the goal of test development is addressed explicitly, the needs of clinicians will continue to be unmet. Even if questions about the factor structure of memory are answered and appropriate memory tests developed, the giant step of relating test performance to everyday memory functioning still remains.

It is clear that the ideal test or test battery is not yet available to assess memory in the elderly. The practitioner, however, is faced with the task of evaluating memory with those instruments that are available. Many of those instruments are useful for specific questions. It is the responsibility of the practitioner to specify as clearly as possible the questions to be answered and then to select the instruments best suited to answer those questions. Obviously, knowledge about the positive and negative attributes of many instruments would be required to optimize the match between questions and instruments. The revised Wechsler Memory Scale is likely to supplant its predecessor as the most widely used battery, and it would be useful to answer some of those questions, but many questions will require the application of some of the other measures described in this chapter.

REFERENCES

Arenberg, D. (1978). Differences and changes with age in the Benton Visual Retention Test. *Journal of Gerontology, 33,* 534-540.

Arenberg, D. (1982). Estimates of age changes on the Benton Visual Retention Test. *Journal of Gerontology, 37,* 87-90.

Arenberg, D. (1987). A note on differences and changes with age in memory. In M.W. Riley, J.D. Matarazzo, & A. Baum (Eds.), *Perspectives on behavioral medicine: The aging dimension* (pp. 39-47). Hillsdale, NJ: Lawrence Erlbaum.

Atkinson, R.C., & Shiffrin, R.M. (1968). Human memory: A proposed system and its control processes. In K.W. Spence & J.T. Spence (Eds.), *The psychology of learning and motivation: Advances in research and theory* (Vol. II, pp. 90-97). New York: Academic Press.

Baltes, P.B., & Willis, S.L. (1982). Plasticity and enhancement of intellectual functioning in old age. In F.I.M. Craik & S. Trehub (Eds.), *Aging and cognitive processes* (pp. 353-389). New York: Plenum.

Benton, A.L. (1974). *The Revised Benton Visual Retention Test.* New York: Psychological Corporation.

Birren, J.E., & Morrison, D.F. (1961). Analysis of the WAIS subtests in relation to age and education. *Journal of Gerontology, 16,* 363-369.

Broadbent, D.E., Cooper, P.F., Fitzgerald, P., & Parkes, K.R. (1982). The Cognitive Failures Questionnaire (CFQ) and its correlates. *British Journal of Clinical Psychology, 21,* 1-16.

Burke, D.M., & Light, L.L. (1981). Memory and aging: The role of retrieval processes. *Psychological Bulletin, 90,* 513-546.

Butters, N., Salmon, D.P., Vullum, C.M., Cairns, P., Troster, A.I., Jacobs, D., Moss, M., & Cermak, L.S. (1988). Differentiation of amnesic and demented patients with the Wechsler Memory Scale-Revised. *Clinical Neuropsychologist, 2,* 133-148.

Canestrari, R.E., Jr. (1968). Age changes in acquisition. In G.A. Talland (Ed.), *Human aging and behavior* (pp. 169-188). New York: Academic Press.

Cerella, J., Poon, L.W., & Fozard, J.L. (1982). Age and iconic read-out. *Journal of Gerontology, 37,* 197-202.

Cohen, J. (1950). Wechsler Memory Scale performance of psychoneurotic, organic, and schizophrenic groups. *Journal of Consulting Psychology, 14,* 371-375.

Craik, F.I.M. (1977). Age differences in human memory. In J.E. Birren & K.W. Schaie (Eds.), *Handbook of the psychology of aging* (pp. 384-420). New York: Van Nostrand Reinhold.

Craik, F.I.M., & Simon, E. (1980). Age differences in memory: The roles of attention and depth of processing. In L.W. Poon, J.L. Fozard, L.S. Cermak, D. Arenberg, & L.W. Thompson (Eds.), *New directions in memory and aging* (pp. 95-112). Hillsdale, NJ: Lawrence Erlbaum.

Craik, F.I.M., & Trehub, S. (Eds.). (1982). *Aging and cognitive processes.* New York: Plenum.

Crossen, J.R., & Wiens, A.N. (1988). Wechsler Memory Scale- Revised: Deficits in performance associated with neurotoxic solvent exposure. *Clinical Neuropsychologist, 2,* 181-187.

Cunningham, W.R. (1986). Psychometric perspectives: Validity and reliability. In L.W. Poon (Ed.), *Handbook for clinical memory assessment of older adults* (pp. 27-31). Washington, DC: American Psychological Association.

Daneman, M., & Carpenter, P.A. (1980). Individual differences in working memory and reading. *Journal of Verbal Learning and Verbal Behavior, 19,* 450-466.

Dixon, R.A., & Hultsch, D.F. (1983a). Metamemory and memory for text relationships in adulthood: A cross-validation study. *Journal of Gerontology, 38,* 689-694.

Dixon, R.A., & Hultsch, D.F. (1983b). Structure and development of metamemory in adulthood. *Journal of Gerontology, 38,* 682- 688.

Dixon, R.A., & Hultsch, D.F. (1984). The Metamemory in Adulthood (MIA) instrument. *Psychological Documents, 14,* 3.

Dixon, R.A., Hultsch, D.F., & Hertzog, C. (1985). *A manual of twenty-five three-tiered structurally equivalent texts for use in aging research.* Berlin: Max Planck Institute for Human Development and Education.

Dujovne, B.E., & Levy, B.I. (1971). The psychometric structure of the Wechsler Memory Scale. *Journal of Clinical Psychology, 27,* 351-354.

Erickson, R.C., Poon, L.W., & Walsh-Sweeney, L. (1980). Clinical memory testing of the elderly. In L.W. Poon, J.L. Fozard, L.S. Cermak, D. Arenberg, & L.W. Thompson (Eds.), *New directions in memory and aging* (pp. 379-402). Hillsdale, NJ: Lawrence Erlbaum.

Erickson, R.C., & Scott, M. (1977). Clinical memory testing: A review. *Psychological Bulletin, 84,* 1130-1149.

Ferris, S.H., Crook, T., Clark, E., McCarthy, M., & Rae, D. (1980). Facial recognition memory deficits in normal aging and senile dementia. *Journal of Gerontology, 35,* 707-714.

Ferris, S.H., Crook, T., Flicker, C., Reisberg, B., & Bartus, R.T. (1986). Assessing cognitive impairment and evaluating treatment effects: Psychometric performance tests. In L.W. Poon (Ed.), *Handbook for clinical memory assessment* (pp. 139-148). Washington, DC: American Psychological Association.

Fischer, J.S. (1988). Using the Wechsler Memory Scale-Revised to detect and characterize memory deficits in multiple sclerosis. *Clinical Neuropsychologist, 2,* 149-172.

Fozard, J.L., & Thomas, J.C. (1975). Psychology of aging: Basic findings and some psychiatric applications. In J.G. Howells (Ed.), *Modern perspectives in the psychiatry of old age* (pp. 107-169). New York: Brunner/Mazel.

Gilewski, M.J. (1983). Self-reported memory functioning in young-old and old-old age: Structural models of predictive factors (Doctoral dissertation, University of Southern California, 1983). *Dissertation Abstracts International, 43,* 4170B.

Gilewski, M.J., & Zelinski, E.M. (1986). Questionnaire assessment of memory complaints. In L.W. Poon (Ed.), *Handbook for clinical memory assessment of older adults* (pp. 93-107). Washington, DC: American Psychological Association.

Gilewski, M.J., Zelinski, E.M., Schaie, K.W., & Thompson, L.W. (1983, August). *Abbreviating the Metamemory Questionnaire: Factor structure and norms for adults.* Paper presented at the Annual Meeting of the American Psychological Association, Anaheim, CA.

Granick, S., & Friedman, A.S. (1967). The effect of education on the decline of psychometric test performance with age. *Journal of Gerontology, 22,* 191-195.

Harris, J.E., & Morris, P.E. (Eds.). (1984). *Everyday memory actions and absentmindedness.* New York: Academic Press.

Hasher, L., & Zacks, R.T. (in press). Working memory, comprehension, and aging: A review and a new view. In G.H. Bower (Ed.), *The psychology of learning and motivation.* Orlando, FL: Academic Press.

Herman, D.O. (1988). Development of the Wechsler Memory Scale- Revised. *Clinical Neuropsychologist, 2,* 102-106.

Herrmann, D.J. (1982). Know thy memory: The use of questionnaires to assess and study memory. *Psychological Bulletin, 92,* 434-452.

Herrmann, D.J. (1984). Questionnaires about memory. In J.E. Harris & P.E. Morris (Eds.), *Everyday memory actions and absentmindedness* (pp. 133-151). New York: Academic Press.

Horn, J.L., Donaldson, G., & Engstrom, R. (1981). Apprehension, memory, and fluid intelligence decline in adulthood. *Research on Aging, 3,* 33-84.

Howes, J.L., & Katz, A.N. (1988). Assessing remote memory with an improved public events questionnaire. *Psychology and Aging, 3,* 142-150.

Hulicka, I.M. (1966). Age differences in Wechsler Memory Scale scores. *Journal of Genetic Psychology, 109,* 135-145.

Hulicka, I.M. (1982). Memory functioning in late adulthood. In F.I.M. Craik & S. Trehub (Eds.), *Aging and cognitive processes* (pp. 331-351). New York: Plenum.

Hulicka, I.M., & Grossman, J.L. (1967). Age group comparisons for the use of mediators in paired-associate learning. *Journal of Gerontology, 22,* 46-51.

Hultsch, D. (1969). Adult age differences in the organization of free recall. *Developmental Psychology, 1,* 673-678.

Hultsch, D. (1975). Adult age differences in retrieval: Trace development and dependent forgetting. *Developmental Psychology, 11,* 197-201.

Hunt, E. (1986). Experimental perspectives: Theoretical memory models. In L.W. Poon (Ed.), *Handbook for clinical memory assessment of older adults* (pp. 43-54). Washington, DC: American Psychological Association.

Kahn, R., & Miller, N.E. (1978). Adaptational factors in memory impairment in the aged. *Experimental Aging Research, 4,* 273-290.

Kausler, D.H. (1982). *Experimental psychology and human aging.* New York: John Wiley.

Klonoff, H., & Kennedy, M. (1965). Memory and perceptual functioning in octogenarians and nonagenarians in the community. *Journal of Gerontology, 20,* 328-333.

Klonoff, H., & Kennedy, M. (1966). A comparative study of cognitive functioning in old age. *Journal of Gerontology, 21,* 239-243.

Labouvie-Vief, G., & Schell, D.A. (1982). Learning and memory in later life: A developmental view. In B.B. Wolman & G. Stricker (Eds.), *Handbook of developmental psychology* (pp. 828-846). Englewood Cliffs, NJ: Prentice-Hall.

Lachman, M.E. (1986). Personal control in later life: Stability, change, and cognitive correlates. In M.M. Baltes & P.E. Baltes (Eds.), *The psychology of control and aging* (pp. 207-236). Hillsdale, NJ: Lawrence Erlbaum.

Lezak, M.D. (1983). *Neuropsychological assessment* (2nd ed.). New York: Oxford University Press.

Meer, B., & Baker, J.A. (1965). Reliability of measurements of intellectual functioning of geriatric patients. *Journal of Gerontology, 20,* 110-114.

Perlmutter, M. (1978). What is memory aging the aging of? *Developmental Psychology, 14,* 330-345.

Piersma, H.I. (1986). Wechsler Memory Scale performance in geropsychiatric patients. *Journal of Clinical Psychology, 42,* 323-327.

Poon, L.W. (Ed.). (1980). *Aging in the 1980's: Psychological issues.* Washington, DC: American Psychological Association.

Poon, L.W. (1985). Differences in human memory with aging: Nature, causes, and clinical implications. In J.E. Birren & K.W. Schaie (Eds.), *Handbook of the psychology of aging* (2nd ed., pp. 427-462). New York: Van Nostrand Reinhold.

Poon, L.W. (Ed.). (1986). *Handbook for clinical memory assessment of older adults.* Washington, DC: American Psychological Association.

Poon, L.W., Fozard, J.L., Cermak, L.S., Arenberg, D., & Thompson, L.W. (Eds.). (1980). *New directions in memory and aging: Proceedings of the George A. Talland Memorial Conference.* Hillsdale, NJ: Lawrence Erlbaum.

Poon, L.W., Fozard, J.L., Paulshock, D.R., & Thomas, J.C. (1979). A questionnaire assessment of age differences in retention of recent and remote events. *Experimental Aging Research, 5,* 401-411.

Poon, L.W., Fozard, J.L. & Treat, N.J. (1978). From clinical and research findings on memory to intervention programs. *Experimental Aging Research, 4,* 235-253.

Poon, L.W., Walsh-Sweeney, L., & Fozard, J.L. (1980). Memory skill training for the elderly: Salient issues on the use of imagery mnemonics. In L.W. Poon, J.L. Fozard, L.S. Cermak, D. Arenberg, & L.W. Thompson (Eds.), *New directions in memory and aging* (pp. 461-484). Hillsdale, NJ: Lawrence Erlbaum.

Prigatano, G.P. (1978). Wechsler Memory Scale: A selective review of the literature. *Journal of Clinical Psychology, 34,* 816-832.

Raskin, A., & Jarvik, L.F. (1979). *Psychiatric symptoms and cognitive loss in the elderly.* Washington, DC: Hemisphere.

Reason, J. (1984). Absent-mindedness and cognitive control. In J.E. Harris & P.E. Morris (Eds.), *Everyday memory actions and absentmindedness* (pp. 113-132). New York: Academic Press.

Riege, W.H. (1982). Self-report and tests of memory aging. *Clinical Gerontologist, 1,* 23-36.

Robertson-Tchabo, E.A., & Arenberg, D. (1987). Cognitive performance. In H.G. Mueller &

V.C. Geoffrey (Eds.), *Communication disorders in aging: Assessment and management* (pp. 72-103). Washington, DC: Gallaudet University Press.

Robertson-Tchabo, E.A., Hausman, C.P., & Arenberg, D. (1976). A classical mnemonic for older learners. *Educational Gerontology, 1,* 215-226.

Rodin, J., Cashman, C., & Desiderato, L. (1987). Intervention and aging: Enrichment and prevention. In M.W. Riley, Matarazzo, J.D., & A. Baum (Eds.), *Perspectives in behavioral medicine: The aging dimension* (pp. 149-172). Hillsdale, NJ: Lawrence Erlbaum.

Rohwer, W.D., Jr. (1973). Elaboration and learning in childhood and adolescence. In H.W. Reese (Ed.), *Advances in child development and behavior* (Vol. 8, pp. 1-57). New York: Academic Press.

Ryan, J.J., & Lewis, C.V. (1988). Comparison of normal controls and recently detoxified alcoholics on the Wechsler Memory Scale-Revised. *Clinical Neuropsychologist, 2,* 173-180.

Salthouse, T.A. (1982). *Adult cognition: An experimental psychology of human aging.* New York: Springer-Verlag.

Salthouse, T.A. (1985). *A theory of cognitive aging.* New York: Elsevier.

Salthouse, T.A., Mitchell, D.R.D., Skovronek, E., & Babcock, R.L. (in press). Effects of adult age and working memory on reasoning and spatial abilities. *Journal of Experimental Psychology: Learning, Memory, and Cognition.*

Schaffer, G., & Poon, L.W. (1982). Individual variability in memory training with the elderly. *Educational Gerontology, 8,* 217-229.

Schaie, K.W. (1977). Quasi-experimental research designs in the psychology of aging. In J.E. Birren & K.W. Schaie (Eds.), *Handbook of the psychology of aging* (pp. 39-58). New York: Van Nostrand Reinhold.

Schaie, K.W. (1978). External validity in the assessment of intellectual development in adulthood. *Journal of Gerontology, 33,* 695-701.

Schonfield, D. (1972). Theoretical nuances and practical old questions: The psychology of aging. *Canadian Psychologist, 13,* 252-266.

Schneider, W., Dumais, S.T., & Shiffrin, R.M. (1984). Automatic and control processing and attention. In R. Parasuraman & D.R. Davies (Eds.), *Varieties of attention* (pp. 1-27). Orlando, FL: Academic Press.

Sehulster, J.R. (1981). Structure and pragmatics of a self- theory of memory. *Memory and Cognition, 9,* 263-276.

Shock, N.W., Greulich, R.C., Andres, R., Arenberg, D., Costa, P.T., Jr., Lakatta, E.G., & Tobin, J.D. (1984). *Normal human aging: The Baltimore Longitudinal Study of Aging* (U.S. Public Health Service Publication No. 84-2450). Washington, DC: U.S. Government Printing Office.

Treat, N.J., Poon, L.W., Fozard, J.L., & Popkin, S.J. (1978). Toward applying cognitive skill training to memory problems. *Experimental Aging Research, 4,* 305-319.

Treat, N.J., & Reese, H.W. (1976). Age, pacing, and imagery in paired-associate learning. *Developmental Psychology, 12,* 119-124.

Walsh, D.A., & Prasse, M.J. (1980). Iconic memory and attentional processes in the aged. In L.W. Poon, J.L. Fozard, L.S. Cermak, D. Arenberg, & L.W. Thompson (Eds.), *New directions in memory and aging* (pp. 153-180). Hillsdale, NJ: Lawrence Erlbaum.

Wechsler, D. (1945). A standardized memory scale for clinical use. *Journal of Psychology, 19,* 87-95.

Wechsler, D. (1955). *Manual for the Wechsler Adult Intelligence Scale.* New York: Psychological Corporation.

Wechsler, D. (1981). *Wechsler Adult Intelligence Scale-Revised* (WAIS-R). New York: Psychological Corporation.

Wechsler, D.A. (1987). *Wechsler Memory Scale-Revised* (WMS-R). San Antonio, TX: Psychological Corporation.

West, R. (1985). *Memory fitness over 40.* Gainesville, FL: Triad.

Willis, S.L. (1987). Cognitive training and everyday competence. *Annual Review of Gerontology and Geriatrics, 7,* 159-188.

Wilson, B., & Moffat, N. (1984). Rehabilitation of memory for everyday life. In J.E. Harris & P.E. Morris (Eds.), *Everyday memory actions and absentmindedness* (pp. 207-233). New York: Academic Press.

Yesavage, J.A., Rose, T.L., & Bower, G.H. (1983). Interactive imagery and affective judgments improve face-name learning in the elderly. *Journal of Gerontology, 38,* 197-203.

Zarit, S.H., Cole, K.D., & Guider, R.L. (1981). Memory training strategies and subjective complaints of memory in the aged. *The Gerontologist, 21,* 158-164.

Zelinski, E.M., Gilewski, M.J., & Thompson, L.W. (1980). Do laboratory tests relate to self-assessment of memory ability in the young and old? In L.W. Poon, J.L. Fozard, L.S. Cermak, D. Arenberg, & L.W. Thompson (Eds.), *New directions in memory and aging: Proceedings of the George A. Talland Memorial Conference* (pp. 519-544). Hillsdale, NJ: Lawrence Erlbaum.

13

Assessment of Older Persons in the Workplace

CLYDE J. LINDLEY, M.A.

Assessment in the workplace represents a challenge to psychologists helping older persons make decisions about continuing employment, re-entry into employment, changing careers, and retirement itself. Three things signify far-reaching implications for employment or continuing employment of older persons. The first is the Age Discrimination in Employment Amendments of 1986 that became effective January 1, 1987. This law abolished mandatory retirement at any age, with a few exceptions—until 1993 for police officers and firefighters and temporarily for college professional staff and certain employees covered by collective bargaining agreements.

The second factor is the so-called "graying of America"—the changing age composition of the U.S. population. The average age of the general population and that of workers will increase in the next few decades, while the number of young workers entering the labor market will decline (Johnston, 1987). The ratio of elderly to working-age persons is increasing dramatically:

> In 1900, there were about seven elderly persons for every 100 persons of working age; in 1986, this ratio was about 20 elderly persons per 100 of working age. By 2020, the ratio will rise to about 29 per 100 and is expected to increase rapidly to 37 per 100 by 2030. (U.S. Senate Special Committee on Aging, 1987-1988)

In the next 20 years fewer young people will be available to seek employment. By the year 2000 it is expected that those persons in the 25-35 age group will drop by 9.5%. The 45-64 age group shows a fairly high increase by the year 2000 and an even greater increase by 2010. And the 65 and older group will increase greatly (Lindley, 1986b). From these population changes, it follows that older persons will be needed in greater numbers in the labor force.

The third consideration is that people are living longer. The current trend toward increases in life expectancy at birth and at age 65 is expected to continue through the year 2050 (Spencer, 1984). Many of these older persons are (and will be) healthier and functioning very effectively in our society.

The increased worker demands created by these trends must be met by the older adult seeking job entry or promotional opportunities. Many older persons who have prior work experience can apply directly for jobs, while other candidates may need retraining and seek help through community or educational counseling or training centers. Some forward-looking and socially interested corporations and governmental agencies are already establishing programs within their workplaces for such counseling and retraining.

Because many older persons are living longer, have good health, and want to or need to work, there are opportunities for them in the workplace. The psychologist, through effective assessment techniques, can assist materially in increasing the effective participation of the older person in the labor force and in making the participation personally satisfying.

GENERAL ASSESSMENT CONSIDERATIONS: PARAMETERS AND TERMINOLOGY

Assessment in the workplace entails the evaluation of job candidates' knowledges, abilities, skills, and other characteristics (KASOCs) for selection, promotion, transfer, training, career development, retirement, separation, or discharge. Assessment functions have recently been extended to the broadest of all responsibilities of personnel, *human resource management* (Lindley & Hunt, 1984).

The older person has historically and typically been defined by chronological age. In population studies, those aged 65 and over are defined as older persons by the U.S. Census Bureau, and the Social Security Administration uses 65 as the age for paying full benefits for retirement. Retirement from the world of work, however, may begin well before age 65. A basic fact about aging is that people age differently (Maddox, 1987); some are old (biologically) well before age 65, while others seem younger at 70 to 75. Further, older persons are very heterogeneous in their characteristics.

The older person in the workplace is the *older worker,* a term that has produced some confusion (Lindley, 1986a). The concept does not imply a worker who is old due to length of service. Length of service in an organization might make a 5-year employee an "older worker" in a newly formed organization or in one with great employee turnover, and a 30-year worker might not yet be at an "older" stage in a long-established firm. For the purposes of this discussion, the term *older worker* will refer to persons 60 years of age and above. Nonetheless, some of the assessment procedures involved in employment decisions of older workers may also apply to those younger than 60 years.

The term *workplace* sounds specific, but it is a compound word, with little to hold its two parts together. Work is anything a person does for other than pure unadulterated pleasure. To add to the confusion—sometimes you work for pleasure. Place is the "where." Where does one do the things that are defined as work? The workplace has undergone tremendous change and changes will continue into the future (Johnston, 1987). The roles of service industries are surpassing the roles of manufacturing industries in jobs likely to be available to middle and lower level older workers. The manufacturing jobs formerly available are being taken over by automation and computerization. Service jobs will be found particularly in the fields of health care, education, child care, retailing, and local government (less in industry and management). New jobs in service industries are demanding increasingly higher skill levels: better reading ability, ability to follow directions, use of basic mathematics (adding, subtracting, multiplying, dividing), and knowledge related to money transactions (making change, etc.). New jobs will put an emphasis upon productivity.

Information technology represents a fundamental transformation of the American economy. Forty percent of new investment now goes to purchase computers, telecommunication equipment, and other electronic labor-saving devices (Office of Technology Assessment, 1988). These changes will "likely reshape virtually every product, every service and every job in the United States" (p. 3). Education is highlighted as playing the key role in this economic transition and in its impact on individuals. "About 45 percent of the job growth between 1980 and 1986 was in professional and managerial occupations, and almost 50 percent of the new jobs created between 1983 and 1986 went to people with at least three years of college education" (Norman, 1988, p. 977). This will invariably have a tremendous influence in development of techniques to assist older workers to learn needed new skills.

An important element in how a person functions at work relates to the organizational climate of the workplace and how the worker reacts to this climate. The impact of organizational climate can be positive or negative. Among various attitudes and perceptions about work climate, a differentiation between organizational climate and psychological climate stands out as a concern. *Organizational climate* refers to the climate stemming from the work setting. It may relate to such things as safety and physical comfort, but it may also pertain to how highly the job demands are structured, the closeness of work supervision, the relative emphasis upon achievement and originality versus conformity, and the managerial style of leadership. Kurt Lewin, the distinguished psychologist, identified three kinds of organizational climates: autocratic, democratic, and laissez-faire (Lewin, Lippet, & White, 1939). *Psychological climate* refers to the meanings attached by individuals to work settings (organizational climates) in which they find themselves. These factors influence work behavior and the thinking and feelings of workers, and they have a direct impact on performance (Lindley, 1984).

Much research has been accomplished in the area of organizational climate and performance. In their book on motivation and organizational climate, Litwin and Stringer (1968) report on the development of a questionnaire for measuring employee perceptions of organizational climate. Schnake (1983) modified the Litwin-Stringer questionnaire, producing an instrument that has had considerable use in business. Schneider and Reichers (1983) studied how climates develop in an organization. Their findings indicate that climates in a group of workers develop from and change depending upon interaction patterns and group membership. Schneider (1987) maintains that the kinds of people in a work organization define the way the place (organization) looks, feels, and behaves. The attributes of people are the important determinants of behavior in an organization. Guion (1973) emphasized that organizational climate is very important in understanding human performance in organizations.

A rather obvious generalization can be made from the foregoing considerations. Various work settings have different organizational climates, and in order to understand them, the specific nature of the work and the specific composition of the worker group must be ascertained. Researchers interested in the older worker have an almost open field for their efforts because relatively little has been established conclusively on the effects of organizational climate on older workers. What is known is that personnel programs will need to emphasize the *human* factor in human resource management (Lindley, 1984), and this is especially important for the older worker.

MYTHS VERSUS REALITIES ABOUT OLDER WORKERS

The many unfounded attitudes and beliefs about older workers generally stem from lack of knowledge and understanding about aging and the aging process (Palmore, 1974, 1977, 1982; Neugarten, 1977; Maddox, 1987; Kimmel, 1988). In summarizing the literature on job interviews of older applicants, Avolio and Barrett concluded that interviewers often view older applicants as "more difficult to train and place into jobs, more resistant to change and less suitable for promotion and expect them to have lower job performance" (1987, p. 56). Stagner (1985) found that employers believe that older persons in the workplace are less capable, less efficient, and less productive. In a simulated hiring study, managers evaluating résumés believed that older candidates are more likely opinionated, less serious, and less ambitious (Craft, Doctors, Shkop, & Benecki, 1979). A widely held stereotype of older employees is that they lack both the motivation and capacity to take advantage of training opportunities; they are rigid, resistant to change, less receptive to new ideas, and less capable of learning compared to younger employees (Rosen & Jerdee, 1976). In real employment interviews, Raza and Carpenter (1987) found that male interviewers gave older applicants lower intelligence ratings and lower hiring recommendations; female interviewers gave older applicants lower attractiveness ratings.

These myths and unfounded attitudes may unfairly affect the admission of older persons as employees in the work force. They may impact the management and treatment of the older worker in the workplace and the circumstances of retirement. These effects are likely to be prevalent when decisions are made subjectively by supervisors and personnel officers. In the process of perceiving or understanding another person while interacting with that person, Jones (1986) indicates that one's own expectancies determine not only the manner of behavior but also provide the stimulus for the perceiver to respond in keeping with the expectancies. Thus, the perceiver responds as if the expectancies were true. Prejudices and stereotypes provide abundant evidence that people see what they expect to see and select evidence that confirms their stereotypes.

The negative image of older workers is related to the traditional stereotype of older people as unhappy, lonely, in poor health with chronic conditions, complainers, cranks, lacking in personal initiative, dependent on others, miserable, and waiting to die. However, research studies of the aging process contradict the many myths and negative views. Old persons are not necessarily unhappy with the process of aging and do not typically feel lonely or isolated. Seventy percent of elderly people in the United States describe their health as excellent. All studies agree that chronological age is not a criterion for functional capacity.

The negative image of aging in America is changing. Today we expect older persons to be more active. Many will continue working full-time or part-time. Many of those who retire will be actively engaged in interacting effectively in their community environment. The myths about older workers are also changing dramatically. In

1985 the American Association of Retired Persons (AARP) initiated a study of perceptions, policies, and practices vis-à-vis older workers in leading American businesses. AARP (1986b) published the highlights of this study in a pamphlet entitled *Workers Over 50: Old Myths, New Realities*. This study surveyed workers over 50 in a random sample of 400 U.S. corporations. Respondents consisted of executives with senior responsibilities for making human resource decisions. The sample of 400 companies was composed of 100 each in four size groupings based upon number of employees (50-99, 100-499, 500-999, 1000+).

It is of special interest to note that 90% of the employers surveyed considered older workers cost effective. They were perceived as valuable for their knowledge and experience and for their favorable work attitudes and habits (attendance, quality of work, loyalty). Perceived, but less frequently, were accountability in a crisis, ability to get along with co-workers, and emotional stability. Some of the findings varied with the size of the employing company. For example, very large companies viewed "knowledge of the business" as more important than did smaller companies. On the other hand, "good work habits" received more attention in smaller companies. On the negative side, the perceived potential weaknesses in older workers included inability to learn new skills quickly and discomfort with new technologies. In large companies, older workers were viewed as lacking a competitive and aggressive spirit, being not so flexible, and lacking in creativity. Counteracting this finding somewhat was the high percentage agreement in all companies (83%) that older workers have special skills for solving new problems based on knowledge/experience.

In a recent article about older workers employed in a large insurance company, Johnson (1988) indicates that the costs of older employees is actually not higher when the value of their experience is considered. Further, he states that older workers are "as physically and mentally able to perform their duties as most younger workers and are fully capable of retraining" (p. 100). It is interesting to note that efforts have been made in this company to improve the health care and economic security of the older employees.

Many employment programs for older workers are operating in small, medium, and large companies representing several different types of business/industry. Ability, not age, is the prime consideration in employing these older workers. AARP (1986a) maintains a computerized system of data on hundreds of older worker employment programs existing in the private sector (National Older Workers System [NOWIS], originally developed by the University of Michigan Institute of Gerontology), and a recent publication discusses current employment programs, titled *Managing a Changing Workforce*. Some examples of the types of programs/jobs for older workers discussed in the AARP publication follow:

Sales jobs. Five hundred members of a sales force of 3,000 are in their 60s or 70s; most work part-time. Eighteen of the firm's top 40 sellers were 60 or over.

Minor home repairs. One hundred sixty persons 65 and over weatherize homes for a power company for customers 60 and older.

Entry level jobs in banks. One seventh of a bank's employees are in their 60s or 70s. (Most work part-time with flexible schedules.) Seventy-five percent of older employees are hired for *entry level jobs.* There has been a dramatic drop in turnover.

Professional jobs—using computers. A computer firm with a large number of professional-level employees uses retired persons on a flexitime and flexiplace option and provides computer terminals for work at home.

Transfer to less stressful job. Some companies have adapted job opportunities for longer service older workers so they can take less physically demanding and stressful positions.

Job sharing. Job sharing permits a pair of older employees to do a single job. "Interoffice messengers" and "foot messengers" pick up and deliver documents throughout a large city. The average age of the 30 workers is 67; the oldest is 83.

Rehearsal for retirement. Retirement rehearsal programs allow an older employee to take an unpaid leave of absence of 3 to 6 months with the option to extend to full retirement or return to full-time or part-time work. Tapering off of schedules prior to retirement is another option.

Such examples illustrate how American business is beginning to realize the potential and actual benefits of older workers.

INTERVIEWS, BIODATA, AND EVALUATIONS OF TRAINING AND EXPERIENCE

Although a full account of assessing older persons in the workplace by means of interviews, biographical data, and evaluations of training and experience is beyond the scope of this chapter, an overview of these techniques will identify their extensive use, frequently in conjunction with psychological tests. The interview is undoubtedly the most widely used selection device even though it has low reliability and is subject to many biases (Arvey, 1979; Arvey & Campion, 1982). Structured interviews and situational interviews have generally increased the reliability (high interrater reliability in judges' ratings of responses to questions) and have very acceptable predictive validity as well as evidence for test fairness and utility (Campion, Pursell, & Brown, 1988; Mauer & Fay, 1988; Latham, Saari, Pursell, & Campion, 1980; Janz, 1982). In my and my colleague's work we have found that this type of interview is well accepted by candidates.

Evaluations of training and experience occur with millions of candidates in both the public and private sector as a means of screening applicants for eligibility to go on to other steps in the employment process or for making final decisions about selection. This technique is utilized frequently for jobs requiring specialized high-level backgrounds, such as engineering, scientific, and research positions, and for trade jobs where a written test might have a discriminatory effect (Davey, 1984). Ash (1983) has contributed to this procedure through a behavioral consistency method of training and experience evaluations. Myers and Fine (1985) developed a content valid Pre-employment Experience Questionnaire that avoids bias, has standardized scoring procedures that are adaptable to a computerized system, and can be used for a wide variety of jobs.

Biographical data, or *biodata,* have been used extensively and in general have been found as valid as many standardized ability tests (Reilly & Chao, 1982). Because much of the life history data in the biodata blank have little direct relationship to job tasks, the items in the questionnaire may not have public acceptability and "be viewed as an irrelevant invasion of personal privacy" (Davey, 1984, p. 369). They also require very large validation samples. Recently Shaffer, Saunders, and Owens

(1986) investigated the accuracy of responses to a biodata questionnaire and found that many of the responses are accurate; they also analyzed the sources of inaccuracy.

SELECTION OF TESTS IN THE WORKPLACE

Tests are used extensively in the workplace in selection, promotion, career development, transfer, and other personnel activities. They are frequently used in conjunction with interviews, assessment centers, and other assessment techniques. The use of tests must conform to the Uniform Guidelines on Employee Selection Procedures (1978), and these legal guidelines apply equally well to the other selection techniques. Tests must be valid, fair, practical, have candidate acceptance, and be defensible in court. The impact of valid selection procedures on work force productivity is considerably greater than most personnel psychologists have believed (Schmidt, Hunter, McKenzie, & Muldrow, 1979). Test selection or development of tests in the workplace involves two tasks: 1) establishing the nature of the job in which the worker is functioning or might function, and 2) evaluating the qualifications of the worker or potential worker to perform the tasks.

The nature of the job is determined by conducting a thorough and detailed job analysis, which becomes the basis for developing the knowledges, abilities, skills, and other characteristics (KASOCs) required by the job. The record of this procedure is necessary for any possible defense of the developed measuring instruments (Hunt & Lindley, 1977). The scope of this chapter does not permit an adequate discussion of job analysis techniques; the reader is referred to Fine and Wiley (1971), Pearlman (1980), Fleishman (1984), Fleishman and Quaintance (1984), Levine (1983), and, for an illustration of the steps used in developing valid selection tests from a content-oriented strategy, Schmitt and Ostroff (1986).

This review of job analysis will be limited to some points related to the broad requirements for a job analysis appropriate for test selection and test construction for the older person:

1) The analysis should be oriented toward the KASOCs *required* by the job in question. This is not as easy as it sounds. It is very important to eliminate KASOCs that are not essential to the performance of an older worker. Because older workers in the job will not usually be available to serve as expert sources for job analysis information, knowledge about older persons' functioning in general may be helpful. It may be that the greater experience of older persons may result in higher quality work, even though the total amount of work accomplished may be less. Additionally, an older worker who lacks a specifically required skill (or who has only a little of the skill) may compensate for the lack by using his or her greater experience and still be able to perform the required work in an acceptable manner. This again emphasizes how important it is to understand the realistic job demands for older employees.

2) For frequently occurring jobs, the analysis should be based upon an extensive body of instances and cases studied, including older persons.

3) The analysis should result from professionally approved methods of securing of basic data.

4) The analysis should show evidence of concerns about the details of jobs likely to be most applicable to the older person as well as the accommodations that may be necessary to secure good performance.

5) The analysis must be specific. One may need to know the duties of specific jobs with details, for example, about physical requirements. If standing for long periods is necessary, this should be stated as a specific job requirement, unless it is possible to modify the job enough so that only occasional standing is necessary. This does not imply that older workers cannot qualify for jobs that require standing, lifting, or pulling, but rather that employers must give attention to the valid demands of a job.

6) The analysis should have been applied in some practical problems of the older person, with published results of related research studies.

These demands may seem to put a strain on the job analyst. So be it. The importance of the job analysis for development of instruments and techniques for human assessment related to job performances cannot be overemphasized. *Most statements in the general literature about the work and work habits of older persons are not based upon job analytic studies.*

Another factor related to job analysis is the overall evaluation of the worker's functioning in the job in the workplace. First of all, the workplace needs to be defined and understood. The same human characteristics and aptitudes do not function equally well in all workplaces. The nature of the workplace is of particular importance in relation to the older worker, who may be less adaptable to varying demands placed upon basic abilities. Modern management responses to the problems have permitted older workers to use flexible working hours, to work part-time, or to work at home for some types of jobs (with adequate supervision and productivity checks). There are numerous examples of workplaces that managers have modified to accommodate the physical strength and stamina limitations of older workers who have needed skills and experiences. But more must be done as the availability of qualified older persons increases.

The social aspects of the workplace present rather different considerations. Older persons need to be accepted by other workers from management on down, their abilities must be recognized and respected, their security concerns need to be considered, and the sources of their job satisfactions must be understood. This implies the current work force needs orientation about older persons to modify any myths that employees may have about older persons and older workers.

Testing Practices in the Workplace

The determination of whether or not a person is qualified for a job is frequently accomplished through psychological testing, supplemented by interviews and ratings of education and experience. Testing for *selection* applies primarily to older persons who have retired and reenter the workplace, to those who are just entering the workplace for the first time, and to those who are considering career changes. Where *promotion* is under consideration, psychological test results are likely to be used in combination with interviews, oral examinations or structured interviews, and/or work performance ratings. Assessment centers have been found useful for predicting managerial success, selection for promotion, for career planning, and in training and development (Klimoski & Brickner, 1987). In addition to usual "assessment exercises" (observations, interviews, behavior ratings, evaluations, etc.), assessment centers may also use psychological tests for more standardized objective evaluations (for reviews of assessment center functioning, see Bray & Grant, 1966; Cascio & Sibley, 1979; Joiner, 1984; Thornton & Byham, 1982; Klimoski & Brickner, 1987; and Sackett, 1987).

In studying testing practices in the workplace, Ryan and Sackett (1987) have reported that the three top purposes of testing in 137 industries were (in order) selection, promotion, and development of employees. These typical findings were not directed toward the older worker, but covered all ages. For the older person already in the workplace, testing is most likely to be utilized in making decisions on promotion (although rarely as a single criterion) and for employee development.

In an agency of appreciable size, psychological testing of older persons in the workplace is most likely to involve middle management concerns. Is the employee measuring up to established demands of the job or special demands of his or her employment? Is he or she oriented toward relationships with the agency and opportunities for advancement? Has he or she shown evidence of leadership ability? Does he or she get along with fellow workers? Is he or she able to handle work-related contacts outside the workplace? Should he or she be encouraged as a promotable employee? Should the agency invest in this employee's development to make him or her a more valuable employee? Evaluations of work performance (discussed later) supplemented by a variety of test results in such areas as mental ability, interests, and personality would be useful in answering these questions.

Many large corporations and large public service agencies have their own staff of psychologists or personnelists to develop their own tests to meet their specific needs, while smaller companies and agencies frequently employ consultants for such test development. Development of these specifically oriented tests starts with an "in-house" job analysis. As with any job analysis, to ensure job-related data on duties and responsibilities as a basis for development of valid tests there must be input from "subject matter experts"—those who perform the job and perform it in an "expert" manner. The subject matter experts are the employees in the job in the specific agencies. Indications are that this in-house procedure creates a confidence on the part of employees that the test is really job related, as indeed it probably is. The author and his associate have used the described in-house test development procedures in a wide variety of jobs in the public and private sectors, a process that has generally included the development of structured interviews and/or performance evaluation systems to be used in conjunction with the tests that are developed.

Despite some advantages of in-house developed tests, commercially available tests may be chosen instead. In the private sector this is probably more frequent than choosing to develop a new test for the specific purpose in mind. The selection of available tests is complicated by the fact that their development and norming usually are not related to the older person. In the absence of appropriate data, what criteria for choosing of a test can be recommended? The following are some suggestions:

Know the situation in which the test(s) is to be given and utilized. Further, the test user must understand the purpose and use to be made of the test(s).

Choose a test that is in wide use. Extensive usage will indicate that many users have confidence in the test in a "variety of situations." Some of the situations may be reasonably close to the situation at hand.

Choose a test with which you are familiar. Familiarity with the test will contribute to the validity of making necessary adaptations for administration to older persons and to interpretation of test results.

Choose a test that ties assessment to the problem at hand, such as enhancing the adjustment and/or productivity of the older worker. This emphasis on the utility of the test(s) is important (Hayes, Nelson, & Jarrett, 1987).

These concerns are primarily cries for adequate training on the part of test users. Do the demands require that only professional psychologists or trained professional technicians can administer any test in an employment agency, a rehabilitation center, or a nursing home? Not necessarily. But there must be professional supervisory and/or administrative overhead in touch with the testing situation and the test administrator. It is recognized that psychological tests differ in administrator demands. Considerable graduate university training plus supervised experience is expected for the administrator of most of the projective personality techniques. Much less may be expected for the administrator of a pencil-and-paper mental status tests in an employment office. (Refer to *Practical Considerations in Testing* in the chapter on "Psychometric Considerations in Testing the Older Person" for additional suggestions.)

Patterns of Test Usage

In deciding upon the selection of tests, a study of test usage in the United States by Lubin, Larsen, and Matarazzo (1984) may be helpful. It is interesting to note from their study that a test developed especially for adults heads the list of the 30 most frequently used test over five decades—the Wechsler Adult Intelligence Scale (WAIS). The five most frequently used among the 30 are all adult applicable and adult oriented. These include the WAIS, the Minnesota Multiphasic Personality Inventory (MMPI), the Bender Visual Motor Gestalt Test, the Rorschach Inkblot Test, and the Thematic Apperception Test (TAT).

Six hundred thirty counseling psychologists completed a questionnaire survey about their use of psychological tests in a study by Watkins, Campbell, and McGregor (1988). Analyzing the questionnaires revealed that the 10 most frequently used tests were the Strong-Campbell Interest Inventory (SCII—81.5%), the MMPI (80.2%), the Wechsler Adult Intelligence Scale-Revised (WAIS-R—79.8%), sentence completion blanks (67.5%), Bender Gestalt (60.2%), the TAT (59.8%), the Sixteen Personality Factor Questionnaire (16PF—56.9%), the Wechsler Intelligence Scale for Children-Revised (WISC-R—54.3%), and the Edwards Personal Preference Schedule (EPPS—53.8%). When asked to recommend tests with which counseling psychology students should be competent, these respondents added the California Psychological Inventory (CPI), Myers-Briggs Type Indicator (MBTI), Millon Clinical Multiaxial Inventory, Kuder Occupational Interest Survey, Rorschach, Draw-A-Person, and House-Tree-Person.

The types of tests used by industrial/organizational psychologists as well as specific choices are indicated in a questionnaire survey of assessment practices done by Ryan and Sackett (1987). From 316 usable questionnaires returned, they found 78.4% used ability tests, 77.8% used personality or interest inventories, and 34.0% used projective tests. The most frequently used ability test was the Watson-Glaser Critical Thinking Appraisal; others mentioned including the Wesman Personnel Classification Test, the Employee Aptitude Series (EAS), and WAIS-R. In order (from 32.8% to 18.0%), the personality tests reported were the 16PF, the Guilford-Zimmerman Temperament Survey (GZTS), the MMPI, the MBTI, and the EPPS.

In testing older persons in the workplace, my colleague and I, in the activities of the Center for Psychological Service, have found certain tests appropriate in the following categories of use:

For evaluating general mental status (intelligence): WAIS and WAIS-R, Wechsler Memory Scale (WMS) and Wechsler Memory Scale-Revised (WMS-R).

For differential aptitudes: Differential Aptitude Test (DAT), U.S. Employment Service General Aptitude Test Battery.

For general informational-educational background: Wide Range Achievement Test-Revised (WRAT-R), ETS Basic Education Tests.

For aptitudes: Clerical Aptitude Test, Center for Psychological Service Test for Ability to Sell.

For differentiated informational-educational background: Stanford Achievement Tests, ETS Cooperative Achievement Tests.

For information related to behavior in situations involving social interactions: Center for Psychological Service Social Intelligence Test.

For vocational interest exploration: Thurstone Vocational Interest Schedule, Kuder Interest-Preference Inventory, SCII.

For psychological adjustment-personality evaluation: GZTS, CPI-Adult Form, MMPI, MBTI, TAT (selected stimulus cards), Rotter Incomplete Sentences Blank, Draw-A-Person, Experimental Circles Drawing Test (Past, Present, and Future Circles).[1]

Specific Issues in Testing Older Workers

An interrelated three-fold challenge is present in testing older workers. The tests available for use can present problems. The older person in general, as a test subject, raises some testing questions. And the older worker is a special older person, about whom we have very little factual (reliable) data in relation to functioning or potential functioning in the workplace. Several problems are currently encountered:

1) The test market of available tests suited to testing the older person has been increasing, but it is still difficult to find tests with appropriate norms and reliability-validity data for testing older persons/workers. Current research in the field of aging may eventually enhance the market. However,

> most ability tests were not designed to assess intelligence in adulthood or to predict adaptation to development challenges posed by novel situations in adult life. . . . The scope of traditional ability tests may be too restricted to tap aspects of intelligence that are important for everyday functioning. (Cornelius & Caspi, 1987, p. 144)

1. With blank sheets of paper furnished, this test requires the subject to draw three circles: one representing the past, one the present, and one the future. Comments are sought, either orally or in writing, on thoughts or reflections in relation to the drawings. Subjective examiner interpretation is a major basis of use. The test is of particular interest in testing older persons because of its wide age range of coverage in "past, present, and future." For older workers, comments on the present and future usually produce pertinent information related to the workplace and work responsibilities, as well as their evaluation of the importance of work in their later years.

2) The stereotypes of older workers (as biologically and irreversibly slowed down, etc.) held by many executives and test administrators may distort test results.

3) Older persons have some disadvantages in functioning on typical objective test techniques, whether the process involves blackening a space on an answer sheet or pressing a computer key. The examiner must ensure that the test technique does not result in a measurement of how to handle the logistics of the test situation rather than whatever construct was actually intended.

4) Sensorimotor deficits (poor vision, poor hearing, motor slowness and incoordination) affect ratings on most psychological tests designed to evaluate "mental" characteristics.

5) "Performance tests," as found in the Wechsler scales, penalize older persons with decreased sensorimotor capacities.

6) Many tests are timed, making speed a factor in the test record whether or not it is crucial in what is being tested.

7) Permissible adaptations of test procedures in testing older workers are seldom available in published test instructions. The examiner must necessarily make adaptations and include these variances in the interpretations.

8) Older workers, for the most part, have limited test-taking experience, so that a test may reflect this lack of experience rather than the ability desired to be evaluated.

9) Testing of older persons should be carried out in an environment in which the older subject is relaxed and comfortable.

10) Older workers are entitled to know as much as is permissible about the nature of tests they are to take and the use to be made of them. Examinees should be informed well ahead of the time of testing and given instructions on how to take a test. When appropriate, a practice test should be administered to provide familiarity with the type of questions as well as in using the answer sheet.

11) In questions of selection, particularly for older workers, tests should be directly job related. An academically oriented test for measuring job potentialities may be fair for an 18-year-old just graduating from high school, but not for a 60-year-old, equally qualified.

12) Job requirements for strength, agility, and endurance must be specifically described. The necessity for much walking, standing, bending, lifting (specify pounds), or outside work in all kinds of weather need to be understood by the older worker. If strength and agility tests are *necessary* in the selection process, older persons would need to take such tests. But it is incumbent on the test administrator to be certain that the strength and agility tests represent critical job requirements.

Misuse of Tests

Psychological tests are not designed for use without some decision-making capabilities on the part of users. Furthermore, users must be possessed of ethical qualifications necessary for adherence to professional principles of test use and for protection of test takers. Some informative case examples of misuse of tests on the part of psychologists are discussed by Eyde and Quaintance (1988). The categories of their cases and brief notes on their examples may furnish guidelines to test evaluators:

1) *Inappropriate use and interpretation of an assessment procedure.* This case involved the sole use of the California Psychological Inventory to assess candidates

for promotion to senior management positions. Use was made without consideration of situational factors involved in the inventory administration process and without knowledge of studies of the influence of such factors on test performance. The psychologist in charge of testing succumbed to management pressure for quick promotional decisions by using the CPI with no other assessment techniques or evidence from such appropriate sources as relevant performance evaluations and supervisors' inputs. Test users bear a heavy responsibility in such cases. They must be alert to personal, social, organizational, financial, and political situations and pressures that might lead to misdirection of their responsibilities.

2) *Lack of competence in test interpretation and misrepresentation.* This case described a personnel psychologist who lacked training in the interpretation of the MMPI and was not eligible to purchase materials related to its use. A trained clinical psychologist working subordinately to the personnel psychologist used and interpreted the MMPI for selection of applicants for nuclear power plant jobs, with respect to their emotional fitness for the work. After financial pressures resulted in the termination of the services of the clinical psychologist, the personnelist continued the use of the MMPI with routinized scoring and interpretations without informing power plant officials of the loss of the clinical psychologist or his own lack of knowledge of the MMPI.

3) *Violation of legal standards and submission to personal pressures.* Moral and legal standards, to which users of psychological tests are bound, require avoiding actions that may violate the legal and/or civil rights of clients or others who may be affected. The older test taker for whom one feels sorry cannot be given advantages to alleviate that sorrow. A psychologist cannot look with any favor toward a client because it would be professionally, politically, or socially advantageous to do so.

4) *Misleading public statements.* Interpreted, this case example says: Do not make self-aggrandizing statements about your own personnel test publications. (The reference here is to ethical standards.)

5) *Lack of competence in test selection and interpretation.* The case is cited of the use in teacher selection of a general verbal and numerical abilities test with no references to evaluation of teacher competency. The test was recommended with a cutoff score for passing by a counseling psychologist.

These cases do not literally illustrate assessments of "older persons in the workplace." However, they do exemplify some of the factors involved in the misuse of tests and how important it is when working with older workers to adhere to the professional guidelines published by the American Psychological Association (1985) for selecting and interpreting psychological tests, and to the principles for the validation and use of personnel selection procedures published by the Society for Industrial and Organizational Psychology (1987).

COMPUTERS IN THE WORKPLACE

Assessment of the older person in the workplace cannot omit serious consideration of the computerization of the workplace. Automation (computerization) of many work functions has taken place in both the public and private sectors, with increased utilization projected for the future. As an example in the personnel field, word processing functions have replaced much of standard typing, and applicant tracking systems have been established to record personnel actions in recruitment, selection, career development, promotion, retirement, and discharge. Computer systems also function within the examination process; that is, sending rejection notices to those applicants who do not meet the minimum qualifications, sending admission notices and scheduling examinations, scoring the examinations, and generating necessary statistical information (Darany, 1984). Similar uses of computers and expansion of computerized work activities in other organizational units besides personnel are taking place. This computerization of work functions has implications for the work activities that will be performed by many older workers. It may be necessary for employers to provide training opportunities for older persons in computer use to secure needed workers.

Guidelines for Psychological Testing Using Computers

Psychological testing in the workplace frequently involves computers, which are used in administration, scoring, and interpretation of test results. The American Psychological Association (1986) has published the *Guidelines for Computer-Based Tests and Interpretations,* designed to assist professionals in applying computer-based assessments competently and to serve the best interests of clients. The guidelines also help test developers to establish and maintain the quality of new products. The psychologist who uses computers, computer services, or computer programs with psychological tests should be aware of the ethical responsibilities (as outlined in the guidelines) that are inherent in such use. The guidelines should be utilized in conjunction with the *Standards for Educational and Psychological Testing* (American Educational Research Association, American Psychological Association, & National Council on Measurement in Education, 1985).

Computer-administered Psychological Tests

When computers are used to administer psychological tests, the 1986 *Guidelines* provide specific suggestions. A few of these will be discussed because of their significance in testing older persons. First, the environment where the testing terminal is located should be free of distractions. Noise, including conversation, may be very disruptive to an older person, especially to one with hearing problems. This display screen should have no glare or reflections, and material to be read should be of adequate size to be easily readable. Visual deterioration with advancing age accounts for reductions in light sensitivity, image formation, color perception, and resistance to glare (Kosnik, Winslow, Kline, Rasinski, & Sekuler, 1988).

As many older examinees will not have used computers before, they may respond more slowly and may need longer practice periods in using the equipment before test administration. Examinees need to devote their full attention to the substance of the test items and not be concerned about how to use the equipment or anxious about what they are expected to do. Older persons should be monitored and offered assistance when needed so that any problem that might affect the psychometric soundness of the score or interpretation can be remedied. (Some computer programs do monitoring automatically.)

Adaptive testing uses the computer to adapt tests to the ability of the person being tested. Based on preliminary data that are entered into the computer before testing, an estimate of the level of item difficulty is made. After the response that the examinee makes to the first item, successive test items are selected that would be appropriate to his or her ability level. With each successive response a more difficult or easier item can be presented and a more reliable estimate made of presenting further questions. As a result, fewer test items need to be presented (less than in a paper-and-pencil test), and generally the results are more reliable. The Armed Forces, the United States Employment Service, and large private testing organizations are experimenting with this approach, the value of which lies in its potential for reducing testing time and costs. Although originally designed for large-scale testing, developments for individual test applications are expected. To date there has not been much experience in adaptive testing with older persons.

Computerized Interpretations of Psychological Tests

The area of computerized interpretations of psychological tests has raised several questions about the ethical, legal, and practical implications of such practices. Matarazzo (1986) believes that computer-generated interpretations of psychological tests offer considerable potential, but states that the current status of the software has not been validated. He warns about the

> pages and pages of today's neatly typed, valid-sounding narrative interpretations that are the products, for the most part, of secretly developed discs of software that have not even been offered for scientific evaluation (as has clinical judgment), let alone even met the most rudimentary acceptable tests of Science. (Matarazzo, 1986, p. 15)

He argues that computerized test interpretations are marketed for use by many health service providers who may not have a background to understand the limitations of such reports. In a similar vein, Hartman (1986) indicates that most of the computer interpretative systems lack demonstrated validity. He also raises the question about legal challenges to a decision based on the computer test results. Who is liable, the psychologist who provided the service or the software manufacturer/programmer, or both? Both Matarazzo and Hartman refer to clinical uses of computers, but their comments apply equally well to assessment in the workplace.

Burke and Normand (1987) provide a very complete overview of the different types of computer systems used for psychological assessment, describe some helpful suggestions in developing and implementing a computer testing system, and discuss the problems associated with these developments. They conclude that computerized psychological testing systems have tremendous potential of being practical, cost effective, and psychometrically sound. They state that this potential can be realized "if proper considerations are made in designing, developing, and implementing these testing systems and if professional standards are maintained by computer test service providers and users" (Burke & Normand, 1987, p. 49). In a similar vein, Skinner and Pakula (1986) recognize the advantages that computers offer in efficiency and productivity of assessment services, but caution that the psychometric aspects of computer development and interpretation have not been rigorously evaluated. Vale, Keller, and Bentz (1986) report the results of developing a computerized system for personnel testing that generates narrative interpretations from a battery of personnel screening tests. They indicate that the computerized reports are very accurate, thorough, and have good readability, but that they are somewhat less coherent than ones done by a psychological expert.

SPECIAL TOPICS IN ASSESSING THE OLDER WORKER

Memory

Memory is an important topic of consideration in assessing older workers (see Lindley, 1987)—for the job analyst, for the assessment specialist, for the training director, for the supervisor, for the employee counselor—because older persons have commonly been thought to be distinguished from younger ones particularly by memory changes and deficits. Modern, carefully planned studies of memory have disproved the older, generally assumed relationships between age and memory loss.

Memory appears expressly or implicitly as an important candidate qualification in a large proportion of jobs. Further, memory is a prime factor in good performance on many selection and promotion tests. The past two decades have witnessed an explosion of interest and attention to studying memory by applied professionals as well as theoretical scientists. Advances in physiological, psychological, and pharmacological studies related to memory have contributed much to understanding some of the employee problems of the older worker. Knowledge of memory processes and their disturbance enhances understanding of employees exhibiting abuse of alcohol, tranquilizers, and amphetamines. Knowledge about memory contributes to the understanding of diseases referred to in personnel records and literature, such as Alzheimer's disease, characteristically occurring in older workers.

Of the many definitions of memory, most center around *learning,* leaving the assumption that memory applies only to things that have been learned. This assumption is probably correct, and a good one for dealing with the function of memory in the older person. But erudite discussions on the part of geneticists and related professionals raise troublesome questions on defining when learning can begin. They need not concern us in the present discussion.

Memory is the power or process of reproducing what has been learned and retained, of carrying out procedures for which training has been given. Memory comprises a store of information as well as the process involved in accessing that stored information, a store of things learned and retained from activity or experience as evidenced by modification of structure or behavior. These definitions emphasize recent trends in definition. As Craik (1984) says about research on age differences in remembering, "The last 20 years of memory research have seen a progressive trend away from theories concerned with structure and mechanism toward theories dealing with processes and operations" (p. 3). This means that more attention is being given to the complexities of memory rather than to just a recording of the recalled elements. The trend has also resulted in increased attention to the neurological bases of memory, moving a long distance from the early search for a localized memory center in the brain. Memory is being looked upon as the process of storing experiences in the brain by some means of encoding them with already existing storages. The process of memory can then be viewed in this sequence of events:

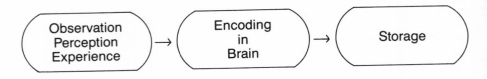

Because memory has long been an established field of concern and investigation in the elderly, the older worker is being prominently included in scientific studies and experimental investigations related to these new concepts on memory.

Viewing memory as a part or as an aspect of intelligence, and viewing intelligence according to Thorndike's breakdown as *abstract, mechanical,* or *social,* one can then think of memory as related to abstract things, mechanical things, or social things. Recognition of these types of memory may be important for selection and placement of personnel into jobs as they demand these three types of memory. The three types are positively related but not at high degrees of correlation. Some people with good abstract memory cannot readily remember faces (a part of social memory). Some older persons may have more trouble with abstract memory than with the other two because of the relatively infrequent abstract-type experiences in their later lives.

Recall and *recognition* are two types of memory. Recall involves the ability to reproduce the thing learned upon request or upon representation of the proper stimulus. Recognition involves the ability to pick out from among things presented the one or ones experienced before. Recognition of the principles as they are involved in personnel testing is illustrated by the use of recall types of examinations versus multiple-choice or true/false examinations (recognition types). Both have their place and advantages, and there is no definitive answer to the question as to which is better.

Short-term and *long-term* memory relate to the length of time between the experience and the memory of it. An example of short-term memory is furnished by job candidates who take a selection examination on the basis of cramming on suggested job descriptions and reading materials, then promptly forget all they have read. Long-term memory taps more encoded stored materials. Employees who function in their jobs primarily as short-term memory adherents cannot be assigned other than routine, immediately-to-be-carried-out duties. They can be expected to have little job ambition to rise above their present job. Such employees have not been interested in encoding much that will enhance their value to their employer or their employing agency.

Only in special situations will the psychologist or counselor need specific evaluation of memory in older adults. Memory needs for jobs in which older workers are hired will have been encompassed in more general tests. In problem situations that might call specifically for memory evaluation, the older worker probably will be referred to a specially trained clinical psychologist or psychiatrist.

Among psychological tests, the commonly used memory measures are individual tests, requiring a one-to-one communication situation. Particularly recommended is the Wechsler Memory Scale-Revised, which has adult norms up to 74 years of age, making it useful in testing older workers as well as younger adults. Its seven parts cover Personal and Current Information, Orientation, Mental Control, Logical Memory, Digits Forward and Backward, Visual Reproduction, and Associative Learning. The test is scored in terms of a Memory Quotient related to one's age group (as in IQs on the WAIS or WAIS-R).

Age Discrimination

Age discrimination occurs when an individual is denied a privilege, opportunity, recognition, or award because of the number of years he or she has lived, without due attention to more valid, just considerations. Age discrimination may apply to any designated age group, but the concern here is with that encompassing the older person. Workplace examples include promoting a less qualified younger employee over an older employee in line for promotion or limiting older workers' attendance at work-training seminars approved for younger workers.

Major concerns call for psychological assessment techniques. The foremost concern is, what should receive attention in lieu of age? The answer is usually an individual's traits, abilities, and personal characteristics. Established standardized assessment techniques, including psychological tests, will add to the accuracy and objectivity of evaluations. One must guard against the selection of tests that in and of themselves are unfairly discriminatory with respect to age.

Because of the pressing nature of these age discrimination problems, local, state, and federal government agencies have all played roles. Of notable importance and influence in employment testing has been the U.S. Equal Employment Opportunity Commission (EEOC). This commission enforces the Uniform Guidelines on Employee Selection (1978) and the age discrimination laws. Since the passage of the Age Discrimination in Employment Act (ADEA), the number of employment-related age discrimination litigation cases has increased dramatically (personal communication, Office of General Consul, U.S. Equal Employment Commission, October, 1986). The purpose of the act (and its amendments) is to provide *fair practices in employment of older persons based on ability rather than age*. As mentioned, the Age Discrimination in Employment Amendments of 1986 abolished mandatory retirement at any age (with the previously noted exceptions). Therefore, it is now illegal to discharge, to refuse to employ, or to deny a promotion to a person because of age. The law is somewhat complex, and the outcome of a complaint may depend on interpretation of the issues involved by the courts. Faley, Kleiman, and Lengnick-Hall (1984) summarized 290 cases reported in *Fair Employment Practice Cases* and found six age-related issues most important to employers and professionals: hiring, demotion, promotion, discharge, termination, and layoff. Fifty-three of the cases were selected for thorough review and analysis. In their review, the authors emphasized two concerns: 1) the evidence considered necessary by the courts to establish that age discrimination has occurred, and 2) employer defenses against age discrimination complaints.

When age is a bona fide occupational qualification (BFOQ) reasonably necessary to the operation of the business, employers may base employment decisions on age if they can justify the reasonableness of their decisions. When the BFOQ concerns public safety, it is easier to justify that hiring and/or discharge decisions are "reasonably necessary." However, the standards used by the courts to judge the validity of age-related BFOQs have varied considerably (Faley et al., 1984).

Cutoff scores in the practical utilization of tests have been viewed as presenting problems in some uses of tests with older persons. Cutoff scores are those that determine the "reject" or "accept" dividing line on an employment test or the "pass" or "fail" on a job training test. These can rarely be defended in a definitive, absolute sense. On job employment or promotion tests, cutoffs are frequently set on the basis of a distribution of candidate scores. If age differences in test scores are not correlated with job success, such a method of setting cutoff scores, it may be claimed, is unfair to older workers. Cascio, Alexander, and Barrett (1988) have summarized and analyzed the related legal, psychometric, and professional literature and developed a set of recommendations regarding acceptable professional practice in this area.

Unsatisfactory Job Performance

Assessment is of prime importance in considering the unsatisfactory worker. Poor performance is cited frequently as the reason for unsatisfactory performance. It is essential to know in what way the work is unsatisfactory—unsatisfactory at doing what? The "what" then becomes the performance criterion for evaluating personal characteristics of the worker in doing the work. Evaluating the personal characteristics of the unsatisfactorily performing worker must be assumed as a responsibility of the psychologist (or consultant psychologist) in the workplace. An accurate and fair evaluation is crucial to dealing with the problems and carrying out appropriate solutions.

Evaluations of unsatisfactory performance should be recorded ratings based on *objective* descriptions of everyday work behavior that is not satisfactory. Such behavioral descriptions (ratings) should be based upon observations made over a period of time, not upon incidental or only occasional observations. Employees should be apprised at the initial and subsequent stages of work performance, to provide the opportunity for changes in work behavior.

Assessment of the older worker is especially necessary because of the increasing number of employees dismissed (fired) for unsatisfactory performance. Of the 3 million persons fired each year in the private sector, Schreiber (1983) estimates that 200,000 are fired unfairly. In countering a charge of discrimination, the employer frequently contends the discharge resulted solely from poor job performance (Barrett & Kernan, 1987). Unsatisfactory work performance may be due to a number of reasons. Broadly classified the reasons relate to 1) the *worker* or 2) aspects of the *work environment*. The two are, of course, related. Neither considered alone can suffice for dealing with problems of acceptable job performance.

Assessment needs to be directed toward determining inherent or practically unchangeable aspects of the nature of the worker, and often more importantly toward what is modifiable. Inherent characteristics of the worker include his or her basic ability and basic aptitudes. These determine whether, under appropriate circumstances of training and environmental conditions, an unsatisfactory employee may be capable of satisfactory work performance. Some worker characteristics that may relate to work efficiency are in an "in between" classification with respect to modifiability. These include, as examples, such things as health problems, some family problems, alcoholism, and other drug abuses.

Characteristics of the worker that potentially are modifiable may include attitudes toward work in general (work ethic), attitude toward the worker's current job, attitude toward management and supervisor, ability to effect appropriate interpersonal relationships, as well as other worker characteristics. Employers or employing agencies should be capable of identifying these worker causes of unsatisfactory work performance. Because of inadequate staff and other curtailments, employers may not be able to enter into employee improvement programs, but they should be aware of the needs and form relationships with community programs related to employee problems.

If valid study has revealed inherent characteristics of a worker as the basis of unsatisfactory work performance, then a reassignment of duties or a job shift or transfer may be in order, or termination of employment considered. Smaller businesses may find reassignment of duties or job shifts impossible, in which case termination of employment may be necessary. Special employee counseling programs or association with professionally trained counselors should be available to assist workers so terminated. The older worker, particularly, is likely to need assistance. It may not be practical or feasible for the older worker to seek a new job, so that other options need to be considered and discussed with the employee.

The work environment may have bad effects upon the worker, as produced by unbearable physical, mental, or emotional demands. The work environment may be of such a nature as to preclude assessment of efficiency level of work performance. The work environment may be relatively ignored by researchers studying broad aspects of work performance, yet study of the work environment is particularly important in assessing worker characteristics and potentialities of older employees. Such employees are less adaptable to changes in the work environment and to the demands of modern personnel policies. Frequent work environment factors related to unsatisfactory worker performance of older persons include physical demands producing undue tiredness or fatigue, unfavorable interpersonal relationships with other workers, and troublesome supervisory relationships. Some of the causal factors are changeable or correctable, both in terms of the worker and the work environment. Careful job analysis studies are necessary for establishing the worker traits and abilities related to satisfactory worker performance. Such studies give the basis for development of appropriate assessment techniques.

Counseling the unsatisfactory worker is the logical outcome of identifying the inadequate work performance. Counseling with appropriate selection and interpretation of tests can be counted upon to contribute importantly to individual treatment and job remedial aims. It may be determined that the unfavorable traits, attitudes, or feelings that have caused the unsatisfactory performance can be corrected, which may require further counseling or remedial training or education. Or it may be determined through employee testing that the unsatisfactory worker is not capable of performing the job. Counseling programs for employees showing unsatisfactory job performance need to be expanded in scope and in executive attitudes toward their potential functions (Cairo, 1983). In the past, most employee counseling programs have emphasized problems related to alcoholism, drug abuse, and mental health problems.

Counseling an unsatisfactory older worker is fraught with difficulties and concerns to the counselor. Major ones have to do with caution in erroneously attributing unsatisfactory work to age itself; with the older worker, blaming work deficiencies upon age is common. However, as noted previously, chronological age is not an accurate gauge of functional age.

Retirement

The congressional law abolishing mandatory-age retirement is not expected to result in a significant increase in the number of older workers in the labor force (U.S. Senate Special Committee on Aging, 1987-1988). A national survey of American attitudes toward retirement found that almost two thirds of retirees left work before age 65 (Harris & Associates, 1979). The new law on age discrimination does have significant aspects for the employee. Although in the survey most of those retired were not employed, about 8% were employed part-time and another 5% were working full-time. Most working people of all ages believe that part-time work is desirable during retirement (Harris & Associates, 1981). In this nationwide poll, almost 75% stated they prefer to continue some kind of paid part-time work after retirement. About the same percentage felt that some kind of flexible work schedule would be beneficial. Other factors such as the need of the older person to work to supplement retirement income and the increasing recognition by employers that older workers make good employees have already resulted in new employment opportunities for older workers. More decision responsibility is left to the employee to determine retirement age and to plan for retirement. The older worker may now have a choice of continuing to work or retiring. As the older worker may continue in the work force longer than formerly possible, the problems of employee interaction and adaption may change. Retraining may be necessary (Lindley, 1986c).

The transition from work to retirement represents a major life change (Vaillant, 1977). This frequently involves adaptation to a basic role change with concomitant integration into a new life-style—new networks of relationships, new behaviors, and new self-perceptions (Schlossberg, 1981). The adaptation that occurs is likely to be influenced by individual personality (Costa, McCrae, & Arenberg, 1983). Older persons differ markedly in their ability to adapt to the changes required by retirement. Some regard it as an opportunity to embark on a long-time goal, while others regard it with fear and trepidation. Some employees like early retirement because it gives them increased time to enjoy leisure activities and to pursue a less pressureful life. Some dislike early retirement because it leaves them an empty life with nothing to do.

The effects of retirement upon the lives of retirees need special consideration in working with the older employee. Some people do not spend a large proportion of their lives at work; they may do many other things. Thus, when they retire, they change little. They go on with the things they have been enjoying. Other people are very much tied up with their work and it constitutes a large part of their lives. For these persons, retirement may have a negative effect upon quality of life. Retired, they withdraw and narrow their role in society, especially if such a result is enhanced by society's attitude toward retirees.

The word "retirement" is not always an accurate descriptor, as there are many different types of retirement with different meanings attached to each. Even in the previously cited Harris surveys of retirement, the respondents included retirees who were working full-time and part-time. Voluntary retirement because of illness is different from voluntary retirement to pursue some recreational or avocational goals. Beehr (1986) indicates that one of the needs of research on retirement is to develop better definitions about the different types of retirement. He suggests that psychologists with industrial/organizational psychology backgrounds have shown very little interest in this area. Beehr further believes that, because retirement is of such importance to employing organizations and the workers therein, I/O psychologists have an opportunity to conduct research that will contribute much more factual and valid information about the process of retirement.

Today many older persons do not retire, and many others continue working part-time after retirement. The timing of retirement can vary greatly, due to several factors such as financial security, health, family circumstances, job level, job conditions, company layoffs, or inability to perform adequately on the job. Pre-retirement programs or retirement counseling programs have been established in many organizations to facilitate the transition for the worker. As mentioned previously, most of the employee counseling programs in private industry and in the government have dealt with alcoholism, situational crises, drug abuse, and mental health disturbances (American Society for Personnel Administration and the Bureau of National Affairs, 1978). Some large corporations have programs aimed at career counseling or career development (Griffith, 1980), and most businesses have some type of retirement planning or orientation programs about retirement (Siegel & Rines, 1978).

Many of the decisions that need to be made about retirement call for assessments of the worker via techniques that include psychological tests. The question of continued employment versus retirement is frequently a major question, perhaps requiring an evaluation of worker effectiveness. Is the worker able to perform the work adequately to justify continued employment? Is work performance unsatisfactory? Many workers who retire from a full-time job want to continue working in a part-time capacity. If this cannot be done without job change, problems arise very similar to those of initial employment, involving analysis of available jobs and evaluating the retiree as a potential worker. Retirement as an event in the worker's career can be eased and made more contributory to continued personal satisfactions and enjoyments by planned psychological evaluations.

CONCLUSION

Assessment in the workplace requires considerable knowledge about the functioning of older workers and an understanding of the limitations of currently available psychological tests. Efforts need to be made to avoid discrimination in employment and to dispel unfounded myths about older workers. Provisions are necessary to enhance the skills of the older person in dealing with the newer methods and technicalities of the modern workplace (Kuhlman, 1988; Mills & Pace, 1988). Worker counseling, especially for the older worker, must be regarded as a continuous process rather than a technique to meet emergencies and job exits. In this way, assessments directed toward longer term goals can be expected to be very rewarding to all those connected with the workplace, from management to the newest or lowest level workers.

REFERENCES

American Association of Retired Persons. (1986a). *Managing a changing workforce.* Washington, DC: Author.

American Association of Retired Persons. (1986b). *Workers over 50: Old myths, new realities.* Washington, DC: Author.

American Psychological Association. (1986). *Guidelines for computer-based tests and interpretations.* Washington, DC: Author.

American Psychological Association, American Educational Research Association, & National Council on Measurement in Education. (1985). *Standards for educational and psychological tests.* Washington, DC: American Psychological Association.

American Society for Personnel Administration and Bureau of National Affairs. (1978). Counseling policies and programs for employees with problems. *Bulletin to Management,* pp. 1-10.

Arvey, R.D. (1979). Unfair discrimination in the employment interview: Legal and psychological aspects. *Psychological Bulletin, 86,* 736-763.

Arvey, R.D., & Campion, J.E. (1982). The employment interview: A summary and review of recent research. *Personnel Psychology, 35,* 281-322.

Ash, R.A. (1983). The behavioral consistency method of training and experience evaluation: Content validity issues and completion rate problems. *Public Personnel Management, 12,* 115-127.

Avolio, B.J., & Barrett, G.V. (1987). Effects of age stereotyping in a simulated interview. *Psychology and Aging, 2,* 56-63.

Barrett, G.V., & Kernan, M.C. (1987). Performance appraisal and terminations: A review of court decisions since *Brito v. Zia* with implications for personnel practices. *Personnel Psychology, 40,* 489-503.

Beehr, T.A. (1986). The process of retirement: A review and recommendations for future investigations. *Personnel Psychology, 39,* 31-55.

Bray, D.W., & Grant, D.L. (1966). The assessment center in the measurement of potential for business management. *Psychological Monographs, 80*(17).

Burke, M.J., & Normand, J. (1987). Computerized psychological testing: Overview and critique. *Professional Psychology: Research and Practice, 18*(1), 42-51.

Cairo, P. (1983). Counseling in industry: A selected review of the literature. *Personnel Psychology, 36,* 1-18.

Campion, M.A., Pursell, E.D., & Brown, B.K. (1988). Structured interviewing: Raising the psychometric properties of the employment interview. *Personnel Psychology, 41,* 25-42.

Cascio, W.F., Alexander, R.A., & Barrett, G.V. (1988). Setting cutoff scores: Legal, psychometric, and professional issues and guidelines. *Personnel Psychology, 41,* 1-23.

Cascio, W.F., & Sibley, V. (1979). Utility of the assessment center as a selection device. *Journal of Applied Psychology, 64,* 107-118.

Cornelius, S.W., & Caspi, A. (1987). Everyday problem solving in adulthood and old age. *Psychology and Aging, 2,* 144-153.

Costa, P.T., McCrae, R.R., & Arenberg, D. (1983). Recent longitudinal research on personality in aging. In K.W. Schaie (Ed.), *Longitudinal studies of adult psychological development* (pp. 222-265). New York: Guilford.

Craft, J.A., Doctors, S.I., Shkop, Y.M., & Benecki, T.J. (1979). Simulated management perceptions, hiring decisions and age. *Aging and Work, 2,* 95-100.

Craik, F. (1984). Age differences in remembering. In L.R. Squire & N. Butters (Eds.), *Neuropsychology of memory* (pp. 3-12). New York: Guilford.

Darany, T.S. (1984). Computer applications to personnel (releasing the genie—harnessing the dragon). *Public Personnel Management, 13,* 451-473.

Davey, B.W. (1984). Personnel testing and the search for alternatives. *Public Personnel Management, 13,* 361-374.

Eyde, L.D., & Quaintance, M.K. (1988). Ethical issues and cases in the practice of personnel psychology. *Professional Psychology Research and Practice, 19*(2), 148-154.

Faley, R.H., Kleiman, L.S., & Lengnick-Hall, M.L. (1984). Age discrimination and personnel psychology: A review and synthesis of the legal literature with implications for future research. *Personnel Psychology, 37,* 327-350.

Fine, S.A., & Wiley, W.W. (1971). *An introduction to functional job analysis methods for manpower analysis* (Monograph No. 4). Kalamazoo, MI: Upjohn Institute.

Fleishman, E.A. (1984). Systems for linking job tasks to personnel requirements. *Public Personnel Management, 13,* 395-408.

Fleishman, E.A., & Quaintance, M.K. (1984). *Taxonomies of human performance: The description of human tasks.* Orlando, FL: Academic Press.

Griffith, A.R. (1980). A survey of career development in corporations. *Personnel and Guidance Journal, 58,* 537-542.

Guion, R.M. (1973). A note on organizational climate. *Organizational Behavior and Human Performance, 9,* 120-125.

Harris, L., & Associates. (1979). *Study of American attitudes towards pensions and retirement.* New York: Johnson & Higgins.

Harris, L., & Associates. (1981). *Aging in the eighties: America in transition.* Washington, DC: National Council on the Aging.

Hartman, D.E. (1986). On the use of clinical psychology software: Practical, legal and ethical concerns. *Professional Psychology: Research and Practice, 17,* 462-465.

Hayes, S.C., Nelson, R.O., & Jarrett, R.B. (1987). The treatment utility of assessment. *American Psychologist, 42,* 963-974.

Hunt, T., & Lindley, C.J. (1977). Documentation of selection and promotion test questions: Are your records sagging? *Public Personnel Management, 6,* 415-421.

Janz, T. (1982). Initial comparisons of patterned description interviews versus unstructured interviews. *Journal of Applied Psychology, 67,* 577-580.

Johnson, H.E. (1988). Older workers help meet employment needs. *Personnel Journal, 67,* 100-105.

Johnston, W.B. (Ed.). (1987). *Workforce 2000.* Indianapolis: Hudson Institute.

Joiner, D.A. (1984). Assessment centers in the public sector: A practical approach. *Public Personnel Management, 13,* 435-450.

Jones, E.J. (1986). Interpreting interpersonal behavior: The effects of expectancies. *Science, 134,* 41-46.

Kimmel, D.C. (1988). Ageism, psychology, and public policy. *American Psychologist, 43,* 175-178.

Klimoski, R., & Brickner, M. (1987). Why do assessment centers work? The puzzle of assessment center validity. *Personnel Psychology, 40,* 243-260.

Kosnik, W., Winslow, L., Kline, D., Rasinski, K., & Sekuler, R. (1988). Visual changes in daily life throughout adulthood. *Journal of Gerontology: Psychological Sciences, 43,* 63-70.

Kuhlman, T.M. (1988). Adapting to technical changes in the workplace. *Personnel, 65,* 67-69.

Latham, G.P., Saari, L.M., Pursell, E.D., & Campion, M.A. (1980). The situational interview. *Journal of Applied Psychology, 65,* 422-427.

Levine, E.L. (1983). *Everything you always wanted to know about job analysis.* Tampa, FL: Mariner.

Lewin, K., Lippett, R., & White, R. (1939). Patterns of aggressive behavior in experimentally created "social climates." *Journal of Social Psychology, 10,* 271-299.

Lindley, C.J. (1984). Putting "human" into human resource management. *Public Personnel Management, 13,* 501-510.

Lindley, C.J. (1986a). The older worker. *IPMA Assessment Council News, 10*(1), 15-16.

Lindley, C.J. (1986b). The older worker. *IPMA Assessment Council News, 10*(2), 8-9.

Lindley, C.J. (1986c). The older worker. *IPMA Assessment Council News, 10*(4), 13-14.

Lindley, C.J. (1987). The older worker—Memory. *IPMA Assessment Council News, 11*(1), 13-15.

Lindley, C.J., & Hunt, T. (Eds.). (1984). Assessment techniques and challenges [Special issue]. *Public Personnel Management, 13.*

Litwin, G.H., & Stringer, R.A. (1986). *Motivation and organizational climate.* Boston: Harvard University Press.

Lubin, B., Larsen, R.M., & Matarazzo, J.D. (1984). Patterns of psychological test usage in the United States: 1935-1982. *American Psychologist, 39,* 451-454.

Maddox, G.L. (1987). Aging differently. *The Gerontologist, 27,* 557-564.

Matarazzo, J.D. (1986). Computerized clinical psychological test interpretations: Unvalidated plus all mean and no sigma. *American Psychologist, 41,* 14-24.

Maurer, S.D., & Fay, C. (1988). Effect of situational interviews, conventional structured interviews, and training on interview rating agreement: An experimental analysis. *Personnel Psychology, 41,* 329-344.

Mills, G.E., & Pace, R.W. (1988). Providing practice for skill development. *Training and Development Journal, 42,* 36-38.

Myers, D.C., & Fine, S.A. (1985). Development of a methodology to obtain and assess applicant experiences for employment. *Public Personnel Management, 14,* 51-64.

Neugarten, B.L. (1979). Time, age, and the life cycle. *American Journal of Psychiatry, 136,* 887-894.

Norman, C. (1988). Rethinking technology's role in economic change. *Science, 240,* 977.

Office of Technology Assessment. (1988). *Technology and the American economic transition.* Washington, DC: Author.

Palmore, E.B. (1974). *Normal aging* (Vol. 2). Durham, NC: Duke University Press.

Palmore, E.B. (1977). Facts on aging: A short quiz. *The Gerontologist, 17,* 315-320.

Palmore, E.B. (1982). Attitudes toward aging. *Research on Aging, 4,* 333-348.

Pearlman, K. (1980). Job families: A review and discussion of their implications for personnel selection. *Psychological Bulletin, 87,* 1-28.

Raza, S.M., & Carpenter, B.N. (1987). A model of hiring decisions in real employment interviews. *Journal of Applied Psychology, 72,* 596-603.

Reilly, R.R., & Chao, G.T. (1982). Validity and fairness of some alternative employee selection procedures. *Personnel Psychology, 35,* 1-61.

Rosen, B., & Jerdee, T.H. (1976). The nature of job-related stereotypes. *Journal of Applied Psychology, 61,* 180-183.

Ryan, A.M., & Sackett, P.R. (1987). A survey of individual assessment practices by I/O psychologists. *Personnel Psychology, 40,* 455-488.

Sackett, P.R. (1987). Assessment centers and content validity: Some neglected issues. *Personnel Psychology, 40,* 13-25.

Schlossberg, N. (1981). A model for analyzing human adaptation to transition. *The Counseling Psychologist, 9,* 2-18.

Schmidt, F.L., Hunter, J.E., McKenzie, R.C., & Muldrow, T.W. (1979). Impact of valid selection procedures on work-force productivity. *Journal of Applied Psychology, 64,* 609-626.

Schmitt, N., & Ostroff, C. (1986). Operationalizing the "behavioral consistency" approach: Selection test development based on a content-oriented strategy. *Personnel Psychology, 39,* 91-108.

Schnake, M.E. (1983). An empirical assessment of the effects of affective response in the measurement of organizational climate. *Personnel Psychology, 36,* 791-807.

Schneider, B. (1987). The people make the place. *Personnel Psychology, 40,* 437-453.

Schneider, B., & Reichers, A.E. (1983). On the etiology of climates. *Personnel Psychology, 36,* 19-39.

Schreiber, N.E. (1983). Wrongful terminations of at-will employees. *Massachusetts Law Review, 68,* 22-35.

Shaffer, G.S., Saunders, V., & Owens, W.A. (1986). Additional evidence for the accuracy of biographical data: Long-term retest and observer ratings. *Personnel Psychology, 39,* 791-809.

Siegel, S.R., & Rines, J.M. (1978). Characteristics of existing and planned pre-retirement programs. *Aging and Work, 2,* 93-99.

Skinner, H.A., & Pakula, A. (1986). Challenge of computers in psychological assessment. *Professional Psychology: Research and Practice, 17,* 44-50.

Society for Industrial and Organizational Psychology, Inc. (1987). *Principles for the validation and use of personnel selection procedures* (3rd ed.). College Park, MD: Author.

Spencer, G. (1984). Projections of the population of the United States by age, sex and race: 1983-2080. *Current Population Reports* (Series P-25, No. 952). Washington, DC: U.S. Bureau of the Census.

Stagner, R. (1985). Aging in industry. In J.E. Birren & K.W. Schaie (Eds.), *Handbook of the psychology of aging* (2nd ed., pp. 789-817). New York: Van Nostrand Reinhold.

Thornton, G.C., III, & Byham, W.C. (1982). *Assessment centers and managerial performance.* New York: Academic Press.

U.S. Senate Special Committee on Aging. (1987-1988). *Aging America: Trends and projections.* Washington, DC: U.S. Department of Health and Human Services.

Uniform guidelines on employee selection procedures. (1978). *Federal Register, 43,* 38290-38315.

Vaillant, G.E. (1977). *Adaptation to life.* Boston: Little, Brown.

Vale, C.D., Keller, L.S., & Bentz, V.J. (1986). Development and validation of a computerized interpretation system for personnel tests. *Personnel Psychology, 39,* 525-542.

Watkins, C.D., Jr., Campbell, V.L., & McGregor, P. (1988). Counseling psychologists' uses and opinions about psychological tests: A contemporary perspective. *The Counseling Psychologist, 16,* 476-486.

14

Counseling and Therapeutic Interventions with Older Adults

MICHAEL DUFFY, PH.D.

Counseling interventions can be viewed as an integral part of the assessment process; assessment is never complete without the intervention process and intervention is a process involving cycles of continuing assessment. This chapter addresses the role of intervention and emphasizes that intervention is a constituent part of assessment and vice versa.

This chapter will also discuss testing as one of many counseling techniques. It is important to note that psychological tests are used differently depending on whether they stand separately as a battery, or whether they are used *within* and as part of the counseling process. A counselor who is working with a client over a period of time in counseling may affect the use made of tests. First, because of the ongoing assessment that good therapy involves, less testing may be called for. Second, because counseling allows an intimate perspective on client dynamics, when tests are used, the counselor is able to use them in a more selective and targeted fashion.

INTERVENTION AS ASSESSMENT

The inherent link between assessment and intervention is made strongly in the work of Kell and Mueller (1966; Mueller & Kell, 1972), where assessment and diagnosis is an incremental process, gradually unfolding throughout the process of therapy. This is unlike the classical approach where assessment/diagnosis is an initial and intact phase, preceding and yielding a reliable treatment plan. These differences point, in turn, to a basic distinction in the meaning of the term *diagnosis*. In one sense, diagnosis is *symptom identification* as described in the *Diagnostic and Statistical Manual of Mental Disorders* (American Psychiatric Association, 1980); in another sense the term *diagnosis* conveys *understanding of the cause or meaning* of those behaviors or symptoms. It makes sense, therefore, that the early identification of the symptomatic pattern of a problem through assessment is later expanded during intervention by an understanding of the context and meaning of the problem in the person's life. These two aspects of the diagnostic process are complementary and both necessary. Symptoms and overt behavior patterns cannot be ignored; by the same token they do not always reveal the full meaning of behavior. Similar symptoms can have very dissimilar meaning and therefore require different treatment; depression, for example, is often a "final common pathway" (Gurland, 1980) of many different disorders. Conversely, dissimilar symptoms can represent essentially similar problems; the symptoms of anxiety are many.

A final point here: if we accept that assessment continues and is expanded during therapy, it is interesting, and paradoxical, that we often gain more understanding by interventions that *fail* to work. A successful intervention confirms our diagnostic hypothesis; case closed! (We might, of course, argue with this assertion.) Paradoxically, an unsuccessful intervention often leads to further enquiry that deepens understanding of the problem and the person. Limited efficacy of medication in treating depression in an older adult may lead to a more realistic appraisal of her social-emotional needs. This is an important issue because therapists often view unsuccessful interventions with a sense of professional failure rather than cues that raise further questions.

AN IMAGE PROBLEM

Counseling older persons simply does not have the "sex appeal" of other specialty areas in the trend-ridden field of the therapies. This author's experience in training professionals in geriatric therapy is consistent; graduate students and professionals approach the area somewhat timidly. There is often an ambivalence about working with older persons. Trainees may be intellectually convinced of the importance of the area but be struggling with aversive reactions to geriatric disability or countertransference-like reactions of young professionals working with older clients. There is also the feeling that therapy with older adults will be totally different and difficult and that therapy techniques learned elsewhere will not be applicable with older clients. Neither of these two fears is justified.

The same point can be made about the applicability of assessment and diagnostic techniques. Psychometrically, it is reasonable to question the age norming of many tests, but this does not imply that these cannot be used. In testing it is always presupposed that the diagnostician take into account characteristics of the test-taker and context of testing.

Working with older persons is much more the same than different as compared with working with younger persons. Descriptions of personality in late life are often negative and largely unsupported by facts: rigid, stubborn, bossy, complaining, dependent, incompetent, and so on. In fact, recent research suggests that personality does not basically change with aging (Neugarten, 1977), but simply becomes more obvious. At younger ages, individuals have greater concerns about being liked, being socially appropriate, and may tend to mask personal characteristics. Self-involved, selfish behavior in a 75-year-old frequently reflects the narcissism of a younger age. The old lady who "jumps line" in the grocery store (and gets away with it!) has probably behaved similarly throughout life, if less obtrusively.

An important element in the disposition to view older persons as "different" is the personal and professional tendency to view others or clients as "them," rather than "us." To be an older person is simply to be myself at a later point of time. Do we think *we* will be so different as we age? Do we believe we will stop feeling, being hurt, being excited, or fail to hold our cherished values? Probably not. We have no reason to believe that our emotional lives will cease to be as rich, complex, and (often) problematic as they are now. It is interesting, therefore, that many therapists believe that therapy with older adults will not reach the same emotional depth as therapy with younger persons. And this belief, of course, will preclude intensive therapy. Similarly, it should not be assumed that established therapeutic techniques will be ineffective with older adults. There is no evidence to support this. All techniques need to be sensitively attuned to the individual and not used mechanically. This general proviso should avoid using inappropriate techniques with persons who happen to be older. These issues related to the negative "image" of counseling older adults often has predictable results. Many therapists simply stay away from working with older adults; other therapists trivialize the process, often infantalizing the older client and failing to reach the full potential of therapeutic change.

REAL DIFFERENCES

In correcting for negative stereotypes it is important not to lose sight of differences that do exist in working with older persons (Duffy, 1988). One important factor is the relatively few older persons who receive mental health care. Only 4% of all community mental health center clients are elderly and only 2% of private psychiatric services (Roybal, 1984). This is not due to simple neglect of older persons, although it needs to be corrected. The fact is that the current cohort of elderly—as opposed to older persons per se—tends not to utilize mental health services. While mental health is intrinsic in human beings, *self-awareness* of mental health differs greatly by culture, context, and history. Although older persons today are acutely aware of physical health needs, they have grown up in a context where happiness, feelings, and emotional wellness were considered (wrongly, of course) a luxury. In terms of Maslow's (1962) hierarchy of needs, concern over emotional and psychological wellness assumes a higher order character. Older persons certainly do seek medical services; they tend not to seek out psychological services. Interestingly, they are overrepresented in public mental hospitals; 30% of patients are over 65 (Gatz, Smyer, & Lawton, 1980) and are probably increasing also in private psychiatric hospitals. This is because they reach these institutions through referral by physicians. In the psychotherapy practice of this author, most older clients are referred either by physicians or family members; they are rarely self-referred.

Apart from utilization of services, there are several other differences characterizing older clients. Age does have a direct effect on such things as decreased acuity in hearing and vision (McFarland, 1968) and limited mobility. Aging can mean hearing loss of sounds at a higher frequency; this tempts the counselor to speak at higher volume, with little success. In fact, we need to speak lower, not louder, and perhaps move closer to the person. Another age change in vision is the need for approximately 50% increase in illumination. In yet another area, aging decreases response time; older persons do not do well in timed tasks—like IQ tests—but frequently surpass younger cohorts in consistency on task and attention to detail (Welford, 1977). It seems also that older persons may be at a disadvantage in recall from secondary memory (after 30 seconds of interpolated activity), but this is less problematic when good retrieval information is given (Craik, 1977). This has implications for both testing and intervention; memory tests based on serial recall will disadvantage older persons and, in turn, recall performance can be improved by the use of cognitive elaboration strategies that help older persons with recall (Weinstein, Duffy, Underwood, McDonald, & Gott, 1981).

Finally, on the asset side, older persons are different in their sheer amount of human experience. Although it is possible, of course, for people not to profit from experience, older persons have had opportunities to learn from life's hazards and problems that simply surpass the young. Older persons are "survivors" of many battles and challenges. Living in a nursing home, for example, with its inherent constraint and loss of freedom, presents crises that would defeat many a younger person. In our legitimate concern over the condition of geriatric patients, we sometimes forget how remarkably gracious is their adjustment to unfortunate circumstances (Duffy, 1988).

COUNSELING OLDER PERSONS

The field of gerontology and therefore geriatric therapy has grown up in an era of interdisciplinary cooperation. The following discussion will overview a series of concepts, techniques, and counseling and assessment approaches and provide resources in the best practice in counseling older adults.

To say this is a series of techniques is somewhat ambiguous. *Technique* is a word with several meanings in counseling and psychotherapy—not to mention the source of some confusion. The term can imply a *structured procedure* such as in behavior therapies, in dynamic therapy methods such as psychodrama, the gestalt "empty chair," or in hypnosis. The word is also applied to *psychological strategy* such as the use of paradox, symptom prescription, or the use of suggestion in therapy. Yet again, used in the singular, *technique* can refer to the therapist's *overall approach* to a given client. This is often its meaning in psychodynamic therapies where the therapist's "posture" toward the client, rather than specific procedures, is a critical issue. This is the case in managing a client's transference to the therapist. The various approaches to working with older persons that follow will use all of these meanings. And, as will be seen, many of the sections are in some sense overlapping; interviewing techniques can also be used in group contexts.

Finally, the techniques or approaches that follow differ in whether they are directed toward individual-clinical or system-level effects. Community psychology and community mental health have contributed much to understanding the futility of interventions at the individual, clinical level, when the problem is systemic in nature. Often forgotten, however, is that sophisticated individual clinical skills are an enormous asset in working with the organizational complexity of systemic intervention. Both are needed; neither alone is adequate.

The Use of Tests in Counseling

Psychological tests often provide the counselor with a wider range of behavior than is not available through interview alone. Often, too (as with the projectives), they provide a more oblique, less direct, and often more revealing perspective on the client's behavior. Given that older persons rarely seek counseling directly, very frequently the first contact with the older client is a request for psychological testing by a concerned family or nursing home. Because of this, using tests in counseling older persons is not less relevant (as is often believed) but more so than with younger clients.

When a psychological assessment of an older person is requested by a family member, physician, or nursing home, the referral question is often related to assessment of cognitive impairment. Answering this question often allows and requires that the counselor assess also areas such as personality, mood, and memory. Moreover this initial assessment is frequently the "foot in the door" for ongoing counseling interventions, which in turn may lead to further pinpointed assessment questions.

Whether assessment techniques are used as a comprehensive battery or in a more piecemeal but targeted way within the process of therapy, the counselor should have at hand a selection of instruments that adequately cover the various domains of geriatric behaviors and clinical questions. These domains include mental status and cognitive functioning; mood; personality; activity and functional status; and psychosocial stressors. So frequent is the request for and need of assessment that this author finds it useful to make up complete packets of the basic test materials and keep them available for ready use.

The basic package should include a measure of mental status. Although mental status examinations are not psychometrically complex devices, they provide a very useful screening measure of cognitive functioning as a first stage in differential diagnosis. The Short Portable Mental Status Questionnaire (SPMSQ; Pfeiffer, 1975) remains a brief and reliable measure, although it is somewhat eclipsed currently by the Mini-Mental State Examination (Folstein, Folstein, & McHugh, 1975), which includes measures of specific cognitive functions such as recall, language, and calculation. Because scores on a mental status examination can also be deflated by functional conditions such as depression and schizophrenia, it is useful to add a neurological screening device such as the Face-Hand Test (Kahn, Goldfarb, Pollack, & Peck, 1960) to crosscheck for organic processes in mental status (Kane & Kane, 1981).

As affective disorders are a major diagnosis with older adults, a measure of depression is essential in the testing repertoire. Here again, because the presence and appearance of depression in geriatric patients can be somewhat obscured and present differently than in younger adults (Hussian, 1981), a test instrument can help isolate indicators of depression. This author finds the Geriatric Depression Scale (Brink, Yesavage, Lum, Heersema, Adey, & Rose, 1982) effective. It is easily administered with older persons and also emphasizes somatic symptomatology, which is prevalent in geriatric depression.

Personality measurement is more complex with older adults. Many of the psychometrically valid instruments such as the Minnesota Multiphasic Personality Inventory (MMPI) have simply not been adequately normed on older groups. It is not at all clear whether normative profiles of older adults on the MMPI are descriptive of late life personality or artifacts of the test itself. The counselor needs to proceed more experimentally in this area. Projective methods such as the Geriatric Sentence Completion Form (LeBray, 1982) and the Senior Apperception Test (SAT; Bellak & Bellak, 1973) can add significantly to the objective measures.

Of course, as was mentioned in the introduction, it is dangerous in assessment to rely too heavily on testing alone. Clinical impressions gained in the context of ongoing counseling and interviewing form the best confirmation of test results. In the differential diagnosis of Alzheimer's disease, for example, the clinical description of symptoms is perhaps the best indicator. The counselor may find it useful to have at hand a semistructured interview format that provides a compendium of symptoms associated with relevant disorders (Gurland et al., 1976).

The style of administering tests, though always critical, is particularly so with geriatric patients. Especially with cognitively impaired elderly, it is important not to let the formality of test administration increase the *appearance* of impairment. Very often it helps to view the testing process, even a formal battery, in a "naturalistic" way, blending the tests into the flow of an ongoing "interview." This is particularly easy where tests are inserted into a counseling process, but even a "one-shot" testing session can become an interesting "conversation" with the older client. Interest, of course, produces diversions and one question on health or mood could (usefully) take up a whole hour. This may be perfect in counseling but slow down a formal assessment. The solution is often simple. Instead of interrupting the client, the counselor can listen carefully (and genuinely) to the clients and find a natural "in" to the next assessment question: ". . . So lacking energy *does* seriously affect you, Mrs. X. . . . Now, let me ask you this also, . . . Do you feel your situation is hopeless?" and so forth.

Interviewing Techniques

Several methods of interviewing older adults have been developed in gerontology that are also useful to mental health counselors. They include oral history, reminiscence, and life review. These techniques are non-invasive and naturalistic in character and are helpful in initial interviews with older persons in circumstances where a more direct focus on mental health would be aversive. Although mental health problems among older persons are very frequent, nursing homes, for example, are physical health care facilities and residents understandably resist characterization as mental health patients. These interviewing techniques serve an assessment as well as a therapeutic function; the purpose of the interview is to gain understanding in order to change behavior.

Oral history is an established method used by historians and anthropologists to tap living history through the oral traditions of a culture. It can also serve, less formally, as a non-threatening entrée and rich source of knowledge and understanding of an older person. "Telling our story" is fascinating to listener and storyteller alike and provides a "window" into what is central to us and therefore recorded in our memories. Doing a *family* history can be particularly evocative of personal memories. This can be done through the use of a structured family history questionnaire (Warren, 1982), through the random selection of cards containing questions about one's family life in "The Ungame" (Zachich, 1975), or in the construction of a genogram (Sherman & Fredman, 1986) of one's family of origin. Another excellent method of stimulating memories of family experiences is the Family Floor Plan (Coppersmith, 1980). In this experience, the drawing of the floor plan of one's childhood home provides a structure to powerfully aid reminiscence.

The phenomenon and technique of *reminiscence,* thus, is essentially similar to oral history and forms its basis. To many younger people reminiscing suggests the caricature of the older person constantly retelling the same story. Robert Butler (1963), however, redefined reminiscence from a "symptom" of living in the past to a natural cognitive process that serves a life-reviewing purpose. It is the opinion of this author that reminiscing is a natural cognitive process among *all ages,* used for a variety of purposes. Reminiscing may help "relocate" to a more pleasant time when our present is less than engaging. We may also reminisce when we have material in our past that is "unfinished" and continues to concern us. It may simply be triggered when present events, emotional or factual, trigger strong associations with past events (Merriam, 1980). It is not surprising that, in geriatric practice, reminiscence has moved from the status of symptom to a valuable tool for remotivating older patients. When used by non-therapists it often focuses on review of factual rather than emotional memories, using a variety of materials including photo albums, music, souvenirs, and videotape documentaries (Woods & Britton, 1985). These are used to stimulate recall and interest. Another popular method is to provide a chronology of significant historical events and play "Where were *you?*" (Ebersole, 1978).

In the hands of a counselor or therapist, these same methods can also serve to stimulate a more psychologically oriented *life review.* In this case, historical facts are secondary to the experiences and emotions that they encapsulate. The purpose here is not just to remotivate and stimulate interest, but to promote therapeutic change. Additional strategies may also intensify this emotional process. Lewis and Butler (1974) suggest making physical or imaginary "pilgrimages" to places in the past, organizing reunions of family, friends, or colleagues, and completing genealogies. Doing this work in groups can intensify the experience; Georgemiller and Maloney (1984) in a controlled clinical study found that group life review, for example, significantly decreased denial of death. The use of denial is a predictable and universal method of coping with uncomfortable or unacceptable material; sensitive life review can make this adaptation unnecessary. Although the effects of reminiscence and life review are not unambiguously supported in group research data, in skilled hands reminiscence and life review are powerful techniques.

An important development in interviewing older adults who are cognitively impaired or confused is validation or fantasy therapy. Developed by Naomi Feil, a geropsychiatric social worker, validation therapy (Feil, 1982) is an application to older adults of an approach to disorientation/confusion that is little used even within general therapeutic circles. It involves the acceptance of a person's inner life and representations as a valid expression of their experience—however illogical, confused, disoriented, dillusional, or paranoid is their expression. A person's fantasies are not challenged but explored sensitively for their meaning in emotional if not logical terms. This approach also recognizes that a person cannot be argued or convinced out of confusion, and that this frequently has the reverse effect. Validation therapy is similar, dynamically, to the concepts of paradoxical intention and symptom prescription (Herr & Weakland, 1979). Feil's work has revolutionized the management of confusion among older adults, especially in nursing homes, which have been dominated by the often inappropriate use of reality orientation. *Looking for Yesterday* (Feil, 1978) is an excellent 30-minute film that portrays the validation therapy approach.

THE PSYCHODYNAMIC APPROACH

Reminiscence, life review, and fantasy therapy all lend themselves well to the psychodynamic approach to geriatric therapy. The term *psychodynamic,* despite popular misconception, is not synonymous with *psychoanalytic;* psychoanalysis is one form of psychodynamic theory and therapy. The psychodynamic approach, as used here, refers to the search for a psychological meaning, context, or cause of human behavior as the basis for intervention; psychoanalysis is one outcome or answer in that search (Duffy, 1984). The psychodynamic approach, in this broader sense, is most clearly different from the strict behaviorist approach of operant and classical conditioning, where psychological meaning is considered conceptually redundant.

It is not possible here to review the many theories and therapies that constitute the psychodynamic tradition; in fact, many other therapeutic modalities described in the chapter share this perspective. There are, however, several major themes and methods that are relevant to working with older persons. One tradition has been the attempt to understand and treat late-life problems as expressions of developmental events. Erikson's (1963) influential concept of life-course stages contributed the late-life stages of ego integrity and generativity. It is curious, however, that many problems of older adults, just like young adults, can be traced to developmental traumata that impact Erikson's *early life* psychosocial tasks, such as basic trust, autonomy, identity, and intimacy (Sherman, 1981). Older adults do not struggle only with late-life developmental issues. Nevertheless, an understanding of late life has been neglected in developmental psychology. Peck (1968) pointed to three major adjustments of late life: ego differentiation versus work-role preoccupation, body transcendence versus body preoccupation, and ego transcendence versus ego preoccupation. These are useful concepts in understanding the psychological issues faced by older adults due often to chronic physical illness and pain.

The transitions of mid and late life, work, parenthood, and so on create disturbing shifts in the inner "ecology" of a person's life (Gutmann, 1981). From the psychodynamic perspective, what is important here is that problems arise from internal processes. External stresses are not always present and are very different in their effect on people.

Clearly the psychodynamic approaches are targeted at "deeper" structures and this has been the source of great controversy: is this deeper analysis possible with older persons? Are they too fixed, too rigid, too old, too confused for psychotherapy? Is basic therapeutic change an unrealistic goal for the geriatric patient? In a work on psychotherapy, Freud (1904/1924) stated that people over 50 years of age lack the mental elasticity for change and learning. However, this view was soon contradicted (Abraham, 1919/1953). Although, even today, few psychotherapists work with older clients for reasons discussed earlier, psychotherapy with older persons is less frequently discounted. As Ingebretsen (1977) said, "age per se indicates nothing definite about the client's power or will to change" (p. 319). There are greater differences *among* older adults than between generations; being "older" is a 40-year age span. It is the experience of this author that not only are generalizations of this magnitude meaningless, but he has seen much therapeutic change in older adults in his own practice.

A body of literature is building on psychotherapy with the elderly. Goldfarb in 1954 (Goldfarb & Sheps, 1954) was describing brief therapy of psychological and somatic disorders, and brief psychodynamic interventions (Kovacs, 1977) have been shown to be successful (Lazarus & Groves, 1987). A recent volume edited by Sadavoy and Leszcz (1987) has provided significant detail to using psychotherapy with the elderly.

Group Approaches

Most practitioners who work with the elderly in groups find this method very effective. Specifically, this author and his graduate student trainees use group formats in treating nursing home patients, and, as long as the leadership is competent, the group method rarely fails. Groups simply work well with older adults. As we age we often become less self-conscious and being in groups becomes less frightening. Perhaps the most powerful argument for using group approaches in counseling is the following: most of what goes wrong in our lives does so in relationships, and most of what goes right does so in relationships! Especially in intensive, controlled contexts, other persons can have powerful therapeutic impact on us. Brink (1979) lists a series of specific advantages to doing group therapy with older persons. Group therapy

1) takes most institutionalized patients out of their withdrawn state;
2) awakens their interest in others;
3) provides opportunities for new friendships;
4) is not as alarming as a private office visit with a therapist;
5) provides group control over excessive dependency and temper tantrums;
6) promotes self-confidence and esteem by having many listeners; and
7) reduces illusions of grandeur and paranoia through realistic mutual criticism.

Groups are perhaps the most widely used therapeutic modality with older adults and have been used in a wide number of contexts and problem areas. Group therapy has been used for psychotic elderly patients (Yalom & Terrazas, 1968), cognitively impaired patients (Allen, 1976; Gilewski, 1986; Shoham & Neuschatz, 1985), older families (Dye & Erber, 1981), older couples (Locker, 1981), mental support (Haber, 1983), and for elderly narcissistic patients (Levine & Poston, 1980). Group therapy has been used in proprietary nursing homes (Saul & Shura, 1974) and in retirement communities (Poggi & Berland, 1985).

In starting a group for older persons it is helpful to be sensitive to how the group is being perceived. Residents in a nursing home (or anyone) will not respond well to being characterized as "people with problems." Some of the interviewing techniques mentioned earlier work well in giving a low-key, naturalistic structure to the new group; once group members are engaged, little structure will be needed. Reminiscence materials ("The Ungame," the Family Floor Plan) provide useful early structure. Alternatively, groups can be structured around refreshments or topics of conversation; this author has had good success with groups identified as "The Coffee Klatch" or "The Conversation Group." Once group cohesion is attained, little rationale or structure is necessary. Groups are natural phenomena and group therapy simply utilizes and enhances these natural processes.

Family and Couples Counseling

Working with older persons in their family has generally received very little attention in psychotherapy and family therapy, but this is changing rapidly. Troubled families, in fact, often bring in an older adult parent for therapy as they struggle with the changing structures created by increased numbers of old-old family members, chronic health problems, providing home health care, and putting parents in nursing homes. Frequently younger family members are agonizing and filled with guilt, horrified at their unsuspected rage at their "loved ones." And as the family tries to cope with these many stressors, it becomes apparent that their ability to do so is severely limited by many unfinished family issues in their family experience. Under particular pressure is the middle-generation female (Duffy & Kurman, 1985), who is often cast as the "family kinkeeper," responsible for older and younger generations, maintaining family organization and communication and, when necessary, being the responsible party in the nursing home. It is not surprising that this can strain the relationship between the family and the nursing home where feelings are frequently displaced (Duffy & Shuttlesworth, 1987; Shuttlesworth, Rubin, & Duffy, 1982).

Support groups for families of Alzheimer's patients are well known. This has been a politically well-supported area with high visibility and many resources. *The 36-Hour Day* (Mace & Rabins, 1981) is an excellent guide for families with a demented parent. Titles like *The Hidden Victims of Alzheimer's Disease: Families under Stress* (Zarit, Orr, & Zarit, 1985) typify a level of public and professional concern for families. It should be remembered, however, that many families with a non-Alzheimer's sick parent in a nursing home or in the home critically need support. To a lesser extent, these issues are receiving attention.

It is important to mention that many pervasive negative images of the contemporary family lack validity (Duffy, 1982). Ideas that imply the breakdown of extended families ties, the isolation of the nuclear family, the facile abandonment of older persons into institutions, the lack of contact between the old and the young, and the decline of family bonds due to institutionalization are largely without support. Too often we judge the norm from the clinical "hard" cases and also simply misjudge the meaning of negative behavior of families. Even apparent neglect, though never justified, can be an avoidance of pain.

It is important not to be constrained by ageism when doing therapy with older families. We need to be as direct, confrontive, and compassionate as with younger families—and carefully avoid infantilizing the older family member. Frequently family therapy assumes the form of multigenerational therapy, which brings a complexity uncomfortable to many family therapists. This complexity can usually be flexibly managed through the structure of therapy: contacting family members strategically through letters, audio-letters, phone calls, time extended sessions, home visits, and audiotaping sessions for absent family members (Duffy, 1986). Although the literature in this area is sparse, recent books by Herr and Weakland (1979) and Brink (1986) are excellent resources. Also, several techniques mentioned in the last section, such as "The Ungame" and the Family Floor Plan, serve as both assessment and therapeutic devices. To these can be added the use of family drawings, which offer insight to the counselor and family members alike and make the process of assessment/intervention engaging and interesting (Oster & Gould, 1987). Sherman and Fredman (1986) and Filsinger (1983) have produced excellent source books on structured techniques on family assessment and therapy.

A central element in the family, its "glue," is the relationship between spouses. The needs of older spouses have been particularly neglected within traditional family therapy. This is critical because there are many transitions in middle and late life, and spouses are often changing in different directions. What may have been a functional relationship in earlier life becomes troubled in late life. Younger family members are often intolerant of the marital stress of older parents. Aggressive interventions are just as necessary with this age group (Crose & Duffy, in press).

Crisis Management

An area of intervention with older persons given little attention is the management of crises. The word "crisis," however, is used so widely and differently as to need definition here. For many, *crisis* is synonymous with *emergency,* given its overtone of urgency and alarm. Other persons use *crisis* synonymously with "a stressful event" or with a set of emotional reactions to that event. Most precisely, a crisis is a *subjective experience of loss of control, helplessness, and perceived inability to cope* that is experienced when faced with a stressful event that extends beyond current coping skills (Duffy & Iscoe, 1988). This is, of course, a normative process, where, through final mastery of the crisis situation, a person gains a new coping skill. It is noteworthy (and fortunate) that older persons are "survivors," because late life presents many stressful events that strain coping capacity. Amster and Krauss (1974) developed a Geriatric Social Readjustment Scale, fashioned after Holmes and Rahe's (1967) work, which lists 35 potentially stressful life events for older persons. It is alarming to note that admission to a nursing home could well involve 25 of their items:

1) Death of a spouse
2) Institutionalization
3) Death of a close family member
4) Major personal injury or illness
5) Major change in financial state
6) Retirement
7) Marital separation from mate
8) Eyesight failing
9) Death of a close friend
10) Major change in health or behavior of family member
11) Major change in gratifying activities
12) Change in sexual behavior
13) Change in responsibilities at work
14) Painful arthritis
15) Feeling of slowing down
16) Change in living conditions or environment
17) Change in social activities
18) Losing driver's license
19) Reaching 65
20) Reaching 70
21) Major change in working hours or conditions
22) Troubles with the boss
23) Holidays or anniversaries
24) Argument with children
25) Argument with spouse

Good preventive care will indicate careful assessment of the level of stress and the number of concurrent psychosocial stressors in older clients. Scales such as Holmes and Rahe's or Amster and Krauss' provide a useful screening device for the clinical indicators of stress and crisis. It is hard to imagine any phase of life where the losses are so numerous or acute. Brief clinical interventions are needed at times of crisis, where the helper "takes over" for the older client in an authoritative manner, reducing the stress and later helping with problem solving. Timely crisis intervention is critical; it may well be that many "nervous breakdowns" are simply masked crises and that hospitalization, even long-term care, resulted from misdiagnosis and over-reaction to crisis experiences.

Expressive Therapies

The use of music, art, drama, or dance to promote therapeutic change is an idea with great promise. The expressive therapies were not developed within mainstream psychology or psychotherapy. Although they have always remained on the fringes of conventional therapy, they are much accepted and useful in working with older adults. This is partly because gerontology has a very interdisciplinary history; as a new specialty, with little established knowledge, there has been a creative incorporation of many contributions. The Gerontological Society of America itself remains interdisciplinary, encompassing biological, medical, and psychosocial sciences, as well as the humanities.

Another reason, of course, for the use of the expressive therapy approach is that it is particularly appropriate where there are verbal or cognitive deficits in performance, which is frequently the case with geriatric patients. Art and music provide nonverbal, non-cognitive avenues to explore and express affect. This approach, of course, is also relevant where an older (or any) person is psychiatrically handicapped—expressive work can help a psychotic patient.

Music therapy is defined by the National Association for Music Therapy as the scientific application of the art of music to accomplish therapeutic aims. While music education is directed to musical skills, music therapy is aimed at non-musical skills using structured music activities. There are many specific therapy goals. The choice of emotionally evocative music can provide a structured, acceptable emotional outlet. The use of music with deaf or hearing-impaired individuals can develop rhythmic skills necessary for motor or language enhancement. Music can be used as a form of nonverbal communication where speech or cognitive process is lost, for example, with Alzheimer's patients. Music therapy has also focused on attending to visual cues and improving gross motor skills, socialization (for example, through dance), self-expression, and memory skills. Music can be used in groups (Moore, 1978) to influence social behavior and as an adjunctive method in reminiscence groups (Hennessy, 1978).

The use of art and drawing historically had a place in psychology's attention to the projective significance of drawing. Art therapy has been used widely for geriatric problems like regression among hospitalized patients, Korsakoff's disease, and aphasia (Weiss, 1984), as well as adjunctively in reality orientation and life review (Zeiger, 1976). Similarly, psychodrama has considerable acceptance within psychotherapy with such techniques as role playing, the "empty chair" technique from gestalt therapy, and even behavior rehearsal. Many difficult feelings can be acted out through an external role that would defy direct expression. Psychodrama has been used in alleviating depression and expressing grief with older persons in nursing homes (Carmen & Nordin, 1984). For anyone interested in drama programs, Weisberg and Wilder's (1985) book, *Creative Arts with Older Adults,* is an excellent, detailed resource.

Finally, expressive therapies with older persons have included dance, writing (Weisberg & Wilder, 1985), systematic relaxation, yoga (Kaye, 1985), exercise (Blumenthal & Williams, 1982), and the powerful impact of touch (Wilson, 1982) in both life and in psychotherapy.

Behavioral Procedures

The purpose at this point in the discussion is not to define a theoretical area but to overview a set of techniques that can be described best as structured procedures. Although a number of these have been described in earlier sections on interviewing, family therapy, and expressive therapies, there are several others that should be mentioned.

Among cognitively oriented procedures, reality orientation (Folsome, 1968), which originally took the field of geriatrics by storm, has now assumed more *real* proportions itself! Its purpose is to eliminate or control confusion in elderly persons by giving consistent cues to time, place, and person in one or both of two formats: 1) in intensive classroom training groups and 2) through 24-hour total environmental cueing using every staff-patient contact (Taulbee, 1976). Although originally believed to help all cognitive confusion, in the experience of this author it works best with beginning stages of memory loss. At this point older persons are often alarmed, highly motivated, and eager to work on orientation. Using reality orientation, however, with advanced Alzheimer's patients or to confront the fantasies of delusional patients is ineffective if not unkind. In these cases the cognitive loss is either chronic or has a psychological meaning that will not yield to confrontation. In restricted circumstances, however, reality orientation is highly necessary and effective and should not be abandoned for a validation/fantasy therapy approach.

Memory and cognitive processes in older persons are perhaps the most researched areas in geropsychology. More recently (Zarit, 1979), these findings have been translated into guidelines for retraining and cognitive therapy for elderly who have cognitive defects. Treatment consists of various information-processing strategies designed to improve memory performance, such as using organizing strategies (e.g., mnemonics) and visual imagery for the recall of shopping lists, names, and faces. These specific cognitive strategies were found more effective than a typical current events group. These strategies, of course, like reality orientation, are inadequate in dealing with persons with advanced dementia. However, cognitive retraining is an area of much promise and appears cost-effective as a treatment strategy (Taylor & Yesavage, 1984).

Woods and Britton (1985) express the opinion that the application of behavior modification to geriatric problems is an area of unfulfilled potential. While behavior therapy procedures have lost some popularity among general contemporary treatment methods, there is an resurgence of interest in the geriatric therapy areas. The recent work of behavior therapists deserves note: Hussian (1981) and Pinkston (Pinkston &

Linsk, 1984) have very current and timely books detailing behavior change strategies for most aspects of working with older persons, including family and individual strategies. Pinkston and Linsk (1984) detail strategies for increasing social contacts, improving self-care, and improving verbal behavior. Hussian (1981) adds behavioral treatments for urinary incontinence, wandering, inappropriate sexual behavior, and repetitive, self-stimulatory behavior.

It is also significant that behaviorists have added greatly to the concept of assessment as well as to that of therapy. Although not opposed to the use of psychometrically designed tests, behaviorists have a predilection for assessment by careful observation and behavior analysis. This is clearly an ideographic rather than nomothetic approach to characterizing behavior and for the design of solutions.

Environmental Intervention

If we define environmental intervention as "effecting change through manipulating a person's environment," we see that many techniques already discussed are environmental. Group methods utilize the social environment, and behaviorist approaches effect behavior through contingency management. The token economy system, often a critical part of milieu therapy, is a clear example of this. So, in general, environmental intervention refers less to a set of techniques as to an attitude in therapy—that our lives are shaped by environmental, and not purely biological or intrapsychic, forces. This, of course, is at the center of the classic nature-nurture, organism-environment controversy within psychology. In most cases behavior is an interaction of organismic and environmental factors. However, what is clear is that the therapeutic care of older adults, especially in institutional settings, cannot afford to neglect the impact of the environment. The remainder of this section will concentrate on a neglected but critical aspect of environmental intervention, variously referred to as the architectural or physical environment.

Institutionalization often represents a crisis in the lives of older persons, and the quality of the physical environment can have a significant impact. A brief view in most proprietary nursing homes, however, will soon suggest that environmental concern is lacking. Buildings meet minimum standards, sometimes with the architect's usual attention to aesthetic factors, but rarely with attention to the functional or mental health needs of residents. If anything, attention of designers is focused on the supposed social interaction needs of the elderly, not recognizing that in a nursing home privacy is at a premium (Duffy, Bailey, Beck, & Barker, 1986). There is increasing indication, however, that residential design factors play a significant role in fostering or hindering the mental health and well-being of residents. It is also critical for older persons who are often more vulnerable to environmental inadequacy due to financial and physical constraints on their mobility. The elderly who live in nursing homes are in double jeopardy.

From an intervention point of view, it makes little sense to do psychotherapy for depression in an older person when it can be more rapidly lifted through an environmental change. Don't adjust to an environment if the environment can be changed! Environmental change can be also an example of a systems-level change, the final intervention approach to be discussed here.

The Perspective of Systems-level Intervention

The old parable of the systems-level approach of community psychology is that after you have pulled your tenth drowning man from the river, it occurs to you to go upstream and build a fence to stop them from falling in! The most effective and economic interventions are systemic—and therefore, preventive. Most precisely, a systems-level intervention does not refer to a particular procedure or technique, but rather the *purpose* and *outcome* of the intervention. A therapeutic intervention in the life of the chief executive officer of a large corporation can have the effect of personal change or organizational change at the level of overall corporate policy!

Systemic change can be at a micro or macro level. It can involve change in a family system by a family therapist or change in a large organization by a corporate consultant. This is an important perspective for therapists, who may easily develop a myopic view of the problem and miss the larger context that explains—and maintains—the problems. This view (Caplan, 1974) has been influential in the community mental health service delivery system, which in turn has reacted to the narrowness of the traditional private, clinical, medical/illness model. Viewed this way, a therapeutic intervention would involve several levels of activity: psychotherapy, advocacy, public speaking, consultation, education and training, organizing, and managing (Knight, 1986). To be directly involved in the distress of an older person through individual counseling may be most satisfying, but it may not be most effective. To help effectively may involve assuming the role of a family therapist, a case manager, or a public policy advocate.

CONCLUSION

To be a therapist or counselor with older persons can mean different things, and usually involves several of the approaches described here. The list is not exhaustive and to some extent represents the special interests of this author. Those who do therapy with older adults, accepting them as adults and capable of change, are relatively few. But the demographics are relentless—our specialty will grow! Psychological assessment (psychological testing) is recognized as an important technique—useful as a contributor to planning therapy and as an integral part of the therapeutic process itself.

REFERENCES

Abraham, K. (1953). *The applicability of psychoanalytic treatment to patients at an advanced age.* New York: Basic Books. (Original work published in 1919)

Allen, K.S. (1976). A group experience for elderly patients with organic brain syndrome. *Health and Social Work, 1*(4), 61-69.

American Psychiatric Association. (1980). *Diagnostic and statistical manual of mental disorders* (3rd ed.). Washington, DC: American Psychiatric Association.

Amster, L.E., & Krauss, H.H. (1974). The relationship between life crises and mental deterioration in old age. *International Journal of Aging and Human Development, 5*(1), 51-55.

Bellak, L., & Bellak, S.S. (1973). *Manual for the Senior Apperception Technique.* Larchmont, NY: CPS.

Blumenthal, J.A., & Williams, R.S. (1982). *Exercise and aging: The use of physical exercise in health enhancement* (Center Reports on Advances in Research, No. 6[3]). Durham, NC: Duke University Center for the Study of Aging and Human Development.

Brink, T.L. (1979). *Geriatric psychotherapy.* New York: Human Sciences.

Brink, T.L. (Ed.). (1986). *Clinical gerontology: A guide to assessment and intervention.* New York: Haworth.

Brink, T.L., Yesavage, J.A., Lum, O., Heersema, P., Adey, M., & Rose T.L. (1982). Screening tests for geriatric depression. *Clinical Gerontologist, 1*(1), 37-43.

Butler, R.N. (1963). The life review: An interpretation of reminiscence in the aged. *Psychiatry, 26,* 65-76.

Caplan, G. (1974). *Support systems and community mental health.* New York: Behavioral Publications.

Carmen, M.B., & Nordin, S.R. (1984). Psychodrama: A therapeutic modality for the elderly in nursing homes. *Clinical Gerontologist, 3*(1), 15-24.

Coppersmith, E. (1980). The Family Floor Plan: A tool for training, assessment, and intervention in family therapy. *Journal of Marital and Family Therapy, 6*(2), 141-145.

Craik, F.I.M. (1977). Age differences in human memory. In J.E. Birren & K.W. Schaie (Eds.), *Handbook of the psychology of aging* (pp. 384-420). New York: Van Nostrand Reinhold.

Crose, R., & Duffy, M. (in press). Separation as a therapeutic strategy in marital therapy with older couples. *Clinical Gerontologist.*

Duffy, M. (1982). Divorce and the dynamics of the family kinship system. *Journal of Divorce, 5*(1/2), 3-18.

Duffy, M. (1984). Aging and the family: Intergenerational psychodynamics. *Psychotherapy: Theory, Research and Practice, 21*(3), 342-346.

Duffy, M. (1986). The techniques and contexts of multigenerational therapy. In T.L. Brink (Ed.), *Clinical gerontology: A guide to assessment and intervention* (pp. 347-362).New York: Haworth.

Duffy, M. (1988). Interviewing older adults. In J. Dillard & R. Reilley (Eds.), *Systematic interviewing: Communication skills for professional effectiveness* (pp. 160-178). Columbus, OH: Charles E. Merrill.

Duffy, M., Bailey, S., Beck, B., & Barker, D.G. (1986). Preferences in nursing home design: A comparison of residents, administrators and designers. *Environment and Behavior, 18*(2), 246-257.

Duffy, M., & Iscoe, I. (1988). *Crisis theory and management: The case of the older person.* Unpublished manuscript, Department of Educational Psychology, Texas A&M University, College Station, TX.

Duffy, M., & Kurman, S. (1985). The middle generation: Stresses within the multigenerational family. *Gerontology Newsletter, 9*(5), 1-10.

Duffy, M., & Shuttlesworth, G.E. (1987). The residents family: Adversary or advocate in long term care. *Journal of Long Term Care Administration, 15*(3), 9-11.

Dye, C.J., & Erber, J.T. (1981). Two group procedures for the treatment of nursing home patients. *The Gerontologist, 21*(5), 539-544.

Ebersole, P.P. (1978). Establishing reminiscing groups. In I.M. Burnside (Ed.), *Working with the elderly: Group processes and techniques* (pp. 236-254). North Scituate, MA: Duxbury.

Erikson, E.H. (1963). *Childhood and society* (2nd ed.). New York: Norton.

Feil, N. (1978). *Looking for yesterday* [Film]. Cleveland: Edward Feil Productions.

Feil, N. (1982). *Validation: The Feil method* [Film]. Cleveland: Edward Feil Productions.

Filsinger, E.E. (1983). *Marriage and family assessment: A source book for family therapy.* Beverly Hills: Sage.

Folsome, J.C. (1968). Reality orientation of the elderly mental patient. *Journal of Geriatric Psychiatry, 1*(2), 291-307.

Folstein, M.F., Folstein, S., & McHugh, P.R. (1975). Mini-Mental State: A practical method for grading the cognitive state of patients for the clinician. *Journal of Psychiatric Research, 12,* 189-198.

Freud, S. (1924). On psychotherapy. In E. Jones (Ed.), *Collected papers of Sigmund Freud* (Vol. 1). London: Hogarth. (Original work published in 1904)

Gatz, M., Smyer, M.A. & Lawton, M.P. (1980). The mental health system and the older adult. In L.W. Poon (Ed.), *Aging in the 1980's: Psychological issues* (pp. 5-18). Washington, DC: American Psychological Association.

Georgemiller, R., & Maloney, H.N. (1984). Group life review and denial of death. *Clinical Gerontologist, 2*(4), 37-49.

Gilewski, M.J. (1986). Group therapy with cognitively impaired older adults. In T.L. Brink (Ed.), *Clinical gerontology: A guide to assessment and intervention* (pp. 281-296). New York: Haworth.

Goldfarb, A.I., & Sheps, J. (1954). Psychotherapy of the aged. III Brief therapy of interrelated psychological and somatic disorders. *Psychosomatic Medicine, 16*(3), 209-219.

Gurland, B.J. (1980). The assessment of mental health status of older adults. In J.E. Birren & R.B. Stone (Eds.), *Handbook of mental health and aging* (pp. 671-700). Englewood Cliffs, NJ: Prentice-Hall.

Gurland, B.J., Fleiss, J.L., Goldberg, K., Sharpe, L., Copeland, J.R.M., Kelleher, M.J., & Kellet, J.M. (1976). A semi-structured clinical interview for the assessment of diagnosis and mental state in the elderly: The Geriatric Mental State Schedule. *Psychological Medicine, 6,* 451-459.

Gutmann, D.L. (1981). Psychoanalysis and aging: A developmental view. In S.I. Greenspan & G.H. Pollack (Eds.), *The course of life: Psychoanalytic contributions toward understanding personality development: Vol. 3. Adulthood and the aging process* (pp. 489-517). Washington, DC: U.S. Government Printing Office.

Haber, D. (1983). Promoting mutual help groups among older persons. *The Gerontologist, 23*(3), 251-253.

Hennessey, M.J. (1978). Music and music therapy groups. In I.M. Burnside (Ed.), *Working with the elderly: Group processes and techniques* (pp. 255-274). North Scituate, MA: Duxbury.

Herr, J.J., & Weakland, J.H. (1979). *Counseling elders and their families.* New York: Springer.

Holmes, T.H., & Rahe, R.H. (1967). The Social Readjustment Rating Scale. *Journal of Psychosomatic Research, 11,* 213-218.

Hussian, R.A. (1981). *Geriatric psychology: A behavioral perspective.* New York: Van Nostrand Reinhold.

Ingebretsen, R. (1977). Psychotherapy with the elderly. *Psychotherapy: Theory, Research and Practice, 14*(4), 319-331.

Kahn, R.L., Goldfarb, A.I., Pollack, M., & Peck, A. (1960). Brief objective measures for determination of mental status in the aged. *American Journal of Psychiatry, 117,* 326-328.

Kane, R.L., & Kane, R.A. (1981). *Assessing the elderly: A practical guide to measurement.* Lexington, MA: Lexington Books.

Kaye, V.G. (1985). An innovative treatment modality for elderly residents of a nursing home. *Clinical Gerontologist, 3*(4), 45-51.

Kell, B.L., & Mueller, W.J. (1966). *Impact and change: A study of counseling relationships.* New York: Appleton-Century-Crofts.

Knight, B. (1986). *Psychotherapy with older adults.* Beverly Hills: Sage.

Kovacs, A.L. (1977). Rapid intervention strategies in work with the aged. *Psychotherapy: Theory, Research and Practice, 14*(4), 368-372.

Lazarus, L.W., & Groves, L. (1987). Brief psychotherapy with the elderly: A study of process and outcome. In J. Sadavoy & M. Leszcz (Eds.), *Treating the elderly with psychotherapy: The scope for change in later life* (pp. 233-264). Madison, WI: International Universities Press.

LeBray, P.R. (1982). *Geriatric Sentence Completion Form.* Odessa, FL: Psychological Assessment Resources.

Levine, B.E., & Poston, M. (1980). A modified group treatment for elderly narcissistic patients. *International Journal of Group Psychotherapy, 30,* 153-167.

Lewis, M.I., & Butler, R.N. (1974, November). Life review therapy: Putting memories to work in individual and group psychotherapy. *Geriatrics,* pp. 165-173.

Locker, R. (1981). Institutionalized elderly: Understanding and helping couples. *Journal of Gerontological Social Work, 3*(4), 37-49.

Mace, N.L., & Rabins, P.V. (1981). *The 36-hour day.* Baltimore: Johns Hopkins University Press.

Maslow, A. (1962). *Toward a psychology of being.* New York: Van Nostrand.

McFarland, R.A. (1968). The sensory and perceptual processes of aging. In K.W. Schaie (Ed.), *Theory and methods of research on aging* (pp. 3-52). Morgantown, WV: West Virginia University Press.

Merriam, S. (1980). The concept and function of reminiscence: A review of the research. *Gerontologist, 20,* 604-608.

Moore, E.C. (1978). Using music with groups of geriatric patients. In I.M. Burnside (Ed.), *Working with the elderly: Group processes and techniques* (pp. 275-291). North Scituate, MA: Duxbury.

Mueller, W.J., & Kell, B.L. (1972). *Coping with conflict: Supervising counselors and psychotherapists.* Englewood Cliffs, NJ: Prentice-Hall.

Neugarten, B. (1977). Personality and aging. In J.E. Birren & K.W. Schaie (Eds.), *Handbook of the psychology of aging* (pp. 626-649). New York: Van Nostrand Reinhold.

Oster, G.D., & Gould, P. (1987). *Using drawings in assessment and therapy.* New York: Brunner/Mazel.

Peck, R.C. (1968). Psychological developments in the second half of life. In B.L. Neugarten (Ed.), *Middle age and aging* (pp. 88-92). Chicago: University of Chicago Press.

Pfeiffer, E. (1975). A short portable mental status questionnaire for the assessment of organic brain deficit in elderly patients. *Journal of the American Geriatrics Society, 23,* 433-441.

Pinkston, E.M., & Linsk, N.L. (1984). *Care of the elderly: A family approach.* New York: Pergamon.

Poggi, R.G., & Berland, D.I. (1985). The therapist's reactions to the elderly. *The Gerontologist, 25*(5), 508-513.

Roybal, E.R. (1984). Federal involvement in the mental health care for the aged. *American Psychologist, 39,* 163-166.

Sadavoy, J., & Leszcz, M. (Eds.). (1987). *Treating the elderly with psychotherapy: The scope for change in later life.* Madison, WI: International Universities Press.

Saul, S.R., & Shura, S. (1974). Group psychotherapy in a proprietary nursing home. *The Gerontologist, 14*(5), 446-450.

Sherman, E. (1981). *Counseling the aging: An integrative approach.* New York: Free Press.

Sherman, R., & Fredman, N. (1986). *Handbook of structured techniques in marriage and family therapy.* New York: Brunner/Mazel.

Shoham, H., & Neuschatz, S. (1985). Group therapy with senile patients. *Social Work, 30*(1), 69-72.

Shuttlesworth, G.E., Rubin, A., & Duffy, M. (1982). Families versus institutions: Incongruent role expectations in the nursing home. *The Gerontologist, 22*(2), 200-208.

Taulbee, L.R. (1976). *The A-B-C's of reality orientation: An instruction manual for rehabilitation of confused elderly persons.* New Port Richey, FL: Author.

Taylor, L.L., & Yesavage, J.A. (1984). Cognitive retraining program for the elderly: A case study of cost-benefit issues. *Clinical Gerontologist, 2*(4), 51-63.

Warren, J.L. (1982). *Self discovery through family history.* College Station, TX: Texas Agricultural Extension Service, Texas A&M University.

Weinstein, C.E., Duffy, M., Underwood, V.L., McDonald, J., & Gott, S.P. (1981). Memory strategies reported by older adults for experimental and everyday learning tasks. *Educational Gerontology: An International Quarterly, 7,* 205-213.

Weisberg, N., & Wilder, R. (Eds.). (1985). *Creative arts with older adults: A sourcebook.* New York: Human Sciences.

Weiss, J.C. (1984). *Expressive therapy with elders and the disabled: Touching the heart of life.* New York: Haworth.

Welford, A.T. (1977). Motor performance. In J.E. Birren & K.W. Schaie (Eds.), *Handbook of the psychology of aging* (pp. 450-496). New York: Van Nostrand Reinhold.

Wilson, J.M. (1982). The value of touch in psychotherapy. *American Journal of Orthopsychiatry, 52*(1), 65-72.

Woods, R.T., & Britton, P.G. (1985). *Clinical psychology with the elderly.* Rockville, MD: Aspen.

Yalom, I.D., & Terrazas, F. (1968). Group therapy for psychotic elderly patients. *American Journal of Nursing, 68*(8), 1690-1694.

Zachich, R. (1975). *The ungame.* (Available from The Ungame Company, P.O. Box 6382, Anaheim, CA 92806)

Zarit, S.H. (1979, April). Helping an aging patient to cope with memory problems. *Geriatrics,* pp. 82-90.

Zarit, S.H., Orr, N.K., & Zarit, J.M. (1985). *The hidden victims of Alzheimer's disease: Families under stress.* New York: New York University Press.

Zeiger, B.L. (1976). Life review in art therapy with the aged. *American Journal of Art Therapy, 15*(2), 47-50.

15

Competence Issues in Older Adults

ISELI K. KRAUSS, ED.D., SAMUEL J. POPKIN, PH.D.

Competence in older adults, judging from the broad literature in which the term figures, has many meanings. Assessment of competence or *competency,* as it is frequently termed, is carried out very differently depending on who is being assessed, who is doing the assessing, and the purpose of the assessment. Unfortunately, the three factors do not always mesh neatly. The result is that older adults are frequently subjected to inappropriate assessment techniques, administered by inappropriate personnel with inappropriate outcomes. It is our purpose here to discuss the various ways in which the term *competence* is used and to describe assessment techniques frequently employed to determine levels of competence in older adults across a range of domains, such as daily living skills, intellectual abilities, social competence, and work competence. The discussion will pay special attention to multiphasic instruments—those designed to assess a variety of aspects of competence in older adults.

Because the living situation and indeed the well-being of a growing number of elderly adults are determined by the courts through guardianship procedures, a portion of the chapter will address the issues raised from the use of these procedures. A major problem with far-reaching implications is that although complex and thorough procedures for the determination of competency exist in treatment and evaluation centers, they are not, as a rule, being used in the legal system.

COMPETENCE

Competence generally refers to a condition of adequacy or sufficiency for a particular set of circumstances. In its broadest sense, it may refer to the ability to carry out the requirements of a productive existence. In a narrower reading, it may refer to the ability to perform quite specific tasks, such as managing a checkbook or bathing, thought to be necessary for an individual to maintain legal control over the conditions of his or her living situation. The terms *competence* and *competency* are considered synonymous with the exception that in legal parlance, competency refers to the ability of an individual to participate in legal affairs on his or her own behalf or to stand trial (Grisso, 1987; Lanyon, 1986). The term *competence* will be used in this chapter unless the discussion refers to the more restrictive legal usage.

Given that competency may vary in its meanings, it is not surprising that the

The authors would like to thank Mrs. Mary Falso for her assistance with the preparation of the manuscript, as well as Bob J. Dvorchak, Raymond Steinberg, H.B. Beels and Son, and *The Oil City Derrick* for their invaluable contributions to the chapter.

range of measures used to assess it is vast. Before considering the types and characteristics of measures used by professionals to determine levels of particular skills within the general domain of competence, an overview of the various uses of the term is appropriate.

Competence and Performance

A distinction between competence and performance is frequently drawn (Schaie, 1978, 1987a, 1987b). Competence refers to underlying abilities that may or may not be evident in any given situation, while performance refers to levels of the ability in question as evidenced on tests or in behavioral situations. Any number of factors may limit the execution of a skill (Krauss, 1984, in press; Schaie, 1980, 1987a). Test characteristics—such as the concepts underlying the test items, importance of speed, print size, and multiple-choice answer sheets—may limit performance through their unfamiliarity and the demands they make on declining physical and sensory abilities of some older adults. Data are now collected in a manner consistent with computerization of the findings. This process may eliminate the use of observational information or behavioral nuance in evaluating assessment data (White, Cartwright, Cornoni-Huntley, & Brock, 1986).

The use of computers for administration of tests presents a whole new range of problems for people with motor and vision problems or those who are not accustomed to computers. Characteristics of the situation such as lighting, tables and chairs, rest periods, or length of the session may also place demands on older adults that would limit their ability to demonstrate their highest skills. The importance of the outcome may also affect the demonstrated level of ability. Finally, temporary or relatively enduring individual characteristics (motivation levels, depression, illness, fatigue) may influence the outcome of assessment. These testing and person factors should be accounted for in any assessment of older adults, but to ignore them or give them token consideration in assessing basic competence of the elderly could have dire consequences. The impact of these factors should be minimized in developing assessment procedures, in administering tests and other behavioral measures, in interpreting results, and in making decisions that affect the lives of older adults based on the findings.

Competence and Adaptation

In a classic discussion of competence, Connolly and Brunner (1974; cited in Schaie, 1987a) distinguish between *knowing that* and the more complex *knowing how.* They believe that competence is not passive, but implies action on the environment in addition to adaptation to it. They suggest that there is a set of skills, some general and some quite specific, that are absolutely required for successful existence in a given society, particularly in technologically advanced societies. Connolly and Brunner propose three requirements for competence: being able to select appropriate factors from a complex environment, initiating a course of action to achieve the desired goals, and using what one has learned from successes and failures in ensuing situations. Building on the work of Connolly and Bruner (1974), Scheidt and Schaie (1978) devised a measure of self-perceived competence across a variety of situations (discussed further later in this chapter).

Competence and adaptation have also been linked by Lawton and Nahemow

(1973; Lawton, 1977). In their scheme, individuals may be found to be more or less able to perform in a set of competencies that range from basic life-sustaining breathing and digesting to complex abilities including cognitive and social processes. Within each type of competence, abilities range from simple to complex (e.g., from basic ambulatory motor skills to highly complex athletic skills). Each progressively complex competence type relies on the one(s) preceding it. Adaptation refers to the relationship between the range of competencies of a given individual and the requirements of the environment within which the individual exists.

Lawton and Nahemow believe that more competent individuals have a greater range of tolerance for difficulties presented by their living situations. They also contend that individuals function at their best when the environment exacts slightly more effort than is completely comfortable; people perform at their highest levels when some, but not too much, effort is required. Not enough environmental stimulation may be as damaging to some people as too much. While the scheme of Lawton and Nahemow is not quantified, it is a framework of considerable value for professionals attempting to assess individuals and their living conditions. As the authors point out, however, means for assessing competence are greater in number and usefulness than means for assessing environments within which the competence must be exercised. Windley (1982) has summarized a number of ways in which environments and their use have been investigated.

Schooler (1987) contends that the more diverse the stimuli in an individual's existence, the greater number of considerations involved in the decision-making processes. Schooler also believes that long-term exposure to simple environments may result in lowered intellectual functioning. Sternberg and Berg (1987) point out, however, that older adults may shape their environments or have them shaped for them in such a way that they may, using relevant competence, adapt to them more successfully than to environments encountered earlier in their lives. In an extreme expression of the interdependence of individuals and their surroundings, Altman and his colleagues state, "Thus persons, psychological processes, and physical and social environments are inseparable from one another and all are necessary definitional features of psychological phenomena" (Altman, Werner, Oxley, & Haggard, 1987, p. 503). In a suggestion that many assessment professionals would find difficult to implement, they claim that measures may need to be changed to account for climate or seasonal variations in situational characteristics or in person factors. (For a theoretical discussion of intelligence and adaptation, see Labouvie-Vief, 1985.) Fortunately, there are indications that psychologists and medical personnel are increasingly viewing individuals as functioning within complex enenvironments of physical, physiological, and social factors (Granick, 1983).

It should be mentioned here that the requirements for competent daily life negotiation will differ as society develops. Shopping, cooking, medication management, financial management, and entertainment, for instance, have changed dramatically in the last decade. People who were perfectly able to manage a comfortable existence in 1985 may have difficulties in 1995, even without declining physical and cognitive abilities. Negotiating the social service system has become a procedural nightmare because of complex and overlapping realms of jurisdiction. Computerization has added a level of mystification for individuals not accustomed to either computers or the social service networks. What a person must be competent for will continue to change as must the relevant assessment techniques (Schaie, 1987a).

Legal Competency

The legal term *competency,* as it is used by forensic psychologists, is not well defined (Lanyon, 1986). Its most frequent uses are as criteria for the ability of an individual to stand trial for alleged crimes or to determine where a criminal defendant should be kept (Horowitz, 1982; Melton, Petrila, Poythress, & Slobogin, 1987). The term is also used, with even less precision, in courtroom proceedings determining the necessity of appointing guardians to older adults. The growing forensic literature (Blau, 1984; Ewing, 1985; Grisso, 1986, 1987; Horowitz, 1982; Lanyon, 1986; Miller, 1985) nearly ignores the issues involved in such assessment. Only minor mention is made of the usefulness of forensic psychologists in the courts' determination of competence of elderly adults outside the criminal justice system. Yet, Grisso (1987) points out that the legal system has an enormous impact on the lives of individuals, a large number of forensic psychologists provide assessments to courts, and these same psychologists may exert a powerful influence on the legal process. Further issues of legal competency will be discussed below.

ASPECTS OF COMPETENCE AND RELEVANT ASSESSMENT METHODS

Intellectual and Cognitive Competence

For extended discussions of intelligence assessment and descriptions of traditional measures used with older adults, the reader is referred to Dye (1982) and Kane and Kane (1981). However, it is important that we address intelligence briefly here, as it is central to competence involved in daily life.

One purpose of most tests of intelligence is to permit comparison, with a high degree of reliability, of interindividual performance on a measure or set of measures. Another common purpose is to compare intraindividual performance on different occasions. A further application is to use the measure to predict future performance outside the testing situation. For these comparisons and predictions to be meaningful, the measures must address a wide range of performance. While some measures are designed to discriminate among individuals at very high levels (e.g., the Miller Analogies Test, the Graduate Record Examination), others are aimed at the general population. When basic competence is to be determined, it is the *lower* end of the population distribution of ability that is of importance. In selecting a measure for use in determining whether a given individual is intellectually competent to understand the requirements of daily life and to formulate and carry out plans for managing it, it becomes irrelevant to know whether that person performs in the top 25% of test takers as opposed to the top 15%.

Another consideration in the choice of measures of intelligence for determining competence is that many intelligence tests were designed to be predictive of academic performance. Tests designed to predict academic performance of young adults will be of limited value in predicting performance of older adults in complex living situations (Schaie, 1987a). For a thorough discussion of internal and external validity considerations as they may affect older adults' tested competency, see Schaie (1980). In the same volume, Miller (1980) presents a cogent analysis of the difficulties encountered in testing older adults. Granick (1983) has proposed a set of guidelines for selecting measures for use with older groups.

Labouvie-Vief (1982) warns that older adults may have restructured the ways in which they conceptualize problems and their own social and moral imperatives. What may appear to be a decline in abilities may be a new way of thinking. Current measures are not designed to accommodate these changes in cognitive structure.

In a recent discussion on the prediction of everyday competence from tests of intelligence, Schaie (1987a) stressed the usefulness of tests measuring performance on a number of well-defined abstract abilities, such as those designed by Thurstone, rather than more global measures such as the Wechsler Adult Intelligence Scale-Revised. His reasoning was that although the Primary Mental Abilities Test (PMA; Thurstone & Thurstone, 1947) did not perform well as an academic predictor, it should be useful in predicting the wider range of complex activities involved in daily life. Schaie has made extensive modifications of the PMA to reduce the elements of the testing procedure that would interfere with optimum performance by older, non-test-wise individuals. The modified measure, the Schaie-Thurstone Adult Mental Abilities Test (STAMAT; Schaie, 1985; Schaie & Willis, 1986) includes measures of vocabulary, spatial orientation, inductive reasoning, numerical skills, and word fluency (Schaie, 1987a).

Psychometric measures of a variety of aspects of intelligence are found in the ADEPT battery (Baltes & Willis, 1982), which was developed specifically to permit a demonstration of "plasticity" over time in older adults. The concept underlying the work of Baltes and Willis is that variability within individuals over time is measurable and modifiable. Using the "fluid-crystallized" distinction of Horn and Cattell (1966, 1967) as a departure point, Baltes and Willis selected a wide range of intellectual measures thought to tap "fluid" abilities (i.e., those that show regular decline with age). Across a series of studies they have demonstrated short-term, positive changes in several fluid abilities with appropriate training. They have also shown that the training enhances performance on measures of related but not identical skills. The measures in the ADEPT battery are eclectic and have been drawn from a number of batteries. Some of the ADEPT measures and training procedures could be used in a competence assessment battery to determine whether a person's fluid abilities could be enhanced over time. They might also help determine the likelihood of decline, improvement, or no change in the near future.

The Krauss Card Tasks of Adult Cognitive Abilities (Krauss, in press) use a variety of playing cards as test materials to assess cognitive performance. Reasoning, spatial memory, spatial rotation, and cognitive flexibility are measured in five subtests. Playing cards were selected because they are familiar to most older adults in the United States, easy to manipulate, and require no reading beyond identification of the cards. Although no single summary score is obtained, performance on each task may be compared to that of other older adults. The measures have been used only for research purposes at this time, but they have been found useful in eliciting interest in older adults who might otherwise not be inclined to invest themselves in any sort of mental testing process or who are unable to manipulate pencils or other test materials.

The Adult Basic Learning Examination (ABLE) was developed specifically for use with adults including the very old. Based on the abilities measured in the widely used Stanford Achievement Tests, the ABLE battery includes measures of vocabulary, reading comprehension, spelling, language, number operations, and problem solving. Items were selected to be of interest to adults and to be representative of the sorts of intellectual operations encountered in daily life. The test is available for three skill levels; a very brief screening test (Select ABLE) may be used to determine which level should be administered. Although this battery employs traditional testing materials, it could be very useful for determining basic competence. A profile of abilities is obtained, and performance may be compared to that of several norm groups as well as to Stanford Achievement norms. This set of measures, like the others discussed here, was developed in part to increase motivation in older adults. Wigdor (1980), however, points out that performance decrements have not been found to be attributable to motivation, but to other factors. Nonetheless, it seems likely that these measures present fewer obstacles to accurate assessment of older adults than those posed by traditional testing materials and content.

All of the tests described here have been developed using traditional psychometric methodology and focusing specifically on older adult samples. By using computer-based methodology, intellectual abilities have also been assessed with information-processing paradigms in which the goal is to determine the speed with which carefully defined, highly practiced mental processes are carried out and, more recently, the particular *way* in which those processes are carried out. Because basic intellectual competence in the daily lives of older adults rarely depends on the speed with which mental operations occur, these assessment methods are not discussed here in any detail. One obvious application for information-processing measures would be to test driving competence in individuals whose reaction time has appeared to slow significantly. Sternberg (1985; Berg & Sternberg, 1985) has proposed that intelligence may be analyzed into its increasingly specific components (including speed and style of processing) and that those components are testable. He reasons that different situations require that different aspects of intelligence be exercised, and that if the required processes are understood and defined, performance on tests of the processes will predict real-world performance.

The above theory offers great promise in understanding both the cognitive processes in older adults and how those processes differ from those of younger adults. It is easily conceivable that at some point it will be possible to assess performance on a small number of basic mental abilities and from the results know how well a given individual would fare in a wide range of environmental situations. At this point, the connections have not been demonstrated.

The measures discussed above take anywhere from one to several hours to complete and provide a wealth of information about intellectual performance. At times, however, a brief screening measure is needed to determine whether an individual is functioning within normal limits. Based on the outcome, the individual may be evaluated more systematically to determine the presence of cognitive dysfunction and its cause. These instruments are in great favor with professionals needing to make speedy determinations of current mental status. Unfortunately, they are sometimes used with no follow-up assessment and stand as the only indices of mental status.

Many of the mental status instruments are based on a series of orientation questions regarding the individual's name, the place where the interview is being carried out, the day and date, and, with a wider frame of reference, the names of the current and past president. In some measures, the individual is asked to count backwards or to perform some very basic cognitive operations such as remembering items previously named. Examples of these measures include the Mental Status Questionnaire (MSQ; Kahn, Goldfarb, Pollack, & Peck, 1960); Philadelphia Geriatric Center Mental Status Questionnaire (Fishback, 1977); Mini-Mental State Examination (Folstein, Folstein, & McHugh, 1975); VIRO (i.e., *V*igor, *I*ntactness, *R*elationship, *O*rientation) Scale (Kastenbaum & Sherwood, 1972); Short Portable Mental Status Questionnaire (SPMSQ; Pfeiffer, 1975); and the Set Test (Isaacs & Akhtar, 1972), all of which are discussed in detail by Kane and Kane (1981). We believe these tests have considerable value as initial measures to determine which successive instruments should be used to assess cognitive competence. We do not concur with Kane and Kane in their regard of these measures as useful in determining the presence of and distinguishing among such syndromes as dementia, depression, and schizophrenia or in differential diagnosis among the dementias (cf. Kane & Kane, 1981, p. 97).

Activities of Daily Living

According to Williams (1983), as many as 40 to 50% of nursing home patients may need less care than is being provided. From a number of perspectives, such excess care has serious drawbacks. As noted previously, behavior may show evidence of decline if it is not exercised (Lawton, 1977; Schooler, 1987). Effective, considerate nursing home care is at a premium and should not be squandered on those who would benefit from less comprehensive care. Certainly, available funds should be reserved for caring for those most in need. The implication for testing the elderly is that careful, thorough, *repeated* assessments should be employed to verify the level of care needed in each case. Equally serious attention should be devoted to making a decision that an individual is incapable of doing the things that need to be carried out on a regular basis if an acceptable living standard is to be maintained. Of course, the crux of the problem is often deciding whose definition of acceptable living standard is to be used. But once that basic determination is made, a reliable, comprehensive measure of functional abilities should be central to competence assessment.

Aside from brief mental status questionnaires, formal or informal assessment of activities of daily living (ADL) may be the most frequently used means to determine the advisability of increasing the level of care provided for an older adult. Virtually every multiphasic assessment battery includes a section for use in determining how well individuals care for their most basic needs. In a 1983 conference on the topic of comprehensive functional assessment sponsored by the National Institute on Aging, several participants discussed the usefulness of such measures. Gurland (1980) points out the importance of assessing ADLs in those individuals with low MSQ scores. He believes that it is quite possible to have adequate self-care skills despite very low tested cognitive awareness because ADLs are less likely to be affected by depression or anxiety. In one of the many conference papers published during 1983 in successive issues of the *Journal of the American Geriatrics Society,* Katz (1983) provides a useful brief history of activity measures and describes the general domains addressed by ADL measures.

Activities of daily living scales generally include the six basic self-care functions of bathing, dressing, toileting, transfer (moving from bed to chair, from wheelchair to bath, etc.), continence, and feeding that have been found to be hierarchically related (Katz, 1983; Katz & Akpom, 1976). Some scales are designed to identify the physical difficulties that contribute to the inability to perform basic functions (e.g., PULSES [Physical condition, Upper extremities, Lower extremities, Sensory, Excretory, mental and emotional Status]; Granger & Greer, 1976) or are more specific. Variations of these scales are used in the OARS Multidimensional Functional Assessment Questionnaire (Duke Older Americans Resources and Services [OARS], 1978), the Long-Term Care Information System Assessment Process (Falcone, 1983), the battery developed by Kane et al. to predict nursing-home patient functioning (Kane, Riegler, Bell, Potter, & Koshland, 1982), and the Philadelphia Geriatric Center Multilevel Assessment Instrument (PMAI; Lawton, Moss, Fulcomer, & Kleban, 1982). Assessment strategies vary and are determined by the rater's direct observation, self-report of the individual being assessed, or by report from skilled and professional staff or family and friends. Scores range from simple yes/no distinctions (patient able to carry out function independently or not) to 7-point rating scales indicating the level and frequency of assistance needed. Katz (1983) refers to a number of additional multiphasic assessment systems that include measures of ADL.

Because functions beyond the basic self-care assessed by ADL measures are required for the maintenance of independent or even partially independent living arrangements, several scales have been derived to assess what have become known as instrumental activities of daily living (IADL). These measures permit assessment of the individual's ability to carry out such activities as meal preparation, shopping, medication management, telephone usage, financial management, and so on. They are useful in determining how well an individual is able to function in his or her current environment, what enhancements or services might be provided to allow the individual to remain in that environment, or what environment might be more conducive to continued or enhanced behavior. The IADL scales are generally outgrowths of the work of Lawton and his colleagues (Lawton & Brody, 1969; Lawton et al., 1982). Versions are found in the PMAI, OARS, and Long-Term Care Information System Assessment Process (Falcone, 1983).

Useful overviews of ADL and IADL scales are provided by Fillenbaum (1987) and Katz (1983). Kane and Kane (1981) discuss measures of these functional abilities extensively; however, the tables in which measures are summarized are difficult to interpret and require scrutiny. Katz (1983) discusses the need to consider carefully the reliability and validity of ADL and IADL scales. He notes that predictive validity information is more readily available for ADL and mobility than for the more complex IADL. ADLs have been found to predict discharge of patients to the community, indicating that basic self-care competence is a significant factor in returning patients to their homes (Kane, Bell, Riegler, Wilson, & Keeler, 1983). A final caveat is that while mobility is covered at least indirectly in ADL and IADL instruments, Katz (1983) suggests it is a factor deserving additional attention. Mobility should certainly be considered in employment or relocation decision-making processes.

Certainly, measures of ADL, mobility, and IADL should be considered in the competence decision-making process. It is interesting that similar measures have been developed by psychologists, social workers, physicians, and members of the nursing profession, all of whom do not often agree on the relative importance of patient characteristics. We are reminded by Besdine (1983) that although elderly adults may have "astonishingly long and impressive problem lists" (p. 652), they may not be functionally hampered. Measures of ADL and IADL are needed to document functional impairment independent of medical history.

Competence and the Workplace

Assessment of competence in the workplace takes on a variety of forms and has many purposes. The topic is discussed extensively by Lindley elsewhere in this book, but some aspects have particular relevance to the discussion of competence assessment here. We believe it is important to understand how work competence assessment may differ significantly from other competence assessments. Kahn (1983) lists paid employment in his categories of productive behaviors, which include unpaid employment, voluntary ongoing optional activity, mutual help, and self-care. The implication is that in and of itself, maintaining a job for which one is regularly paid indicates a level of functional competence different from the other categories, although Kahn does not claim that the categories are linear, hierarchical, or without overlap. But being able to perform work for pay on a regular basis would certainly indicate greater competence than not being able to work. As stated earlier, competence assessment generally refers to the determination of the very basic ability levels. Workplace competence assessment may be concerned with a much wider range of abilities, some of which may be particularly specific, than might be the case with other types of competence. For instance, memory for particular types of terms may be involved rather than generalized memory skills. In legal matters of competence, it is important that the abilities tested have been demonstrated to be critical to job performance (Walker & Lazer, 1978).

Job competence according to Walker and Lazer (1978) consists of the skills, objectives, knowledge, and perhaps values required for a specific position. Once those components are known, assessment systems may be devised to identify individuals who have the required characteristics. But minimum performance levels are less likely than higher levels to be the focus of work-related assessment. If there are several workers available for the prospective positions, even higher skill levels will be required.

Assessment in such instances is of particular relevance to the older worker. While it is to the advantage of both employer and employee that skills and job requirements are well matched, the match may be harder to determine for older workers. If, as stated previously, older adults are hampered by aspects of traditional testing materials and situations, should specialized ones be used in determining competence of the older worker? The answer is yes and no. If non-substantive measurement factors that are likely to be troublesome for older individuals are not relevant to job performance, other measures should be selected or devised. For example, if knowledge relevant to a particular position is being assessed with a multiple-choice test printed in small type, and reading small type is not part of the job requirements, other measures should be used. If, however, reading fine type is part and parcel of the activities required by the job, the traditional measure may be more appropriate. As another example, if speed of response is critical to job performance, as in air traffic control, speeded measures of some substantive skill would be appropriate. We should expect to find increasing reliance on computerized testing in the workplace, which will add to the difficulties of older adults not accustomed to computer operations.

Assessment of functional age has been widely discussed, probably because the concept is designed to be age-irrelevant and therefore appealing to gerontologists. An individual is characterized by ages his or her ability levels represent, not by chronological age. Thus, a 65-year-old individual could have the upper body strength typical of 55-year-olds, memory skills typical of 75-year-olds, and so on. Jobs are then characterized by typical age-level skill requirements. People and jobs are matched by functional ages. Although large demonstration projects have indicated that functional age assessments are heuristic (Dirken, 1972; Meier & Kerr, 1976), their complexity, the lack of applicability of some functional measurements to many jobs, their expense, and the need for continued modification of measures due to changing job characteristics make their value doubtful in most situations (Siegler, 1987). Many of the functional age systems rely heavily on traditional measures that present many of the assessment problems referred to above. The concept of functional age still has strong appeal and should not be dismissed (Salthouse, 1986). For a theoretical discussion of the concept of functional age, see Salthouse (1986), and for a more complete discussion of the applications of functional age technology, see Stagner (1985).

Bray and Howard (1983) have developed a multidimensional tool for assessing the competence of managerial staff members. Assessment was carried out periodically over a number of years and tracked levels and change in cognitive skills, motivation, career orientation, administrative and interpersonal skills, performance stability, and dependency. Although not every employer will have the resources to carry out such a broad assessment, the domains should be understood to be contributing to the work performance of older as well as younger employees. Sales productivity may have risen at a slower pace for older workers, but other factors may more than compensate for the difference.

In an intriguing discussion of experience and competence in older adults, Salthouse (1987) suggests that older adults frequently use compensatory strategies to allow them to perform competently despite declining skills that are basic to performance. Experience over time may lead the individual to restructure the way the task is performed. As Salthouse noted, "Adults of all ages appear to benefit from experience" (1987, p. 157). Although the basic skills related to a task or type of work may be assessed with measures known to identify them, compensation may not be. Thus, an individual may perform poorly on a measure on which he or she had previously performed well. He or she may have learned, perhaps unknowingly, ways of performing the tasks themselves that depend on skills or combinations of skills that have not declined. If so, test performance may be less predictive of job performance of older employees than it is for younger employees.

Based on these considerations, it cannot be assumed that a measure designed to assess skills known to predict work performance in young adults will perform the same function as reliably or with validity for older adults. Assessments should be made over time to indicate change (Krauss, 1980) and separate predictive measures may even be needed. Test and testing characteristics should be carefully selected and monitored to be certain the competence of the older worker is being fairly assessed (Krauss, 1984). Given the aging of the work force, it is likely that assessment of greater than minimal competence of older workers will be increasingly important. Means must be found to ensure appropriate placement of older workers in training programs, post-retirement work situations, or alternative work situations prior to retirement.

Social Competence

The social milieu of the elderly adult may provide a strong support system or it may contribute significantly to the difficulties the individual has in managing an effective life-style. Considering the possibilities from another perspective, an individual with strong social skills may thrive in a socially impoverished environment as well as in a rich social setting, while another with less highly developed or neglected social skills may have interpersonal difficulties regardless of the social surroundings. Therefore, it is not enough to tally the number of family members in the same residence or within a half-hour drive, or to observe social interaction in brief patient assessment settings; it is critical to understand the individual and the setting. How social competence is defined will depend directly on the situation in which the competence is to be exercised. Even then, there are no simple definitions and therefore no simple assessment solutions. Rubenstein (1983) includes social interaction networks and social support needs and resources in his listing of measurable dimensions in geriatric assessment; his confidence is encouraging. Berkman (1983), while echoing Rubenstein's emphasis on the importance of social interaction, indicated that the measurement task is not simple. Her critical concern, beyond the familiar claim of lack of validation, is that the important dimensions or characteristics of social networks are not yet identified.

In attempts to determine the extent and nature of social interactions, investigators have generally resorted to questionnaires and observations. Berkman (1983) has outlined a number of factors to be considered in an analysis of social networks: size of network, frequency of contact, density, intimacy, durability, geographic dispersion, and reciprocity. She cautions that social networks and social support are not identical, as the former may exist but not provide the latter. The relative importance of various segments of a social network—spouse, family members, group affiliations, and so on—should be included in an assessment. Berkman (1983; Berkman & Breslow, 1983) discusses her longitudinal research in which a social network index was developed for use with older adults. Within stratified samples of elders, lack of social support was found to be related to mortality.

In their listing of factors to be considered in assessing social interaction and support, Bengtson and Schrader (1982) include strength of family associations, extent of agreement on general values or orientation, and subjective judgments of the quality of interaction among others. Clashing belief systems could easily undermine an otherwise supportive living arrangement and family harmony. The ability of an older individual and those around him or her to adjust to or tolerate very different values may be critical in determining social competence in a given situation.

Bengtson and Schrader (1982) and Graney (1982) discuss a variety of measures of family structure and social participation. Given the range of reliability and validity problems inherent in measures of social networks, support, and activity (Berkman, 1983; Kane & Kane, 1981), professionals must be exceptionally cautious in selecting measures and making competence judgments based on them. Social assessments may provide valuable supplementary data that would lend support to or indicate a contradiction in competence decision-making processes. If only one instrument is to be used, a social network or activity measure should not be the one; if several are to be used, those that examine the social context and social functioning must be included.

Multidimensional Assessment Instruments

It is our specific recommendation that professionals who examine the competence of older adults consider the use of available multidimensional instruments. These measures have been developed largely for exclusive use with older adults and attend to some of the problems involved in geriatric assessment discussed earlier. They have been designed to be comprehensive but not burdensome on the test administrator or the person tested. Many take into account the mutual influence of physical and psychosocial factors that may be more prevalent in the global functioning of older adults than in younger ones (Rubenstein, 1983). Finally, and perhaps of greatest importance, these measures typically are concerned more with assessment of functions than with reductionistic diagnosis. Such procedures are more likely to address the question "competent to do *what?*"

There are several multidimensional assessment instruments reported in the literature, and some will be described here. Fillenbaum's (1987) review identifies the domains typically covered by these measures: 1) activities of daily living, 2) physical health, 3) mental health, 4) social resources, 5) economic resources, 6) environmental factors, and 7) level of strain on the caregiver. The tests do vary with respect to their degree of emphasis on these dimensions, their direct observation of the individual in question, their reliance on trained professionals to administer the procedure, and their established degree of validity and reliability.

The Duke University Older Americans Research and Services Questionnaire (Duke OARS, 1978) emerged from an extensive clinical research effort directed largely at adults over age 55. The questionnaire is comprised of Parts A and B. The former addresses the functional status of the adult in five areas: social (which includes data on network and support systems), economic (including determination of income adequacy), mental health (including measures of mental status and well-being), physical health, and activities of daily living. In Part B, additional demographic and background data are included. Furthermore, the subject is rated on the use of and need for 24 different services. Both Parts A and B have been factor analyzed and reveal distinct scales on which the subject may be rated. The OARS questionnaire has demonstrated reasonable validity, test-retest reliability, and inter- and intrarater reliability.

Lawton et al. (1982) report the development of their Multilevel Assessment Instrument (MAI). They designed the MAI to address critical domains of functioning, including behavioral competence, psychological well-being, perceived quality of life, and critical factors in the objective environment. Furthermore, their project was intended to improve upon the psychometric integrity of existing multidimensional techniques and to investigate the utility of abbreviated forms of the instrument. Much of the MAI borrows from prior instruments. The *physical health* domain includes self-rated health, health behavior, and a checklist of health conditions. *Cognition* includes mental status and cognitive symptoms. *Activities of daily living* examine physical self-maintenance and instrumental activities of daily living (see previous discussion of IADLs). The MAI also explores *time use,* focusing on non-instrumental use of free time. *Social interaction* examines relations with family and friends. *Personal adjustment* items explore general morale and the presence of psychiatric symptoms. Finally, the *perceived environment* domain evaluates housing quality, neighborhood quality, and the subject's personal security.

Responses to the MAI were compared among three criterion groups that were assumed to represent different levels of "general competence." The study revealed generally favorable MAI reliability (test-retest reliability was poor on the physical self-maintenance ADL index), and several tests of validity were encouraging on all domains but the social scale. Short forms of the MAI appeared to decrease the power of the instrument but were acceptable for use in some of the dimensions evaluated (ADLs, cognition, personal adjustment, and physical health).

The Long-Term Care Information System (LTCIS; Falcone, 1984) is an extensive data-gathering instrument, primarily used to make accurate assessment of older adults' functional status and their specific service needs. A number of areas are covered in the LTCIS. *Demographic and identifying information* has a special focus on support networks and current living arrangements. *Medical data* cover traditional areas of health functioning and identify particular health risks. *Functional status* indexes address activities of daily living across a number of dimensions (including, for example, orientation, mobility level, and communication of needs). The instrument further assesses *services currently received,* such as therapies, medications, nutritional supplements, and so on.

The survey data from the LTCIS are directly linked to the delineation of 11 services of which the adult may be in need. These possible interventions are tempered by the personal resources of the individual assessed so that realistic options for further care are chosen. The LTCIS was designed to allow for periodic reassessment of abilities and liabilities, with the rationale that personal resources and environments change across time and should be reviewed.

Thus, the LTCIS may be a useful tool in structuring the evaluations of frail older adults' competence in a number of discrete behavioral areas. However, it is clear that one outcome of the survey (and perhaps of similar instruments) may be the need for additional assessment. For example, knowing that an individual is rated as "disoriented in all spheres all of the time" provides little understanding of this symptom's diagnostic significance. More substantial neuropsychological and medical evaluation might be required to clarify the etiology of the observed disorientation. Falcone notes that the assessment procedure "has been successfully tested for statistical significance" (1984, p. 370), but specific data on LTCIS validity and reliability are not provided.

Kane et al. (1982) undertook a project to develop a structured interview measure that would cover multiple areas of functioning in older adults requiring long-term care. The instrument was to be used as part of a research effort to evaluate the prediction of various treatment outcomes for nursing home patients. Unlike Falcone's (1984) LTCIS, Kane et al.'s measure was designed to be administered by nonservice providers. Their technical report describes well the rationale behind their choice of measures and administration procedures.

Six domains comprise the structured interview. As was true of Lawton et al.'s (1982) MAI, many items were borrowed from other test instruments or surveys. First, *administrative data* consist of traditional socioeconomic factors. Items in the *physical domain* include a description of abilities with activities of daily living, the self-report of health status, and a measure of general well-being. The *psychological domain* addresses both cognition and affect. The cognition measures include a simple mental status questionnaire, items that help rule out the presence of a dementia, and some brief memory measures. The affective status items focus in on symptoms of depression and anxiety and other indicators of general well-being. *Social health* data are also considered in the interview and are rated in terms of participation in various activities common to nursing home environments. *Life satisfaction* measures are included, using an adaptation of a satisfaction inventory. Finally, interviewers are encouraged to make relevant observations of behavior throughout the interview. Kane et al. provide thorough, encouraging data on the validity and reliability of their instrument.

We have recently learned of a "Client Care Assessment" package that is actually being used in California's probate court cases concerning guardianship decisions (M. White, personal communication, December 21, 1987). The instrument is a very detailed questionnaire, computer programmed and using various decision trees to assist the investigator in determining levels of competence. The Client Care Assessment program focuses largely on ADLs and IADLs and the mental status exam. Ultimately, decisions about functional level are determined bv the investigator, who may override and alter decisions made by the computer program's recommendations for further assessment. A revision of the original survey is anticipated in March of 1988 (I. Bryman, personal communication, February 8, 1988).

LEGAL ISSUES

There are few consistencies in the processes of determining legal competency. Practices vary widely from state to state and even within states in how competency is determined and regulated. The importance of the legal designation of incompetency is evident from two consequences of such a decision: once a person is declared incompetent, he or she is not entitled to legal representation in most states, and an initial finding of incompetence is rarely reversed even though some of the contributory causes of incompetency are reversible (Associated Press, 1987a).

From a year-long investigation of the legal procedures involved in guardianship cases across the United States, the Associated Press (1987a) learned that laws determining who needs guardianship are vague, and the standards by which medical and psychological assessments are made are poorly upheld. They also report an "insensitivity toward the elderly" in competency procedures (Associated Press, 1987b). Elderly individuals are very poorly represented in hearings that will determine the conditions in which they will live. In summarizing the results of examination of 2,200 guardianship files, Bayles and McCartney (1987) reported that nearly half of the guardianship hearings were carried out without representation for the individual in question. In 25% of the cases, no hearing was held. The National Senior Citizens Law Center found that in Los Angeles, 96% of those for whom guardianship was proposed were not represented (Associated Press, 1987c).

For our purposes, the manner of the determination of competency in these court cases is of paramount concern: the focus is on who makes the assessment and what are the criteria. Bayles and McCartney (1987) found that testimony as to the competency of the individual was presented by physicians, attorneys, lay individuals, and in some cases by the person seeking guardianship. They found that specialists such as pediatricians and plastic surgeons have offered testimony to the courts. Thirty-four percent of the cases did not include a doctor's opinion of any sort. Examinations tended to be brief medical or psychiatric assessments; 11 states require no supporting evidence beyond that presented by the person submitting the petition (Associated Press, 1987b).

The listed causes of incompetency have tended to be vague or general and to include such judgments as inability to care for self or finances (19%), senility or dementia (16%), or even "old age" (8%) (Associated Press, 1987a). In 25 states, according to the American Bar Association, "advanced age" is sufficient cause for a judgment of incompetency (Associated Press, 1987b). Ohio permits a judgment of "improvidence"; Massachusetts, "spendthrift"; and several states, "habitual drunkard" (Associated Press, 1987b). Not surprisingly, abuses of these diverse systems are reported to be widespread.

Some states and communities have made significant attempts to institute reforms. In Los Angeles county, for example, conservators, popularly called "public guardians," are provided for those people who have no other source of legal protection. The county probate court sends investigators to assess a range of abilities in individuals being considered for mental health conservatorship (Bayles & McCartney, 1987; R. Steinberg, personal communication, December 4, 1987; M. White, personal communication, January 28, 1988). The assessment tool is described above. The aim of the court is to place the individual in the "least restrictive environment" (R. Steinberg, personal communication, December 4, 1987). Probate conservatorship, primarily concerned with asset management, does not require assessment.

Following reforms, New Hampshire law requires quite specific evidence of the abilities of individuals thought to be incompetent; testimony of doctors or psychiatrists is no longer sufficient evidence on which to base a judgment of incompetency. Examples of the kinds of tasks on which a person is evaluated are consenting to medical treatment, possessing or managing property, and making contracts. As in California, the goal is to provide the "least restrictive environment" (Associated Press, 1987a).

From the Associated Press reports, it is obvious that guardianship procedures frequently fail to protect the rights of those they are designed to benefit. Only rarely are comprehensive assessment procedures involved in the legal decision-making process. From the forensic psychology literature, we have learned that determination of competency in criminal court cases has received much greater attention than in guardianship cases. Even when knowledgeable individuals are part of the process, there may be substantial problems. In the words of Watson (1984), expert witnesses and lawyers "pass each other like the proverbial ships in the night" as they often fail to communicate effectively to each other and the courts.

What is so distressing about these competency proceedings is that across the country, teams of professionals are skilled at making exactly the type of assessments the courts need for competency hearings. A number of the comprehensive measures we have discussed here and others could be used by the courts or designated agencies to determine, with acceptable reliability and validity, whether or not an individual is capable of managing his or her own affairs. They could be used to determine partial or temporary incompetency and could be administered over several occasions to determine whether significant changes have occurred that might indicate greater or lesser competence.

Because each state is responsible for its own competency legislation, it is not likely that uniform standards will be adopted in the near future or that the expertise of professionals familiar with complex assessments of competence will be drawn upon to lend substance to competency determinations. Recent hearings in the U.S. House of Representatives have led to discussions on the possibility of initiating federal standards on guardianship (Associated Press, 1987c), but there would still be 50 independent legal systems establishing criteria and procedures.

RECOMMENDATIONS FOR COMPETENCE ASSESSMENT

The first question in any assessment of competence should be "competence for what?" Consistent with the foregoing arguments that an individual and his or her surroundings are inexorably interdependent, just what the person is forced to contend with must be known and evaluated. After that is done, the relevant skills may be assessed, the supports offered by the environment noted, the lack of congruence between environmental demands and evident skills plus supports determined, available remedies identified, possible solutions proposed, the feasibility of these solutions determined, and a course of action offered. Physical domains, psychological domains including cognitive and affective functioning, and social domains should be investigated in the assessment process. The possibility of change in or even reversal of current status must be an integral part of any competence assessment system.

The selection of measures may differ depending on the purpose of the assessment. Kane et al. (1982) have suggested several criteria for measures to assess competence in the determination of probable treatment outcomes. We concur with some of the criteria that guided their project, including the following:

1) Measures must cover a range of domains of functioning.

2) They must be reliable both between and within interviewers/examiners.

3) They must measure what they purport to measure (i.e., show validity).

4) They must be sufficiently broad-based to examine the range of behaviors of the target population of interest.

While we subscribe to many of the criteria proposed by Kane et al., others used in the development of their instrument are questionable when the purpose of the assessment is to establish competence. We believe that the consequences of finding one "incompetent" are so drastic that every precaution should be taken to ensure that the determination is appropriate. Unlike Kane et al., we argue that professionals should administer the measures whenever possible. Furthermore, brevity of assessment should not take precedence over its accuracy. In addition, we propose that assessment findings be couched in a common language (Falcone, 1983, 1984), one that is acceptable to medical, psychological, and social professionals and interpretable by legal professionals. Follow-up testing should be systematically incorporated into competence assessment. Courts will have to recognize that deficits and conditions are sometimes reversible, both before and following court procedures.

We now offer a summary of several recommendations for assessment of competence. Some of these guidelines have been proposed by Falcone (1983), some by Kane et al. (1982), and some are original. None is to be ignored when an individual is being judged able or unable to be responsible for aspects of his or her own existence:

1) The nature and extent of the competence being assessed must be operationally defined.

2) Several domains—including physical, social, environmental, cognitive, and affective factors—should be incorporated into the assessment system.

3) Although multiple domains are assessed, the use of single instruments that address relevant domains is preferable to the use of extensive batteries of tests.

4) Tests used should demonstrate acceptable reliability and predictive validity.

5) Measures should be age-appropriate for the behaviors in question.

6) Test administration should be conducted by appropriate professionals, although relevant information should be gathered from more than one source.

7) Although brief screening measures are useful, they should not be the only measures employed.

8) The language in which assessment results are reported must be understandable by a range of professionals.

9) The individual should be the focus of the assessment, not the needs of the reporting professional.

10) Reversibility of outcome must be considered a legitimate possibility in every assessment case.

11) Follow-up assessment of functions must be incorporated into the competence determination system.

12) One goal of competence assessment must be to assist in determining the "least restrictive environment" for the individual in question.

REFERENCES

Altman, I., Werner, C.M., Oxley, D., & Haggard, L.M. (1987). "Christmas Street" as an example of transactionally oriented research. *Environment and Behavior, 19,* 501-524.
Associated Press. (1987, September 20). *Guardianship files.* New York: Author.
Associated Press. (1987, September 23). Elderly granted fewer courtroom rights than criminals. *Syracuse Herald-Journal,* p. A17.
Associated Press. (1987, September 27). House panel hears sad tales, warnings about guardianship. *Syracuse Herald American,* p. A13.
Baltes, P.B., & Willis, S.L. (1982). Plasticity and enhancement of intellectual functioning in old age: Penn State's Adult Development and Enrichment Program (ADEPT). In F.I.M.

Craik & S.E. Trehub (Eds.), *Aging and cognitive processes* (pp. 353-389). New York: Plenum.

Bayles, F., & McCartney, S. (1987, September 23). Guardians of the elderly. Part I. *Syracuse Herald-Journal*, pp. A1, A16.

Bengston, V.L., & Schrader, S.S. (1982). Parent-child relations. In D.J. Mangen & W.A. Peterson (Eds.), *Research instruments in social gerontology: Vol. 2. Social roles and social participation* (pp. 115-185). Minneapolis: University of Minnesota Press.

Berg, C.A., & Sternberg, R.J. (1985). A triarchic theory of intellectual development during adulthood. *Developmental Review, 5*, 334-370.

Berkman, L.F. (1983). The assessment of social networks and social support in the elderly. *Journal of the American Geriatrics Society, 31*, 743-749.

Berkman, L.F., & Breslow, L. (1983). *Health and ways of living: The Alameda County study.* New York: Oxford University Press.

Besdine, R.W. (1983). The educational utility of comprehensive functional assessment in the elderly. *Journal of the American Geriatrics Society, 31*(11), 651-656.

Blau, T.H. (1984). Psychology tests in the courtroom. *Professional Psychology: Research and Practice, 15*, 176-186.

Bray, D.W., & Howard, A. (1983). The AT&T longitudinal studies of managers. In K.W. Schaie (Ed.), *Longitudinal studies of adult psychological development* (pp. 266-312). New York: Guilford.

Connolly, K., & Brunner, J. (1974). Competence: Its nature and nurture. In K. Connolly & J. Brunner (Eds.), *The growth of competence* (pp. 3-7). New York: Academic Press.

Dirkin, J.M. (Ed.). (1972). *Functional age of industrial workers.* Groninn, The Netherlands: Wolters-Noodhoff.

Duke Older American Resources and Services. (1978). *Multidimensional functional assessment: The OARS methodology* (2nd ed.). Durham, NC: Center for the Study of Aging and Human Development, Duke University.

Dye, C.J. (1982). Intellectual functioning. In D.J. Mangen & W.A. Peterson (Eds.), *Research instruments in social gerontology: Vol. 2. Social roles and social participation* (pp. 25-77). Minneapolis: University of Minnesota Press.

Ewing, C.P. (1985). Mental health clinicians and the law: An overview of current law governing professional practice. In C.P. Ewing (Ed.), *Psychology, psychiatry, and the law: A clinical and forensic handbook* (pp. 527-560). Sarasota, FL: Professional Resource Exchange.

Falcone, A. (1984, November-December). Care based on need. *Geriatric Nursing*, pp. 376-379.

Falcone, A.R. (1983). Comprehensive functional assessment as an administrative tool. *Journal of the American Geriatrics Society, 31*, 642-650.

Fillenbaum, G.G. (1987). Multidimensional functional assessment. In G.L. Maddox (Ed.), *The encyclopedia of aging* (pp. 460-462). New York: Springer.

Fishback, D.B. (1977). Mental status questionnaires for organic brain syndrome with a new visual counting test. *Journal of the American Geriatrics Society, 25*, 167-170.

Folstein, M.F., Folstein, S., & McHugh, P.R. (1975). Mini-Mental State: A practical method for grading the cognitive state of patients for the clinician. *Journal of Psychiatric Research, 12*, 189-198.

Graney, M.J. (1982). Social participation roles. In D.J. Mangen & W.A. Peterson (Eds.), *Research instruments in social gerontology: Vol. 2. Social roles and social participation* (pp. 9-42). Minneapolis: University of Minnesota Press.

Granger, C.V., & Greer, D.S., (1976). Functional status measurement and medical rehabilitation outcomes. *Archives of Physical Medicine and Rehabilitation, 57*, 103-109.

Granick, S. (1983). Psychologic assessment technology for geriatric practice. *Journal of the American Geriatrics Society, 31*, 728-742.

Grisso, T. (1986). *Evaluating competencies: Forensic assessments and instruments.* New York: Plenum.

Grisso, T. (1987). The economic and scientific future of forensic psychological assessment. *American Psychologist, 42*, 831-839.

Gurland, B.J. (1980). The assessment of the mental health status of older adults. In J.E. Birren & R.B. Sloane (Eds.), *Handbook of mental health and aging* (pp. 671-700). Englewood Cliffs, NJ: Prentice-Hall.

Horn, J.L., & Cattell, R.B. (1966). Refinement and test of the theory of fluid and crystallized general intelligences. *Journal of Educational Psychology, 58*, 253-270.

Horn, J.L., & Cattell, R.B. (1967). Age differences in fluid and crystallized intelligence. *Acta Psychologica, 26*, 107-129.

Horowitz, R.J. (1982). Testing: The armamentarium of psychology. In F.R. Fields & R.J. Horowitz (Eds.), *Psychology and professional practice: The interface of psychology and the law* (pp. 17-31). Westport, CT: Quorum Books.

Isaacs, B., & Akhtar, A.J. (1972). The Set Test. *Age and Ageing, 1*, 222-226.

Kahn, R.L. (1983). Productive behavior: Assessment, determinants, and effects. *Journal of the American Geriatrics Society, 31*, 750-757.

Kahn, R.L., Goldfarb, A.I., Pollack, M., & Peck, A. (1960). Brief objective measure for the determination of mental status in the aged. *American Journal of Psychology, 117*, 326-328.

Kane, R.L., Bell, R., Riegler, S., Wilson, A., & Keeler, E. (1983). Predicting the outcomes of nursing home patients. *The Gerontologist, 23*(2), 200-206.

Kane, R.L, & Kane, R.A. (1981). *Assessing the elderly: A practical guide to management.* Lexington, MA: D.C. Heath.

Kane, R.L., Riegler, S., Bell, R., Potter, R., & Koshland, C. (1982). *Predicting the course of nursing home patients: A progress report* (N-1786-NCHSR). Santa Monica, CA: Rand Corporation.

Kastenbaum, R., & Sherwood, S. (1972). VIRO: A scale for assessing the interview behavior of elderly people. In D.P. Kent, R. Kastenbaum, & S. Sherwood (Eds.), *Research planning and action for the elderly: The power and potential of social science* (pp. 166-200). New York: Behavioral Publications.

Katz, S. (1983). Assessing self-maintenance: Activities of daily living, mobility, and instrumental activities of daily living. *Journal of the American Geriatrics Society, 31*(12), 721-727.

Katz, S., & Akpom, C.A. (1976). A measure of primary socio-biological functions. *International Journal of Health Services, 6*, 493-507.

Krauss, I.K. (1980). Assessment for retirement. In P.K. Ragan (Ed.), *Policy issues in aging, work, and retirement* (pp. 111-126). Lexington, MA: Lexington Press.

Krauss, I.K. (1984). Assessing cognitive skills of older workers. *Personnel Selection and Training Bulletin, 5*, 210-219.

Krauss, I.K. (in press). Testing cognitive skills with playing cards. In J.D. Sinnott (Ed.), *Everyday problem solving: Theory and applications.* New York: Praeger.

Labouvie-Vief, G. (1982). Dynamic development and mature autonomy. *Human Development, 25*, 161-191.

Labouvie-Vief, G. (1985). Intelligence and cognition. In J.E. Birren & K.W. Schaie (Eds.), *Handbook of the psychology of aging* (2nd ed., pp. 500-530). New York: Van Nostrand Reinhold.

Lanyon, R.I. (1986). Psychological assessment procedures in court related settings. *Professional Psychology: Research and Practice, 17,* 260-268.

Lawton, M.P. (1977). The impact of the environment on aging and behavior. In J.E. Birren & K.W. Schaie (Eds.), *Handbook of the psychology of aging* (pp. 276-301). New York: Van Nostrand Reinhold.

Lawton, M.P., & Brody, E.M. (1969). Assessment of older people: Self-maintaining and instrumental activities of daily living. *The Gerontologist, 9,* 179-186.

Lawton, M.P., Moss, M., Fulcomer, M., & Kleban, M.H. (1982). A research and service oriented multilevel assessment instrument. *Journal of Gerontology, 37*(1), 91-99.

Lawton, M.P., & Nahemow, L. (1973). Ecology and the aging process. In C. Eisdorfer & M.P. Lawton (Eds.), *The psychology of adult development and aging* (pp. 619-674). Washington, DC: American Psychological Association.

Meier, E.L., & Kerr, E.A. (1976). Capabilities of middle-aged and older workers: A survey of the literature. *Industrial Gerontology, 3,* 147-156.

Melton, G.B., Petrila, J., Poythress, N.G., & Slobogin, C. (1987). *Psychological evaluation for the courts: A handbook for mental health professionals and lawyers.* New York: Guilford.

Miller, E. (1980). Cognitive assessment of the older adult. In J.E. Birren & R.B. Sloane (Eds.), *Handbook of mental health and aging* (pp. 520-536). Englewood Cliffs, NJ: Prentice-Hall.

Miller, R.D. (1985). Clinical and legal aspects of civil commitment. In C.P. Ewing (Ed.), *Psychology, psychiatry, and the law: A clinical and forensic handbook* (pp. 149-180). Sarasota, FL: Professional Resource Exchange.

Pfeiffer, E. (1975). A short portable mental status questionnaire for the assessment of organic brain deficit in elderly patients. *Journal of the American Geriatrics Society, 23,* 433-441.

Rubenstein, L. (1983). The clinical effectiveness of multidimensional geriatric assessment. *Journal of the American Geriatrics Society, 31*(12), 758-762.

Salthouse, T.A. (1986). Functional age: Examination of a concept. In J.E. Birren, P.K. Robinson, & J.E. Livingston (Eds.), *Age, health, and employment* (pp. 78-92). Englewood Cliffs, NJ: Prentice-Hall.

Salthouse, T.A. (1987). Age, experience and compensation. In C. Schooler & K.W. Schaie (Eds.), *Cognitive functioning and social structure over the life course* (pp. 142-157). Norwood, NJ: Ablex.

Schaie, K.W. (1978). External validity. *Journal of Gerontology, 33,* 695-701.

Schaie, K.W. (1980). Intelligence and problem solving. In J.E. Birren & R.B. Sloane (Eds.), *Handbook of mental health and aging* (pp. 262-284). Englewood Cliffs, NJ: Prentice-Hall.

Schaie, K.W. (1985). *Manual for the Schaie-Thurstone Test of Adult Mental Abilities (STAMAT).* Palo Alto, CA: Consulting Psychologists Press.

Schaie, K.W. (1987a). Applications of psychometric intelligence to the prediction of everyday competence in the elderly. In C. Schooler & K.W. Schaie (Eds.), *Cognitive functioning and social structure over the life course* (pp. 50-58). Norwood, NJ: Ablex.

Schaie, K.W. (1987b). Intelligence. In G.L. Maddox (Ed.), *The encyclopedia of aging* (pp. 357-358). New York: Springer.

Schaie, K.W., & Willis, S.L. (1986). Can decline in adult intellectual functioning be reversed? *Developmental Psychology, 22,* 223-232.

Scheidt, R.J., & Schaie, K.W. (1978). A situational taxonomy for the elderly: Generating situational criteria. *Journal of Gerontology, 33,* 848-857.

Schooler, C. (1987). Cognitive effects of complex environments during the life span: A review and theory. In C. Schooler & K.W. Schaie (Eds.), *Cognitive functioning and social structure over the life course* (pp. 24-49). Norwood, NJ: Ablex.

Siegler, I.C. (1987). Functional age. In G.L. Maddox (Ed.), *The encyclopedia of aging* (pp. 464-465). New York: Springer.

Stagner, R. (1985). Aging in industry. In J.E. Birren & K.W. Schaie (Eds.), *Handbook of the psychology of aging* (2nd ed., pp. 789- 817). New York: Van Nostrand Reinhold.

Sternberg, R.J. (1985). *Beyond IQ: A triarchic theory of human intelligence.* New York: Cambridge University Press.

Sternberg, R.J., & Berg, C.J. (1987). What are theories of adult intellectual development theories of? In C. Schooler & K.W. Schaie (Eds.), *Cognitive functioning and social structure over the life course* (pp. 3-23). Norwood, NJ: Ablex.

Thurstone, L.L., & Thurstone, T.G. (1947). *Primary mental abilities.* Chicago: Science Research Associates.

Walker, J.W., & Lazer, H.L. (1978). *The end of mandatory retirement: Implications for management.* New York: John Wiley.

Watson, A.S. (1984). Comment. *American Journal of Psychiatry, 141,* 58-60.

White, L.R., Cartwright, W.S., Cornoni-Huntley, J., & Brock, D.B. (1986). Epidemiology of aging. In C. Eisdorfer (Ed.), *Annual Review of Gerontology and Geriatrics, 6,* 215-311.

Wigdor, B. (1980). Drives and motivation. In J.E. Birren & R.B. Sloane (Eds.), *Handbook of mental health and aging* (pp. 245-261). Englewood Cliffs, NJ: Prentice-Hall.

Williams, T.F. (1983). Comprehensive functional assessment: An overview. *Journal of the American Geriatrics Society, 31*(11), 637-641.

Windley, P.G. (1982). Environments. In D.J. Mangen & W.A. Peterson (Eds.), *Research instruments in social gerontology: Vol. 2. Social roles and social participation* (pp. 383-413). Minneapolis: University of Minnesota Press.

Appendix: Test Directory and Index

Refer to pages(s)	*Test Title*

143

ADJECTIVE CHECK LIST (ACL) *Harrison G. Gough and Alfred B. Heilbrun, Jr.*

Describes self and relations with others. Used for personality assessment and research.

300-item paper-pencil test of up to 37 dimensions of personality, including 4 Method of Response scales, 15 Need scales, 9 Topical scales, 5 Transactional scales, and 4 Origence-Intellectence scales. Items are adjectives that are checked if they apply to self, but they may be answered with reference to others. Scores need not be obtained on all 37 scales. Self-administered. Suitable for group use. Hand scoring requires users to prepare their own stencils; computer scoring available from publisher. Available in Spanish. Untimed (15-20 minutes). Manual $13.00; 25 check lists (hand scored) $7.00; 50 profiles $11.00. *Publisher:* Consulting Psychologists Press, Inc.

281, 282

ADULT BASIC LEARNING EXAMINATION, SECOND EDITION (ABLE) *Bjorn Karlsen and Eric F. Gardner*

Measures adult achievement in basic learning.

Multiple-item paper-pencil measure of vocabulary knowledge, reading comprehension, spelling, arithmetic computation, and problem-solving skills. Test is divided into three levels: Level 1, for adults with from 1 to 4 years of formal education; Level 2, for adults with from 5 to 8 years of schooling; and Level 3, for those with at least 8 years of schooling and who may or may not have graduated from high school. Because the vocabulary test is dictated, no reading is required. The Arithmetic Problem-Solving test is dictated at Level 1. A short screening test, SelectABLE, is available for use in determining the appropriate level of ABLE for each applicant. The test is available in two alternate forms, E and F, at each level. SelectABLE is available in only one form. Examiner required. Suitable for group use. Untimed (SelectABLE 15 minutes; Level 1, 2 hours, 10 minutes; Levels 2 and 3, 2 hours, 55 minutes). Scored by hand key or may be computer scored; Levels 2 and 3 self-scored. Specimen set (Level 1, 2, 3 test booklets for Form E; directions for administration for Levels 1, 2, 3; group record, hand-scorable answer sheet, and ready score answer sheet for Level 2; SelectABLE ready-scale answer sheet) $23.00. *Publisher:* The Psychological Corporation

Refer to pages(s)	*Test Title*

12

AFFECT BALANCE SCALE (ABS)   *Leonard R. Derogatis*

Evaluates psychological adjustment and well-being in terms of mood and affect balance.

40-item paper-pencil self-report adjective mood scale assessing four positive affect dimensions (joy, contentment, vigor, and affection) and four negative affect dimensions (anxiety, depression, guilt, and hostility). Scoring and interpretation procedures are structured on the concept that healthy psychological adjustment is based on the presence of active positive emotions and the relative absence of negative emotions. The overall score of the test is expressed as the Affect Balance Index, reflecting the balance between positive and negative affects in terms of standardized scores. SCORABS Version 2.1 is a computer scoring program designed for IBM XT/AT systems. It generates eight positive and negative Primary Affect Dimension scores, positive and negative Affect Total scores, and an Affect Balance Index. Examiner required. Suitable for group use. Untimed (3-5 minutes). Scored via examiner evaluation. 100 test forms $28.00; 100 profile sheets $20.00. *Publisher:* Clinical Psychometric Research, Inc.

144

ANXIETY SCALE FOR THE BLIND   *Richard E. Hardy*

Measures manifest anxiety among blind and partially sighted people. Used for clinical evaluations by psychologists, psychiatrists, and other qualified counselors.

78-item true-false test measuring the level of anxiety present in blind and partially sighted children and recently modified adults. The subject is given a roll of tickets to be placed to the right or left of the table to indicate true or false as the items are read. Originally developed for use in residential schools with students of high-school age, the test may be used in other contexts as well. The test is still experimental in nature and must be used only by psychologists, psychiatrists, and other qualified counselors. Examiner required. Not suitable for group use. Untimed. Scored via examiner evaluation. Scale $3.60. *Publisher:* American Foundation for the Blind

80, 102, 103, 168, 169, 194, 195

BECK DEPRESSION INVENTORY   *Aaron T. Beck*

Measures an individual's level of depression. Used for treatment planning and evaluation in mental health settings.

21-item inventory assessing the severity of an individual's complaints, symptoms, and concerns related to his current level of depression. The symptoms assessed are sadness, pessimism, sense of failure, dissatisfaction, feelings of guilt, expectation of punishment, self-dislike, self-accusations, suicidal ideas, crying, irritability, social withdrawal, indecisiveness, change in body image, work difficulty, insomnia, loss of appetite, weight loss, somatic preoccupation, fatigability, and loss of libido. A microcomputer printout indicates the severity of the depressed mood, lists major symptom complaints, and shows a table of responses. Questions are presented on an eighth-grade reading level. Self-administered. Not

Refer to pages(s)	*Test Title*

suitable for group use. Untimed (15-20 minutes). Microcomputer scored. Contact publisher for cost. *Publisher:* Center for Cognitive Therapy

BENDER VISUAL MOTOR GESTALT TEST   *Lauretta Bender*

Assesses the visual-motor functions of individuals ages 3-adult. Also used to evaluate developmental problems in children, learning disabilities, retardation, psychosis, and organic brain disorders.

Test consists of nine gestalt cards. The examiner presents the cards to the subject one at a time and in order, and the subject reproduces on blank paper the configuration or design shown on each card. Responses are scored according to the development of the concepts of form, shape, and pattern and orientation in space. Analysis of performance may indicate the presence of psychosis and maturational lags. Examiner required. Slides may be used for group administration. Untimed (15-20 minutes). Scored via examiner evaluation; scoring service available. Test cards with manual of instructions $5.00; monograph $12.00; slides with manual of instructions $15.00. *Publisher:* American Orthopsychiatric Association, Inc.

BOOKLET CATEGORY TEST   *Nick A. DeFilippis and Elizabeth McCampbell*

Diagnoses brain dysfunction. Used for clinical assessment of brain damage.

208-item test of concept formation and abstract reasoning. Figures are presented one at at time to the subject, who responds with a number between 1 and 4. This is the booklet version of the Halstead Category Test. The first four subtests may be used to predict total error scores if time limitations do not allow administration of the entire test. Examiner required. Not suitable for group use. Untimed (30-60 minutes). Scored via examiner evaluation. Complete set (2-volume manual, 25 scoring forms) $125.00. *Publisher:* Psychological Assessment Resources, Inc.

BOSTON DIAGNOSTIC APHASIA EXAMINATION
Harold Goodglass and Edith Kaplan

Assesses the functioning of aphasic patients. Used for clinical evaluations.

Multiple-item oral-response paper-pencil and task-performance test yielding 43 scores relating to recognized aphasic syndromes, including severity rating, fluency, auditory comprehension, naming, oral reading, repetition, paraphasia, automatized speech, reading comprehension, writing, and music. The test also provides the following seven ratings: melodic line, phrase length, articulatory agility, grammatical form, paraphrasia in running speech, word finding, and auditory comprehension. The test manual includes information on the nature of aphasic deficits, common clusters of defects, statistical information, administration and scoring procedures, and illustrations of test profiles that correspond to

Refer to pages(s)	*Test Title*

major aphasic syndromes. Examiner required. Not suitable for group use. Untimed. Scored via examiner evaluation. Complete set (manual, examination booklets, and Boston Naming Test) $32.50; 25 examination booklets $15.00. *Publisher:* Lea and Febiger

59

BOSTON NAMING TEST *Edith Kaplan, Harold Goodglass, and Sandra Weintraub*

Used with learning disabled, brain-damaged, dementing, and aphasic populations.

60-item wide-range picture naming test used as part of language assessment in populations at risk for brain damage. The 60 pictures are contained in a single test booklet. Examiner required. Not suitable for group use. Available in Spanish. Untimed (30 minutes). Scored via examiner evaluation. 25 answer booklets $6.00. *Publisher:* Lea and Febiger

195

BRIEF SYMPTOM INVENTORY (BSI) *Leonard R. Derogatis*

Evaluates psychological symptomatic distress. Used with medical and psychiatric patients and adult and adolescent non-patients.

53-item paper-pencil self-report inventory assessing symptomatic distress in terms of nine symptom dimensions (somatization, obsessive-compulsive, interpersonal sensitivity, depression, anxiety, hostility, phobic anxiety, paranoid ideation, and psychoticism) and three global indices of distress (global severity index, positive symptom index, and positive symptom total). This inventory is a brief form of the SCL-90-R and may be used in conjunction with the matching observer's scales in the Psychopathology Rating Scales Series (the SCL-90-R Analogue and the Hopkins Psychiatric Rating Scale). SCORBSI Version 2.1 is a computer scoring program for use with IBM PC/XT systems. Examiner required. Suitable for group use. Available in over 20 languages. Untimed (10-12 minutes). Scored via examiner evaluation. Manual $17.50; 100 test forms $30.00; 100 score/profile forms $22.00; SCORBSI Version 2.1 $125.00. *Publisher:* Clinical Psychometric Research, Inc.

143, 241, 242, 243

CALIFORNIA PSYCHOLOGICAL INVENTORY, 1987 REVISED EDITION *Harrison G. Gough*

Assesses personality characteristics important for daily living. Used in business, schools and colleges, clinics and counseling agencies, and research.

468-item true-false paper-pencil test measuring behavioral tendencies along 20 scales: Dominance, Capacity for Status, Sociability, Social Presence, Self-acceptance, Independence, Empathy, Responsibility, Socialization, Self-control, Good Impression, Communality, Well-being, Tolerance, Achievement via Independence, Intellectual Efficiency, Psychological-mindedness, Flexibility, and Femininity/Masculinity. Revised edition contains semantic changes in 29 items and two additional scales (Empathy and Independence). In addition, three new independent themes representing the CPI's conceptual foundations have been introduced to organize results and aid interpretation. Three scoring reports are available: Profile Report, Gough Interpretive Report, and McAllister Interpretive Report. Self-administered. Suitable for group use. Available in French, Spanish, Italian, and German. Untimed (45-60 minutes). Scored by hand key or may be computer scored. Administrator's Guide $15.00; hand-scoring stencils $40.00; 25 test booklets $20.00; 100 profiles (specify male or female) $15.00; 50 non-prepaid answer sheets $7.50. *Publisher:* Consulting Psychologists Press, Inc.

84

CALIFORNIA VERBAL LEARNING TEST, RESEARCH EDITION   *Dean C. Delis, Joel H. Kramer, Edith Kaplan, and Beth A. Ober*

Assesses verbal learning and memory deficits and aids in designing and monitoring rehabilitation. Used with the elderly and the neurologically impaired.

Multi-trial verbal learning task consisting of 16 categorized words used in immediate and delayed free recall, cued recall, and recognition trials. A second word list also is presented to obtain interference measures. Indices of learning strategies, error types, primacy/recency effects, and other process data are provided. Examiner required. Not suitable for group use. Untimed (35 minutes). Scored via examiner evaluation or may be computer scored. 25 record booklets $20.00; 25 scorings/reports $75.00; manual $15.00. *Publisher:* The Psychological Corporation

96, 168

CENTER FOR EPIDEMIOLOGIC STUDIES—DEPRESSION SCALE (CES-D)   *Center for Epidemiologic Studies*

Measures symptoms associated with depression in adults. Used to identify high-risk groups for research and screening.

20-item paper-pencil test in which the subject is asked to rank experiences and feelings for the past week on a 3-point scale ranging from "less than once a day" (0) to "most or all of the time" (3). Questions deal with symptoms of depressed mood, lack of energy, insomnia, and appetite loss. The scale may be read to a subject by an examiner or completed in privacy by the client. Scales are weighted for scoring and interpretation. Self-administered. Suitable for group use. Available in Spanish. Untimed (5 minutes). Scored by hand key. Contact publisher for cost. *Publisher:* Epidemiology and Psychopathology, Research Branch, National Institute of Mental Health

242

CLERICAL APTITUDE TEST   *Andrew Kobal, J. Wayne Wrightstone, and Andrew J. MacElroy*

Assesses aptitude for clerical work. Used for screening job applicants.

Three-part paper-pencil test measuring clerical aptitudes, including business practice, number checking, and date, name, and address checking. Scores correlate with job success. Examiner required. Suitable for group use. Timed (40 minutes). Scored by hand key. Specimen set $4.00; 25 tests $8.75. *Publisher:* Psychometric Affiliates

CLIFTON ASSESSMENT PROCEDURES FOR THE ELDERLY (CAPE) *A.H. Pattie and C.J. Gilleard*

Assesses level of dependency in the elderly. Used by general practitioners, community nurses, health visitors, occupational therapists, social workers, and hospital personnel.

Two multiple-item paper-pencil rating scales assessing cognitive and behavioral competence in the elderly. The Cognitive Assessment Scale is a short psychological test comprised of three sections: information/orientation, mental ability, and psychomotor (utilizing the Gibson Spiral Maze). The Behavioral Rating Scale consists of 18 items measuring physical disability, apathy, communication difficulties, and social disturbance. The scoring procedure relates the level of cognitive and behavioral dependency to likely need for community or hospital care. Examiner required. Not suitable for group use. Untimed (varies). Scored via examiner evaluation. Contact publisher for cost. *Publisher:* Hodder and Stoughton Educational; distributed in the U.S. by The Psychological Corporation

DEPRESSION ADJECTIVE CHECK LIST (DACL) *Bernard Lubin*

Differentiates between depressed and nondepressed highschool and college students and adults. Used for counseling, group screening, and large-scale depression studies.

Multiple-item paper-pencil checklist measuring transient depressive moods, feelings, or emotions. Seven parallel forms allow repeated measurement of these factors. The subject responds by checking adjectives on the checklist that describe feelings at the time of testing. Seven parallel forms, A, B, C, D (32 items each) and E, F, G (34 items each), allow repeated measurement. None of the adjectives appear on more than one of Forms A, B, C, or D or on more than one of Forms E, F, or G. Norms are presented for male and female normals and for depressed patients. Examiner/self-administered. Suitable for group use. Untimed (5 minutes per form). Scored by hand key. Specimen set (manual, one copy of all forms) $5.50; 25 checklists (specify form) $6.50; key $2.50; manual $3.00. *Publisher:* Educational and Industrial Testing Service

DIFFERENTIAL APTITUDE TESTS (DAT) *G.K. Bennett, H.G. Seashore, and A.G. Wesman*

Assesses aptitude. Used for educational and vocational guidance in junior and senior high schools.

Multiple-item paper-pencil test of eight abilities: verbal reasoning, numerical ability, abstract reasoning, clerical speed and accuracy, mechanical reasoning, space relations, spelling, and language usage. A ninth score, an Index of Scholastic Ability, is obtained by summing the Verbal Reasoning and Numerical Ability scores. Materials include two alternate and equivalent forms, V and W. The Career Planning Questionnaire is optional. Forms V and W supersede Forms S and T. Examiner required. Suitable for group use. Timed (complete battery, 3 hours or longer). Scoring options include hand key, machine scoring, or computer scoring. Specimen set (test, directions, administrator's handbook, MRC and NCS answer documents and sheets, list of correct answers, order for scoring service, sample profile forms) $13.00; Career Planning Service Information Packet (counselor's manual, directions, glossary, sample career planning report, explanation of school summary report, MRC answer document with MRC sheet, orientation booklet) $10.00. *Publisher:* The Psychological Corporation

241, 242

EDWARDS PERSONAL PREFERENCE SCHEDULE (EPPS)
A.L. Edwards

Assesses an individual's personality. Used for both personal counseling and personality research.

Paper-pencil forced-choice test designed to show the relative importance of 15 needs and motives: achievement, deference, order, exhibition, autonomy, affiliation, intraception, succorance, dominance, abasement, nurturance, change, endurance, heterosexuality, and aggression. Self-administered. Suitable for group use. Untimed (45 minutes). Scored by hand key. Specimen set (schedule booklet, hand-scorable answer document and template; IBM 805 and NCS answer documents, manual) $19.00. *Publisher:* The Psychological Corporation

144

EMOTIONAL FACTORS INVENTORY   *Mary K. Bauman*

Measures emotional and personality factors of visually handicapped individuals.

170-item paper-pencil or oral response questionnaire assessing the personal and emotional adjustment of visually impaired individuals. The questionnaire yields scores on the following seven scales: sensitivity, somatic symptoms, social competency, attitudes of distrust, feelings of inadequacy, depression, and attitudes concerning blindness. A validation score is also obtained. The questionnaire is presented in large-print format. Instructions for tape recording the questions are included. Supplementary materials provided in the test kit include a discussion of the inventory, instructions for administering and scoring the inventory, and a comparative study of personality factors in blind, other handicapped, and nonhandicapped individuals. Examiner required. The paper-pencil version is suitable for group use. Untimed (varies). Scored via examiner evaluation. Test kit (test booklet, scoring overlays, 10 IBM answer sheets, supplementary materials, and norms) $15.00. *Publisher:* Associated Services for the Blind

Refer to pages(s)	*Test Title*

241

EMPLOYEE APTITUDE SURVEY TEST #1—VERBAL COMPREHENSION *G. Grimsley, F.L. Ruch, N.D. Warren, and J.S. Ford*

Measures ability to use and understand the relationships between words. Used for selection and placement of executives, secretaries, professional personnel, and high-level office workers. Also used in career counseling.

30-item paper-pencil multiple-choice test measuring word-relationship recognition, reading speed, and ability to understand instructions. Each item consists of a word followed by a list of four other words from which the examinee must select the one meaning the same or about the same as the first word. The test is available in two equivalent forms. Examiner required. Suitable for group use. Timed (5 minutes). Scored by hand key or may be computer scored. 25 tests $23.75. *Publisher:* Psychological Services, Inc.

241

EMPLOYEE APTITUDE SURVEY TEST #2—NUMERICAL ABILITY *G. Grimsley, F.L. Ruch, and N.D. Warren*

Measures basic mathematical skills. Used for selection and placement of executives, supervisors, engineers, accountants, sales, and clerical workers. Also used in career counseling.

75-item paper-pencil multiple-choice test arranged in three 25-item parts assessing addition, subtraction, multiplication, and division skills. Part I covers whole numbers, Part II decimal fractions, and Part III common fractions. The test is available in two equivalent forms. Examiner required. Suitable for group use. Available in Spanish and French. Timed (10 minutes). Scored by hand key or may be computer scored. 25 tests $23.75. *Publisher:* Psychological Services, Inc.

241

EMPLOYEE APTITUDE SURVEY TEST #3—VISUAL PURSUIT *G. Grimsley, F.L. Ruch, N.D. Warren, and J.S. Ford*

Measures speed and accuracy in visually tracing lines through complex designs. Used for selection and placement of drafters, design engineers, technicians, and related positions. Also used in career counseling.

30-item paper-pencil multiple-choice test consisting of a maze of lines that weave their way from their starting points (numbered 1 to 30) on the right-hand side of the page to a column of boxes on the left. The task is to identify for each starting point the box on the left at which the line ends. Examinees are encouraged to trace with their eyes, not their pencils. The test is available in two equivalent forms. Examiner required. Suitable for group use. Available in Spanish and French. Timed (5 minutes). Scored by hand key or may be computer scored. 25 tests $23.75. *Publisher:* Psychological Services, Inc.

241

EMPLOYEE APTITUDE SURVEY TEST #4—VISUAL SPEED AND ACCURACY *G. Grimsley, F.L. Ruch, and N.D. Warren*

Measures ability to see details quickly and accurately. Used to select bookkeepers, accountants, general office clerks, stenographers, office machine operators, and supervisors. Also used in career planning.

150-item paper-pencil multiple-choice test in which each item consists of two series of numbers and symbols that the subject must compare and determine whether they are "the same" or "different." The test may be administered to applicants for sales, supervisory, and executive positions with the expectation that their scores will be above average. The test is available in two equivalent forms. Examiner required. Suitable for group use. Available in Spanish. Timed (5 minutes). Scored by hand key or may be computer scored. 25 tests $23.75. *Publisher:* Psychological Services, Inc.

241

EMPLOYEE APTITUDE SURVEY TEST #5—SPACE VISUALIZATION   G. Grimsley, F.L. Ruch, N.D. Warren, and J.S. Ford

Measures ability to visualize and manipulate objects in three dimensions by viewing a two-dimensional drawing. Used to select employees for jobs requiring mechanical aptitude, such as drafters, engineers, and personnel in technical positions. Also used in career counseling.

50-item paper-pencil multiple-choice test consisting of 10 perspective line-drawings of stacks of blocks. The blocks are all the same size and rectangular in shape so that they appear to stack neatly and distinctly. Five of the blocks in each stack are lettered. The subjects must look at each lettered block and determine how many other blocks in the stack the lettered block touches. The test is available in two equivalent forms. Examiner required. Suitable for group use. Available in Spanish. Timed (5 minutes). Scored by hand key or may be computer scored. 25 tests $23.75. *Publisher:* Psychological Services, Inc.

241

EMPLOYEE APTITUDE SURVEY TEST #6—NUMERICAL REASONING   G. Grimsley, F.L. Ruch, N.D. Warren, and J.S. Ford

Measures the ability to analyze logical relationships and discover principles underlying such relationships. Used to select for technical, supervisory, and executive positions. Predictive of on-the-job trainability. Also used in career counseling.

20-item paper-pencil multiple-choice test in which each item consists of a series of seven numbers followed by a question mark where the next number of the series should be. Examinees must determine the pattern of each series and select (from five choices) the number that correctly fills the blank. Logic and deduction, rather than computation, are emphasized. The test is available in two equivalent forms. Examiner required. Suitable for group use. Available in Spanish and French. Timed (5 minutes). Scored by hand key or may be computer scored. 25 tests $23.75. *Publisher:* Psychological Services, Inc.

Refer to pages(s)	*Test Title*

241

EMPLOYEE APTITUDE SURVEY TEST #7—VERBAL REASONING   *G. Grimsley, F.L. Ruch, N.D. Warren, and J.S. Ford*

Measures ability to analyze information and make valid judgments about that information. Used to select employees for jobs requiring the ability to organize, evaluate, and utilize information, such as executive, administrative, supervisory, scientific, accounting, and technical maintenance personnel. Also used in career counseling.

30-item paper-pencil multiple-choice test consisting of six lists of facts (one-sentence statements) with five possible conclusions for each list of facts. The subject reads each list of facts and then looks at each conclusion and decides whether it is definitely true, definitely false, or unknown from the given facts. The test is available in two equivalent forms. Examiner required. Suitable for group use. Available in Spanish and French. Timed (5 minutes). Scored by hand key or may be computer scored. 25 tests $23.75. *Publisher:* Psychological Services, Inc.

241

EMPLOYEE APTITUDE SURVEY TEST #8—WORD FLUENCY   *G. Grimsley, F.L. Ruch, N.D. Warren, and J.S. Ford*

Measures flexibility and ease in verbal communication. Used to select sales representatives, journalists, field representatives, technical writers, receptionists, secretaries, and executives. Also used in career counseling.

Open-ended paper-pencil test measuring word fluency by determining how many words beginning with one specific letter, given at the beginning of the test, a person can produce in a 5-minute test period (75 answer spaces are provided). Examiner required. Suitable for group use. Timed (5 minutes). Scored by hand key. 25 tests $23.75. *Publisher:* Psychological Services, Inc.

241

EMPLOYEE APTITUDE SURVEY TEST #9—MANUAL SPEED AND ACCURACY   *G. Grimsley, F.L. Ruch, N.D. Warren, and J.S. Ford*

Measures ability to make fine-finger movements rapidly and accurately. Used to select clerical workers, office machine operators, electronics and small parts assemblers, and employees for similar precision jobs involving repetitive tasks. Also used in career counseling.

Multiple-item paper-pencil test consisting of a straightforward array of evenly spaced lines of 750 small circles. The applicant must place a pencil dot in as many of the circles as possible in five minutes. Examiner required. Suitable for group use. Available in Spanish. Timed (5 minutes). Scored by hand key. 25 tests $23.75. *Publisher:* Psychological Services, Inc.

Refer to pages(s)	*Test Title*

EMPLOYEE APTITUDE SURVEY TEST #10—SYMBOLIC
REASONING   *G. Grimsley, F.L. Ruch, N.D. Warren, and J.S.
Ford*

Measures ability to manipulate abstract symbols and use them
to make valid decisions. Used to evaluate candidates for positions
requiring a high level of reasoning ability, such as troubleshooters,
computer programmers, accountants, engineers, and scientific personnel. Used in career counseling.

30-item paper-pencil multiple-choice test consisting of a list of
abstract symbols (and their coded meanings) used to establish relationships in the pattern of "A" to "B" to "C." Given the statement,
the examinee must decide whether a proposed relationship between
"A" and "C" is true, false, or unknown from the given statement.
The test is available in two equivalent forms. Examiner required.
Suitable for group use. Available in Spanish and French. Timed (5
minutes). Scored by hand key or may be computer scored. 25 tests
$23.75. *Publisher:* Psychological Services, Inc.

FACIAL RECOGNITION TEST   *Arthur L. Benton*

Assesses a subject's capacity to identify and discriminate photographs of unfamiliar human faces.

Multiple-item multiple-choice test consisting of three parts:
matching identical front-view photographs, matching front-view
with three-quarter-view photographs, and matching front-view
photographs taken under different lighting conditions. The test is
available in a 27-item short form and a 54-item long form (from
which the first 13 stimulus and response pictures presented comprise the short form). The test is administered orally by the examiner. Each correct response is assigned a score of 1; scores are
corrected for age and education. Materials required include a spiral-
bound booklet containing stimulus photographs and corresponding
response choices, a record sheet, and a manual. Examiner required.
Not suitable for group use. Untimed (varies). Scored via examiner
evaluation. Contact publisher for cost. *Publisher:* Oxford University Press

FULD OBJECT-MEMORY EVALUATION   *Paula Altman Fuld*

Measures memory and learning in adults regardless of vision,
hearing, or language handicaps, cultural differences, or inattention
problems.

Ten common objects in a bag are presented to the patient to
determine whether he can identify them by touch. The patient
names the item and then pulls it out of the bag to see if he was right.
After being distracted, the patient is asked to recall the items from
the bag. The patient is given four additional chances to learn and
recall the objects. The test provides separate scores for long-term
storage, retrieval, consistency of retrieval, and failure to recall
items even after being reminded. The test also provides a chance to
observe naming ability, left-right orientation, stereognosis, and verbal fluency. Examiner required. Not suitable for group use. Timed

(60 seconds for each first trial, 30 seconds for each second trial). Scored via examiner evaluation. Complete kit (testing materials, manual, record forms) $22.25; 30 record forms $6.25. *Publisher:* Stoelting Company

GENERAL APTITUDE TEST BATTERY (GATB)
U.S. Employment Service

Measures vocational aptitudes of literate individuals who need help choosing an occupation. Used for counseling.

434-item paper-pencil test consisting of 284 multiple-choice questions, 150 dichotomous-choice questions, and two dexterity formboards. Twelve subtests measure nine vocational aptitudes: General Learning Ability, Verbal, Numerical, Spatial, Form Perception, Clerical Perception, Motor Coordination, Finger Dexterity, and Manual Dexterity. Occupational Aptitude Patterns (OAP) indicate the aptitude requirements for groups of occupations. There are 66 OAPs covering 97% of all non-supervisory occupations. The GATB is scored in terms of OAPs. Results of the battery indicate the individual's likelihood of success in the various occupations. Use in the United States must be authorized by State Employment Service Agencies and in Canada by the Canadian Employment and Immigration Commission. Examiner required. Suitable for group use. Available in Spanish and French. Timed (varies). Scored by hand key or may be computer scored. Contact publisher for cost; available from State Employment Service Agencies only. *Publisher:* U.S. Department of Labor

GERIATRIC DEPRESSION SCALE   *T.L. Brink, J. Yesavage, P. Heersema, O. Lum, M. Adey, T.L. Rose, V.O. Leirer, and V. Huang*

Diagnoses depression in the elderly.

30-item oral-response test assessing the level of depression in older adults. Questions seek "yes" or "no" responses. The test can be administered in oral or written format. It also can be used with other age groups, including adolescents, but loses validity as dementia increases. Spanish and French translations are available. Examiner required. Not suitable for group use. Untimed (5-15 minutes). Scored via examiner evaluation. Free. *Publisher:* T.L. Brink

GERIATRIC SENTENCE COMPLETION FORM (GSCF)
Peter LeBray

Assesses the personal and social adjustment of elderly adults. Used by clinicians working with the elderly in hospitals, long-term care facilities, out-patient settings, community care programs, and private offices.

30-item oral-response or paper-pencil projective test assessing elderly individuals' adjustment in four domains: physical, psychological, social, and temporal. The individual is asked to complete fragmentary sentence stems by using either written or verbal responses. The manual includes information on the development,

Test Title

structure, administration, and interpretation of the test and a number of clinical case illustrations. Examiner required. Suitable for group use. Untimed (varies). Scored via examiner evaluation. Manual, 50 forms $8.95. *Publisher:* Psychological Assessment Resources, Inc.

GOODENOUGH-HARRIS DRAWING TEST
Florence L. Goodenough and Dale B. Harris

Assesses mental ability without requiring verbal skills.

Measures intelligence through three drawing tasks in three tests: Goodenough Draw-A-Man Test, Draw-A-Woman Test, and the experimental Self-Drawing Scale. The man and woman drawings may be scored for the presence of up to 73 characteristics. Materials include Quality Scale Cards, which are required for the short-scoring method. Separate norms are available for males and females. Examiner required. Suitable for group use. Untimed (10-15 minutes). Scored by hand key. Examiner's kit (test booklet, manual, Quality Scale Cards) $39.00; 35 tests $29.00; manual $20.00; Quality Scale Cards $25.00; text $49.00. *Publisher:* The Psychological Corporation

GUILFORD-ZIMMERMAN TEMPERAMENT SURVEY
(GZTS) *J.P. Guilford and Wayne S. Zimmerman*

Measures personality traits. Used for personnel selection, vocational guidance, and clinical practice.

300-item paper-pencil measure of 10 factor-analytically derived traits that have proven to be most uniquely measurable: general activity, restraint, ascendance, sociability, emotional stability, objectivity, friendliness, thoughtfulness, personal relations, and masculinity/femininity. The test is restricted to APA members. Examiner required. Suitable for group use. Untimed (45 minutes). Scored by hand key or may be computer scored. 25 tests $18.00; 25 answer sheets $6.00; 25 profile charts $5.00; manual $6.00; scoring set $7.00. *Publisher:* Sheridan Psychological Services, Inc.

HALSTEAD CATEGORY TEST *Michael Hill*

Assesses individuals' perceptual ability to categorize graphic items.

Multiple-item computer-administered test measuring an individual's ability to categorize along a number of different dimensions. The client observes a series of graphic items on the screen and chooses whether an object belongs to or differs from a set of objects. The series gradually increases in difficulty. Fifty sets of client scores may be saved on disk for later examination. Available for use with the Apple II+, IIe, and IIc computers and the IBM PC and compatible computers. Examiner required. Not suitable for group use. Untimed. Computer scored. $199.00. *Publisher:* Precision People, Inc.

| *Test Title*

HALSTEAD-REITAN NEUROPSYCHOLOGICAL TEST
BATTERY   *Reitan Neuropsychology Laboratory and others*

Evaluates brain function and dysfunction in adults. Used for clinical evaluation.

Battery of tests assessing adult neuropsychological functioning, including the Halstead Neuropsychological Test Battery, the Wechsler Adult Intelligence Scale, the Trail Making Test, the Reitan-Indiana Aphasia Screening Test, various tests of sensory-perceptual functions, and the Minnesota Multiphasic Personality Inventory. Materials include a Category Test projection box with electric control mechanism and projector; 208 adult category slides in carousels; Tactual Performance Test (10-hole board, stand, 10 blocks); manual finger tapper; tape cassette for Speech-Sounds Perception Test; Tactile Form Recognition Test; and a manual for administration and scoring. The components may be ordered separately. Examiner required. Not suitable for group use. Timed/untimed (varies). Scored via examiner evaluation. Adult battery $1,106.00. *Publisher:* Reitan Neuropsychology Laboratory

HAND TEST, REVISED 1983   *Edwin E. Wagner*

Measures an individual's attitudes and action tendencies that are likely to be expressed in overt behavior, particularly aggression. Used for diagnosis and screening.

10-item oral-response projective test using picture cards that present line drawings of hands in various positions. For each card, the subject explains what the hand is doing. The tenth card, which is blank, requires the subject to imagine a hand and describe what it is doing. Responses are scored on a variety of qualitative and quantitative indices to measure potential behavior toward persons and objects in the environment, pathological inefficiency, and social withdrawal. Reading skill is not required. Examiner required. Not suitable for group use. Untimed (10 minutes). Scored via examiner evaluation. Kit (25 scoring booklets, set of picture cards, manual) $39.50. *Publisher:* Western Psychological Services

HAPTIC INTELLIGENCE SCALE FOR ADULT BLIND
Harriet C. Shurrager and Phil S. Shurrager

Measures the intelligence of blind and partially sighted adults. Used as a substitute for or supplement to the Wechsler Adult Intelligence Scale.

Seven nonverbal (except for instructions) task assessments measuring the intelligence of blind and partially sighted adults. The subtests are Digit Symbol, Object Assembly, Block Design, Plan-of-Search, Object Completion, Pattern Board, and Bead Arithmetic. Wechsler's procedures were followed in establishing age categories and statistical treatment of the data. Examiner required. Not suitable for group use. Timed (1 hour, 30 minutes). Scored via examiner evaluation. Complete kit (25 record blanks, testing materials, manual) $525.00. *Publisher:* Stoelting Company

Refer to pages(s)	*Test Title*

HOUSE-TREE-PERSON TECHNIQUE   *John N. Buck*

Assesses personality disturbances in individuals ages 3 and older in psychotherapy, school, and research settings. May be used with the culturally disadvantaged, educationally deprived, mentally retarded, and aged.

Multiple-item paper-pencil and oral-response test providing a projective study of personality. The test consists of two steps. The first, which is nonverbal, creative, and almost completely unstructured, requires the subject to make a freehand drawing of a house, a tree, and a person. The second step, which is verbal, apperceptive, and more formally structured, gives the subject an opportunity to describe, define, and interpret the drawings and their respective environments. Examiner required. Not suitable for group use. Untimed (15-20 minutes). Scored by hand key; examiner evaluated. Complete set (manual for administering and scoring; interpretive catalogs and manuals, 25 drawing forms, 25 interrogation folders, 25 scoring folders, 25 post-drawing interrogation folders, 25 two-copy drawing forms) $140.00. *Publisher:* Western Psychological Services

INCOMPLETE SENTENCES BLANK   *Julian B. Rotter*

Studies personality by using sentence completion.

40-item paper-pencil test of personality. Items are stems of sentences to be completed by the subject. Responses may be classified into three categories: conflict or unhealthy responses, neutral responses, and positive or healthy responses. The test is available in high-school, college, and adult forms. Self-administered. Suitable for group use. Untimed (20-40 minutes). Scored by hand key; examiner evaluated. 25 blanks (specify form) $13.00; manual $20.00. *Publisher:* The Psychological Corporation

KOHS BLOCK DESIGN TEST   *S. C. Kohs*

Measures intelligence of persons with a mental age of 3-19 years. Used for testing individuals with language and hearing handicaps, the disadvantaged, and non-English-speaking individuals.

Multiple-item task-assessment test consisting of 17 cards containing colored designs and 16 colored blocks that the subject uses to duplicate the designs on the cards. Performance is evaluated for attention, adaptation, and auto-criticism. This test also is included in the Merrill-Palmer and Arthur Performance scales. The complete set includes cubes, cards, manual, and 50 record blanks. Examiner required. Suitable for group use. Timed (40 minutes or less). Scored via examiner evaluation. Complete kit $85.00. *Publisher:* Stoelting Company

KUDER OCCUPATIONAL INTEREST SURVEY, FORM DD (KOIS), REVISED   *Frederic Kuder*

Measures how an individual's interests compare with those of satisfied workers in a number of occupational fields or students in

| | *Test Title* |

various college majors. Used with high-school and college students and adults for career planning, vocational guidance, and academic counseling.

100-item paper-pencil inventory assessing the subject's interests in a number of areas related to occupational fields and college majors. Items list three activities and the examinee indicates for each which activity he likes the most and which he likes the least. The Report Form lists scores on occupational and college major scales separately, in rank order for each student. All respondents receive scores on all scales, including some nontraditional occupations for men and women. Optional interpretive guides include an interpretive audiocassette, Fast Fax, Expanding Your Future, and Counseling with the Kuder Occupational Interest Survey, Form DD. A sixth-grade reading level is required. Self-administered. Suitable for group use. Timed (30-40 minutes). Computer scored. Materials and scoring for 20 persons $73.50; audiocassette $16.75; Expanding Your Future $12.00; Counseling with KOIS $5.25; Fast Fax for KOIS Occupations and College Majors $10.00; no charge for general manual if requested when ordering. *Publisher:* Science Research Associates, Inc.

LURIA-NEBRASKA NEUROPSYCHOLOGICAL BATTERY
Charles J. Golden, Arnold D. Purisch, and Thomas A. Hammeke

Assesses a broad range of neuropsychological functions for individuals ages 15 and older. Used to diagnose specific cerebral dysfunction and to select and assess rehabilitation programs.

Multiple-item verbal, observational test available in two forms: Form I (269 items) and Form II (279 items). The discrete, scored items produce a profile for Motor, Rhythm, Tactile, Visual, Receptive Speech, Expressive Speech, Writing, Reading, Arithmetic, Memory, Intellectual, Pathognomonic, Left Hemisphere, Right Hemisphere, Impairment, and Profile Evaluation scales. Form II also assesses intermediate memory. Test materials include six stimulus cards, tape cassette, comb, quarter, and stopwatch. Microcomputer software is available for computer scoring and interpretation of both forms. Examiner required. Not suitable for group use. Untimed (1½-2½ hours). Scored by hand key or may be computer scored. Complete kit Form I (manual, stimulus cards including Christensen cards, tape cassette, 10 scoring booklets, 10 response booklets, 2 answer sheets including publisher scoring and reports) $310.00; complete kit Form II (stimulus cards, tape cassette, manual, 10 patient response booklets, 10 scoring booklets, 2 answer sheets including publisher scoring and reports) $275.00. *Publisher:* Western Psychological Services

MILLON CLINICAL MULTIAXIAL INVENTORY-II
(MCMI-II) *Theodore Millon*

Diagnoses adults with personality disorders. Used in private or group practice, mental health centers, out-patient clinics, and general and psychiatric hospitals and clinics with individuals in assessment or treatment programs.

175-item paper-pencil true-false test (revised version of the MCMI) evaluating adults with emotional or interpersonal problems. Contains 25 scales measuring state and trait features of personality: 10 clinical personality pattern scales (Schizoid, Avoidant, Dependent, Histrionic, Narcissistic, Antisocial, Aggressive/Sadistic, Compulsive, Passive/Aggressive, and Self-defeating), 3 modifier indices (Disclosure, Desirability, and Debasement), 3 severe pathology scales (Schizotypal, Borderline, and Paranoid), 6 clinical syndrome scales (Anxiety Disorder, Somatoform Disorder, Hypomanic Disorder, Dysthymic Disorder, Alcohol Dependence, and Drug Dependence), and 3 severe syndrome scales (Thought Disorder, Major Depression, and Delusional Disorder). A validity index is included. This new edition is intended to reflect proposed DSM-III-R changes. Of the 175 items in the revised edition, 45 are new or reworded. MCMI-II also has a new scoring method and a revised interpretive report. Self-administered. Suitable for group use. Untimed (20-30 minutes). Computer scored. Manual $16.00; interpretive report $19.85-$27.95 depending on quantity and scoring method; profile report $5.45-$7.85 depending on quantity and scoring method. *Publisher:* National Computer Systems/PAS Division

MINNESOTA MULTIPHASIC PERSONALITY INVENTORY (MMPI)   *Starke R. Hathaway and Charnley McKinley*

Assesses individual personality. Used for clinical diagnosis and research in psychopathology.

550-item true-false test of 10 clinical variables or factors of personality: hypochondriasis, depression, hysteria, psychopathic-deviate, masculinity-femininity, paranoia, psychasthenia, schizophrenia, hypomania, and social introversion. Scores also are obtained on four validity scales: Question (?), Lie (L), Validity (F), and Defensiveness (K). Materials include 50 cards to which the individual responds. Personality scores are plotted on a profile sheet reflecting standard deviations from the mean. Group forms are also available. Examiner required. Available in 45 languages. Untimed (1 hour, 30 minutes). Scored by hand key (examiner evaluated) or may be computer scored. 25 recording sheets $5.00; item cards $54.00; answer keys (includes manual) $18.00. *Publisher:* University of Minnesota Press; distributed exclusively by NCS Interpretive Scoring Systems

MULTIPLE AFFECT ADJECTIVE CHECK LIST (MAACL) *Marvin Zuckerman and Bernard Lubin*

Measures anxiety, depression, and hostility in high-school and college students and adults. Used for clinical evaluation and research application.

132-item paper-pencil inventory measuring affects of Anxiety (A), Depression (D), and Hostility (H). The Today Now form measures current affect states and requires examinees to check the

	Test Title

adjectives that describe how they feel at the time of testing. The In General form instructs subjects to check those adjectives that describe a more general state of their feelings. The new MAACL-R contains trait and state forms shown to differentiate patients with affective disorders from other types of patients and normals. Scales on the MAACL-R are Anxiety (A), Depression (D), Hostility (H), Positive Affect (PA), and Sensation Seeking (SS). The two summary scores are Dysphoria (A + D + H) and Positive Affect and Sensation Seeking (PA + SS). Examiner/self-administered. Suitable for group use. Untimed (5 minutes per form). Scored by hand key or may be computer scored. Contact publisher for cost. *Publisher:* Educational and Industrial Testing Service

MYERS-BRIGGS TYPE INDICATOR (MBTI)
Isabel Briggs Myers and Katharine C. Briggs

Measures personality dispositions and interests based on Jung's theory of types. Used in personal, vocational, and marital counseling, executive development programs, educational settings, and research.

166- to 126-item paper-pencil or computer-administered test of four bipolar aspects of personality: Introversion-Extraversion, Sensing-Intuition, Thinking-Feeling, and Judging-Perceptive. Subjects are classified as one of two "types" on each scale. Results for the four scales may be expressed as continuous scores or reduced to a 4-letter code or "type." Individual report forms contain a profile sheet with a brief interpretation of the scores and a chart explanation of each of the 16 MBTI types. Materials include Form F (166 items) and Form G (126 items). A software package containing a diskette, user's guide, and carrying case is available for use with IBM PCs and compatibles. Self-administered. Suitable for group use. Untimed (20-30 minutes). Scored by hand key or may be computer scored. Scoring service also available. Manual $20.00; 50 individual report forms $5.50; *Introduction to Type* $1.25; 25 question booklets (specify Form F or G) $10.00; 50 answer sheets (specify form) $7.00. *Publisher:* Consulting Psychologists Press, Inc.

NURSES' OBSERVATION SCALE FOR INPATIENT
EVALUATION   *Gilbert Honigfeld, Roderic D. Gillis, and*
C. James Klett

Assesses the ward behavior of psychiatric inpatients. Used by nursing personnel to evaluate patient status and change.

30-item paper-pencil observational inventory assessing inpatient psychiatric behavior. Measures six factors: social competence, social interest, personal neatness, irritability, manifests psychosis, and retardation. Scale items consist of statements about the patient's ward behavior and are rated on 5-point scale from 0 (never) to 4 (always). Factor scores are based on two raters' combined scores in which each item receives unit weight. A global score, Total Patient Assets, is also calculated as a composite of the six factor scores. Examiner required. Not suitable for group use. Untimed (varies).

Scored via examiner evaluation. Contact publisher for cost. *Publisher:* Behavior Arts Center

OARS MULTIDIMENSIONAL FUNCTIONAL ASSESSMENT QUESTIONNAIRE *Center for the Study of Aging and Human Development, Duke University*

Assesses the functional status of adults, particularly the elderly. Suitable for use with visually, physically, mentally, and hearing-impaired populations.

101-item criterion-referenced paper-pencil and oral-response test assessing five areas of functioning: social (13 items), economic (20 items), mental health (15 items), physical health (22 items), and activities of daily living (ADL; 14 items). The test also contains a 24-item services section, demographic information, and interviewer sections. The test yields both subscore ratings and summary ratings on 6-point scales for social, economic, mental health, physical health, and ADL. A scoring service is available from the publisher. A videocassette is available for training purposes. Examiner/self-administered. Not suitable for group use. Available in Spanish, Portuguese, and French. Untimed (45 minutes). Scored via examiner evaluation or may be computer scored. Free use of questionnaires with permission of Director of Center; contact publisher for cost of training. *Publisher:* Center for the Study of Aging and Human Development, Duke University

PROFILE OF MOOD STATES (POMS) *Douglas M. McNair, Maurice Lorr, and Leo Droppleman*

Assesses dimensions of affect or mood in individuals ages 18 and older. Used to measure outpatients' response to various therapeutic approaches, including drug evaluation studies.

65-item paper-pencil test measuring six dimensions of affect or mood: tension-anxiety, depression-dejection, anger-hostility, vigor-activity, fatigue-inertia, and confusion-bewilderment. An alternative POMS-Bipolar Form measures the following mood dimensions in terms of six bipolar affective states identified in recent research: composed-anxious, elated-depressed, agreeable-hostile, energetic-tired, clearheaded-confused, and confident-unsure. The POMS-Bipolar Form is currently available for research use. Examiner required. Suitable for group use. Untimed (3-5 minutes). Scored by hand key or may be computer scored. Specimen set (manual, all forms) $5.25; 25 inventories (specify college or outpatient) $6.50; 25 profile sheets $4.75; keys $12.00; manual $3.00. *Publisher:* Educational and Industrial Testing Service

PROVERBS TEST *Donald R. Gorham*

Assesses abstract verbal functioning. Used for individual clinical evaluation, screening, and clinical research.

12- or 40-item power test measuring verbal comprehension. The subject is required to explain the meanings of proverbs. The 12-

item free-answer format allows the subject to respond in his or her own words. A 40-item multiple-choice format is also available. The free-response forms are scored for abstractness and pertinence on a 3-point scale. The multiple-choice form is scored with a hand stencil. Forms I, II, and III are available for free-answer administration. Examiner required. Only the multiple-choice form is suitable for group use. Untimed (individual test, 10-30 minutes; group multiple-choice test, 20-40 minutes). Scored by hand key; examiner evaluated. Complete kit (general manual, clinical manual, 10 each of Forms I, II, III, scoring cards, 10 free-response form booklets, scoring stencils) $13.00; 100 test blanks $18.00; 25 test booklets (specify Form I, II, or III) $8.00; 100 answer sheets $8.00. *Publisher:* Psychological Test Specialists

128

QUICK TEST (QT) *R.B. Ammons and C.H. Ammons*

Assesses individual intelligence. May be used for evaluation of the severely physically handicapped, individuals with short attention spans, or uncooperative subjects.

50-item test of general intelligence. The subject looks at plates with four line drawings and indicates which picture best illustrates the meaning of a given word. The subject usually responds by pointing. The test requires no reading, writing, or speaking. Usual administration involves the presentation of 15 to 20 of the items. Items are administered until the subject scores six consecutive passes and six consecutive failures. Materials include plates with stimulus pictures and three alternate forms. Examiner required. Suitable for group use. Untimed (3-10 minutes). Scored by hand key; examiner evaluated. Complete kit (3 plates, 100 record sheets, instruction cardboard, item cardboard) $16.00; 100 record sheets $10.00; 3 plates $4.00; instruction cardboard $0.80; item cardboard $0.70; manual $5.00. *Publisher:* Psychological Test Specialists

63

RANDT MEMORY TEST *C.T. Randt and E.R. Brown*

Measures memory processes in neurologically impaired populations, including the elderly.

Computer-administered test of memory changes in areas including process of association, primary memory deficits, recall vs. recognition memory, and transfer to and retrieval from secondary store memory. Test materials include picture recognition cards, documentation, a program for test administration control, response recording, and computation of scaled scores, standard scores, and summary of test scores. Examiner/self-administered. Not suitable for group use. Untimed (varies). Scored by hand key or may be computer scored. Test, manual scoring $75.00; Apple computer scoring program $40.00. *Publisher:* Life Science Associates

Refer to pages(s)	*Test Title*

128, 158

REVISED BETA EXAMINATION *D.E. Kellogg and N.W. Morton*

Measures mental ability of nonreading applicants. Used for testing applicants in settings with large numbers of unskilled workers.

Six separately timed paper-pencil tests of mental ability, including mazes, coding, paper formboards, picture completion, clerical checking, and picture absurdities. Directions are given orally to the applicant. Examiner required. Suitable for group use. Available in Spanish. Untimed (30 minutes). Scored by hand key. Specimen set (test, demonstration booklet, manual) $19.00; 25 tests, demonstration booklet, manual, key $51.00. *Publisher:* The Psychological Corporation

61, 62, 63, 79, 209, 210, 211, 212, 213, 214

REVISED VISUAL RETENTION TEST *Arthur L. Benton*

Measures visual memory, visual perception, and visuoconstructive abilities. Used as a supplement to mental examinations. Also useful in experimental research.

10-item test of visual perception, visual memory, and visuoconstructive abilities. Items are designs that are shown to the subject one by one. The subject studies each design and reproduces it as exactly as possible by drawing it on plain paper. Materials include design cards and three alternate and equivalent forms, C, D, and E. Examiner required. Not suitable for group use. Untimed (5 minutes). Scored via examiner evaluation. Complete set (manual, 3 forms of design cards, 50 record forms) $59.00; manual $25.00; 50 record forms $15.00. *Publisher:* The Psychological Corporation

18, 99, 129, 130, 140, 159, 160, 194, 241

RORSCHACH INKBLOT TEST *Hermann Rorschach*

Evaluates personality through projective technique. Used in clinical evaluation.

10-card oral-response projective personality test in which the subject is asked to interpret what he sees in 10 inkblots, based on the assumption that the individual's perceptions and associations are selected and organized in terms of motivations, impulses, and other underlying aspects of personality. Extensive scoring systems have been developed. Although many variations are in use, this entry refers only to the psychodiagnostic plates first published in 1921. Materials include inquiry charts, tabulation sheets, and a set of 10 inkblots. A set of 10 Kodaslides of the inkblots may be imported on request. Trained examiner required. Not suitable for group use. Untimed. Scored via examiner evaluation. $56.00 U.S. currency. *Publisher:* Verlag Hans Huber; distributed in North America by Hans Huber Publishers, Inc.

281

SCHAIE-THURSTONE ADULT MENTAL ABILITIES TEST (STAMAT) *K. Warner Schaie*

Measures five separate factors of intelligence.
Multiple-item paper-pencil test in two forms measuring ver-

bal, spatial, reasoning, number, and word fluency abilities of adults. Form A (adult) is the original Thurstone Primary Mental Abilities Test, Form 11-17, with new adult norms. Form OA (older adult) is a large-print version of the original test plus two additional scales relevant for adults ages 55 and older. Instructions have been written to enhance performance by older adults. Examiner required. Suitable for group use. Timed (Form A, 26 minutes; Form B, 37 minutes). Scored by hand key. Specimen set 21.00; manual $13.00; 25 Form OA test booklets (includes scoring instructions) $40.00; 25 Form A booklets $31.50; Form A score key $4.50; 25 profiles $5.25; 50 Form A answer sheets $9.50. *Publisher:* Consulting Psychologists Press, Inc.

97, 98, 102, 104

SCHEDULE FOR AFFECTIVE DISORDERS AND SCHIZOPHRENIA (SADS)   *Jean Endicott and The Department of Research Assessment and Training*

Describes the psychopathology of the past week and the current episode of illness. Used as an aid in diagnosing and estimating prognosis and severity.

Measure of recent psychopathology consisting of over 200 scales and many checklist items. The examiner rates the items based on a subject interview, case records, and a clinical workup. The instrument is similar in concept to the Schedule for Affective Disorders and Schizophrenia—Lifetime Version (SADS-L) and the Schedule for Affective Disorders and Schizophrenia—Change Version (SADS-C). The instrument must be used in conjunction with the Research Diagnostic Criteria (RDC). Examiner required. Not suitable for group use. Untimed (1½-2 hours). Scored via examiner evaluation; computer scored for summary scale. SADS booklet $2.00; SADS score sheet $0.30; SADS, SAD-L, RDC suggested procedures $0.50; SADS, SAD-L instructions $0.50; summary scale booklet $1.50; editing/coding instructions $0.40; FORTRAN program $125.00 plus postage and handling. *Publisher:* Department of Research Assessment and Training, New York State Psychiatric Unit

75, 102, 103, 168, 169

SELF-RATING DEPRESSION SCALE   *William W.K. Zung*

Assesses intensity of depressive symptoms of subjects of all ages (except the extremely debilitated), but is best suited for those ages 20 to 64. Used for clinical diagnosis and research on depression.

20-item paper-pencil measure of specific characteristics of depression. Subjects respond "none or a little of the time," "some of the time," "good part of the time," or "most or all of the time" to each item, according to the way they felt a week prior to taking the test. Examiner required. Suitable for group use. Available in Chinese, Czech, Dutch, French, German, Italian, Japanese, Slovak, Spanish, Swedish, and Thai. Scored by hand key. Test booklet contains sample test, scoring transparency, 12 test/answer sheets, and examiner information. Contact publisher for cost. *Publisher:* William W.K. Zung.

132, 194, 262   SENIOR APPERCEPTION TECHNIQUE (SAT)
                        Leopold Bellak and Sonya Sorel Bellak

Assesses personality in individuals age 60 and older. Used by psychiatrists, psychologists, physicians, nurses, and social workers for clinical evaluation and diagnosis.

16-item oral-response projective personality test measuring the traits, attitudes, and psychodynamics involved in the personalities of individuals age 60 and older. Each test item consists of a picture of human figures in situations of concern to the elderly. The examinee is asked to tell a story about each picture. The test also includes informational material on technique, administration, research possibilities, and a bibliography. Examiner required. Not suitable for group use. Available in Spanish and Japanese. Untimed (20-30 minutes). Scored via examiner evaluation. Complete kit (pictures, manual) $16.00. *Publisher:* C.P.S., Inc.

62   SERIAL DIGIT LEARNING TEST   *Arthur L. Benton*

Measures short-term memory in a clinical assessment of mental status.

Examiner presents either eight (Form SD8) or nine (Form SD9) randomly selected single digits for a varying number of trials up to a maximum of 12 trials. Three alternate versions are provided for each form, the selection of which is based primarily on the subject's age and educational level. Generally, Form SD9 is given to patients under age 65 who have 12 or more years of education and Form SD8 to those age 65 or older and those under age 65 with less than 12 years of education. The manual provides exceptions to these criteria. Testing is discontinued after two consecutive correct repetitions. One point is scored for each "near-correct" response; correct repetitions are credited two points. Examiner required. Not suitable for group use. Untimed (5-10 minutes). Scored via examiner evaluation. Contact publisher for cost. *Publisher:* Oxford University Press

126, 143, 241, 242   SIXTEEN PERSONALITY FACTOR QUESTIONNAIRE
                        Raymond B. Cattell and IPAT Staff

Evaluates the normal adult personality. Used for personnel selection and placement, vocational and educational guidance, marriage counseling, clinical evaluations, and research.

Multiple-item paper-pencil test measuring 16 primary personality traits, including levels of assertiveness, emotional maturity, shrewdness, self-sufficiency, tension, anxiety, neuroticism, and rigidity. Five forms are available: Forms A and B (187 items, seventh-grade reading level), Forms C and D (105 items, sixth-grade reading level), and Form E (128 items, third-grade reading level). Six computer reports are available: Personal Career Development Profile, Karson Clinical Report, Marriage Counseling Report, 16PF Narrative Scoring Report, Human Resources Development Report, and Law Enforcement and Development Report. A videotape presenting the Form A test booklet in American Sign Language is available. Form E test booklet also is available on cassette tape. Examiner/self-administered. Suitable for group use. Available in Spanish and 40 other languages. Untimed (45-60 minutes). Scored by hand key or may be computer scored. 25 reusable test booklets (specify form) $19.00; 25 machine-scorable answer sheets (specify form) $7.50; 50 hand-scorable answer sheets (specify form) $8.50; 50 profile sheets $8.50; 50 hand-scorable answer-profile sheets (specify form) $12.00; scoring keys $13.00. *Publisher:* Institute for Personality and Ability Testing, Inc.

242

SOCIAL INTELLIGENCE TEST   *F.A. Moss, Thelma Hunt, and K. Omwake*

Assesses basic social perceptions and judgments of students.

Multiple-item paper-pencil test measuring five factors: judgment in social situations, recognition of mental state of speaker, observation of human behavior, memory for names and faces, and sense of humor. Percentile norms are provided for high-school, college, and adult populations. Three editions are available: Second Edition (Long Form); Shortened Edition (omits Memory for Names and Faces factor); and Special Edition (contains only Judgment in Social Situations and Observation of Human Behavior). A complete specimen set contains all three forms. Examiner required. Suitable for group use. Timed (50 minutes). Scored by hand key. Specimen set $5.00. *Publisher:* Center for Psychological Service

158

STANDARD PROGRESSIVE MATRICES   *J.C. Raven*

Measures an individual's mental ability through assessment of nonverbal abstract reasoning tasks. Used for school and vocational counseling and placement.

60-item paper-pencil nonverbal test in five sets of 12 problems each. In each problem, the subject is presented with a pattern or figure design with a missing part. The subject selects one of six possible parts as the correct one. The patterns are arranged from simple to complex. The test often is used with the Mill Hill Vocabulary Scale. U.S. norms are available. Examiner required. Suitable for group use. Untimed (45 minutes). Scored by hand key or may be machine scored. Specimen set (book of tests, 5 each of combined matrices and Mill Hill Vocabulary record forms, Sections 1, 3, and 5a of manual, sample machine-scorable record form) 15.20 plus VAT; 25 tests 65.00; 50 record forms 4.50; plastic marking key 6.70 plus VAT. *Publisher:* H.K. Lewis & Co., Ltd.; distributed in the U.S. by The Psychological Corporation

169

STATE-TRAIT ANXIETY INVENTORY (STAI)
Charles D. Spielberger

Evaluates individual anxiety levels as an aid to clinical screening for anxiety-prone students, as an indicator of current anxiety level of therapy and counseling clients, and as a research tool.

20-item paper-pencil test of two aspects of anxiety: state (current level of anxiety, or S-Anxiety) and trait (anxiety-proneness, or

T-Anxiety). The T-Anxiety scale asks the subject to indicate how he "generally" feels; the S-Anxiety scale asks how he feels "at a particular moment in time." Form Y is a revision of the original Form X in which six items on each scale have been changed. Self-administered. Suitable for group use. Form X is no longer available in English; a Spanish version is available. Untimed (15 minutes). Scored by hand key. Specimen set (tests, manual, key) $8.00; 25 tests $5.00; key $1.25; manual $7.00; 25 tests in Spanish $5.25; Spanish manual $14.75. *Publisher:* Consulting Psychologists Press, Inc.

STRONG-CAMPBELL INTEREST INVENTORY (SCII)
E.K. Strong, Jr., Jo-Ida C. Hansen, and David P. Campbell

Measures occupational interests in a wide range of career areas. Used to make long-range curricular and occupational choices and for employee placement, career guidance, career development, and vocational rehabilitation placement.

325-item paper-pencil multiple-choice test requiring the examinee to respond either "like," "indifferent," or "dislike" to items covering a broad range of familiar occupational tasks and day-to-day activities. General topics include occupations, school subjects, activities, leisure activities, types of people, preference between two activities, and personal characteristics. Respondents are scored on 6 general occupational themes, 23 basic interest scales, and 207 occupational scales. Scoring services also provide 11 additional non-occupational and administrative indexes as a further guide to interpretation. Self-administered. Suitable for group use. Available in Spanish. Untimed (25-30 minutes). Computer scored. Specimen prepaid scoring packet (descriptive brochure, test booklet, answer sheet to be returned for free profile and interpretive report) $7.00; User's Guide $12.00; manual $13.50; 25 reusable test booklets (specify standard or Spanish version) $9.25. *Publisher:* Distributed exclusively by Consulting Psychologists Press, Inc.

TEST OF TEMPORAL ORIENTATION   *Arthur L. Benton*

Assesses the accuracy of a patient's temporal orientation. Used as a component of a mental status examination.

5-item oral-response test in which the examiner asks temporal orientation questions (day of week, day of month, month, year, and time of day) and assigns points based on criteria provided in the manual. The test is used to disclose and interpret minor as well as gross temporal disorientation within a prescribed range of normal variation. The total number of error points constitutes the patient's obtained score, resulting in classifications ranging from normal to severely defective. Examiner required. Not suitable for group use. Untimed (varies). Scored via examiner evaluation. Contact publisher for cost. *Publisher:* Oxford University Press

| *Refer to pages(s)* | *Test Title* |

THEMATIC APPERCEPTION TEST (TAT)
Henry Alexander Murray

Assesses personality through projective technique focusing on dominant drives, emotions, sentiments, complexes, attitudes, and conflicts.

20-item projective-type test in which a subject is shown pictures one at a time and asked to make up a story about each picture. The examiner records the subject's stories for later analysis. The projective test seeks to measure, among other things, the subject's temperament, level of emotional maturity, observational ability, intellectuality, imagination, psychological insight, creativity, sense of reality, and factors of family and psychic dynamics. Generally the subject is asked to make up stories based on 10 cards in each of two sessions. A trained examiner is required. Not suitable for groups. Untimed (1 hour per series). Scored via examiner evaluation. Specimen set $12.50; manual $1.50. *Publisher:* Harvard University Press

TWITCHELL-ALLEN THREE-DIMENSIONAL PERSONALITY TEST, 1985 REVISION   *Doris Twitchell-Allen*

Diagnoses critical areas of personality in children and adults. Used by teachers and human service personnel to provide guidance in terms of an individual's current functional status and more permanent characteristics of personality.

Four action and oral-response tests providing a projective evaluation of an individual's personality. Test materials consist of 28 small objects, all of an ambiguous or abstract nature (some are suggestive of human forms). The four subtests are Naming Test, Story Production, Fein Testing Limits 1 (for intrafamilial relations), and Fein Testing Limits 2. The examiner records the following types of responses: gestures, general behavior, constructions with test forms, vocalizations (everything the subject says, not just the stories and names), sequence, and time. May be administered to the blind with only minor procedural adaptations. Examiner required. Not suitable for group use. Untimed (1 hour). Scored via examiner evaluation; may be computer scored. Complete set (carrying case, instructions, 5 sets of recording forms) $115.00. *Publisher:* Doris Twitchell-Allen, Ph.D.

WATSON-GLASER CRITICAL THINKING APPRAISAL
Goodwin Watson and Edward M. Glaser

Assesses critical thinking abilities. Used for evaluation of gifted and talented individuals and to select candidates for positions in which analytic reasoning is an important part of the job.

80-item paper-pencil test measuring five aspects of the ability to think critically: inference, recognition of assumptions, deduction, interpretation, and evaluation of arguments. The subject responds to the exercises, which include problems, statements, arguments, and interpretation of material encountered on a daily basis. Two alternate and equivalent forms, A and B, are available.

Test Title

Examiner required. Suitable for group use. Untimed (50 minutes). Scored by hand key or may be machine scored. 35 tests $59.00; 35 OpScan answer documents $19.00; key $10.00; manual $12.00; class record $3.00 (specify form for each item ordered); specimen kit (test booklet, answer document, key, manual, class record) $20.00. *Publisher:* The Psychological Corporation

WECHSLER ADULT INTELLIGENCE SCALE (WAIS)
David Wechsler

Measures intelligence in adolescents and adults.

Eleven subtests divided into two major divisions yielding a Verbal IQ, a Performance IQ, and a Full Scale IQ for individuals ages 16 and older. The verbal section of the test consists of the following subtests: Information, Comprehension, Arithmetic, Similarities, Digit Span, and Vocabulary. The performance or nonverbal section of the test consists of the following subtests: Digit Symbol, Picture Completion, Block Design, Picture Arrangement, and Object Assembly. Some units of the test require verbal responses from the subject, and others require the subject to manipulate test materials to demonstrate performance ability. Examiner required. Not suitable for group use. Available in Spanish. Untimed (1 hour). Scored via examiner evaluation. Complete set (all necessary equipment, manual, 25 record forms, without attache case) $275.00; attache case $55.00. *Publisher:* The Psychological Corporation

WECHSLER ADULT INTELLIGENCE SCALE-REVISED
(WAIS-R)   *David Wechsler*

Assesses intelligence in adolescents and adults.

Eleven subtests divided into two major divisions yielding a Verbal IQ, a Performance IQ, and a Full Scale IQ for individuals ages 16 and older. The verbal section of the test consists of the following subtests: Information, Comprehension, Arithmetic, Similarities, Digit Span, and Vocabulary. The performance or nonverbal section of the test consists of the following subtests: Digit Symbol, Picture Completion, Block Design, Picture Arrangement, and Object Assembly. Some units of the test require verbal responses from the subject, and others require the subject to manipulate test materials to demonstrate performance ability. The WAIS-R is a revision of the 1955 edition of the WAIS. Examiner required. Not suitable for group use. Available in Spanish. Untimed (1 hour, 15 minutes). Scored via examiner evaluation. Complete set (all necessary equipment, manual, 25 record forms with attache case) $298.00; complete without attache case $275.00; manual $39.00. *Publisher:* The Psychological Corporation

WECHSLER MEMORY SCALE (WMS)   *David Wechsler and C.P. Stone*

Assesses memory functions. Used for adult subjects with special problems, such as aphasics, the elderly, and organically brain-injured individuals.

| *Test Title*

A short, standardized scale featuring seven subtests assessing memory functions and yielding a Memory Quotient. Two alternate forms, I and II, are available. Examiner required. Not suitable for group use. Untimed. Scored via examiner evaluation. Specimen set (manual, design cards, both record forms) $20.00; 50 record forms $35.00 (specify Form I or II); manual $15.00. *Publisher:* The Psychological Corporation

WECHSLER MEMORY SCALE-REVISED (WMS-R)
David Wechsler and C.P. Stone

Assesses memory functioning. Used with aphasic and organically brain-injured individuals and with the elderly.

10-subtest verbal and nonverbal scale assessing memory functioning. Three new subtests have been added: Figural Memory, Visual Paired Associates, and Visual Memory Span. The Logical Memory, Verbal Paired Associates, Visual Paired Associates, and Visual Reproduction subtests are administered twice to provide separate estimates of immediate and delayed recall. The revised edition also contains more explicit scoring guidelines for the Logical Memory and Visual Reproduction subtests. Test is to be used only by persons with at least a master's degree in psychology or a related discipline. Examiner required. Not suitable for group use. Untimed (50 minutes, including 30-minute delayed recall procedure). Scored via examiner evaluation. Complete set (35 record forms, carrying case) $189.00; manual $40.00; 25 record forms $19.00. *Publisher:* The Psychological Corporation

WESMAN PERSONNEL CLASSIFICATION TEST (PCT)
A.G. Wesman

Assesses general mental ability. Used for selection of employees for sales, supervisory, and managerial positions.

Multiple-item paper-pencil test of two major aspects of mental ability: verbal and numerical. The verbal items are analogies. The numerical items test basic math skills and understanding of quantitative relationships. Three forms, A, B, and C, are available. The verbal part of Form C is somewhat more difficult than the verbal parts of Forms A and B. Examiner required. Suitable for group use. Timed (Verbal, 18 minutes; Numerical, 10 minutes). Scored by hand key. Specimen set (one each of materials for all 3 forms, keys and manual) $17.00; 25 tests, manual, booklet, key (specify form) $34.00. *Publisher:* The Psychological Corporation

WIDE RANGE ACHIEVEMENT TEST-REVISED (WRAT-R)
Sarah Jastak and Gary S. Wilkinson

Measures the basic educational skills of word recognition, spelling, and arithmetic. Used to identify individuals with learning difficulties and for educational placement, measuring school achievement, vocational assessment, and job placement and training.

Refer to pages(s)	*Test Title*

Three paper-pencil subtests (50-100 items per subtest) assessing coding skills: Reading, Spelling, and Arithmetic. The test consists of two levels, Level I (ages 5-11) and Level II (ages 12-adult). Optional word lists for both levels of the reading and spelling tests are offered on plastic cards, and a recorded pronunciation of the lists is provided on cassette tape. The tape itself can be used to administer the spelling section. Use is restricted to educational and psychological professionals. A large-print edition is available. Examiner required. The spelling and arithmetic subtests are suitable for group use; the reading subtest must be individually administered. Timed (10 minutes per subtest). Scored via examiner evaluation. Manual $20.00; 25 test forms $8.00. *Publisher:* Jastak Assessment Systems

27, 60, 145

WISCONSIN CARD SORTING TEST (WCST)
David A. Grant and Esta A. Berg

Assesses perseveration and abstract thinking. Used for neuropsychological assessment of individuals suspected of having brain lesions involving the frontal lobes.

Multiple-task nonverbal test in which the subject matches cards in two response decks to one of four stimulus cards for color, form, or number. Responses are recorded on a form for later scoring. The test provides measures of overall success and particular sources of difficulty. When used in conjunction with more comprehensive ability testing, the test can help discriminate frontal from nonfrontal lesions. A computerized version operates on Apple II systems with a color monitor, two floppy disk drives, and a paddle. The scoring program operates on IBM PC systems with 256K and two disk drives. Examiner required. Not suitable for group use. Untimed. Scored via examiner evaluation or may be computer scored. Complete kit (2 card decks, 50 response and scoring forms, manual) $85.00; manual $10.00. *Publisher:* Psychological Assessment Resources, Inc.

Note: Descriptions in this section are limited to published and commercially available tests; the unpublished measures cited or recommended by the chapter authors are found in the General Index.

Test Publisher/Distributor Directory

AMERICAN FOUNDATION FOR THE BLIND, 15 West 16th Street, New York, New York 10011; (212)620-2000

AMERICAN ORTHOPSYCHIATRIC ASSOCIATION, INC., 19 West 44th Street, Suite 1616, New York, New York 10036; (212)54-5770

ASSOCIATED SERVICES FOR THE BLIND, 919 Walnut Street, Philadelphia, Pensylvania 19107; (215)627-0600

BEHAVIOR ARTS CENTER, 77 Lyons Place, Westwood, New Jersey 07675; (201)664-3237

T.L. BRINK, 1044 Sylvan, San Carlos, California 94070; (415)592-3570

CENTER FOR COGNITIVE THERAPY, 133 South 36th Street, Room 602, Philadelphia, Pennsylvania 19104; (215)898-4100

CENTER FOR PSYCHOLOGICAL SERVICE, 1511 K Street, N.W., Suite 430, Washington, D.C. 20005; (202)347-4069

CENTER FOR THE STUDY OF AGING AND HUMAN DEVELOPMENT, DUKE UNIVERSITY MEDICAL CENTER, Box 3003, Attn: OARS Coordinator, Durham, North Carolina 27710; (919)684-3204

CLINICAL PSYCHOMETRIC RESEARCH, INC. P.O. Box 619, Riderwood, Maryland 21139; (301)321-6165

CONSULTING PSYCHOLOGISTS PRESS, INC., 577 College Avenue, P.O. Box 60070, Palo Alto, California 94306; (415)857-1444

C.P.S., INC., P.O. Box 83, Larchmont, New York 10538; no business phone

DEPARTMENT OF RESEARCH ASSESSMENT AND TRAINING, NEW YORK STATE PSYCHIATRIC UNIT, 722 West 168th Street, Room 341, New York, New York 10032; (212)960-5534

EDUCATIONAL AND INDUSTRIAL TESTING SERVICE, P.O. Box 7234, San Diego, California 92107; (619) 222-1666

EPIDEMIOLOGY AND PSYCHOPATHOLOGY, RESEARCH BRANCH, DIVISION OF CLINICAL RESEARCH, NATIONAL INSTITUTE OF MENTAL HEALTH, 5600 Fishers Lane, Room 10C-05, Rockville, Maryland 20857; (301)443-4513

HANS HUBER PUBLISHERS, INC., 14 Bruce Park Avenue, Toronto, Ontario M4P253, Canada; (416)482-6339

HARVARD UNIVERSITY PRESS, 79 Garden Street, Cambridge, Massachusetts 02138; (617) 495-2600

HODDER AND STOUGHTON EDUCATIONAL, Mill Road, Dunton Green, Seven Oaks, Kent TN13 2YD, England; (0732)450111

INSTITUTE FOR PERSONALITY AND ABILITY TESTING, INC., 1602 Coronado Drive, P.O. Box 188, Champaign, Illinois 61820; (217)352-4739

JASTAK ASSOCIATES, INC., 1526 Gilpin, Wilmington, Delaware 19806; (302)652-4990

LEA AND FEBIGER, 600 Washington Square, Philadelphia, Pennsylvania 19106; (215)922-1330

H.K. LEWIS & CO., LTD., 136 Gower Street, London WCIE 6BS, England; (01)387-4282

LIFE SCIENCE ASSOCIATES, One Fenimore Road, Bayport, New York 11705; (516)472-2111

NATIONAL COMPUTER SYSTEMS/PAS DIVISION, P.O. Box 1416, Minneapolis, Minnesota 55440; (800)328-6759, in Minnesota (612)933-2800

OXFORD UNIVERSITY PRESS, 200 Madison Avenue, New York, New York 10016; (212) 679-7300

PRECISION PEOPLE, INC., 3452 North Ride Circle S., Jacksonville, Florida 32217; (904) 262-1096

PSYCHOLOGICAL ASSESSMENT RESOURCES, INC., P.O. Box 998, Odessa, Florida 33556; (813)977-3395

THE PSYCHOLOGICAL CORPORATION, A Subsidiary of Harcourt, Brace, Jovanovich, Inc., 555 Academic Court, San Antonio, Texas 78204; (800)228-0752

PSYCHOLOGICAL SERVICES, INC., Test Publication Division, 100 West Broadway, Suite 1100, Glendale, California 91210; (818)244-0033

PSYCHOLOGICAL TEST SPECIALISTS, Box 9229, Missoula, Montana 59807; no business phone

PSYCHOMETRIC AFFILIATES, P.O. Box 807, Murfreesboro, Tennessee 37133; (615) 890-6296 or 898-2565

REITAN NEUROPSYCHOLOGY LABORATORY, 1338 East Edison Street, Tucson, Arizona 85719; (602)795-3717

SCIENCE RESEARCH ASSOCIATES, INC., 155 North Wacker Drive, Chicago, Illinois 60606; (312)984-7000, (800)621-0664

SHERIDAN PSYCHOLOGICAL SERVICES, INC., P.O. Box 6101, Orange, California 92667; (714)639-2595

STOELTING COMPANY, 1350 South Kostner Avenue, Chicago, Illinois 60623; (312)522-4500

DORIS TWITCHELL-ALLEN, PH.D., Bangor Mental Health Institute, P.O. Box 926, Bangor, Maine 04401; (207)947-6981

U.S. DEPARTMENT OF LABOR, 200 Constitution Avenue, N.W., Room N-4460, Washington, D.C. 20213; (202)535-0192

UNIVERSITY OF MINNESOTA PRESS, 2037 University Avenue S.E., Minneapolis, Minnesota 55414; (612)373-3266

VERLAG HANS HUBER, Langgassstrasse 76, 3000 Bern 9, Switzerland

WESTERN PSYCHOLOGICAL SERVICES, A Division of Manson Western Corporation, 12031 Wilshire Boulevard, Los Angeles, California 90025; (213)478-2061

WILLIAM W.K. ZUNG, M.D., Veterans Administration Medical Center, 508 Fulton Street, Durham, North Carolina 27705; (919)286-0411

Names Index

General Index

About the Contributors

DAVID ARENBERG, PH.D., has been Chief of the Cognition Section, Gerontology Research Center, at the National Institute on Aging since 1969, where previously he had served as a research psychologist. Dr. Arenberg completed his doctoral work at Duke University on the developmental effects of delayed breathing at birth, and his subsequent professional research has included numerous longitudinal studies on various effects and dimensions of aging. He is a Fellow of the Gerontological Society and of the American Psychological Association, in which he has chaired several committees within the division on Adult Development and Aging. Dr. Arenberg has authored or co-authored over 50 journal articles and book chapters and has served as associate editor of the *Journal of Gerontology,* as an editorial advisory board member for *Educational Gerontology* and the *Journal of Gerontology,* and as consulting editor and acting associate editor for *Psychology and Aging.*

KENNETH D. COLE, PH.D., is the program director of Interdisciplinary Team Training in Geriatrics at the Sepulveda, California, Veterans Administration Medical Center and is associated with Sepulveda's Geriatric Research, Education, and Clinical Center. In addition, Dr. Cole is a clinical associate professor in the department of psychology at the University of Southern California, where he also received his Ph.D. in clinical psychology with a subspecialty in life-span developmental psychology. After earning his doctorate, Dr. Cole was a staff psychologist at Pasadena Guidance Clinics, where he treated adults of all ages and began aging programs for the agency. Currently, he is in private practice specializing in adult developmental and later life concerns. His teaching and research interests include psychotherapy supervision, interdisciplinary team development and communication, consultation-liaison psychiatry, atypical presentations of mood disorders and psychoses in later years, and adjustment processes throughout the life span.

MICHAEL DUFFY, PH.D., is Associate Professor and Director of Training of the Counseling Psychology Program in the Department of Educational Psychology at Texas A&M University. He holds a postgraduate diploma in child clinical psychology from University College, Dublin, Ireland, and a doctorate in counseling psychology from the University of Texas at Austin. Dr. Duffy has specialized extensively in the mental health of older adults and conducts research, teaches a practicum, and maintains an active inpatient and outpatient practice in psychotherapy with older adults. He has published widely in this area and has led committees on the professional development of geropsychology in the American Psychological Association and Texas Psychological Association.

CAROL J. DYE, PH.D., is Assistant Chief and Director of Intern Training at the St. Louis Veterans Administration Medical Center. She received her doctorate in clinical psychology with a specialty in gerontology at Washington University in St. Louis. Since that time she has worked as a clinical psychologist with persons of all ages, seeing older adults almost exclusively for the last 15 years. In addition to her clinical work, Dr. Dye has taught courses at all three of the major universities in the St. Louis area and has given numerous workshops through the Veterans Administration and other agencies interested in the problems of aging. Her research focuses on applied problems of the aging process, and her publications include journal articles and chapters in books on aging. Dr. Dye is a Fellow of the American Psychological Association, the Gerontological Society of America, and the Missouri Psychological Association.

MARLA HASSINGER, PH.D., is a clinical geropsychologist on staff at the UCLA Geriatric Outpatient Clinic of the Neuropsychiatric Institute and Hospital. She received her doctoral degree in clinical-aging psychology from the University of Southern California in 1985 and pursued postdoctoral training in geropsychology through the UCLA Department of Psychiatry and Biobehavioral Sciences. She is the co-author of a chapter on clinical assessment in the *Handbook of the Psychology of Aging* (3rd ed.). Her areas of specialization include cognitive and psychodiagnostic assessment, group psychotherapy, and expansion of community-based mental health programs for the elderly. She has given lectures on normal age changes in learning and memory to both the general public and professionals in a variety of settings.

CHRISTOPHER HERTZOG, PH.D., is Associate Professor of Psychology at the Georgia Institute of Technology. He received his doctorate in psychology, with a specialization in adult development and aging, from the University of Southern California. His dissertation, completed under K. Warner Schaie, applied structural equation models to Schaie's longitudinal data on intellectual change in adults. As a National Institute on Aging PHS postdoctoral fellow, Dr. Hertzog studied cognitive psychology and information processing models of intelligence at the University of Washington. Formerly an assistant professor of human development at The Pennsylvania State University, his work at Georgia Tech currently is supported by a Research Career Development Award from the National Institute on Aging, and he manages two funded research projects that study individual differences in aging, cognition, and intelligence.

THELMA HUNT, PH.D., M.D., is Director of the Center for Psychological Service, a consulting firm in Washington, D.C. She received her doctorates in psychology and medicine from George Washington University, where she is now Professor Emeritus of Psychology. She was on the professional staff of the psychology department at George Washington University for more than 30 years, serving as chairman for over 20 years. Her consulting work and other professional activities focus primarily on the areas of clinical psychology, psychological testing, and personnel psychology. In addition to her consulting work, Dr. Hunt conducts psychological evaluations of individual clients, many of whom are elderly. She is a Fellow of the American Psychological Association, an honorary life member of the International Personnel Management Association, and a Fellow and Fifty Year Honorary Member of the American Association for Advance for Science. In addition, she is a member of the American Medical Women's Association, the American Association on Mental Deficiency, and several regional and local psychological and testing associations. Dr. Hunt received the Stockberger Achievement Award from the International Personnel Management Association in 1984 and was honored for participation as an Eminent Woman in the American Psychological Association program in 1985. Dr. Hunt has edited, authored, and co-authored several book chapters and articles on psychological assessment and measurement, and she co-edited the special assessment issue of *Public Personnel Management* with Clyde J. Lindley in 1984. Dr. Hunt is a test author and was the co-director for the development of several examinations for the Civil Service Commission.

ISELI K. KRAUSS, ED.D., obtained a master's degree in industrial psychology from New York University and her doctorate in educational psychology from Rutgers University. After postdoctoral training in aging at the Andrus Gerontology Center of the University of Southern California, she joined the psychology faculty there. Later, she was a psychology faculty member at Syracuse University. She has authored the Krauss Card Tasks of Adult Cognitive Abilities for use with older adults and has developed a portable computerized system for the assessment of reaction time and cognitive skills. Dr. Krauss has been awarded numerous fellowships and research grants for her work on intellectual functioning in older adults.

ASENATH LA RUE, PH.D., is Associate Professor of Psychiatry at the Neuropsychiatric Institute, University of California, Los Angeles. She received her doctorate in developmental psychology from the University of Iowa. Dr. La Rue's research interests include neuropsychological assessment of older adults and longitudinal investigations of dementia and depression. She is on the editorial board of *Alzheimer's Disease and Associated Disorders* and is associate director of the UCLA postgraduate training program in clinical aging.

CLYDE J. LINDLEY, M.A., is Associate Director of the Center for Psychological Service in Washington, D.C., where he has served as a consultant to federal, state, county, and city personnel departments since 1975. Mr. Lindley received his master's degree in clinical psychology at the University of Iowa and had completed his course work toward a doctorate in psychology at the University of Minnesota when his studies were interrupted by service in the U.S. Army, where he served as director of one of the largest counseling programs in the country. From 1946-75, Mr. Lindley served in the Veterans Administration Department of Medicine and Surgery, Central Office, as Executive Secretary of the Mental Health and Behavioral Sciences Service and was editor of the six-volume *National VA Research Conferences on Chemotherapy in Psychiatry;* in the Office of Planning as Associate Director of Planning; and in the Office of the Chief Medical Director as Executive Director of the top Medical Advisory Group. He is a member of the American Psychological Association (Division of Counseling Psychology and Division of Adult Development and Aging), the Society for Industrial and Organizational Psychology, and the American Association for Counseling and Development, and has served as president of the American Board on Counseling Services and the National Capitol Area American Personnel and Guidance Association. Mr. Lindley's present work and interests focuses on personnel assessment and human resource management but also includes the psychological evaluation of individual clients, many of whom are older persons. He has contributed significantly in the development of tests and interview techniques for personnel selection and promotion. The International Personnel Management Association recognized Mr. Lindley's outstanding contributions in the area of public personnel work by awarding him an Honorary Life Membership. He is the editor of *IPMA Assessment Council News,* is a member of the editorial board of *Public Personnel Management,* and has published widely on personnel assessment and other personnel-related topics.

BERNICE A. MARCOPULOS, PH.D., is Research Health Scientist Specialist at the Palo Alto Veterans Administration Medical Center, Older Adult and Family Research and Resource Center, Division of Gerontology, Stanford University School of Medicine. She received her doctoral training in neuropsychology from the University of Victoria in British Columbia, Canada. Dr. Marcopulos's major research and clinical interests are the diagnosis and treatment of geriatric depression and neuropsychological assessment to examine brain-behavior relationships in older adults.

SAMUEL J. POPKIN, PH.D., is a staff clinical geropsychologist at the Pittsburgh (Highland Drive) Veterans Administration Medical Center and is a faculty member of the University of Pittsburgh Medical School. He received his doctorate from the clinical aging program at the University of Southern California and completed a clinical geropsychology postdoctoral fellowship at UCLA's Neuropsychiatric Institute and Hospital in 1985. Dr. Popkin designed and directs the Older Adult Rehabilitation Service, a program of outpatient and intermediate-care psychological services. His research publications and professional presentations focus largely on the relationship between metamemory and memory performance in older adults. He also has published on select topics concerning the applied psychology of aging. Dr. Popkin's current clinical and research interests are in memory aging, the assessment of dementia and depression in older adults, and psychodynamic therapeutic interventions in adulthood.

JOHN D. RANSEEN, PH.D., is Neuropsychology Section Chairman and Director of Clinical Training, Predoctoral Internship Program, at the Veterans Administration Medical Center in Lexington, Kentucky. In addition, he is Assistant Professor of Psychiatry and Neurology at the Unversity of Kentucky Medical Center. Dr. Ranseen received his doctorate in clinical psychology at Ohio University in Athens, Ohio, and currently is involved in neuropsychological assessment, consultation, and treatment planning for both inpatients and outpatients from neurology, neurosurgery, psychiatry, and general medical units. He has authored journal articles, book chapters, and numerous presentations on neuropsychologcial topics, and his professional affiliations include the American Psychological Association, the International Neuropsychological Society, the National Academy of Neuropsychologists, and the National Head Injury Foundation.

E. A. ROBERTSON-TCHABO, PH.D., is Associate Professor and Assistant Director, Graduate Studies and Research, in the Department of Human Development at the University of Maryland. She received her doctorate in psychology from the University of Southern California, Los Angeles, and completed additional formal training in programs sponsored by the Gerontological Society and by the Harvard University School of Medicine. Previously she served as a research psychologist in the Laboratory of Neurosciences at the National Institute on Aging. Her publications include numerous book chapters and journal articles, and she has made invited presentations at both national and international gerontological conferences. Dr. Robertson-Tchabo is a Fellow of the Gerontological Society and a frequent consultant on aging issues concerns, and she currently serves as a reviewer for the *Journal of Gerontology, Experimental Aging Research,* and *Educational Gerontology.*

JAMES M. SCHEAR, PH.D., is Director of the Neuropsychology Laboratory (Uptown Division) and Neuropsychology Research at the Veterans Administration Medical Center, and Assistant Professor of Psychiatry and Health Behavior at the Medical College of Georgia in Augusta, Georgia. Dr. Schear received his doctorate from Duke University, where he was awarded an American Psychological Association Dissertation Support Fellowship at the Center for the Study of Aging and Human Development for his work on verbal and spatial memory as a function of age. He was awarded a postdoctoral fellowship in neuropsychology at the University of Pittsburgh School of Medicine, Western Psychiatric Institute and Clinic, in Pittsburgh, Pennsylvania. Dr. Schear has received continuous funding from the Veterans Administration Medical Research Service since joining the VA in 1980. He co-edited *Clinical Neuropsychology: A Multidisciplinary Approach* and has published on various neuropsychological topics in aging, assessment, and neuropsychiatry.

DAVID SCHLENOFF, ED.D., is Director of Psychology at the Rehabilitation Hospital of York in York, Pennsylvania. Previously, he worked as a clinical psychologist with the Veterans Administration Medical Center at Perry Point, Maryland, and with the Baltimore City Public School System. Dr. Schlenoff received his doctoral training at George Washington University, where he was granted a Rehabilitation Services Administration fellowship for research related to disability and employment. He has published widely and has made numerous professional presentations in the areas of rehabilitation counseling and psychology. In addition, he has served on the editorial board of *Rehabilitation Literature,* as an editorial reviewer for the *Journal of Counseling Psychology,* and as a psychological consultant to *Runners World Magazine.* Dr. Schlenoff is a member of the American Psychological Association and the National Rehabilitation Association.

FREDERICK A. SCHMITT, PH.D., is Director of the Neuropsychology Service at the University of Kentucky Albert B. Chandler Medical Center, an assistant professor in neurology, and an associate of the Sanders-Brown Center on Aging in Lexington, Kentucky. He holds joint appointments in the departments of psychology and psychiatry and is also a Senior Fellow in the Center for the Study of Aging and Human Development at Duke University Medical Center. Dr. Schmitt's research interests include developmental changes in cognition associated with disease (dementia, stroke, cancer), aging, and medical interventions.

STEVE SHINDELL, PH.D., is the staff clinical psychologist at the Western Blind Rehabilitation Center located at the Palo Alto Veterans Administration Medical Center. He received his doctorate in clinical psychology from the University of Arizona and his internship training at the Palo Alto VA Medical Center. In addition to his primary clinical responsibilities, Dr. Shindell is the principal investigator of two studies currently funded by the National Institute for Disability and Rehabilitation Research and the Veterans Administration, and he is the coordinator of clinical services for the Vision and Aging Unit. He is active in the American Psychological Association Division of Rehabilitation Psychology and is the author of numerous articles, serves on the editorial board of *Rehabilitation Psychology,* and is the editor of *Rehabilitation Psychology News.* Dr. Shindell's primary research interests include the effect of community and social forces on the life satisfaction and quality of life of people after the onset of severe physical or sensory disability.

GLENN SMITH, PH.D., is an instructor in the Department of Rehabilitation Medicine at the Spain Rehabilitation Center, University of Alabama at Birmingham. He completed his doctoral training in clinical psychology at the University of Nebraska-Lincoln and completed his internship at the University of California, Los Angeles Neuropsychiatric Institute. His training emphases were in the areas of geropsychology and neuropsychology. Dr. Smith's research interests include investigation of brain-behavior relationships in general and neuropsychological models of emotion in particular.

McCAY VERNON, PH.D., is Professor of Psychology at Western Maryland College and also maintains a private practice. He earned his doctorate in psychology at the Claremont Graduate School and University Center in California following master's degrees from Gallaudet University and Florida State University in deafness and psychology, respectively. Dr. Vernon's honors include fellowship status in the American Psychological Association, the Declaration of Merit from the World Federation of Deaf, the Medal of Honor from the British Deaf Association, an Honorary Doctor of Letters from Gallaudet University, and the Distinguished Service Award from the National Association of the Deaf. His numerous publications include books, book chapters, journal articles, and documentary film scripts. Currently he is the editor-in-chief of the *American Annals of the Deaf.* Dr. Vernon's specialities are hearing impairment, deaf-blindness, psychodiagnostics, and forensic psychology.